THE GOAL
THIRD REVISED EDITION

Other North River Press Books by
Eliyahu M. Goldratt

The Race (with Robert E. Fox)
Theory of Constraints
The Haystack Syndrome
It's Not Luck
Critical Chain
Necessary But Not Sufficient
Production the TOC Way
Essays on the Theory of Constraints
Late Night Discussions

THE GOAL
A Process of Ongoing Improvement
THIRD REVISED EDITION

By
Eliyahu M. Goldratt
and
Jeff Cox

With interviews by David Whitford,
Editor at Large, Fortune Small Business

North River Press

Additional copies can be obtained from your local
bookstore or the publisher:

**The North River Press
Publishing Corporation
P.O. Box 567
Great Barrington, MA 01230
(800) 486-2665 or (413) 528-0034**

www.northriverpress.com

Manufactured in the United States of America

Library of Congress Cataloging-in-Publication Data

Goldratt, Eliyahu M., 1948-
   The goal: a process of ongoing improvement

I. Cox, Jeff, 1951-. II. Title
PR9510.9.G64G61986   823   86-12566
ISBN: 0-88427-178-1

INTRODUCTION

The Goal is about science and education. I believe that these two words have been abused to the extent that their original meanings have been lost in a fog of too much respect and mystery. Science for me, and for the vast majority of respectable scientists, is not about the secrets of nature or even about truths. Science is simply the method we use to try and postulate a minimum set of assumptions that can explain, through a straightforward logical derivation, the existence of many phenomena of nature.

The Law of Conservation of Energy of physics is not truth. It is just an assumption that is valid in explaining a tremendous amount of natural phenomena. Such an assumption can never be proven since even an infinite number of phenomena that can be explained by it does not prove its universal application. On the other hand, it can be disproved by just a single phenomenon that cannot be explained by the assumption. This disproving does not detract from the validity of the assumption. It just highlights the need or even the existence of another assumption that is *more* valid. This is the case with the assumption of the conservation of energy which was replaced by Einstein's more global—more valid —postulation of the conservation of energy and mass. Einstein's assumption is not true to the same extent that the previous one was not "true".

Somehow we have restricted the connotation of science to a very selective, limited assemblage of natural phenomena. We refer to science when we deal with physics, chemistry or biology. We should also realize that there are many more phenomena of nature that do not fall into these categories, for instance those phenomena we see in organizations, particularly those in industrial organizations. If these phenomena are not phenomena of nature, what are they? Do we want to place what we see in organizations to the arena of fiction rather than into reality?

This book is an attempt to show that we can postulate a very small number of assumptions and utilize them to explain a very large spectrum of industrial phenomena. You the reader can judge whether or not the logic of the book's derivation from its assumptions to the phenomena we see daily in our plants is so flawless that you call it common sense. Incidentally, common sense is not so common and is the highest praise we give to a chain of logical conclusions. If you do, you basically have taken science from the ivory tower of academia and put it where it belongs, within the reach of every one of us and made it applicable to what we see around us.

What I have attempted to show with this book is that no exceptional brain power is needed to construct a new science or to expand on an existing one. What is needed is just the courage to face inconsistencies and to avoid running away from them just because "that's the way it was always done". I dared to interweave into the book a family life struggle, which I assume is quite familiar to any manager who is to some extent obsessed with his work. This was not done just to make the book more popular, but to highlight the fact that we tend to disqualify many phenomena of nature as irrelevent as far as science is concerned.

I have also attempted to show in the book the meaning of education. I sincerely believe that the only way we can learn is through our deductive process. Presenting us with final conclusions is not a way that we learn. At best it is a way that we are trained. That's why I tried to deliver the message contained in the book in the Socratic way. Jonah, in spite of his knowledge of the solutions, provoked Alex to derive them by supplying the question marks instead of the exclamation marks. I believe that because of this method, you the reader will deduce the answers well before Alex Rogo succeeds in doing so. If you find the book entertaining maybe you will agree with me that this is the way to educate, this is the way we should attempt to write our textbooks. Our textbooks should not present us with a series of end results but rather a plot that enables the reader to go through the deduction process himself. If I succeed by this book to change somewhat your perception of science and education, this is my true reward.

INTRODUCTION TO THE FIRST EDITION

"The Goal" is about New global principles of manufacturing. It's about people trying to understand what makes their world tick so that they can make it better. As they think logically and consistently about their problems they are able to determine "cause and effect" relationships between their actions and the results. In the process they deduce some basic principles which they use to save their plant and make it successful.

I view science as nothing more than an understanding of the way the world is and *why* it is that way. At any given time our scientific knowledge is simply the current state of the art of our understanding. I do not believe in absolute truths. I fear such beliefs because they block the search for better understanding. Whenever we think we have final answers progress, science, and better understanding ceases. Understanding of our world is not something to be pursued for its own sake, however. Knowledge should be pursued, I believe, to make our world better—to make life more fulfilling.

There are several reasons I chose a novel to explain my understanding of manufacturing—how it works (reality) and why it works that way. First, I want to make these principles more understandable and show how they can bring order to the chaos that so often exists in our plants. Second, I wanted to illustrate the power of this understanding and the benefits it can bring. The results achieved are not fantasy; they have been, and are being, achieved in real plants. The western world does not have to become a second or third rate manufacturing power. If we just understand and apply the correct principles, we can compete with anyone. I also hope that readers would see the validity and value of these principles in other organizations such as banks, hospitals, insurance companies and our families. Maybe the same potential for growth and improvement exists in all organizations.

Finally, and most importantly, I wanted to show that we can

all be outstanding scientists. The secret of being a good scientist, I believe, lies not in our brain power. We have enough. We simply need to look at reality and think logically and precisely about what we see. The key ingredient is to have the courage to face inconsistencies between what we see and deduce and the way things are done. This challenging of basic assumptions is essential to breakthroughs. Almost everyone who has worked in a plant is at least uneasy about the use of cost accounting efficiencies to control our actions. Yet few have challenged this sacred cow directly. Progress in understanding requires that we challenge basic assumptions about how the world is and why it is that way. If we can better understand our world and the principles that govern it, I suspect all our lives will be better.

Good luck in your search for these principles and for your own understanding of "The Goal."

ABOUT THE AUTHOR

Dr. Eli Goldratt's book, *The Goal* has been a best seller since 1984 and is recognized as one of the best-selling management books of all time. Recently, the Japanese edition of *The Goal* sold over 500,000 copies in less than one year after being released.

Eli Goldratt is the author of many other books including the business novels, *It's Not Luck* (the sequel to *The Goal*), *Critical Chain,* and *Necessary but Not Sufficient.* His books have been translated into 27 languages and sales have exceeded 6 million copies worldwide. His latest book is, *Necessary but Not Sufficient,* which focuses on the low rate of return obtained by companies on their huge investments in IT and enterprise resource planning (ERP) systems.

Eli Goldratt is the founder of TOC for education; a non-profit organization dedicated to bringing TOC thinking and tools to teachers and their students (www.tocforeducation.com). Dr. Goldratt currently spends his time promoting TOC for Education and The Goldratt Group while he continues to write, lecture and consult.

For more information on Eli Goldratt and his current projects visit his web site at: www.eligoldratt.com.

THE GOAL
THIRD REVISED EDITION

1

I come through the gate this morning at 7:30 and I can see it from across the lot: the crimson Mercedes. It's parked beside the plant, next to the offices. And it's in *my* space. Who else would do that except Bill Peach? Never mind that the whole lot is practically empty at that hour. Never mind that there are spaces marked "Visitor." No, Bill's got to park in the space with my title on it. Bill likes to make subtle statements. So, okay, he's the division vice-president, and I'm just a mere plant manager. I guess he can park his damn Mercedes wherever he wants.

I put my Mazda next to it (in the space marked "Controller"). A glance at the license as I walk around it assures me it has to be Bill's car because the plate says "NUMBER 1." And, as we all know, that's absolutely correct in terms of who Bill always looks out for. He wants his shot at CEO. But so do I. Too bad that I may never get the chance now.

Anyway, I'm walking up to the office doors. Already the adrenalin is pumping. I'm wondering what the hell Bill is doing here. I've lost any hope of getting any work done this morning. I usually go in early to catch up on all the stuff I'm too busy to do during the day, because I can really get a lot done before the phone rings and the meetings start, before the fires break out. But not today.

"Mr. Rogo!" I hear someone calling.

I stop as four people come bursting out of a door on the side of the plant. I see Dempsey, the shift supervisor; Martinez, the union steward; some hourly guy; and a machining center foreman named Ray. And they're all talking at the same time. Dempsey is telling me we've got a problem. Martinez is shouting about how there is going to be a walkout. The hourly guy is saying something about harassment. Ray is yelling that we can't finish some damn thing because we don't have all the parts. Suddenly I'm in the middle of all this. I'm looking at them; they're looking at me. And I haven't even had a cup of coffee yet.

When I finally get everyone calmed down enough to ask what's going on, I learn that Mr. Peach arrived about an hour before, walked into my plant, and demanded to be shown the status of Customer Order Number 41427.

Well, as fate would have it, nobody happened to know about Customer Order 41427. So Peach had everybody stepping and fetching to chase down the story on it. And it turns out to be a fairly big order. Also a late one. So what else is new? Everything in this plant is late. Based on observation, I'd say this plant has four ranks of priority for orders: Hot . . . Very Hot . . . Red Hot . . . and Do It NOW! We just can't keep ahead of anything.

As soon as he discovers 41427 is nowhere close to being shipped, Peach starts playing expeditor. He's storming around, yelling orders at Dempsey. Finally it's determined almost all the parts needed are ready and waiting—stacks of them. But they can't be assembled. One part of some sub-assembly is missing; it still has to be run through some other operation yet. If the guys don't have the part, they can't assemble, and if they can't assemble, naturally, they can't ship.

They find out the pieces for the missing subassembly are sitting over by one of the n/c machines, where they're waiting their turn to be run. But when they go to that department, they find the machinists are *not* setting up to run the part in question, but instead some other do-it-now job which somebody imposed upon them for some other product.

Peach doesn't give a damn about the other do-it-now job. All he cares about is getting 41427 out the door. So he tells Dempsey to direct his foreman, Ray, to instruct his master machinist to forget about the other super-hot gizmo and get ready to run the missing part for 41427. Whereupon the master machinist looks from Ray to Dempsey to Peach, throws down his wrench, and tells them they're all crazy. It just took him and his helper an hour and a half to set up for the *other* part that everyone needed so desperately. Now they want to forget about it and set up for something else instead? The hell with it! So Peach, always the diplomat, walks past my supervisor and my foreman, and tells the master machinist that if he doesn't do what he's told, he's fired. More words are exchanged. The machinist threatens to walk off the job. The union steward shows up. Everybody is mad. Nobody is working. And now I've got four upset people greeting me bright and early in front of an idle plant.

"So where is Bill Peach now?" I ask.

"He's in your office," says Dempsey.

"Okay, would you go tell him I'll be in to talk to him in a minute," I ask.

Dempsey gratefully hurries toward the office doors. I turn to Martinez and the hourly guy, who I discover is the machinist. I tell them that as far as I'm concerned there aren't going to be any firings or suspensions—that the whole thing is just a misunderstanding. Martinez isn't entirely satisfied with that at first, and the machinist sounds as if he wants an apology from Peach. I'm not about to step into that one. I also happen to know that Martinez can't call a walkout on his own authority. So I say if the union wants to file a grievance, okay; I'll be glad to talk to the local president, Mike O'Donnell, later today, and we'll handle everything in due course. Realizing he can't do anything more before talking to O'Donnell anyway, Martinez finally accepts that, and he and the hourly guy start walking back to the plant.

"So let's get them back to work," I tell Ray.

"Sure, but uh, what should we be working on?" asks Ray. "The job we're set up to run or the one Peach wants?"

"Do the one Peach wants," I tell him.

"Okay, but we'll be wasting a set-up," says Ray.

"So we waste it!" I tell him. "Ray, I don't even know what the situation is. But for Bill to be here, there must be some kind of emergency. Doesn't that seem logical?"

"Yeah, sure," says Ray. "Hey, I just want to know what to do."

"Okay, I know you were just caught in the middle of all this," I say to try to make him feel better. "Let's just get that setup done as quick as we can and start running that part."

"Right," he says.

Inside, Dempsey passes me on his way back to the plant. He's just come from my office and he looks like he's in a hurry to get out of there. He shakes his head at me.

"Good luck," he says out of the corner of his mouth.

The door to my office is wide open. I walk in, and there he is. Bill Peach is sitting behind my desk. He's a stocky, barrel-chested guy with thick, steely-gray hair and eyes that almost match. As I put my briefcase down, the eyes are locked onto me with a look that says *This is your neck, Rogo.*

"Okay, Bill, what's going on?" I ask.

He says, "We've got things to talk about. Sit down."

I say, "I'd like to, but you're in my seat."

It may have been the wrong thing to say.

"You want to know why I'm here?" he says. "I'm here to save your lousy skin."

I tell him, "Judging from the reception I just got, I'd say you're here to ruin my labor relations."

He looks straight at me and says, "If you can't make some things happen around here, you're not going to have any labor to worry about. Because you're not going to have this plant to worry about. In fact, you may not have a job to worry about, Rogo."

"Okay, wait a minute, take it easy," I say. "Let's just talk about it. What's the problem with this order?"

First of all, Bill tells me that he got a phone call last night at home around ten o'clock from good old Bucky Burnside, president of one of UniCo's biggest customers. Seems that Bucky was having a fit over the fact that this order of his (41427) is seven weeks late. He proceeded to rake Peach over the coals for about an hour. Bucky apparently had gone out on a limb to sway the order over to us when everybody was telling him to give the business to one of our competitors. He had just had dinner with several of his customers, and they had dumped all over him because their orders were late—which, as it happens, was because of us. So Bucky was mad (and probably a little drunk). Peach was able to pacify him only by promising to deal with the matter personally and by guaranteeing that the order would be shipped by the end of today, no matter what mountains had to be moved.

I try to tell Bill that, yes, we were clearly wrong to have let this order slide, and I'll give it my personal attention, but did he have to come in here this morning and disrupt my whole plant?

So where was I last night, he asks, when he tried to call me at home? Under the circumstances, I can't tell him I have a personal life. I can't tell him that the first two times the phone rang, I let it ring because I was in the middle of a fight with my wife, which, oddly enough, was about how little attention I've been giving her. And the third time, I didn't answer it because we were making up.

I decide to tell Peach I was just late getting home. He doesn't press the issue. Instead, he asks how come I don't know what's going on inside my own plant. He's sick and tired of hearing complaints about late shipments. Why can't I stay on top of things?

"One thing I do know," I tell him, "is that after the second round of layoffs you forced on us three months ago, along with the order for a twenty percent cutback, we're lucky to get anything out the door on time."

"Al," he says quietly, "just build the damn products. You hear me?"

"Then give me the people I need!" I tell him.

"You've got enough people! Look at your efficiencies, for god's sake! You've got room for improvement, Al," he says. "Don't come crying to me about not enough people until you show me you can effectively use what you've got."

I'm about to say something when Peach holds up his hand for me to shut my mouth. He stands up and goes over to close the door. Oh shit, I'm thinking.

He turns by the door and tells me, "Sit down."

I've been standing all this time. I take a seat in one of the chairs in front of the desk, where a visitor would sit. Peach returns behind the desk.

"Look, Al, it's a waste of time to argue about this. Your last operations report tells the story," says Peach.

I say, "Okay, you're right. The issue is getting Burnside's order shipped—"

Peach explodes. "Dammit, the issue is not Burnside's order! Burnside's order is just a symptom of the problem around here. Do you think I'd come down here just to expedite a late order? Do you think I don't have enough to do? I came down here to light a fire under you and everybody else in this plant. This isn't just a matter of customer service. Your plant is losing money."

He pauses for a moment, as if he had to let that sink in. Then —bam—he pounds his fist on the desk top and points his finger at me.

"And if you can't get the orders out the door," he continues, "then I'll show you how to do it. And if you still can't do it, then I've got no use for you *or* this plant."

"Now wait a minute, Bill—"

"Dammit, I don't have a minute!" he roars. "I don't have time for excuses anymore. And I don't need explanations. I need performance. I need shipments. I need income!"

"Yes, I know that, Bill."

"What you may not know is that this division is facing the worst losses in its history. We're falling into a hole so deep we may never get out, and your plant is the anchor pulling us in."

I feel exhausted already. Tiredly I ask him, "Okay, what do

you want from me? I've been here six months. I admit it's gotten worse instead of better since I've been here. But I'm doing the best I can."

"If you want the bottom line, Al, this is it: You've got three months to turn this plant around," Peach says.

"And suppose it can't be done in that time?" I ask.

"Then I'm going to go to the management committee with a recommendation to close the plant," he says.

I sit there speechless. This is definitely worse than anything I expected to hear this morning. And, yet, it's not really that surprising. I glance out the window. The parking lot is filling with the cars of the people coming to work first shift. When I look back, Peach has stood up and is coming around the desk. He sits down in the chair next to me and leans forward. Now comes the reassurance, the pep talk.

"Al, I know that the situation you inherited here wasn't the best. I gave you this job because I thought you were the one who could change this plant from a loser to . . . well, a small winner at least. And I still think that. But if you want to go places in this company, you've got to deliver results."

"But I need time, Bill."

"Sorry, you've got three months. And if things get much worse, I may not even be able to give you that."

I sit there as Bill glances at his watch and stands up, discussion ended.

He says, "If I leave now, I'll only miss my first meeting."

I stand up. He walks to the door.

Hand on the knob, he turns and says with a grin, "Now that I've helped you kick some ass around here, you won't have any trouble getting Bucky's order shipped for me today, will you?"

"We'll ship it, Bill," I say.

"Good," he says with wink as he opens the door.

A minute later, I watch from the window as he gets into his Mercedes and drives toward the gate.

Three months. That's all I can think about.

I don't remember turning away from the window. I don't know how much time has passed. All of a sudden, I'm aware that I'm sitting at my desk and I'm staring into space. I decide I'd better go see for myself what's happening out in the plant. From the shelf by the door, I get my hard hat and safety glasses and head out. I pass my secretary.

"Fran, I'll be out on the floor for a little while," I tell her as I go by.

Fran looks up from a letter she's typing and smiles.

"Okey-dokey," she says. "By the way, was that Peach's car I saw in your space this morning?"

"Yes, it was."

"Nice car," she says and she laughs. "I thought it might be yours when I first saw it."

Then I laugh. She leans forward across the desk.

"Say, how much would a car like that cost?" she asks.

"I don't know exactly, but I think it's around sixty thousand dollars," I tell her.

Fran catches her breath. "You're kidding me! That much? I had no idea a car could cost that much. Wow. Guess I won't be trading in my Chevette on one of those very soon."

She laughs and turns back to her typing.

Fran is an "okey-dokey" lady. How old is she? Early forties I'd guess, with two teen-aged kids she's trying to support. Her ex-husband is an alcoholic. They got divorced a long time ago . . . since then, she's wanted nothing to do with a man. Well, almost nothing. Fran told me all this herself on my second day at the plant. I like her. I like her work, too. We pay her a good wage . . . at least we do now. Anyway, she's still got three months.

Going into the plant is like entering a place where satans and angels have married to make kind of a gray magic. That's what it always feels like to me. All around are things that are mundane and miraculous. I've always found manufacturing plants to be fascinating places—even on just a visual level. But most people don't see them the way I do.

Past a set of double doors separating the office from the plant, the world changes. Overhead is a grid of lamps suspended from the roof trusses, and everything is cast in the warm, orange hues of sodium-iodine light. There is a huge chain-link cage which has row after row of floor-to-roof racks loaded with bins and cartons filled with parts and materials for everything we make. In a skinny aisle between two racks rides a man in the basket of a forklift crane that runs along a track on the ceiling. Out on the floor, a reel of shiny steel slowly unrolls into the machine that every few seconds says "Ca-chunk."

Machines. The plant is really just one vast room, acres of space, filled with machines. They are organized in blocks and the blocks are separated by aisles. Most of the machines are painted in solid Mardi Gras colors—orange, purple, yellow, blue. From some of the newer machines, ruby numbers shine from digital displays. Robotic arms perform programs of mechanical dance.

Here and there, often almost hidden among the machines, are the people. They look over as I walk by. Some of them wave; I wave back. An electric cart whines past, an enormous fat guy driving it. Women at long tables work with rainbows of wire. A grimy guy in amorphous coveralls adjusts his face mask and ignites a welding torch. Behind glass, a buxom, red-haired woman pecks the keys on a computer terminal with an amber display.

Mixed with the sights is the noise, a din with a continuous underlying chord made by the whirr of fans, motors, the air in the ventilators—it all sounds like an endless breath. At random comes a BOOM of something inexplicable. Behind me ring the alarm bells of an overhead crane rumbling up its track. Relays click. The siren sounds. From the P.A. system, a disembodied voice talks like God, intermittently and incomprehensibly, over everything.

Even with all that noise, I hear the whistle. Turning, I see the unmistakable shape of Bob Donovan walking up the aisle. He's some distance away. Bob is what you might call a mountain of a man, standing as he does at six-foot-four. He weighs in at about 250 pounds, a hefty portion of which is beer gut. He isn't the prettiest guy in the world . . . I think his barber was trained by the Marines. And he doesn't talk real fancy; I suspect it's a point of pride with him. But despite a few rough edges, which he guards closely, Bob is a good guy. He's been production manager here for nine years. If you need something to happen, all you do is talk to Bob and if it can be done, it will be by the next time you mention it.

It takes a minute or so for us to reach each other. As we get closer, I can see he isn't very cheerful. I suppose it's mutual.

"Good morning," says Bob.

"I'm not sure what's good about it," I say. "Did you hear about our visitor?"

"Yeah, it's all over the plant," says Bob.

"So I guess you know about the urgency for shipping a certain order number 41427?" I ask him.

He starts to turn red. "That's what I need to talk to you about."

"Why? What's up?"

"I don't know if word reached you yet, but Tony, that master machinist Peach yelled at, quit this morning," says Bob.

"Aw, shit," I mutter.

"I don't think I have to tell you that guys like that are not a dime a dozen. We're going to have a tough time finding a replacement," says Bob.

"Can we get him back?"

"Well, we may not want him back," says Bob. "Before he quit, he did the set-up that Ray told him to do, and put the machine on automatic to do its run. The thing is, he didn't tighten two of the adjusting nuts. We got little bits of machine tool all over the floor now."

"How many parts do we have to scrap?"

"Well, not that many. It only ran for a little while."

"Will we have enough to fill that order?" I ask him.

"I'll have to check," he says. "But, see, the problem is that the machine itself is down and it may stay down for some time."

"Which one is it?" I ask.

"The NCX-10," he says.

I shut my eyes. It's like a cold hand just reached inside me and grabbed the bottom of my stomach. That machine is the only one of its type in the plant. I ask Bob how bad the damage is. He says, "I don't know. They've got the thing half torn apart out there. We're on the phone with the manufacturer right now."

I start walking fast. I want to see it for myself. God, are we in trouble. I glance over at Bob, who is keeping pace with me.

"Do you think it was sabotage?" I ask.

Bob seems surprised. "Well, I can't say. I think the guy was just so upset he couldn't think straight. So he screwed it up."

I can feel my face getting hot. The cold hand is gone. Now I'm so pissed off at Bill Peach that I'm fantasizing about calling him on the phone and screaming in his ear. It's his fault! And in my head I see him. I see him behind my desk and hear him telling me how he's going to show me how to get the orders out the door. Right, Bill. You really showed me how to do it.

2

Isn't it strange to feel your own world is falling apart while those of the people close to you are rock steady? And you can't figure out why they're not affected the way you are. About 6:30, I slip away from the plant to run home and grab some dinner. As I come through the door, Julie looks up from the television.

"Hi," she says. "Like my hair?"

She turns her head. The thick, straight brown hair she used to have is now a mass of frizzed ringlets. And it isn't all the same color anymore. It's lighter in places.

"Yeah, looks great," I say automatically.

"The hairdresser said it sets off my eyes," she says, batting her long lashes at me. She has big, pretty blue eyes; they don't need to be "set off" in my opinion, but what do I know?

"Nice," I say.

"Gee, you're not very enthusiastic," she says.

"Sorry, but I've had a rough day."

"Ah, poor baby," she says. "But I've got a great idea! We'll go out to dinner and you can forget all about it."

I shake my head. "I can't. I've got to eat something fast and get back to the plant."

She stands up and puts her hands on her hips. I notice she's wearing a new outfit.

"Well you're a lot of fun!" she says. "And after I got rid of the kids, too."

"Julie, I've got a crisis on my hands. One of my most expensive machines went down this morning, and I need it to process a part for a rush order. I've got to stay on top of this one," I tell her.

"Okay. Fine. There is nothing to eat, because I thought we were going out," she says. "Last night, you said we were going out."

Then I remember. She's right. It was part of the promises when we were making up after the fight.

"I'm sorry. Look, maybe we can go out for an hour or so," I tell her.

"That's your idea of a night on the town?" she says. "Forget it, Al!"

"Listen to me," I tell her. "Bill Peach showed up unexpectedly this morning. He's talking about closing the plant."

Her face changes. Did it brighten?

"Closing the plant . . . really?" she asks.

"Yeah, it's getting very bad."

"Did you talk to him about where your next job would be?" she asks.

After a second of disbelief, I say, "No, I didn't talk to him about my next job. My job is *here*—in this town, at this plant." ·

She says, "Well, if the plant is going to close, aren't you interested in where you're going to live next? I am."

"He's only talking about it."

"Oh," she says.

I feel myself glaring at her. I say, "You really want to get out of this town as fast as you can, don't you?"

"It isn't my home town, Al. I don't have the same sentimental feelings for it you do," she says.

"We've only been here six months," I say.

"Is that all? A mere six months?" she says. "Al, I have no friends here. There's nobody except you to talk to, and you're not home most of the time. Your family is very nice, but after an hour with your mother, I go crazy. So it doesn't feel like six months to me."

"What do you want me to do? I didn't ask to come here. The company sent me to do a job. It was the luck of the draw," I say.

"Some luck."

"Julie, I do not have time to get into another fight with you," I tell her.

She's starting to cry.

"Fine! Go ahead and leave! I'll just be here by myself," she crys. "Like every night."

"Aw, Julie."

I finally go put my arms around her. We stand together for a few minutes, both of us quiet. When she stops crying, she steps back and looks up at me.

"I'm sorry," she says. "If you have to go back to the plant, then you'd better go."

"Why don't we go out tomorrow night?" I suggest.

She turns up her hands. "Fine . . . whatever."

I turn, then look back. "Will you be okay?"

"Sure. I'll find something to eat in the freezer," she says.

I've forgotten about dinner by now. I say, "Okay, I'll probably pick up something on my way back to the plant. See you later tonight."

Once I'm in the car, I find I've lost my appetite.

Ever since we moved to Bearington, Julie has been having a hard time. Whenever we talk about the town, she always complains about it, and I always find myself defending it.

It's true I was born and raised in Bearington, so I do feel at home here. I know all the streets. I know the best places to go to buy things, the good bars and the places you stay out of, all that stuff. There is a sense of ownership I have for the town, and more affection for it than for some other burg down the highway. It was home for eighteen years.

But I don't think I have too many illusions about it. Bearington is a factory town. Anyone passing through probably wouldn't see anything special about the place. Driving along, I look around and have much the same reaction. The neighborhood where we live looks like any other American suburb. The houses are fairly new. There are shopping centers nearby, a litter of fast-food restaurants, and over next to the Interstate is a big mall. I can't see much difference here from any of the other suburbs where we've lived.

Go to the center of town and it *is* a little depressing. The streets are lined with old brick buildings that have a sooty, crumbling look to them. A number of store fronts are vacant or covered with plywood. There are plenty of railroad tracks, but not many trains.

On the corner of Main and Lincoln is Bearington's one high-rise office building, a lone tower on the skyline. When it was being built some ten years ago, the building was considered to be a very big deal around here, all fourteen stories of it. The fire department used it as an excuse to go buy a brand new fire engine, just so it would have a ladder long enough to reach to the top. (Ever since then, I think they've secretly been waiting for a fire to break out in the penthouse just to use the new ladder.) Local boosters immediately claimed that the new office tower was some kind of symbol of Bearington's vitality, a sign of re-birth in an old industrial town. Then a couple of years ago, the building management erected an enormous sign on the roof which says in red block letters: "Buy Me!" It gives a phone number. From the

Interstate, it looks like the whole town is for sale. Which isn't too far from the truth.

On my way to work each day, I pass another plant along the road to ours. It sits behind a rusty chain-link fence with barbed wire running along the top. In front of the plant is a paved parking lot—five acres of concrete with tufts of brown grass poking through the cracks. Years have gone by since any cars have parked there. The paint has faded on the walls and they've got a chalky look to them. High on the long front wall you can still make out the company name; there's darker paint where the letters and logo had once been before they were removed.

The company that owned the plant went south. They built a new plant somewhere in North Carolina. Word has it they were trying to run away from a bad situation with their union. Word also has it that the union probably will catch up with them again in about five years or so. But meanwhile they'll have bought themselves five years of lower wages and maybe fewer hassles from the work force. And five years seem like eternity as far as modern management planning is concerned. So Bearington got another industrial dinosaur carcass on its outskirts and about 2,000 people hit the street.

Six months ago, I had occasion to go inside the plant. At the time, we were just looking for some cheap warehouse space nearby. Not that it was my job, but I went over with some other people just to look the place over. (Dreamer that I was when I first got here, I thought maybe someday we'd need more space to expand. What a laugh that is now.) It was the silence that really got to me. Everything was so quiet. Your footsteps echoed. It was weird. All the machines had been removed. It was just a huge empty place.

Driving by it now, I can't help thinking, that's going to be us in three months. It gives me a sick feeling.

I hate to see this stuff happening. The town has been losing major employers at the rate of about one a year ever since the mid-1970s. They fold completely, or they pull out and go elsewhere. There doesn't seem to be any end to it. And now it may be our turn.

When I came back to manage this plant, the Bearington *Herald* did a story on me. I know, big deal. But I was kind of a minor celebrity for a while. The local boy had made it big. It was sort of a high-school fantasy come true. I hate to think that the next time my name is in the paper, the story might be about the plant closing. I'm starting to feel like a traitor to everybody.

Donovan looks like a nervous gorilla when I get back to the plant. With all the running around he's done today, he must have lost five pounds. As I walk up the aisle toward the NCX-10, I watch him shifting his weight from one leg to the other. Then he paces for a few seconds and stops. Suddenly he darts across the aisle to talk to someone. And then he takes off to check on something. I give him a shrill, two-finger whistle, but he doesn't hear it. I have to follow him through two departments before I can catch up with him—back at the NCX-10. He looks surprised to see me.

"We going to make it?" I ask him.

"We're trying," he says.

"Yeah, but can we do it?"

"We're doing our best," he says.

"Bob, are we going to ship the order tonight or not?"

"Maybe."

I turn away and stand there looking at the NCX-10. Which is a lot to look at. It's a big hunk of equipment, our most expensive n/c machine. And it's painted a glossy, distinctive lavender. (Don't ask me why.) On one side is a control board filled with red, green, and amber lights, shiny toggle switches, a jet black keyboard, tape drives, and a computer display. It's a sexy-looking machine. And the focus of it all is the metal-working being done in the middle of it, where a vise holds a piece of steel. Shavings of metal are being sliced away by a cutting tool. A steady wash of turquoise lubricant splashes over the work and carries away the chips. At least the damn thing is working again.

We were lucky today. The damage wasn't as bad as we had first thought. But the service technician didn't start packing his tools until 4:30. By then, it was already second shift.

We held everybody in assembly on overtime, even though overtime is against current division policy. I don't know where we'll bury the expense, but we've to go get this order shipped tonight. I got four phone calls today just from our marketing manager, Johnny Jons. He too has been getting his ear chewed—from Peach, from his own sales people, and from the customer. We absolutely must ship this order tonight.

So I'm hoping nothing else goes wrong. As soon as each part

is finished, it's individually carried over to where it's fitted into the subassembly. And as soon as that happens, the foreman over there is having each subassembly carted down to final assembly. You want to talk about efficiency? People hand-carrying things one at a time, back and forth . . . our output of parts per employee must be ridiculous. It's crazy. In fact, I'm wondering, where did Bob get all the people?

I take a slow look around. There is hardly anybody working in the departments that don't have something to do with 41427. Donovan has stolen every body he could grab and put them all to work on this order. This is not the way it's supposed to be done.

But the order ships.

I glance at my watch. It's a few minutes past 11:00 P.M. We're on the shipping dock. The doors on the back of the tractor-trailer are being closed. The driver is climbing up into his seat. He revs the engine, releases the brakes, and eases out into the night.

I turn to Donovan. He turns to me.

"Congratulations," I tell him.

"Thanks, but don't ask me how we did it," he says.

"Okay, I won't. What do you say we find ourselves some dinner?"

For the first time all day, Donovan smiles. Way off in the distance, the truck shifts gears.

We take Donovan's car because it's closer. The first two places we try are closed. So then I tell Donovan just to follow my directions. We cross the river at 16th Street and drive down Bessemer into South Flat until we get to the mill. Then I tell Donovan to hang a right and we snake our way through the side streets. The houses back in there are built wall to wall, no yards, no grass, no trees. The streets are narrow and everyone parks in the streets, so it makes for some tedious maneuvering. But finally we pull up in front of Sednikk's Bar and Grill.

Donovan takes a look at the place and says, "You sure this is where we want to be?"

"Yeah, yeah. Come on. They've got the best burgers in town," I tell him.

Inside, we take a booth toward the rear. Maxine recognizes me and comes over to make a fuss. We talk for a minute and then Donovan and I order some burgers and fries and beer.

Donovan looks around and says, "How'd you know about this place?"

I say, "Well, I had my first shot-and-a-beer over there at the bar. I think it was the third stool on the left, but it's been a while."

Donovan asks, "Did you start drinking late in life, or did you grow up in this town?"

"I grew up two blocks from here. My father owned a corner grocery store. My brother runs it today."

"I didn't know you were from Bearington," says Donovan.

"With all the transfers, it's taken me about fifteen years to get back here," I say.

The beers arrive.

Maxine says, "These two are on Joe."

She points to Joe Sednikk who stands behind the bar. Donovan and I wave out thanks to him.

Donovan raises his glass, and says, "Here's to getting 41427 out the door."

"I'll drink to that," I say and clink my glass against his.

After a few swallows, Donovan looks much more relaxed. But I'm still thinking about what went on tonight.

"You know, we paid a hell of a price for that shipment," I say. "We lost a good machinist. There's the repair bill on the NCX-10. Plus the overtime."

"Plus the time we lost on the NCX-10 while it was down," adds Donovan. Then he says, "But you got to admit that once we got rolling, we really moved. I wish we could do that every day."

I laugh. "No thanks. I don't need days like this one."

"I don't mean we need Bill Peach to walk into the plant every day. But we *did* ship the order," says Donovan.

"I'm all for shipping orders, Bob, but not the way we did it tonight," I tell him.

"It went out the door, didn't it?"

"Yes, it did. But it was the way that it happened that we can't allow."

"I just saw what had to be done, put everybody to work on it, and the hell with the rules," he says.

"Bob, do you know what our efficiencies would look like if we ran the plant like that every day?" I ask. "We can't just dedicate the entire plant to one order at a time. The economies of scale would disappear. Our costs would go—well, they'd be even worse than they are now. We can't run the plant just by the seat-of-the-pants."

Donovan becomes quiet. Finally he says, "Maybe I learned too many of the wrong things back when I was an expeditor."

"Listen, you did a hell of a job today. I mean that. But we set policy for a purpose. You should know that. And let me tell you that Bill Peach, for all the trouble he caused to get one order shipped, would be back here pounding on our heads at the end of the month if we didn't manage the plant for efficiency."

He nods slowly, but then he asks, "So what do we do the next time this happens?"

I smile.

"Probably the same damn thing," I tell him. Then I turn and say, "Maxine, give us two more here, please. No, on second thought, we're going to save you a lot of walking. Make it a pitcher."

So we made it through today's crisis. We won. Just barely. And now that Donovan is gone and the effects of the alcohol are wearing off, I can't see what there was to celebrate. We managed to ship one very late order today. Whoopee.

The real issue is I've got a manufacturing plant on the critical list. Peach has given it three months to live before he pulls the plug.

That means I have two, maybe three more monthly reports in which to change his mind. After that, the sequence of events will be that he'll go to corporate management and present the numbers. Everybody around the table will look at Granby. Granby will ask a couple of questions, look at the numbers one more time, and nod his head. And that will be it. Once the executive decision has been made, there will be no changing it.

They'll give us time to finish our backlog. And then 600 people will head for the unemployment lines—where they will join their friends and former co-workers, the *other* 600 people whom we have already laid off.

And so the UniWare Division will drop out of yet another market in which it can't compete. Which means the world will no longer be able to buy any more of the fine products we can't make cheap enough or fast enough or good enough or something enough to beat the Japanese. Or most anybody else out there for that matter. That's what makes us another fine division in the UniCo "family" of businesses (which has a record of earnings growth that looks like Kansas), and that's why we'll be just

another fine company in the Who-Knows-What Corporation after the big boys at headquarters put together some merger with
some other loser. That seems to be the essence of the company's
strategic plan these days.

What's the matter with us?

Every six months it seems like some group from corporate is
coming out with some new program that's the latest panacea to
all our problems. Some of them seem to work, but none of them
does any good. We limp along month after month, and it never
gets any better. Mostly it gets worse.

Okay. Enough of the bitching, Rogo. Try to calm down. Try
to think about this rationally. There's nobody around. It's late. I
am alone finally . . . here in the coveted corner office, throne
room of my empire, such as it is. No interruptions. The phone is
not ringing. So let's try to analyze the situation. Why can't we
consistently get a quality product out the door on time at the cost
that can beat the competition?

Something is wrong. I don't know what it is, but something
basic is very wrong. I must be missing something.

I'm running what *should* be a good plant. Hell, it is a good
plant. We've got the technology. We've got some of the best n/c
machines money can buy. We've got robots. We've got a computer system that's supposed to do everything but make coffee.

We've got good people. For the most part we do. Okay, we're
short in a couple of areas, but the people we have are good for
the most part, even though we sure could use more of them. And
I don't have too many problems with the union. They're a pain in
the ass sometimes, but the competition has unions too. And, hell,
the workers made some concessions last time—not as many as
we'd have liked, but we have a livable contract.

I've got the machines. I've got the people. I've got all the
materials I need. I know there's a market out there, because the
competitors' stuff is selling. So what the hell is it?

It's the damn competition. That's what's killing us. Ever
since the Japanese entered our markets, the competition has been
incredible. Three years ago, they were beating us on quality and
product design. We've just about matched them on those. But
now they're beating us on price and deliveries. I wish I knew
their secret.

What can I possibly do to be more competitive?

I've done cost reduction. No other manager in this division has cut costs to the degree I have. There is nothing left to trim.

And, despite what Peach says, my efficiencies are pretty damn good. He's got other plants with worse, I know that. But the better ones don't have the competition I do. Maybe I could push efficiencies some more, but . . . I don't know. It's like whipping a horse that's already running as fast as it can.

We've just got to do something about late orders. Nothing in this plant ships until it's expedited. We've got stacks and stacks of inventory out there. We release the materials on schedule, but nothing comes out the far end when it's supposed to.

That's not uncommon. Just about every plant I know of has expeditors. And you walk through just about any plant in America about our size and you'll find work-in-process inventory on the same scale as what we have. I don't know what it is. On the one hand, this plant is no worse than most of the ones I've seen— and, in fact, it's better than many. But we're losing money.

If we could just get our backlog out the door. Sometimes it's like little gremlins out there. Every time we start to get it right, they sneak around between shifts when nobody is looking and they change things just enough so everything gets screwed up. I swear it's got to be gremlins.

Or maybe I just don't know enough. But, hell, I've got an engineering degree. I've got an MBA. Peach wouldn't have named me to the job if he hadn't thought I was qualified. So it can't be me. Can it?

Man, how long has it been since I started out down there in industrial engineering as a smart kid who knew everything— fourteen, fifteen years? How many long days have there been since then?

I used to think if I worked hard I could do anything. Since the day I turned twelve I've worked. I worked after school in my old man's grocery store. I worked through high school. When I was old enough, I spent my summers working in the mills around here. I was always told that if I worked hard enough it would pay off in the end. That's true, isn't it? Look at my brother; he took the easy way out by being the first born. Now he owns a grocery store in a bad neighborhood across town. But look at me. I worked hard. I sweated my way through engineering school. I got a job with a big company. I made myself a stranger to my wife and kids. I took all the crap that UniCo could give me and said,

"I can't get enough! Give me more!" Boy, am I glad I did! Here I am, thirty-eight years old, and I'm a crummy plant manager! Isn't that wonderful? I'm really having fun now.

Time to get the hell out of here. I've had enough fun for one day.

3

I wake up with Julie on top of me. Unfortunately, Julie is not being amorous; she is reaching for the night table where the digital alarm clock says 6:03 A.M. The alarm buzzer has been droning for three minutes. Julie smashes the button to kill it. With a sigh, she rolls off of me. Moments later, I hear her breathing resume a steady pace; she is asleep again. Welcome to a brand new day.

About forty-five minutes later, I'm backing the Mazda out of the garage. It's still dark outside. But a few miles down the road the sky lightens. Halfway to the city, the sun rises. By then, I'm too busy thinking to notice it at first. I glance to the side and it's floating out there beyond the trees. What makes me mad sometimes is that I'm always running so hard that—like most other people, I guess—I don't have time to pay attention to all the daily miracles going on around me. Instead of letting me eyes drink in the dawn, I'm watching the road and worrying about Peach. He's called a meeting at headquarters for all the people who directly report to him—in essence, his plant managers and his staff. The meeting, we are told, is to begin promptly at 8:00 A.M. The funny thing is that Peach is not saying what the meeting is about. It's a big secret—you know: hush-hush, like maybe there's a war on or something. He has instructed us to be there at eight and to bring with us reports and other data that'll let us go through a thorough assessment of all the division's operations.

Of course, all of us have found out what the meeting is about. At least we have a fairly good idea. According to the grapevine, Peach is going to use the meeting to lay some news on us about how badly the division performed in the first quarter. Then he's going to hit us with a mandate for a new productivity drive, with targeted goals for each plant and commitments and all that great stuff. I suppose that's the reason for the commandment to be there at eight o'clock on the button with numbers in hand; Peach must've thought it would lend a proper note of discipline and urgency to the proceedings.

The irony is that in order to be there at such an early hour, half the people attending will have had to fly in the night before. Which means hotel bills and extra meals. So in order to announce to us how badly the division is doing, Peach is going to pay out a couple of grand more than he would have had to pay if he'd begun the meeting an hour or two later.

I think that Peach may be starting to lose it. Not that I suspect him of drifting toward a breakdown or anything. It's just that everything seems to be an over-reaction on his part these days. He's like a general who knows he is losing the battle, but forgets his strategy in his desperation to win.

He was different a couple of years ago. He was confident. He wasn't afraid to delegate responsibility. He'd let you run your own show—as long as you brought in a respectable bottom line. He tried to be the "enlightened" manager. He wanted to be open to new ideas. If some consultant came in and said, "Employees have to feel good about their work in order to be productive," Peach would try to listen. But that was when sales were better and budgets were flush.

What does he say now?

"I don't give a damn if they feel good," he says. "If it costs an extra nickel, we're not paying for it."

That was what he said to a manager who was trying to sell Peach on the idea of a physical fitness center where employees could work out, the premise being that everyone would do better work because healthy employees are happy employees, etc. Peach practically threw him out of his office.

And now he's walking into my plant and wreaking havoc in the name of improving customer service. That wasn't even the first fight I've had with Peach. There have been a couple of others, although none as serious as yesterday's. What really bugs me is I used to get along very well with Peach. There was a time when I thought we were friends. Back when I was on his staff, we'd sit in his office at the end of the day sometimes and just talk for hours. Once in a while, we'd go out and get a couple of drinks together. Everybody thought I was brown-nosing the guy. But I think he liked me precisely because I wasn't. I just did good work for him. We hit it off together.

Once upon a time, there was a crazy night in Atlanta at the annual sales meeting, when Peach and I and a bunch of wackos from marketing stole the piano from the hotel bar and had a sing-along in the elevator. Other hotel guests who were waiting for an elevator would see the doors open, and there we'd be, midway through the chorus of some Irish drinking song with

Peach sitting there at the keyboard tickling those ivories. (He's a pretty good piano player, too). After an hour, the hotel manager finally caught up with us. By then, the crowd had grown too big for the elevator, and we were up on the roof singing to the entire city. I had to pull Bill out of this fight with the two bouncers whom the manager had enlisted to kill the party. What a night that was. Bill and I ended up toasting each other with orange juice at dawn in some greasy-spoon diner on the wrong end of town.

Peach was the one who let me know that I really had a future with this company. He was the guy who pulled me into the picture when I was just a project engineer, when all I knew was how to try hard. He was the one who picked me to go to headquarters. It was Peach who set it up so I could go back and get my MBA.

Now we're screaming at each other. I can't believe it.

By 7:50, I'm parking my car in the garage under the UniCo building. Peach and his division staff occupy three floors of the building. I get out of the car and get my briefcase from the trunk. It weighs about ten pounds today, because it's full of reports and computer printouts. I'm not expecting to have a nice day. With a frown on my face, I start to walk to the elevator.

"Al!" I hear from behind me.

I turn; it's Nathan Selwin coming toward me. I wait for him.

"How's it going?" he asks.

"Okay. Good to see you again," I tell him. We start walking together. "I saw the memo on your appointment to Peach's staff. Congratulations."

"Thanks," he says. "Of course, I don't know if it's the best place to be right now with everything that's going on."

"How come? Bill keeping you working nights?"

"No, it's not that," he says. Then he pauses and looks at me. "Haven't you heard the news?"

"What about?"

He stops suddenly and looks around. There is nobody else around us.

"About the division," he says in a low voice.

I shrug; I don't know what he's talking about.

"The whole division is going to go on the block," he says. "Everybody on Fifteen is crapping in their pants. Peach got the word from Granby a week ago. He's got till the end of the year to improve performance, or the whole division goes up for sale. And I don't know if it's true, but I heard Granby specifically say that if the division goes, Peach goes with it."

"Are you sure?"

Nathan nods and adds, "Apparently it's been in the making for quite a while."

We start walking again.

My first reaction is that it's no wonder Peach has been acting like a madman lately. Everything he's worked for is in jeopardy. If some other corporation buys the division, Peach won't even have a job. The new owners will want to clean house and they're sure to start at the top.

And what about me; will I have a job? Good question, Rogo. Before hearing this, I was going on the assumption that Peach would probably offer me some kind of position if the plant is shut down. That's usually the way it goes. Of course, it may not be what I want. I know there aren't any UniWare plants out there in need of a manager. But I figured maybe Peach would give me my old staff job back—although I also know it's already been filled and I've heard that Peach is very satisfied with the guy. Come to think of it, he did kind of threaten yesterday with his opening remarks that I might not have a job.

Shit, I could be on the street in three months!

"Listen, Al, if anybody asks you, you didn't hear any of this from me," says Nat.

And he's gone. I find myself standing alone in the corridor on the fifteenth floor. I don't even remember having gotten on the elevator, but here I am. I vaguely recall Nat talking to me on the way up, saying something about everybody putting out their resumés.

I look around, feel stupid, wonder where I'm supposed to be now, and then I remember the meeting. I head down the hall where I see some others going into a conference room.

I go in and take a seat. Peach is standing at the far end of the table. A slide projector sits in front of him. He's starting to talk. A clock on the wall indicates it's exactly eight o'clock.

I look around at the others. There are about twenty of them, most of them looking at Peach. One of them, Hilton Smyth, is looking at me. He's a plant manager, too, and he's a guy I've never liked much. For one thing, I resent his style—he's always promoting some new thing he's doing, and most of the time what he's doing isn't any different from the things everyone else is doing. Anyway, he's looking at me as if he's checking me out. Is it because I look a little shaken? I wonder what he knows. I stare back at him until he turns toward Peach.

When I'm finally able to tune into what Peach is saying, I find he's turning the discussion over to the division controller, Ethan Frost, a thin and wrinkled old guy who, with a little makeup, could double for the Grim Reaper.

The news this morning befits the messenger. The first quarter has just ended, and it's been a terrible one everywhere. The division is now in real danger of a shortfall in cash. All belts must be tightened.

When Frost is done, Peach stands and proceeds to deliver some stern talk about how we're going to meet this challenge. I try to listen, but after his first couple of sentences, my mind drops out. All I hear are fragments.

". . . imperative for us to minimize the downside risk . . ." ". . . acceptable to our current marketing posture . . ." ". . . without reducing strategic expense . . ." ". . . required sacrifices . . ." ". . . productivity improvements at all locations . . ."

Graphs from the slide projector begin to flash on the screen. A relentless exchange of measurements between Peach and the others goes on and on. I make an effort, but I just can't concentrate.

". . . first quarter sales down twenty-two percent compared to a year ago . . ." ". . . total raw materials' costs increased . . ." ". . . direct labor ratios of hours applied to hours paid had a three-week high . . ." ". . . now if you look at numbers of hours applied to production versus standard, we're off by over twelve percent on those efficiencies . . ."

I'm telling myself that I've got to get hold of myself and pay attention. I reach into my jacket to get a pen to take some notes.

"And the answer is clear," Peach is saying. "The future of our business depends upon our ability to increase productivity."

But I can't find a pen. So I reach into my other pocket. And I pull out the cigar. I stare at it. I don't smoke anymore. For a few seconds I'm wondering where the hell this cigar came from.

And then I remember.

4

Two weeks ago, I'm wearing the same suit as now. This is back in the good days when I think that everything will work out. I'm traveling, and I'm between planes at O'Hare. I've got some time, so I go to one of the airline lounges. Inside, the place is jammed with business types like me. I'm looking for a seat in this place, gazing over the three-piece pinstripes and the women in conservative blazers and so on, when my eye pauses on the yarmulke worn by the man in the sweater. He's sitting next to a lamp, reading, his book in one hand and his cigar in the other. Next to him there happens to be an empty seat. I make for it. Not until I've almost sat down does it strike me I think I know this guy.

Running into someone you know in the middle of one of the busiest airports in the world carries a shock with it. At first, I'm not sure it's really him. But he looks too much like the physicist I used to know for him to be anyone but Jonah. As I start to sit down, he glances up at me from his book, and I see on his face the same unspoken question: Do I know you?

"Jonah?" I ask him.

"Yes?"

"I'm Alex Rogo. Remember me?"

His face tells me that he doesn't quite.

"I knew you some time ago," I tell him. "I was a student. I got a grant to go and study some of the mathematical models you were working on. Remember? I had a beard back then."

A small flash of recognition finally hits him. "Of course! Yes, I do remember you. 'Alex,' was it?"

"Right."

A waitress asks me if I'd like something to drink. I order a scotch and soda and ask Jonah if he'll join me. He decides he'd better not; he has to leave shortly.

"So how are you these days?" I ask.

"Busy," he says. "Very busy. And you?"

"Same here. I'm on my way to Houston right now," I say. "What about you?"

"New York," says Jonah.

He seems a little bored with this line of chit-chat and looks as if he'd like to finish the conversation. A second of quiet falls between us. But, for better or worse, I have this tendency (which I've never been able to bring under control) of filling silence in a conversation with my own voice.

"Funny, but after all those plans I had back then of going into research, I ended up in business," I say. "I'm a plant manager now for UniCo."

Jonah nods. He seems more interested. He takes a puff on his cigar. I keep talking. It doesn't take much to keep me going.

"In fact, that's why I'm on my way to Houston. We belong to a manufacturers' association, and the association invited UniCo to be on a panel to talk about robotics at the annual conference. I got picked by UniCo, because my plant has the most experience with robots."

"I see," says Jonah. "Is this going to be a technical discussion?"

"More business oriented than technical," I say. Then I remember I have something I can show him. "Wait a second. . . ."

I crack open my briefcase on my lap and pull out the advance copy of the program the association sent me.

"Here we are," I say, and read the listing to him. " 'Robotics: Solution to America's Productivity Crisis in the new millenium . . . a panel of users and experts discusses the coming impact of industrial robots on American manufacturing.' "

But when I look back to him, Jonah doesn't seem very impressed. I figure, well, he's an academic person; he's not going to understand the business world.

"You say your plant uses robots?" he asks.

"In a couple of departments, yes," I say.

"Have they really increased productivity at your plant?"

"Sure they have," I say. "We had—what?" I scan the ceiling for the figure. "I think it was a thirty-six percent improvement in one area."

"Really . . . thirty-six percent?" asks Jonah. "So your company is making thirty-six percent more money from your plant just from installing some robots? Incredible."

I can't hold back a smile.

"Well . . . no," I say. "We all wish it were that easy! But it's a lot more complicated than that. See, it was just in one department that we had a thirty-six percent improvement."

Jonah looks at his cigar, then extinguishes it in the ashtray.

"Then you didn't really increase productivity," he says.

I feel my smile freeze.

"I'm not sure I understand," I say.

Jonah leans forward conspiratorially and says, "Let me ask you something—just between us: Was your plant able to ship even one more product per day as a result of what happened in the department where you installed the robots?"

I mumble, "Well, I'd have to check the numbers . . ."

"Did you fire anybody?" he asks.

I lean back, looking at him. What the hell does he mean by that?

"You mean did we lay anybody off? Because we installed the robots?" I say. "No, we have an understanding with our union that nobody will be laid off because of productivity improvement. We shifted the people to other jobs. Of course, when there's a business downturn, we lay people off."

"But the robots themselves didn't reduce your plant's people expense," he says.

"No," I admit.

"Then, tell me, did your inventories go down?" asks Jonah.

I chuckle.

"Hey, Jonah, what is this?" I say to him.

"Just tell me," he says. "Did inventories go down?"

"Offhand, I have to say I don't think so. But I'd really have to check the numbers."

"Check your numbers if you'd like," says Jonah. "But if your inventories haven't gone down . . . and your employee expense was not reduced . . . and if your company isn't selling more products—which obviously it can't, if you're not shipping more of them—then you can't tell me these robots increased your plant's productivity."

In the pit of my stomach, I'm getting this feeling like you'd probably have if you were in an elevator and the cable snapped.

"Yeah, I see what you're saying, in a way," I tell him. "But my efficiencies went up, my costs went down—"

"Did they?" asks Jonah. He closes his book.

"Sure they did. In fact, those efficiencies are averaging well above ninety percent. And my cost per part went down considerably. Let me tell you, to stay competitive these days, we've got to do everything we can to be more efficient and reduce costs."

My drink arrives; the waitress puts it on the table beside me. I hand her a ten and wait for her to give me the change.

"With such high efficiencies, you must be running your robots constantly," says Jonah.

"Absolutely," I tell him. "We have to. Otherwise, we'd lose our savings on our cost per part. And efficiencies would go down. That applies not only to the robots, but to our other production resources as well. We have to keep producing to stay efficient and maintain our cost advantage."

"Really?" he says.

"Sure. Of course, that's not to say we don't have our problems."

"I see," says Jonah. Then he smiles. "Come on! Be honest. Your inventories are going through the roof, are they not?"

I look at him. How does he know?

"If you mean our work-in-process—"

"All of your inventories," he says.

"Well, it depends. Some places, yes, they are high," I say.

"And everything is always late?" asks Jonah. "You can't ship anything on time?"

"One thing I'll admit," I tell him, "is that we have a heck of a problem meeting shipping dates. It's a serious issue with customers lately."

Jonah nods, as if he had predicted it.

"Wait a minute here . . . how come you know about these things?" I ask him.

He smiles again.

"Just a hunch," says Jonah. "Besides, I see those symptoms in a lot of the manufacturing plants. You're not alone."

I say, "But aren't you a physicist?"

"I'm a scientist," he says. "And right now you could say I'm doing work in the science of organizations—manufacturing organizations in particular."

"Didn't know there was such a science."

"There is now," he says.

"Whatever it is you're into, you put your finger on a couple of my biggest problems, I have to give you that," I tell him. "How come—"

I stop because Jonah is exclaiming something in Hebrew. He's reached into a pocket of his trousers to take out an old watch.

"Sorry, Alex, but I see I'm going to miss my plane if I don't hurry," he says.

He stands up and reaches for his coat.

"That's too bad," I say. "I'm kind of intrigued by a couple of things you've said."

Jonah pauses.

"Yes, well, if you could start to think about what we've been discussing, you probably could get your plant out of the trouble it's in."

"Hey, maybe I gave you the wrong impression," I tell him. "We've got a few problems, but I wouldn't say the plant is in *trouble*."

He looks me straight in the eye. He knows what's going on, I'm thinking.

"But tell you what," I hear myself saying, "I've got some time to kill. Why don't I walk you down to your plane? Would you mind?"

"No, not at all," he says. "But we have to hurry."

I get up and grab my coat and briefcase. My drink is sitting there. I take a quick slurp off the top and abandon it. Jonah is already edging his way toward the door. He waits for me to catch up with him. Then the two of us step out into the corridor where people are rushing everywhere. Jonah sets off at a fast pace. It takes an effort to keep up with him.

"I'm curious," I tell Jonah, "what made you suspect something might be wrong with my plant?"

"You told me yourself," Jonah says.

"No, I didn't."

"Alex," he says, "it was clear to me from your own words that you're not running as efficient a plant as you think you are. You are running exactly the opposite. You are running a very *in*-efficient plant."

"Not according to the measurements," I tell him. "Are you trying to tell me my people are wrong in what they're reporting . . . that they're lying to me or something?"

"No," he says. "It is very unlikely your people are lying to you. But your measurements definitely are."

"Yeah, okay, sometimes we massage the numbers here and there. But everybody has to play that game."

"You're missing the point," he says. "You *think* you're running an efficient plant . . . but your thinking is wrong."

"What's wrong with my thinking? It's no different from the thinking of most other managers."

"Yes, exactly," says Jonah.

"What's that supposed to mean?" I ask; I'm beginning to feel somewhat insulted by this.

"Alex, if you're like nearly everybody else in this world, you've accepted so many things without question that you're not really thinking at all," says Jonah.

"Jonah, I'm thinking all the time," I tell him. "That's part of my job."

He shakes his head.

"Alex, tell me again why you believe your robots are such a great improvement."

"Because they increased productivity," I say.

"And what is productivity?"

I think for a minute, try to remember.

"According to the way my company is defining it," I tell him, "there's a formula you use, something about the value added per employee equals. . . ."

Jonah is shaking his head again.

"Regardless of how your company defines it, that is not what productivity really is," he says. "Forget for just a minute about the formulas and all that, and just tell me in your own words, from your experience, what does it mean to be productive?"

We rush around a corner. In front of us, I see, are the metal detectors and the security guards. I had intended to stop and say good-bye to him here, but Jonah doesn't slow down.

"Just tell me, what does it mean to be productive?" he asks again as he walks through the metal detector. From the other side he talks to me. "To *you* personally, what does it mean?"

I put my briefcase on the conveyor and follow him through. I'm wondering, what does he want to hear?

On the far side, I'm telling him, "Well, I guess it means that I'm accomplishing something."

"Exactly!" he says. "But you are accomplishing something in terms of what?"

"In terms of goals," I say.

"Correct!" says Jonah.

He reaches under his sweater into his shirt pocket and pulls out a cigar. He hands it to me.

"My compliments," he says. "When you are productive you are accomplishing something in terms of your goal, right?"

"Right," I say as I retrieve my briefcase.

We're rushing past gate after gate. I'm trying to match Jonah stride for stride.

And he's saying, "Alex, I have come to the conclusion that productivity is the act of bringing a company closer to its goal. Every action that brings a company closer to its goal is productive. Every action that does not bring a company closer to its goal is not productive. Do you follow me?"

"Yeah, but . . . really, Jonah, that's just simple common sense," I say to him.

"It's simple logic is what it is," he says.

We stop. I watch him hand his ticket across the counter.

"But it's too simplified," I tell him. "It doesn't tell me anything. I mean, if I'm moving toward my goal I'm productive and if I'm not, then I'm not productive—so what?"

"What I'm telling you is, productivity is meaningless unless you know what your goal is," he says.

He takes his ticket and starts to walk toward the gate.

"Okay, then," I say. "You can look at it this way. One of my company's goals is to increase efficiencies. Therefore, whenever I increase efficiencies, I'm being productive. It's logical."

Jonah stops dead. He turns to me.

"Do you know what your problem is?" he asks me.

"Sure," I say. "I need better efficiencies."

"No, that is not your problem," he says. "Your problem is you don't know what the goal is. And, by the way, there is only one goal, no matter what the company."

That stumps me for a second. Jonah starts walking toward the gate again. It seems everyone else has now gone on board. Only the two of us are left in the waiting area. I keep after him.

"Wait a minute! What do you mean, I don't know what the goal is? I know what the goal is," I tell him.

By now, we're at the door of the plane. Jonah turns to me. The stewardess inside the cabin is looking at us.

"Really? Then, tell me, what is the goal of your manufacturing organization?" he asks.

"The goal is to produce products as efficiently as we can," I tell him.

"Wrong," says Jonah. "That's not it. What is the real goal?"

I stare at him blankly.

The stewardess leans through the door.

"Are either of you going to board this aircraft?"

Jonah says to her, "Just a second, please." Then he turns to me. "Come on, Alex! Quickly! Tell me the real goal, if you know what it is."

"Power?" I suggest.

He looks surprised. "Well . . . not bad, Alex. But you don't get power just by virtue of manufacturing something."

The stewardess is pissed off. "Sir, if you're not getting on this aircraft, you have to go back to the terminal," she says coldly.

Jonah ignores her. "Alex, you cannot understand the meaning of productivity unless you know what the goal is. Until then, you're just playing a lot of games with numbers and words."

"Okay, then it's market share," I tell him. "That's the goal."

"Is it?" he asks.

He steps into the plane.

"Hey! Can't you tell me?" I call to him.

"Think about it, Alex. You can find the answer with your own mind," he says.

He hands the stewardess his ticket, looks at me and waves good-bye. I raise my hand to wave back and discover I'm still holding the cigar he gave me. I put it in my suit jacket pocket. When I look up again, he's gone. An impatient gate-agent appears and tells me flatly she is going to close the door.

5

It's a good cigar.

For a connoisseur of tobacco, it might be a little dry, since it spent several weeks inside my suit jacket. But I sniff it with pleasure during Peach's big meeting, while I remember that other, stranger, meeting with Jonah.

Or was it really more strange than this? Peach is up in front of us tapping the center of a graph with a long wood pointer. Smoke whirls slowly in the beam of the slide projector. Across from me, someone is poking earnestly at a calculator. Everyone except me is listening intently, or jotting notes, or offering comments.

". . . consistent parameters . . . essential to gain . . . matrix of advantage . . . extensive pre-profit recovery . . . operational indices . . . provide tangential proof. . . ."

I have no idea what's going on. Their words sound like a different language to me—not a foreign language exactly, but a language I once knew and only vaguely now recall. The terms seem familiar to me. But now I'm not sure what they really mean. They are just words.

You're just playing a lot of games with numbers and words.

For a few minutes there in Chicago's O'Hare, I did try to think about what Jonah had said. He'd made a lot of sense to me somehow; he'd had some good points. But it was like somebody from a different world had talked to me. I had to shrug it off. I had to go to Houston and talk about robots. It was time to catch my own plane.

Now I'm wondering if Jonah might be closer to the truth than I first thought. Because as I glance from face to face, I get this gut hunch that none of us here has anything more than a witch doctor's understanding of the medicine we're practicing. Our tribe is dying and we're dancing in our ceremonial smoke to exorcise the devil that's ailing us.

What is the real goal? Nobody here has even asked anything that basic. Peach is chanting about cost opportunities and "productivity" targets and so on. Hilton Smyth is saying hallelujah to whatever Peach proclaims. Does anyone genuinely understand what we're doing?

At ten o'clock, Peach calls a break. Everyone except me exits for the rest rooms or for coffee. I stay seated until they are out of the room.

What the hell am I doing here? I'm wondering what good it is for me—or any of us—to be sitting here in this room. Is this meeting (which is scheduled to last for most of the day) going to make my plant competitive, save my job, or help anybody do anything of benefit to anyone?

I can't handle it. I don't even know what productivity is. So how can this be anything except a total waste? And with that thought I find myself stuffing my papers back into my briefcase. I snap it closed. And then I quietly get up and walk out.

I'm lucky at first. I make it to the elevator without anyone saying anything to me. But while I'm waiting there, Hilton Smyth comes strolling past.

"You're not bailing out on us, are you Al?" he asks.

For a second, I consider ignoring the question. But then I realize Smyth might deliberately say something to Peach.

"Have to," I say to him. "I've got a situation that needs my attention back at the plant."

"What? An emergency?"

"You can call it that."

The elevator opens its doors. I step in. Smyth is looking at me with a quizzical expression as he walks by. The doors close.

It crosses my mind that there is a risk of Peach firing me for walking out of his meeting. But that, to my current frame of mind as I walk through the garage to my car, would only shorten three months of anxiety leading up to what I suspect might be inevitable.

I don't go back to the plant right away. I drive around for a while. I point the car down one road and follow it until I'm tired of it, then take another road. A couple of hours pass. I don't care where I am; I just want to be out. The freedom is kind of exhilarating until it gets boring.

As I'm driving, I try to keep my mind off business. I try to clear my head. The day has turned out to be nice. The sun is out. It's warm. No clouds. Blue sky. Even though the land still has an early spring austerity, everything yellow-brown, it's a good day to be playing hooky.

I remember looking at my watch just before I reach the plant gates and seeing that it's past 1 P.M. I'm slowing down to make the turn through the gate, when—I don't know how else to say it—it just doesn't feel right. I look at the plant. And I put my foot down on the gas and keep going. I'm hungry; I'm thinking maybe I should get some lunch.

But I guess the real reason is I just don't want to be found yet. I need to think and I'll never be able to do it if I go back to the office now.

Up the road about a mile is a little pizza place. I see they're open, so I stop and go in. I'm conservative; I get a medium pizza with double cheese, pepperoni, sausage, mushrooms, green peppers, hot peppers, black olives and onion, and—mmmmmmmmm —a sprinkling of anchovies. While I'm waiting, I can't resist the Munchos on the stand by the cash register, and I tell the Sicilian who runs the place to put me down for a couple of bags of beer nuts, some taco chips, and—for later—some pretzels. Trauma whets my appetite.

But there's one problem. You just can't wash down beer nuts with soda. You need beer. And guess what I see in the cooler. Of course, I don't usually drink during the day . . . but I look at the way the light is hitting those frosty cold cans. . . .

"Screw it."

I pull out a six of Bud.

Twenty-three dollars and sixty-two cents and I'm out of there.

Just before the plant, on the opposite side of the highway, there is a gravel road leading up a low hillside. It's an access road to a substation about half a mile away. So on impulse, I turn the wheel sharply. The Mazda goes bouncing off the highway onto the gravel and only a fast hand saves my pizza from the floor. We raise some dust getting to the top.

I park the car, unbutton my shirt, take off my tie and coat to save them from the inevitable, and open up my goodies.

Some distance below, down across the highway, is my plant. It sits in a field, a big gray steel box without windows. Inside, I know, there are about 400 people at work on day shift. Their cars are parked in the lot. I watch as a truck backs between two others sitting at the unloading docks. The trucks bring the materials which the machines and people inside will use to make something. On the opposite side, more trucks are being filled with what they have produced. In simplest terms, that's what's happening. I'm supposed to manage what goes on down there.

I pop the top on one of the beers and go to work on the pizza.

The plant has the look of a landmark. It's as if it has always been there, as if it will always be there. I happen to know the plant is only about fifteen years old. And it may not be here as many years from now.

So what is the goal?

What are we supposed to be doing here?

What keeps this place working?

Jonah said there was only one goal. Well, I don't see how that can be. We do a lot of things in the course of daily operations, and they're all important. Most of them anyway . . . or we wouldn't do them. What the hell, they all could be goals.

I mean, for instance, one of the things a manufacturing organization must do is buy raw materials. We need these materials in order to manufacture, and we have to obtain them at the best cost, and so purchasing in a cost-effective manner is very important to us.

The pizza, by the way, is primo. I'm chowing down on my second piece when some tiny voice inside my head asks me, But is this the goal? Is cost-effective purchasing the reason for the plant's existence?

I have to laugh. I almost choke.

Yeah, right. Some of the brilliant idiots in Purchasing sure do act as if that's the goal. They're out there renting warehouses to store all the crap they're buying so cost-effectively. What is it we have now? A thirty-two-month supply of copper wire? A seven-month inventory of stainless steel sheet? All kinds of stuff. They've got millions and millions tied up in what they've bought —and at terrific prices.

No, put it that way, and economical purchasing is definitely not the goal of this plant.

What else do we do? We employ people—by the hundreds here, and by the tens of thousands throughout UniCo. We, the people, are supposed to be UniCo's "most important asset," as some P.R. flack worded it once in the annual report. Brush off the bull and it is true the company couldn't function without good people of various skills and professions.

I personally am glad it provides jobs. There is a lot to be said for a steady paycheck. But supplying jobs to people surely isn't why the plant exists. After all, how many people have we laid off so far?

And anyway, even if UniCo offered lifetime employment like some of the Japanese companies, I still couldn't say the goal is jobs. A lot of people seem to think and act as if that were the goal (empire-building department managers and politicians just to name two), but the plant wasn't built for the purpose of paying wages and giving people something to do.

Okay, so why was the plant built in the first place?

It was built to produce products. Why can't that be the goal? Jonah said it wasn't. But I don't see why it isn't the goal. We're a manufacturing company. That means we have to manufacture something, doesn't it? Isn't that the whole point, to produce products? Why else are we here?

I think about some of the buzzwords I've been hearing lately.

What about quality?

Maybe that's it. If you don't manufacture a quality product all you've got at the end is a bunch of expensive mistakes. You have to meet the customer's requirements with a quality product, or before long you won't have a business. UniCo learned its lesson on that point.

But we've already learned that lesson. We've implemented a major effort to improve quality. Why isn't the plant's future secure? And if quality were truly the goal, then how come a company like Rolls Royce very nearly went bankrupt?

Quality alone cannot be the goal. It's important. But it's not the goal. Why? Because of costs?

If low-cost production is essential, then efficiency would seem to be the answer. Okay . . . maybe it's the two of them together: quality and efficiency. They do tend to go hand-in-hand. The fewer errors made, the less re-work you have to do, which can lead to lower costs and so on. Maybe that's what Jonah meant.

Producing a quality product efficiently: that must be the goal. It sure sounds good. "Quality and efficiency." Those are two nice words. Kind of like "Mom and apple pie."

I sit back and pop the top on another beer. The pizza is now just a fond memory. For a few moments I feel satisfied.

But something isn't sitting right. And it's more than just indigestion from lunch. To efficiently produce quality products sounds like a good goal. But can that goal keep the plant working?

I'm bothered by some of the examples that come to mind. If the goal is to produce a quality product efficiently, then how come Volkswagen isn't still making Bugs? That was a quality product that could be produced at low cost. Or, going back a ways, how come Douglas didn't keep making DC-3's? From everything I've heard, the DC-3 was a fine aircraft. I'll bet if they had kept making them, they could turn them out today a lot more efficiently than DC-10's.

It's not enough to turn out a quality product on an efficient basis. The goal has to be something else.

But what?

As I drink my beer, I find myself contemplating the smooth finish of the aluminum beer can I hold in my hand. Mass production technology really is something. To think that this can until recently was a rock in the ground. Then we come along with some know-how and some tools and turn the rock into a lightweight, workable metal that you can use over and over again. It's pretty amazing—

Wait a minute, I'm thinking. That's it!

Technology: that's really what it's all about. We have to stay on the leading edge of technology. It's essential to the company. If we don't keep pace with technology, we're finished. So that's the goal.

Well, on second thought . . . that isn't right. If technology is the real goal of a manufacturing organization, then how come the most responsible positions aren't in research and development? How come R&D is always off to the side in every organization chart I've ever seen? And suppose we did have the latest of every kind of machine we could use—would it save us? No, it wouldn't. So technology is important, but it isn't the goal.

Maybe the goal is some combination of efficiency, quality and technology. But then I'm back to saying we have a lot of important goals. And that really isn't saying anything, aside from the fact that it doesn't square with what Jonah told me.

I'm stumped.

I gaze down the hillside. In front of the big steel box of the plant there is a smaller box of glass and concrete which houses the offices. Mine is the office on the front left corner. Squinting at it, I can almost see the stack of phone messages my secretary is bringing in my wheelbarrow.

Oh well. I lift my beer for a good long slug. And as I tilt my head back, I see them.

Out beyond the plant are two other long, narrow buildings. They're our warehouses. They're filled to the roof with spare parts and unsold merchandise we haven't been able to unload yet. Twenty million dollars in finished-goods inventory: quality products of the most current technology, all produced efficiently, all sitting in their boxes, all sealed in plastic with the warranty cards and a whiff of the original factory air—and all waiting for someone to buy them.

So that's it. UniCo obviously doesn't run this plant just to fill a warehouse. The goal is sales.

But if the goal is sales, why didn't Jonah accept market share as the goal? Market share is even more important as a goal than sales. If you have the highest market share, you've got the best sales in your industry. Capture the market and you've got it made. Don't you?

Maybe not. I remember the old line, "We're losing money, but we're going to make it up with volume." A company will sometimes sell at a loss or at a small amount over cost—as UniCo has been known to do—just to unload inventories. You can have a big share of the market, but if you're not making money, who cares?

Money. Well, of course . . . money is the big thing. Peach is going to shut us down because the plant is costing the company too much money. So I have to find ways to reduce the money that the company is losing. . . .

Wait a minute. Suppose I did some incredibly brilliant thing and stemmed the losses so we broke even. Would that save us? Not in the long run, it wouldn't. The plant wasn't built just so it could break even. UniCo is not in business just so it can break even. The company exists to make money.

I see it now.

The goal of a manufacturing organization is to make money.

Why else did J. Bartholomew Granby start his company back in 1881 and go to market with his improved coal stove? Was it for the love of appliances? Was it a magnanimous public gesture to bring warmth and comfort to millions? Hell, no. Old J. Bart did it to make a bundle. And he succeeded—because the stove was a gem of a product in its day. And then investors gave him more money so they could make a bundle and J. Bart could make an even bigger one.

But is making money the only goal? What are all these other things I've been worrying about?

I reach for my briefcase, take out a yellow legal pad and take a pen from my coat pocket. Then I make a list of all the items people think of as being goals: cost-effective purchasing, employing good people, high technology, producing products, producing quality products, selling quality products, capturing market share. I even add some others like communications and customer satisfaction.

All of those are essential to running the business successfully. What do they all do? They enable the company to make money. But they are not the goals themselves; they're just the means of achieving the goal.

How do I know for sure?

Well, I don't. Not absolutely. But adopting "making money" as the goal of a manufacturing organization looks like a pretty good assumption. Because, for one thing, there isn't one item on that list that's worth a damn if the company isn't making money.

Because what happens if a company doesn't make money? If the company doesn't make money by producing and selling products, or by maintenance contracts, or by selling some of its assets, or by some other means . . . the company is finished. It will cease to function. Money must be the goal. Nothing else works in its place. Anyway, it's the one assumption I have to make.

If the goal is to make money, then (putting it in terms Jonah might have used), an action that moves us toward making money is productive. And an action that takes away from making money is non-productive. For the past year or more, the plant has been moving away from the goal more than toward it. So to save the plant, I have to make it productive; I have to make the plant make money for UniCo. That's a simplified statement of what's happening, but it's accurate. At least it's a logical starting point.

Through the windshield, the world is bright and cold. The sunlight seems to have become much more intense. I look around as if I have just come out of a long trance. Everything is familiar, but seems new to me. I take my last swallow of beer. I suddenly feel I have to get going.

6

By my watch, it's about 4:30 when I park the Mazda in the plant lot. One thing I've effectively managed today is to evade the office. I reach for my briefcase and get out of the car. The glass box of the office in front of me is silent as death. Like an ambush. I know they're all inside waiting for me, waiting to pounce. I decide to disappoint everyone. I decide to take a detour through the plant. I just want to take a fresh look at things.

I walk down to a door into the plant and go inside. From my briefcase, I get the safety glasses I always carry. There is a rack of hard hats by one of the desks over by the wall. I steal one from there, put it on, and walk inside.

As I round a corner and enter one of the work areas, I happen to surprise three guys sitting on a bench in one of the open bays. They're sharing a newspaper, reading and talking with each other. One of them sees me. He nudges the others. The newspaper is folded away with the grace of a snake disappearing in the grass. All three of them nonchalantly become purposeful and go off in three separate directions.

I might have walked on by another time. But today it makes me mad. Dammit, the hourly people know this plant is in trouble. With the layoffs we've had, they have to know. You'd think they'd all try to work harder to save this place. But here we've got three guys, all of them making probably ten or twelve bucks an hour, sitting on their asses. I go and find their supervisor.

After I tell him that three of his people are sitting around with nothing to do, he gives me some excuse about how they're mostly caught up on their quotas and they're waiting for more parts.

So I tell him, "If you can't keep them working, I'll find a department that can. Now find something for them to do. You use your people, or lose 'em—you got it?"

From down the aisle, I look over my shoulder. The super now has the three guys moving some materials from one side of the aisle to the other. I know it's probably just something to keep them busy, but what the hell; at least those guys are working. If I hadn't said something, who knows how long they'd have sat there?

Then it occurs to me: those three guys are doing something now, but is that going to help us make money? They might be working, but are they productive?

For a moment, I consider going back and telling the supervisor to make those guys actually produce. But, well . . . maybe there really isn't anything for them to work on right now. And even though I could perhaps have those guys shifted to someplace where they could produce, how would I know if that work is helping us make money?

That's a weird thought.

Can I assume that making people work and making money are the same thing? We've tended to do that in the past. The basic rule has been just keep everybody and everything out here working all the time; keep pushing that product out the door. And when there isn't any work to do, make some. And when we can't make work, shift people around. And when you still can't make them work, lay them off.

I look around and most people *are* working. Idle people in here are the exception. Just about everybody is working nearly all the time. And we're not making money.

Some stairs zig-zag up one of the walls, access to one of the overhead cranes. I climb them until I am halfway to the roof and can look out over the plant from one of the landings.

Every moment, lots and lots of things are happening down there. Practically everything I'm seeing is a variable. The complexity in this plant—in *any* manufacturing plant—is mind-boggling if you contemplate it. Situations on the floor are always changing. How can I possibly control what goes on? How the hell am I supposed to know if any action in the plant is productive or non-productive toward making money?

The answer is supposed to be in my briefcase, which is heavy in my hand. It's filled with all those reports and printouts and stuff that Lou gave me for the meeting.

We do have lots of measurements that are supposed to tell us if we're productive. But what they really tell us are things like whether somebody down there "worked" for all the hours we paid him or her to work. They tell us whether the output per hour met our standard for the job. They tell us the "cost of products," they tell us "direct labor variances," all that stuff. But how do I really know if what happens here is making money for us, or whether we're just playing accounting games? There must be a connection, but how do I define it?

I shuffle back down the stairs.

Maybe I should just dash off a blistering memo on the evil of reading newspapers on the job. Think that'll put us back in the black?

By the time I finally set foot inside my office, it is past five o'clock and most of the people who might have been waiting for me are gone. Fran was probably one of the first ones out the door. But she has left me all their messages. I can barely see the phone under them. Half of the messages seem to be from Bill Peach. I guess he caught my disappearing act.

With reluctance, I pick up the phone and dial his number. But God is merciful. It rings for a straight two minutes; no answer. I breathe quietly and hang up.

Sitting back in my chair, looking out at the reddish-gold of late afternoon, I keep thinking about measurements, about all the ways we use to evaluate performance: meeting schedules and due dates, inventory turns, total sales, total expenses. Is there a simplified way to know if we're making money?

There is a soft knock at the door.

I turn. It's Lou.

As I mentioned earlier, Lou is the plant controller. He's a paunchy, older man who is about two years away from retirement. In the best accountants' tradition, he wears horn-rimmed bifocal glasses. Even though he dresses in expensive suits, somehow he always seems to look a little frumpled. He came here from corporate about twenty years ago. His hair is snow white. I think his reason for living is to go to the CPA conventions and bust loose. Most of the time, he's very mild-mannered—until you try to put something over on him. Then he turns into Godzilla.

"Hi," he says from the door.

I roll my hand, motioning him to come in.

"Just wanted to mention to you that Bill Peach called this afternoon," says Lou. "Weren't you supposed to be in a meeting with him today?"

"What did Bill want?" I ask, ignoring the question.

"He needed some updates on some figures," he says. "He seemed kind of miffed that you weren't here."

"Did you get him what he needed?" I ask.

"Yeah, most of it," Lou says. "I sent it to him; he should get it in the morning. Most of it was like the stuff I gave you."

"What about the rest?"

"Just a few things I have to pull together," he says. "I should have it sometime tomorrow."

"Let me see it before it goes, okay?" I say. "Just so I know."

"Oh, sure," says Lou.

"Hey, you got a minute?"

"Yeah, what's up?" he asks, probably expecting me to give him the rundown on what's going on between me and Peach.

"Sit down," I tell him.

Lou pulls up a chair.

I think for a second, trying to phrase this correctly. Lou waits expectantly.

"This is just a simple, fundamental question," I say.

Lou smiles. "Those are the kind I like."

"Would you say the goal of this company is to make money?"

He bursts out laughing.

"Are you kidding?" he asks. "Is this a trick question?"

"No, just tell me."

"Of course it's to make money!" he says.

I repeat it to him: "So the goal of the company is to make money, right?"

"Yeah," he says. "We have to produce products, too."

"Okay, now wait a minute," I tell him. "Producing products is just a means to achieve the goal."

I run through the basic line of reasoning with him. He listens. He's a fairly bright guy, Lou. You don't have to explain every little thing to him. At the end of it all, he agrees with me.

"So what are you driving at?"

"How do we know if we're making money?"

"Well, there are a lot of ways," he says.

For the next few minutes, Lou goes on about total sales, and market share, and profitability, and dividends paid to stockholders, and so on. Finally, I hold up my hand.

"Let me put it this way," I say. "Suppose you're going to rewrite the textbooks. Suppose you don't have all those terms and you have to make them up as you go along. What would be the minimum number of measurements you would need in order to know if we are making money?"

Lou puts a finger alongside his face and squints through his bifocals at his shoe.

"Well, you'd have to have some kind of absolute measurement," he says. "Something to tell you in dollars or yen or whatever just how much money you've made."

"Something like net profit, right?" I ask.

"Yeah, net profit," he says. "But you'd need more than just that. Because an absolute measurement isn't going to tell you much."

"Oh yeah?" I say. "If I know how much money I've made, why do I need to know anything else? You follow me? If I add up what I've made, and I subtract my expenses, and I get my net profit—what else do I need to know? I've made, say, $10 million, or $20 million, or whatever."

For a fraction of a second, Lou gets a glint in his eye like I'm real dumb.

"All right," he says. "Let's say you figure it out and you come up with $10 million net profit . . . an absolute measurement. Offhand, that sounds like a lot of money, like you really raked it in. But how much did you start with?"

He pauses for effect.

"You see? How much did it take to make that $10 million? Was it just a million dollars? Then you made ten times more money than you invested. Ten to one. That's pretty goddamned good. But let's say you invested a billion dollars. And you only made a lousy ten million bucks? That's pretty bad."

"Okay, okay," I say. "I was just asking to be sure."

"So you need a relative measurement, too," Lou continues. "You need something like return on investment . . . ROI, some comparison of the money made relative to the money invested."

"All right, but with those two, we ought to be able to tell how well the company is doing overall, shouldn't we?" I ask.

Lou nearly nods, then he gets a faraway look.

"Well. . . ." he says.

I think about it too.

"You know," he says, "it is possible for a company to show net profit and a good ROI and still go bankrupt."

"You mean if it runs out of cash," I say.

"Exactly," he says. "Bad cash flow is what kills most of the businesses that go under."

"So you have to count cash flow as a third measurement?"

He nods.

"Yeah, but suppose you've got enough cash coming in every month to meet expenses for a year," I tell him. "If you've got enough of it, then cash flow doesn't matter."

"But if you don't, nothing else matters," says Lou. "It's a measure of survival: stay above the line and you're okay; go below and you're dead."

We look each other in the eye.

"It's happening to us, isn't it?" Lou asks.

I nod.

Lou looks away. He's quiet.

Then he says, "I knew it was coming. Just a matter of time."

He pauses. He looks back to me.

"What about us?" he asks. "Did Peach say anything?"

"They're thinking about closing us down."

"Will there be a consolidation?" he asks.

What he's really asking is whether he'll have a job.

"I honestly don't know, Lou," I tell him. "I imagine some people might be transferred to other plants or other divisions, but we didn't get into those kinds of specifics."

Lou takes a cigarette out of the pack in his shirt pocket. I watch him stamp the end of it repeatedly on the arm of his chair.

"Two lousy years to go before retirement," he mutters.

"Hey, Lou," I say, trying to lift him out of despair, "the worst it would probably mean for you would be an early retirement."

"Dammit!" he says. "I don't *want* an early retirement!"

We're both quiet for some time. Lou lights his cigarette. We sit there.

Finally I say, "Look, I haven't given up yet."

"Al, if Peach says we're finished—"

"He didn't say that. We've still got time."

"How much?" he asks.

"Three months," I say.

He all but laughs. "Forget it, Al. We'll never make it."

"I said I'm not giving up. Okay?"

For a minute, he doesn't say anything. I sit there knowing I'm not sure if I'm telling him the truth. All I've been able to do so far is figure out that we have to make the plant make money. Fine, Rogo, now *how* do we do it? I hear Lou blow a heavy breath of smoke.

With resignation in his voice, he says, "Okay, Al. I'll give you all the help I can. But. . . ."

He leaves the sentence unfinished, waves his hand in the air.

"I'm going to need that help, Lou," I tell him. "And the first thing I need from you is to keep all this to yourself for the time being. If the word gets out, we won't be able to get anyone to lift a finger around here."

"Okay, but you know this won't stay a secret for long," he says.

I know he's right.

"So how do you plan on saving this place?" Lou asks.

"The first thing I'm trying to do is get a clear picture of what we have to do to stay in business," I say.

"Oh, so that's what all this stuff with the measurements is about," he says. "Listen, Al, don't waste your time with all that. The system is the system. You want to know what's wrong? I'll tell you what the problem is."

And he does. For about an hour. Most of it I've heard before, it's the kind of thing everybody's heard: It's all the union's fault; if everybody would just work harder; nobody gives a damn about quality; look at foreign labor—we can't compete on costs alone; and so on, and so on. He even tells me what sorts of self-flagellation we should administer in order to chasten ourselves. Mostly Lou is blowing off steam. That's why I let him talk.

But I sit there wondering. Lou actually is a bright guy. We're all fairly bright; UniCo has lots of bright, well-educated people on the payroll. And I sit here listening to Lou pronounce his opinions, which all sound good as they roll off his tongue, and I wonder why it is that we're slipping minute by minute toward oblivion, if we're really so smart.

Sometime after the sun has set, Lou decides to go home. I stay. After Lou has gone, I sit there at my desk with a pad of paper in front of me. On the paper, I write down the three measurements which Lou and I agreed are central to knowing if the company is making money: net profit, ROI and cash flow.

I try to figure out if there is one of those three measurements which can be favored at the expense of the other two and allow me to pursue the goal. From experience, I happen to know there are a lot of games the people at the top can play. They can make the organization deliver a bigger net profit this year at the expense of net profit in years to come (don't fund any R&D, for instance; that kind of thing). They can make a bunch of no-risk decisions and have any one of those measurements look great while the others stink. Aside from that, the ratios between the three might have to vary according to the needs of the business.

But then I sit back.

If I were J. Bart Granby III sitting high atop my company's corporate tower, and if my control over the company were secure, I wouldn't want to play any of those games. I wouldn't want to see one measurement increase while the other two were ignored. I would want to see increases in net profit *and* return on investment *and* cash flow—all three of them. And I would want to see all three of them increase all the time.

Man, think of it. We'd *really* be making money if we could have all of the measurements go up simultaneously and forever.

So this is the goal:

To make money by increasing net profit, while simultaneously increasing return on investment, and simultaneously increasing cash flow.

I write that down in front of me.

I feel like I'm on a roll now. The pieces seem to be fitting together. I have found one clear-cut goal. I've worked out three related measurements to evaluate progress toward the goal. And I have come to the conclusion that simultaneous increases in all three measurements are what we ought to be trying to achieve. Not bad for a day's work. I think Jonah would be proud of me.

Now then, I ask myself, how do I build a direct connection between the three measurements and what goes on in my plant? If I can find some logical relationship between our daily operations and the overall performance of the company then I'll have a basis for knowing if something is productive or non-productive . . . moving toward the goal or away from it.

I go to the window and stare into the blackness.

Half an hour later, it is as dark in my mind as it is outside the window.

Running through my head are ideas about profit margins and capital investments and direct labor content, and it's all very conventional. It's the same basic line of thinking everyone has been following for a hundred years. If I follow it, I'll come to the same conclusions as everyone else and that means I'll have no truer understanding of what's going on than I do now.

I'm stuck.

I turn away from the window. Behind my desk is a bookcase; I pull out a textbook, flip through it, put it back, pull out another, flip through it, put it back.

Finally, I've had it. It's late.

I check my watch—and I'm shocked. It's past ten o'clock. All of a sudden, I realize I never called Julie to let her know I wasn't going to be home for dinner. She's really going to be pissed off at me; she always is when I don't call.

I pick up the phone and dial. Julie answers.

"Hi," I say. "Guess who had a rotten day."

"Oh? So what else is new?" she says. "It so happens my day wasn't too hot either."

"Okay, then we both had rotten days," I tell her. "Sorry I didn't call before. I got wrapped up in something."

Long pause.

"Well, I couldn't get a babysitter anyway," she says.

Then it dawns on me; our postponed night out was supposed to be tonight.

"I'm sorry, Julie. I really am. It just completely slipped my mind," I tell her.

"I made dinner," she says. "When you hadn't shown up after two hours, we ate without you. Yours is in the microwave if you want it."

"Thanks."

"Remember your daughter? The little girl who's in love with you?" Julie asks.

"You don't have to be sarcastic."

"She waited by the front window for you all evening until I made her go to bed."

I shut my eyes.

"Why?" I ask.

"She's got a surprise to show you," says Julie.

I say, "Listen, I'll be home in about an hour."

"No rush," says Julie.

She hangs up before I can say good-bye.

Indeed, there is no point in rushing home at this stage of the game. I get my hard hat and glasses and take a walk out into the plant to pay a visit to Eddie, my second shift supervisor, and see how everything is going.

When I get there, Eddie is not in his office; he's out dealing with something on the floor. I have him paged. Finally, I see him coming from way down at the other end of the plant. I watch him as he walks down. It's a five-minute wait.

Something about Eddie has always irritated me. He's a competent supervisor. Not outstanding, but he's okay. His work is not what bothers me. It's something else.

I watch Eddie's steady gait. Each step is very regular.

Then it hits me. That's what irritates me about Eddie: it's the way he walks. Well, it's more than that; Eddie's walk is symbolic of the kind of person he is. He walks a little bit pigeon-toed. It's as if he's literally walking a straight and narrow line. His hands cross stiffly in front of him, seeming to point at each foot. And he does all this like he read in a manual someplace that this is how walking is supposed to be done.

As he approaches, I'm thinking that Eddie has probably never done anything improper in his entire life—unless it was expected of him. Call him Mr. Regularity.

We talk about some of the orders going through. As usual, everything is out of control. Eddie, of course, doesn't realize this. To him, everything is normal. And if it's normal, it must be right.

He's telling me—in elaborate detail—about what is running tonight. Just for the hell of it, I feel like asking Eddie to define what he's doing tonight in terms of something like net profit.

I want to ask him, "Say, Eddie, how's our impact on ROI been in the last hour? By the way, what's your shift done to improve cash flow? Are we making money?"

It's not that Eddie hasn't heard of those terms. It's just that those concerns are not part of his world. His world is one measured in terms of parts per hour, man-hours worked, numbers of orders filled. He knows labor standards, he knows scrap factors, he knows run times, he knows shipping dates. Net profit, ROI, cash flow—that's just headquarters talk to Eddie. It's absurd to think I could measure Eddie's world by those three. For Eddie, there is only a vague association between what happens on his shift and how much money the company makes. Even if I could open Eddie's mind to the greater universe, it would still be very difficult to draw a clear connection between the values here on the plant floor and the values on the many floors of UniCo head-quarters. They're too different.

In the middle of a sentence, Eddie notices I'm looking at him funny.

"Something wrong?" asks Eddie.

7

When I get home, the house is dark except for one light. I try to keep it quiet as I come in. True to her word, Julie has left me some dinner in the microwave. As I open the door to see what delectable treat awaits me (it seems to be some variety of mystery meat) I hear a rustling behind me. I turn around, and there stands my little girl, Sharon, at the edge of the kitchen.

"Well! If it isn't Miz Muffet!" I exclaim. "How is the tuffet these days?"

She smiles. "Oh . . . not bad."

"How come you're up so late?" I ask.

She comes forward holding a manila envelope. I sit down at the kitchen table and put her on my knee. She hands the envelope to me to open.

"It's my report card," she says.

"No kidding?"

"You have to look at it," she tells me.

And I do.

"You got all A's!" I say.

I give her a squeeze and big kiss.

"That's terrific!" I tell her. "That's very good, Sharon. I'm really proud of you. And I'll bet you were the only kid in your class to do this well."

She nods. Then she has to tell me everything. I let her go on, and half an hour later, she's barely able to keep her eyes open. I carry her up to her bed.

But tired as I am, I can't sleep. It's past midnight now. I sit in the kitchen, brooding and picking at dinner. My kid is getting A's in the second grade while I'm flunking out in business.

Maybe I should just give up, use what time I've got to try to land another job. According to what Selwin said, that's what everyone at headquarters is doing. Why should I be different?

For a while, I try to convince myself that a call to a headhunter is the smart thing to do. But, in the end, I can't. A job with another company would get Julie and me out of town, and maybe fortune would bring me an even better position than I've got now (although I doubt it; my track record as a plant manager hasn't exactly been stellar.) What turns me against the idea of looking for another job is I'd feel I were running away. And I just can't do that.

It's not that I feel I owe my life to the plant or the town or the company, but I do feel some responsibility. And aside from that, I've invested a big chunk of my life in UniCo. I want that investment to pay off. Three months is better than nothing for a last chance.

My decision is, I'm going to do everything I can for the three months.

But that decided, the big question arises: what the hell can I really do? I've already done the best I can with what I know. More of the same is not going to do any good.

Unfortunately, I don't have a year to go back to school and re-study a lot of theory. I don't even have the time to read the magazines, papers, and reports piling up in my office. I don't have the time or the budget to screw around with consultants, making studies and all that crap. And anyway, even if I did have the time and money, I'm not sure any of those would give me a much better insight than what I've got now.

I have the feeling there are some things I'm not taking into account. If I'm ever going to get us out of this hole, I can't take anything for granted; I'm going to have to watch closely and think carefully about what is basically going on . . . take it one step at a time.

I slowly realize that the only tools I have—limited as they may be—are my own eyes and ears, my own hands, my own voice, my own mind. That's about it. I am all I have. And the thought keeps coming to me: I don't know if that's enough.

When I finally crawl into bed, Julie is a lump under the sheets. She is exactly the way I left her twenty-one hours ago. She's sleeping. Lying beside her on the mattress, still unable to sleep, I stare at the dark ceiling.

That's when I decide to try to find Jonah again.

8

Two steps after rolling out of bed in the morning, I don't like moving at all. But in the midst of a morning shower, memory of my predicament returns. When you've only got three months to work with, you don't have much time to waste feeling tired. I rush past Julie—who doesn't have much to say to me—and the kids, who already seem to sense that something is wrong, and head for the plant.

The whole way there I'm thinking about how to get in touch with Jonah. That's the problem. Before I can ask for his help, I've got to find him.

The first thing I do when I get to the office is have Fran barricade the door against the hordes massing outside for frontal attack. Just as I reach my desk, Fran buzzes me; Bill Peach is on the line.

"Great," I mutter.

I pick up the phone.

"Yes, Bill."

"Don't you *ever* walk out of one of my meetings again," rumbles Peach. "Do you understand me?"

"Yes, Bill."

"Now, because of your untimely absence yesterday, we've got some things to go over," he says.

A few minutes later, I've pulled Lou into the office to help me with the answers. Then Peach has dragged in Ethan Frost and we're having a four-way conversation.

And that's the last chance I have to think about Jonah for the rest of the day. After I'm done with Peach, half a dozen people come into my office for a meeting that has been postponed since last week.

The next thing I know, I look out the window and it's dark outside. The sun has set and I'm still in the middle of my sixth meeting of the day. After everyone has gone, I take care of some paperwork. It's past seven when I hop in the car to go home.

While waiting in traffic for a long light to turn green, I finally have the opportunity to remember how the day began. That's when I get back to thinking about Jonah. Two blocks later, I remember my old address book.

I pull over at a gas station and use the pay phone to call Julie.

"Hello," she answers.

"Hi, it's me," I say. "Listen, I've got to go over to my mother's for something. I'm not sure how long I'll be, so why don't you go ahead and eat without me."

"The next time you want dinner—"

"Look, don't give me any grief, Julie; this is important."

There is a second of silence before I hear the click.

It's always a little strange going back to the old neighborhood, because everywhere I look is some kind of memory waiting just out of sight in my mind's eye. I pass the corner where I had the fight with Bruno Krebsky. I drive down the street where we played ball summer after summer. I see the alley where I made out for the first time with Angelina. I go past the utility pole upon which I grazed the fender of my old man's Chevy (and subsequently had to work two months in the store for free to pay for the repair). All that stuff. The closer I get to the house, the more memories come crowding in, and the more I get this feeling that's kind of warm and uncomfortably tense.

Julie hates to come here. When we first moved to town, we used to come down every Sunday to see my mother and Danny and his wife, Nicole. But there got to be too many fights about it, so we don't make the trip much anymore.

I park the Mazda by the curb in front of the steps to my mother's house. It's a narrow, brick row house, about the same as any other on the street. Down at the corner is my old man's store, the one my brother owns today. The lights are off down there; Danny closes at six. Getting out of my car, I feel conspicuous in my suit and tie.

My mother opens the door.

"Oh my god," she says. She clutches her hands over her heart. "Who's dead?"

"Nobody died, Mom," I say.

"It's Julie, isn't it," she says. "Did she leave you?"

"Not yet," I say.

"Oh," she says. "Well, let me see . . . it isn't Mothers' Day . . ."

"Mom, I'm just here to look for something."

"Look for something? Look for what?" she asks, turning to let me in. "Come in, come in. You're letting all the cold inside. Boy, you gave me a scare. Here you are in town and you never come to see me anymore. What's the matter? You too important now for your old mother?"

"No, of course not, Mom. I've been very busy at the plant," I say.

"Busy, busy," she says leading the way to the kitchen. "You hungry?"

"No, listen, I don't want to put you to any trouble," I say.

She says, "Oh, it's no trouble. I got some ziti I can heat up. You want a salad too?"

"No, listen, a cup of coffee will be fine. I just need to find my old address book," I tell her. "It's the one I had when I was in college. Do you know where it might be?"

We step into the kitchen.

"Your old address book . . ." she muses as she pours a cup of coffee from the percolator. "How about some cake? Danny brought some day-old over last night from the store."

"No thanks, Mom. I'm fine," I say. "It's probably in with all my old notebooks and stuff from school."

She hands me the cup of coffee. "Notebooks . . ."

"Yeah, you know where they might be?"

Her eyes blink. She's thinking.

"Well . . . no. But I put all that stuff up in the attic," she says.

"Okay, I'll go look there," I say.

Coffee in hand, I head for the stairs leading to the second floor and up into the attic.

"Or it might all be in the basement," she says.

Three hours later—after dusting through the drawings I made in the first grade, my model airplanes, an assortment of musical instruments my brother once attempted to play in his quest to become a rock star, my yearbooks, four steamer trunks filled with receipts from my father's business, old love letters, old snapshots, old newspapers, old you-name-it—the address book is still at large. We give up on the attic. My mother prevails upon me to have some ziti. Then we try the basement.

"Oh, look!" says my mother.

"Did you find it?" I ask.

"No, but here's a picture of your Uncle Paul before he was arrested for embezzlement. Did I ever tell you that story?"

After another hour, we've gone through everything, and I've had a refresher course in all there is to know about Uncle Paul. Where the hell could it be?

"Well, I don't know," says my mother. "Unless it could be in your old room."

We go upstairs to the room I used to share with Danny. Over in the corner is the old desk where I used to study when I was a kid. I open the top drawer. And, of course, there it is.

"Mom, I need to use your phone."

My mother's phone is located on the landing of the stairs between the floors of the house. It's the same phone that was installed in 1936 after my father began to make enough money from the store to afford one. I sit down on the steps, a pad of paper on my lap, briefcase at my feet. I pick up the receiver, which is heavy enough to bludgeon a burglar into submission. I dial the number, the first of many.

It's one o'clock by now. But I'm calling Israel, which happens to be on the other side of the world from us. And vice versa. Which roughly means their days are our nights, our nights are their mornings, and consequently, one in the morning is not such a bad time to call.

Before long, I've reached a friend I made at the university, someone who knows what's become of Jonah. He finds me another number to call. By two o'clock, I've got the tablet of paper on my lap covered with numbers I've scribbled down, and I'm talking to some people who work with Jonah. I convince one of them to give me the number where I can reach him. By three o'clock, I've found him. He's in London. After several transfers here and there across some office of some company, I'm told that he will call me when he gets in. I don't really believe that, but I doze by the phone. And forty-five minutes later, it rings.

"Alex?"

It's his voice.

"Yes, Jonah," I say.

"I got a message you had called."

"Right," I say. "You remember our meeting in O'Hare."

"Yes, of course I remember it," he says. "And I presume you have something to tell me now."

I freeze for a moment. Then I realize he's referring to his question, what is the goal?

"Right," I say.

"Well?"

I hesitate. My answer seems so ludicrously simple I am suddenly afraid that it must be wrong, that he will laugh at me. But I blurt it out.

"The goal of a manufacturing organization is to make money," I say to him. "And everything else we do is a means to achieve the goal."

But Jonah doesn't laugh at me.

"Very good, Alex. Very good," he says quietly.

"Thanks," I tell him. "But, see, the reason I called was to ask you a question that's kind of related to the discussion we had at O'Hare."

"What's the problem?" he asks.

"Well, in order to know if my plant is helping the company make money, I have to have some kind of measurements," I say. "Right?"

"That's correct," he says.

"And I know that up in the executive suite at company headquarters, they've got measurements like net profit and return on investment and cash flow, which they apply to the overall organization to check on progress toward the goal."

"Yes, go on," says Jonah.

"But where I am, down at the plant level, those measurements don't mean very much. And the measurements I use inside the plant . . . well, I'm not absolutely sure, but I don't think they're really telling the whole story," I say.

"Yes, I know exactly what you mean," says Jonah.

"So how can I know whether what's happening in my plant is truly productive or non-productive?" I ask.

For a second, it gets quiet on the other end of the line. Then I hear him say to somebody with him, "Tell him I'll be in as soon as I'm through with this call."

Then he speaks to me.

"Alex, you have hit upon something very important," he says. "I only have time to talk to you for a few minutes, but perhaps I can suggest a few things which might help you. You see, there is more than one way to express the goal. Do you understand? The goal stays the same, but we can state it in different ways, ways which mean the same thing as those two words, 'making money.' "

"Okay," I answer, "so I can say the goal is to increase net profit, while simultaneously increasing both ROI and cash flow, and that's the equivalent of saying the goal is to make money."

"Exactly," he says. "One expression is the equivalent of the other. But as you have discovered, those conventional measurements you use to express the goal do not lend themselves very well to the daily operations of the manufacturing organization. In fact, that's why I developed a different set of measurements."

"What kind of measurements are those?" I ask.

"They're measurements which express the goal of making money perfectly well, but which also permit you to develop operational rules for running your plant," he says. "There are three of them. Their names are throughput, inventory and operational expense."

"Those all sound familiar," I say.

"Yes, but their definitions are not," says Jonah. "In fact, you will probably want to write them down."

Pen in hand, I flip ahead to a clean sheet of paper on my tablet and tell him to go ahead.

"Throughput," he says, "is the rate at which the system generates money through *sales*."

I write it down word for word.

Then I ask, "But what about production? Wouldn't it be more correct to say—"

"No," he says. "Through *sales*—not production. If you produce something, but don't sell it, it's not throughput. Got it?"

"Right. I thought maybe because I'm plant manager I could substitute—"

Jonah cuts me off.

"Alex, let me tell you something," he says. "These definitions, even though they may sound simple, are worded very precisely. And they should be; a measurement not clearly defined is worse than useless. So I suggest you consider them carefully as a group. And remember that if you want to change one of them, you will have to change at least one of the others as well."

"Okay," I say warily.

"The next measurement is inventory," he says. "Inventory is all the money that the system has invested in purchasing things which it intends to sell."

I write it down, but I'm wondering about it, because it's very different from the traditional definition of inventory.

"And the last measurement?" I ask.

"Operational expense," he says. "Operational expense is all the money the system spends in order to turn inventory into throughput."

"Okay," I say as I write. "But what about the labor invested in inventory? You make it sound as though labor is operational expense?"

"Judge it according to the definitions," he says.

"But the value added to the product by direct labor has to be a part of inventory, doesn't it?"

"It might be, but it doesn't have to be," he says.

"Why do you say that?"

"Very simply, I decided to define it this way because I believe it's better not to take the *value* added into account," he says. "It eliminates the confusion over whether a dollar spent is an investment or an expense. That's why I defined inventory and operational expense the way I just gave you."

"Oh," I say. "Okay. But how do I relate these measurements to my plant?"

"Everything you manage in your plant is covered by those measurements," he says.

"Everything?" I say. I don't quite believe him. "But going back to our original conversation, how do I use these measurements to evaluate productivity?"

"Well, obviously you have to express the goal in terms of the measurements," he says, adding, "Hold on a second, Alex." Then I hear him tell someone, "I'll be there in a minute."

"So how do I express the goal?" I ask, anxious to keep the conversation going.

"Alex, I really have to run. And I know you are smart enough to figure it out on your own; all you have to do is think about it," he says. "Just remember we are always talking about the organization as a whole—not about the manufacturing department, or about one plant, or about one department within the plant. We are not concerned with local optimums."

"Local optimums?" I repeat.

Jonah sighs. "I'll have to explain it to you some other time."

"But, Jonah, this isn't enough," I say. "Even if I can define the goal with these measurements, how do I go about deriving operational rules for running my plant?"

"Give me a phone number where you can be reached," he says.

I give him my office number.

"Okay, Alex, I really do have to go now," he says.

"Right," I say. "Thanks for—"

I hear the click from far away.

"—talking to me."

I sit there on the steps for some time staring at the three definitions. At some point, I close my eyes. When I open them again, I see beams of sunlight below me on the living room rug. I haul myself upstairs to my old room and the bed I had when I was a kid. I sleep the rest of the morning with my torso and limbs painstakingly arranged around the lumps in the mattress.

Five hours later, I wake up feeling like a waffle.

9

It's eleven o'clock when I wake up. Startled by what time it is, I fall onto my feet and head for the phone to call Fran, so she can let everyone know I haven't gone AWOL.

"Mr. Rogo's office," Fran answers.

"Hi, it's me," I say.

"Well, hello stranger," she says. "We were just about ready to start checking the hospitals for you. Think you'll make it in to-day?"

"Uh, yeah, I just had something unexpected come up with my mother, kind of an emergency," I say.

"Oh, well, I hope everything's all right."

"Yeah, it's, ah, taken care of now. More or less. Anything going on that I should know about?"

"Well . . . let's see," she says, checking (I suppose) my mes-sage slips. "Two of the testing machines in G-aisle are down, and Bob Donovan wants to know if we can ship without testing."

"Tell him absolutely not," I say.

"Okay," says Fran. "And somebody from marketing is calling about a late shipment."

My eyes roll over.

"And there was a fist fight last night on second shift . . . Lou still needs to talk to you about some numbers for Bill Peach . . . a reporter called this morning asking when the plant was going to close; I told him he'd have to talk to you . . . and a woman from corporate communications called about shooting a video tape here about productivity and robots with Mr. Granby," says Fran.

"With *Granby?*"

"That's what she said," says Fran.

"What's the name and number?"

She reads it to me.

"Okay, thanks. See you later," I tell Fran.

I call the woman at corporate right away. I can hardly believe the chairman of the board is going to come to the plant. There must be some mistake. I mean, by the time Granby's limo pulls up to the gate, the whole plant might be closed.

But the woman confirms it; they want to shoot Granby here sometime in the middle of next month.

"We need a robot as a suitable background for Mr. Granby's remarks," says the woman.

"So why did you pick Bearington?" I ask her.

"The director saw a slide of one of yours and he likes the color. He thinks Mr. Granby will look good standing in front of it," she says.

"Oh, I see," I tell her. "Have you talked to Bill Peach about this?"

"No, I didn't think there was any need for that," she says. "Why? Is there a problem?"

"You might want to run this past Bill in case he has any other suggestions," I tell her. "But it's up to you. Just let me know when you have an exact date so I can notify the union and have the area cleaned up."

"Fine. I'll be in touch," she says.

I hang up and sit there on the steps muttering, "So . . . he likes the color."

"What was that all about on the phone just now?" my mother asks. We're sitting together at the table. She's obliged me to have something to eat before I leave.

I tell her about Granby coming.

"Well that sounds like a feather in your cap, the head man—what's his name again?" asks my mother.

"Granby."

"Here he's coming all the way to your factory to see you," she says. "It must be an honor."

"Yeah, it is in a way," I tell her. "But actually he's just coming to have his picture taken with one of my robots."

My mother's eyes blink.

"Robots? Like from out-of-space?" she asks.

"No, not from outer space. These are industrial robots. They're not like the ones on television."

"Oh." Her eyes blink again. "Do they have faces?"

"No, not yet. They mostly have arms . . . which do things like welding, stacking materials, spray painting, and so on.

They're run by computer and you can program them to do different jobs," I explain.

Mom nods, still trying to picture what these robots are.

"So why's this Granby guy want to have his picture taken with a bunch of robots who don't even have faces?" she asks.

"I guess because they're the latest thing, and he wants to tell everybody in the corporation that we ought to be using more of them so that—"

I stop and glance away for a second, and see Jonah sitting there smoking his cigar.

"So that what?" asks my mother.

"Uh . . . so that we can increase productivity," I mumble, waving my hand in the air.

And Jonah says, have they really increased productivity at your plant? Sure they have, I say. We had—what?—a thirty-six percent improvement in one area. Jonah puffs his cigar.

"Is something the matter?" my mother asks.

"I just remembered something, that's all."

"What? Something bad?" she asks.

"No, an earlier conversation I had with the man I talked to last night," I say.

My mother puts her hand on my shoulder.

"Alex, what's wrong?" she's asking. "Come on, you can tell me. I know something's wrong. You show up out of the blue on my doorstep, you're calling people all over the place in the middle of the night. What is it?"

"See, Mom, the plant isn't doing so well . . . and, ah . . . well, we're not making any money."

My mother's brow darkens.

"Your big plant not making any money?" she asks. "But you're telling me about this fancy guy Granby coming, and these robot things, whatever they are. And you're not making any money?"

"That's what I said, Mom."

"Don't these robot things work?"

"Mom—"

"If they don't work, maybe the store will take them back."

"Mom, will you forget about the robots!"

She shrugs. "I was just trying to help."

I reach over and pat her hand.

"Yes, I know you were," I say. "Thanks. Really, thanks for

everything. Okay? I've got to get going now. I've really got a lot of work to do."

I stand up and go to get my briefcase. My mother follows. Did I get enough to eat? Would I like a snack to take with me for later in the day? Finally, she takes my sleeve and holds me in one place.

"Listen to me, Al. Maybe you've got some problems. I know you do, but this running all over the place, staying up all night isn't good for you. You've got to stop worrying. It's not going to help you. Look what worrying did to your father," she says. "It killed him."

"But, Mom, he was run over by a bus."

"So if he hadn't been so busy worrying he would have looked before he crossed the street."

I sigh. "Yeah, well, Mom, you may have a point. But it's more complicated than you think."

"I mean it! No worrying!" she says. "And this Granby fellow, if he's making trouble for you, you let me know. I'll call him and tell him what a worker you are. And who should know better than a mother? You leave him to me. I'll straighten him out."

I smile. I put my arm around her shoulders.

"I bet you would, Mom."

"You know I would."

I tell Mom to call me as soon as her phone bill arrives in the mail, and I'll come over and pay it. I give her a hug and a kiss good-bye, and I'm out of there. I walk out into the daylight and get into the Mazda. For a moment, I consider going straight to the office. But a glance at the wrinkles in my suit and a rub of the stubble on my chin convinces me to go home and clean up first.

Once I'm on my way, I keep hearing Jonah's voice saying to me: "So your company is making thirty-six percent more money from your plant just by installing some robots? Incredible." And I remember that I was the one who was smiling. I was the one who thought *he* didn't understand the realities of manufacturing. Now I feel like an idiot.

Yes, the goal is to make money. I know that now. And, yes, Jonah, you're right; productivity did not go up thirty-six percent just because we installed some robots. For that matter, did it go up at all? Are we making *any* more money because of the robots? And the truth is, I don't know. I find myself shaking my head.

But I wonder how Jonah knew? He seemed to know right away that productivity hadn't increased. There were those questions he asked.

One of them, I remember as I'm driving, was whether we had been able to sell any more products as a result of having the robots. Another one was whether we had reduced the number of people on the payroll. Then he had wanted to know if inventories had gone down. Three basic questions.

When I get home, Julie's car is gone. She's out some place, which is just as well. She's probably furious at me. And I simply do not have time to explain right now.

After I'm inside, I open my briefcase to make a note of those questions, and I see the list of measurements Jonah gave me last night. From the second I glance at those definitions again, it's obvious. The questions match the measurements.

That's how Jonah knew. He was using the measurements in the crude form of simple questions to see if his hunch about the robots was correct: did we sell any more products (i.e., did our throughput go up?); did we lay off anybody (did our operational expense go down?); and the last, exactly what he said: did our inventories go down?

With that observation, it doesn't take me long to see how to express the goal through Jonah's measurements. I'm still a little puzzled by the way he worded the definitions. But aside from that, it's clear that every company would want to have its throughput go up. Every company would also want the other two, inventory and operational expense, to go down, if at all possible. And certainly it's best if they all occur simultaneously—just as with the trio that Lou and I found.

So the way to express the goal is this?

Increase throughput while simultaneously reducing both inventory and operating expense.

That means if the robots have made throughput go up and the other two go down, they've made money for the system. But what's really happened since they started working?

I don't know what effect, if any, they've had on throughput. But off the top of my head, I know inventories have generally increased over the past six or seven months, although I can't say for sure if the robots are to blame. The robots *have* increased our depreciation, because they're new equipment, but they haven't directly taken away any jobs from the plant; we simply shifted people around. Which means the robots had to increase operational expense.

Okay, but efficiencies have gone up because of the robots. So maybe that's been our salvation. When efficiencies go up, the cost-per-part has to come down.

But did the cost really come down? How could the cost-per-part go down if operational expense went up?

By the time I make it to the plant, it's one o'clock, and I still haven't thought of a satisfactory answer. I'm still thinking about it as I walk through the office doors. The first thing I do is stop by Lou's office.

"Have you got a couple minutes?" I ask.

"Are you kidding?" he says. "I've been looking for you all morning."

He reaches for a pile of paper on the corner of his desk. I know it's got to be the report he has to send up to division.

"No, I don't want to talk about that right now," I tell him. "I've got something more important on my mind."

I watch his eyebrows go up.

"More important than this report for Peach?"

"Infinitely more important than that," I tell him.

Lou shakes his head as he leans back in his swivel chair and gestures for me to have a seat.

"What can I do for you?"

"After those robots out on the floor came on line, and we got most of the bugs out and all that," I say, "what happened to our sales?"

Lou's eyebrows come back down again; he's leaning forward and squinting at me over his bifocals.

"What kind of question is that?" he asks.

"A smart one, I hope," I say. "I need to know if the robots had any impact on our sales. And specifically if there was any increase after they came on line."

"Increase? Just about all of our sales have been level or in a downhill slide since last year."

I'm a little irritated.

"Well, would you mind just checking?" I ask.

He holds up his hands in surrender.

"Not at all. Got all the time in the world."

Lou turns to his computer, and after looking through some

files, starts printing out handfuls of reports, charts, and graphs. We both start leafing through. But we find that in every case where a robot came on line, there was no increase in sales for any product for which they made parts, not even the slightest blip in the curve. For the heck of it, we also check the shipments made from the plant, but there was no increase there either. In fact, the only increase is in overdue shipments—they've grown rapidly over the last nine months.

Lou looks up at me from the graphs.

"Al, I don't know what you're trying to prove," he says. "But if you want to broadcast some success story on how the robots are going to save the plant with increased sales, the evidence just doesn't exist. The data practically say the opposite."

"That's exactly what I was afraid of," I say.

"What do you mean?"

"I'll explain it in a minute. Let's look at inventories," I tell him. "I want to find out what happened to our work-in-process on parts produced by the robots."

Lou gives up.

"I can't help you there," he says. "I don't have anything on inventories by part number."

"Okay, let's get Stacey in on this."

Stacey Potazenik manages inventory control for the plant. Lou makes a call and pulls her out of another meeting.

Stacey is a woman in her early 40's. She's tall, thin, and brisk in her manner. Her hair is black with strands of gray and she wears big, round glasses. She is always dressed in jackets and skirts; never have I seen her in a blouse with any kind of lace, ribbon or frill. I know almost nothing about her personal life. She wears a ring, but she's never mentioned a husband. She rarely mentions anything about her life outside the plant. I do know she works hard.

When she comes in to see us, I ask her about work-in-process on those parts passing through the robot areas.

"Do you want exact numbers?" she asks.

"No, we just need to know the trends," I say.

"Well, I can tell you without looking that inventories went up on those parts," Stacey says.

"Recently?"

"No, it's been happening since late last summer, around the

end of the third quarter," she says. "And you can't blame me for it—even though everyone always does—because I fought it every step of the way."

"What do you mean?"

"You remember, don't you? Or maybe you weren't here then. But when the reports came in, we found the robots in welding were only running at something like thirty percent efficiency. And the other robots weren't much better. Nobody would stand for that."

I look over at Lou.

"We had to do something," he says. "Frost would have had my head if I hadn't spoken up. Those things were brand new and very expensive. They'd never pay for themselves in the projected time if we kept them at thirty percent."

"Okay, hold on a minute," I tell him. I turn back to Stacey. "What did you do then?"

She says, "What *could* I do? I had to release more materials to the floor in all the areas feeding the robots. Giving the robots more to produce increased their efficiencies. But ever since then, we've been ending each month with a surplus of those parts."

"But the important thing was that efficiencies did go up," says Lou, trying to add a bright note. "Nobody can find fault with us on that."

"I'm not sure of that at all any more," I say. "Stacey, why are we getting that surplus? How come we aren't consuming those parts?"

"Well, in a lot of cases, we don't have any orders to fill at present which would call for those parts," she says. "And in the cases where we do have orders, we just can't seem to get enough of the other parts we need."

"How come?"

"You'd have to ask Bob Donovan about that," Stacey says.

"Lou, let's have Bob paged," I say.

Bob comes into the office with a smear of grease on his white shirt over the bulge of his beer gut, and he's talking nonstop about what's going on with the breakdown of the automatic testing machines.

"Bob," I tell him, "forget about that for now."

"Something else wrong?" he asks.

"Yes, there is. We've just been talking about our local celebrities, the robots," I say.

Bob glances from side to side, wondering, I suppose, what we've been saying.

"What are you worried about them for?" he asks. "The robots work pretty good now."

"We're not so sure about that," I say. "Stacey tells me we've got an excess of parts built by the robots. But in some instances we can't get enough of certain other parts to assemble and ship our orders."

Bob says, "It isn't that we can't *get* enough parts—it's more that we can't seem to get them when we need them. That's true even with a lot of the robot parts. We'll have a pile of something like, say, a CD-50 sit around for months waiting for control boxes. Then we'll get the control boxes, but we won't have something else. Finally we get the something else, and we build the order and ship it. Next thing you know, you're looking around for a CD-50 and you can't find any. We'll have tons of CD-45's and 80's, but no 50's. So we wait. And by the time we get the 50's again, all the control boxes are gone."

"And so on, and so on, and so on," says Stacey.

"But, Stacey, you said the robots were producing a lot of parts for which we don't have product orders," I say. "That means we're producing parts we don't need."

"Everybody tells me we'll use them eventually," she says. Then she adds, "Look, it's the same game everybody plays. Whenever efficiencies take a drop, everybody draws against the future forecast to keep busy. We build inventory. If the forecast doesn't hold up, there's hell to pay. Well, that's what's happening now. We've been building inventory for the better part of a year, and the market hasn't helped us one damn bit."

"I know, Stacey, I know," I tell her. "And I'm not blaming you or anybody. I'm just trying to figure this out."

Restless, I get up and pace.

I say, "So the bottom line is this: to give the robots more to do, we released more materials."

"Which, in turn, increased inventories," says Stacey.

"Which has increased our costs," I add.

"But the cost of those parts went down," says Lou.

"Did it?" I ask. "What about the added carrying cost of inventory? That's operational expense. And if that went up, how could the cost of parts go down?"

"Look, it depends on volume," says Lou.

"Exactly," I say. "*Sales* volume . . . that's what matters. And when we've got parts that can't be assembled into a product and sold because we don't have the other components, or because we don't have the orders, then we're increasing our costs."

"Al," says Bob, "are you trying to tell us we got screwed by the robots?"

I sit down again.

"We haven't been managing according to the goal," I mutter.

Lou squints. "The goal? You mean our objectives for the month?"

I look around at them.

"I think I need to explain a few things."

10

An hour and a half later, I've gone over it all with them. We're in the conference room, which I've commandeered because it has a whiteboard. On that whiteboard, I've drawn a diagram of the goal. Just now I've written out the definitions of the three measurements.

All of them are quiet. Finally, Lou speaks up and says, "Where the heck did you get these definitions anyway?"

"My old physics teacher gave them to me."

"Who?" asks Bob.

"Your old physics teacher?" asks Lou.

"Yeah," I say defensively. "What about it?"

"So what's his name?" asks Bob.

"Or what's 'her' name," says Stacey.

"His name is Jonah. He's from Israel."

Bob says, "Well, what I want to know is, how come in throughput he says 'sales'? We're manufacturing. We've got nothing to do with sales; that's marketing."

I shrug. After all, I asked the same question over the phone. Jonah said the definitions were precise, but I don't know how to answer Bob. I turn toward the window. Then I see what I should have remembered.

"Come here," I say to Bob.

He lumbers over. I put a hand on his shoulder and point out the window. "What are those?" I ask him.

"Warehouses," he says.

"For what?"

"Finished goods."

"Would the company stay in business if all it did was manufacture products to fill those warehouses?"

"Okay, okay," Bob says sheepishly, seeing the meaning now. "So we got to sell the stuff to make money."

Lou is still staring at the board.

"Interesting, isn't it, that each one of those definitions contains the word *money*," he says. "Throughput is the money coming in. Inventory is the money currently inside the system. And operational expense is the money we have to pay out to make throughput happen. One measurement for the incoming money, one for the money still stuck inside, and one for the money going out."

"Well, if you think about all the investment represented by what we've got sitting out there on the floor, you know for sure that inventory is money," says Stacey. "But what bothers me is that I don't see how he's treating value added to materials by direct labor."

"I wondered the same thing, and I can only tell you what he told me," I say.

"Which is?"

"He said he thinks that it's just better if value added isn't taken into account. He said that it gets rid of the 'confusion' about what's an investment and what's an expense, I say.

Stacey and the rest of us think about this for a minute. The room gets quiet again.

Then Stacey says, "Maybe Jonah feels direct labor shouldn't be a part of inventory because the time of the employees isn't what we're really selling. We 'buy' time from our employees, in a sense, but we don't sell that time to a customer—unless we're talking about service."

"Hey, hold it," says Bob. "Now look here: if we're selling the product, aren't we also selling the time invested in that product?"

"Okay, but what about idle time?" I ask.

Lou butts in to settle it, saying, "All this is, if I understand it correctly, is a different way of doing the accounting. All employee time—whether it's direct or indirect, idle time or operating time, or whatever—is *operational expense,* according to Jonah. You're still accounting for it. It's just that his way is simpler, and you don't have to play as many games."

Bob puffs out his chest. "Games? We, in operations, are honest, hard-working folk who do not have time for games."

"Yeah, you're too busy turning idle time into process time with the stroke of a pen," says Lou.

"Or turning process time into more piles of inventory," says Stacey.

They go on bantering about this for a minute. Meanwhile, I'm thinking there might be something more to this besides simplification. Jonah mentioned *confusion* between investment and expense; are we confused enough now to be doing something we shouldn't? Then I hear Stacey talking.

"But how do we know the value of our finished goods?" she asks.

"First of all, the market determines the value of the product," says Lou. "And in order for the corporation to make money, the value of the product—and the price we're charging—has to be greater than the combination of the investment in inventory and the total operational expense per unit of what we sell."

I see by the look on Bob's face that he's very skeptical. I ask him what's bothering him.

"Hey, man, this is crazy," Bob grumbles.

"Why?" asks Lou.

"It won't work!" says Bob. "How can you account for everything in the whole damn system with three lousy measurements?"

"Well," says Lou as he ponders the board. "Name something that won't fit in one of those three."

"Tooling, machines . . ." Bob counts them on with his fingers. "This building, the whole plant!"

"Those are in there," says Lou.

"Where?" asks Bob.

Lou turns to him. "Look, those things are part one and part the other. If you've got a machine, the depreciation on that machine is operational expense. Whatever portion of the investment still remains in the machine, which could be sold, is inventory."

"Inventory? I thought inventory was products, and parts and so on," says Bob. "You know, the stuff we're going to sell."

Lou smiles. "Bob, the whole plant is an investment which can be sold—for the right price and under the right circumstances."

And maybe sooner than we'd like, I think.

Stacey says, "So investment is the same thing as inventory."

"What about lubricating oil for the machines?" asks Bob.

"It's operational expense," I tell him. "We're not going to sell that oil to a customer."

"How about scrap?" he asks.

"That's operational expense, too."

"Yeah? What about what we sell to the scrap dealer?"

"Okay, then it's the same as a machine," says Lou. "Any money we've lost is operational expense; any investment that we can sell is inventory."

"The carrying costs have to be operational expense, don't they?" asks Stacey.

Lou and I both nod.

Then I think about the "soft" things in business, things like knowledge—knowledge from consultants, knowledge gained from our own research and development. I throw it out to them to see how they think those things should be classified.

Money for knowledge has us stumped for a while. Then we decide it depends, quite simply, upon what the knowledge is used for. If it's knowledge, say, which gives us a new manufacturing process, something that helps turn inventory into throughput, then the knowledge is operational expense. If we intend to sell the knowledge, as in the case of a patent or a technology license, then it's inventory. But if the knowledge pertains to a product which UniCo itself will build, it's like a machine—an investment to make money which will depreciate in value as time goes on. And, again, the investment that can be sold is inventory; the depreciation is operational expense.

"I got one for you," says Bob. "Here's one that doesn't fit: Granby's chauffeur."

"What?"

"You know, the old boy in the black suit who drives J. Bart Granby's limo for him," says Bob.

"He's operational expense," says Lou.

"Like hell he is! You tell me how Granby's chauffeur turns inventory into throughput," says Bob, and looks around as if he's really got us on this one. "I bet his chauffeur doesn't even know that inventory and throughput exist."

"Unfortunately, neither do some of our secretaries," says Stacey.

I say, "You don't have to have your hands on the product in order to turn inventory into throughput. Every day, Bob, you're out there helping to turn inventory into throughput. But to the people on the floor, it probably looks like all you do is walk around and make life complicated for everyone."

"Yeah, no appreciation from nobody," Bob pouts, "but you still haven't told me how the chauffeur fits in."

"Well, maybe the chauffeur helps Granby have more time to think and deal with customers, etc., while he's commuting here and there," I suggest.

"Bob, why don't you ask Mr. Granby next time you two have lunch," says Stacey.

"That's not as funny as you think," I say. "I just heard this morning that Granby may be coming here to make a video tape on robots."

"Granby's coming here?" asks Bob.

"And if Granby's coming, you can bet Bill Peach and all the others will be tagging along," says Stacey.

"Just what we need," grumbles Lou.

Stacey turns to Bob. "You see now why Al's asking questions about the robots. We've got to look good for Granby."

"We do look good," says Lou. "The efficiencies there are quite acceptable; Granby will not be embarrassed by appearing with the robots on tape."

But I say, "Dammit, I don't care about Granby and his video-tape. In fact, I will lay odds that the tape will never be shot here anyway, but that's beside the point. The problem is that every-body—including me until now—has thought these robots have been a big productivity improvement. And we just learned that they're not productive in terms of the goal. The way we've been using them, they're actually *counter*-productive."

Everyone is silent.

Finally, Stacey has the courage to say, "Okay, so somehow we've got to make the robots productive in terms of the goal."

"We've got to do more than that," I say. I turn to Bob and Stacey. "Listen, I've already told Lou, and I guess this is as good a time as any to tell the both of you. I know you'll hear it eventually anyhow."

"Hear what?" asks Bob.

"We've been given an ultimatum by Peach—three months to turn the plant around or he closes us down for good," I say.

Both of them are stunned for a few moments. Then they're both firing questions at me. I take a few minutes and tell them what I know—avoiding the news about the division; I don't want to send them into panic.

Finally, I say, "I know it doesn't seem like a lot of time. It isn't. But until they kick me out of here, I'm not giving up. What you decide to do is your own business, but if you want out, I suggest you leave now. Because for the next three months, I'm going to need everything you can give me. If we can make this place show any progress, I'm going to go to Peach and do what-ever I have to to make him give us more time."

"Do you really think we can do it?" asks Lou.

"I honestly don't know," I say. "But at least now we can see some of what we're doing wrong."

"So what can we do that's different?" asks Bob.

"Why don't we stop pushing materials through the robots and try to reduce inventories?" suggests Stacey.

"Hey, I'm all for lower inventory," says Bob. "But if we don't produce, our efficiencies go down. Then we're right back where we started."

"Peach isn't going to give us a second chance if all we give him is lower efficiencies," says Lou. "He wants higher efficiencies, not lower."

I run my fingers through my hair.

Then Stacey says, "Maybe you should try calling this guy, Jonah, again. He seems like he's got a good handle on what's what."

"Yeah, at least we could find out what he has to say," says Lou.

"Well, I talked to him last night. That's when he gave me all this stuff," I say, waving to the definitions on the board. "He was supposed to call me . . ."

I look at their faces.

"Well, okay, I'll try him again," I say and reach for my briefcase to get the London number.

I put through a call from the phone in the conference room with the three of them listening expectantly around the table. But he isn't there anymore. Instead I end up talking to some secretary.

"Ah, yes, Mr. Rogo," she says. "Jonah tried to call you, but your secretary said you were in a meeting. He wanted to talk to you before he left London today, but I'm afraid you've missed him."

"Where is he going to be next?" I ask.

"He was flying to New York. Perhaps you can catch him at his hotel," she says.

I take down the name of the hotel and thank her. Then I get the number in New York from directory assistance, and expecting only to be able to leave a message for him, I try it. The switchboard puts me through.

"Hello?" says a sleepy voice.

"Jonah? This is Alex Rogo. Did I wake you?"

"As a matter of fact, you did."

"Oh, I'm sorry—I'll try not to keep you long. But I really need to talk to you at greater length about what we were discussing last night," I tell him.

"Last night?" he asks. "Yes, I suppose it was 'last night' your time."

"Maybe we could make arrangements for you to come to my plant and meet with me and my staff," I suggest.

"Well, the problem is I have commitments lined up for the next three weeks, and then I'm going back to Israel," he says.

"But, you see, I can't wait that long," I say. "I've got some major problems I have to solve and not a lot of time. I understand now what you meant about the robots and productivity. But my staff and I don't know what the next step should be and . . . uh, well, maybe if I explained a few things to you—"

"Alex, I would like to help you, but I also need to get some sleep. I'm exhausted," he says. "But I have a suggestion: if your schedule permits, why don't I meet with you here tomorrow morning at seven for breakfast at my hotel."

"Tomorrow?"

"That's right," he says. "We'll have about an hour and we can talk. Otherwise . . ."

I look around at the others, all of them watching me anxiously. I tell Jonah to hold on for a second.

"He wants me to come to New York tomorrow," I tell them. "Can anybody think of a reason why I shouldn't go?"

"Are you kidding?" says Stacey.

"Go for it," says Bob.

"What have you got to lose?" says Lou.

I take my hand off the mouthpiece. "Okay, I'll be there," I say.

"Excellent!" Jonah says with relief. "Until then, good night."

When I get back to my office, Fran looks up with surprise from her work.

"So there you are!" she says and reaches for the message slips. "This man called you twice from London. He wouldn't say whether it was important or not."

I say, "I've got a job for you: find a way to get me to New York tonight."

11

But Julie does not understand.

"Thanks for the advance notice," she says.

"If I'd known earlier, I'd have told you," I say.

"Everything is unexpected with you lately," she says.

"Don't I always tell you when I know I've got trips coming up?"

She fidgets next to the bedroom door. I'm packing an overnight bag which lies open on the bed. We're alone; Sharon is down the street at a friend's house, and Davey is at band practice.

"When is this going to end?" she asks.

I stop midway through taking some underwear from a drawer. I'm getting irritated by the questions because we just went over the whole thing five minutes ago. Why is it so hard for her to understand?

"Julie, I don't know." I say. "I've got a lot of problems to solve."

More fidgeting. She doesn't like it. It occurs to me that maybe she doesn't trust me or something.

"Hey, I'll call you as soon as I get to New York," I tell her. "Okay?"

She turns as if she might walk out of the room.

"Fine. Call," she says, "but I might not be here."

I stop again.

"What do you mean by that?"

"I might be out someplace," she says.

"Oh," I say. "Well, I guess I'll have to take my chances."

"I guess you will," she says, furious now, on her way out the door.

I grab an extra shirt and slam the drawer shut. When I finish packing, I go looking for her. I find her in the living room. She stands by the window, biting the end of her thumb. I take her hand and kiss the thumb. Then I try to hug her.

"Listen, I know I've been undependable lately," I say. "But this is important. It's for the plant—"

She shakes her head, pulls away. I follow her into the kitchen. She stands with her back to me.

"Everything is for your job," she says. "It's all you think about. I can't even count on you for dinner. And the kids are asking me why you're like this—"

There is a tear forming in the corner of her eye. I reach to wipe it away, but she brushes my hand aside.

"No!" she says. "Just go catch your plane to wherever it is you're going."

"Julie—"

She walks past me.

"Julie, this is not fair!" I yell at her.

She turns to me.

"That's right," she says. "*You* are not being fair. To me or to your children."

She goes upstairs without looking back. And I don't even have time to settle this; I'm already late for my flight, I pick up my bag in the hall, sling it over my shoulder, and grab my briefcase on my way out the door.

At 7:10 the next morning, I'm waiting in the hotel lobby for Jonah. He's a few minutes late, but that's not what's on my mind as I pace the carpeted floor. I'm thinking about Julie. I'm worried about her . . . about us. After I checked into my room last night, I tried to call home. No answer. Not even one of the kids picked up the phone. I walked around the room for half an hour, kicked a few things, and tried calling again. Still no answer. From then until two in the morning, I dialed the number every fifteen minutes. Nobody home. At one point I tried the airlines to see if I could get on a plane back, but nothing was flying in that direction at that hour. I finally fell asleep. My wake-up call got me out of bed at six o'clock. I tried the number twice before I left my room this morning. The second time, I let it ring for five minutes. Still no answer.

"Alex!"

I turn. Jonah is walking toward me. He's wearing a white shirt—no tie, no jacket—and plain trousers.

"Good morning," I say as we shake hands. I notice his eyes are puffy, like those of someone who hasn't had a lot of sleep; I think that mine probably look the same.

"Sorry I'm late," he says. "I had dinner last night with some associates and we got into a discussion which went, I believe, until three o'clock in the morning. Let's get a table for breakfast."

I walk with him into the restaurant and the maitre d' leads us to a table with a white linen cloth.

"How did you do with the measurements I defined for you over the telephone?" he asks after we've sat down.

I switch my mind to business, and tell him how I expressed the goal with his measurements. Jonah seemed very pleased.

"Excellent," he says. "You have done very well."

"Well, thanks, but I'm afraid I need more than a goal and some measurements to save my plant."

"To save your plant?" he asks.

I say, "Well . . . yes, that's why I'm here. I mean, I didn't just call you to talk philosophy."

He smiles. "No, I didn't think you tracked me down purely for the love of truth. Okay, Alex, tell me what's going on."

"This is confidential," I say to him. Then I explain the situation with the plant and the three-month deadline before it gets closed. Jonah listens attentively. When I've finished, he sits back.

"What do you expect from me?" he asks.

"I don't know if there is one, but I'd like you to help me find the answer that will let me keep my plant alive and my people working," I say.

Jonah looks away for a moment.

"I'll tell you *my* problem," he says. "I have an unbelievable schedule. That's why we're meeting at this ungodly hour, incidentally. With the commitments I already have, there is no way I can spend the time to do all the things you probably would expect from a consultant."

I sigh, very disappointed. I say, "Okay, if you're too busy—"

"Wait, I'm not finished," he says. "That doesn't mean you can't save your plant. I don't have time to solve your problems for you. But that wouldn't be the best thing for you anyway—"

"What do you mean?" I interrupt.

Jonah holds up his hands. "Let me finish!" he says. "From what I've heard, I think you can solve your own problems. What I will do is give you some basic rules to apply. If you and your people follow them intelligently, I think you will save your plant. Fair enough?"

"But, Jonah, we've only got three months," I say.

He nods impatiently. "I know, I know," he says. "Three months is more than enough time to show improvement . . . if you are diligent, that is. And if you aren't, then nothing I say could save you anyway."

"Oh, you can count on our diligence, for sure," I say.

"Shall we try it then?" he asks.

"Frankly, I don't know what else to do," I say. Then I smile. "I guess I'd better ask what this is going to cost me. Do you have some kind of standard rate or something?"

"No, I don't," he says. "But I'll make a deal with you. Just pay me the value of what you learn from me."

"How will I know what that is?"

"You should have a reasonable idea after we've finished. If your plant folds, then obviously the value of your learning won't have been much; you won't owe me anything. If, on the other hand, you learn enough from me to make billions, then you should pay me accordingly," he says.

I laugh. What have I got to lose?

"Okay, fair enough," I say finally.

We shake hands across the table.

A waiter interrupts to ask if we're ready to order. Neither of us have opened the menus, but it turns out we both want coffee. The waiter informs us there's a ten-dollar minimum for sitting in the dining room. So Jonah tells him to bring us both our own pots of coffee and a quart of milk. He gives us a dirty look and vanishes.

"Now then," Jonah says. "Where shall we begin . . ."

"I thought maybe first we could focus on the robots," I tell him.

Jonah shakes his head.

"Alex, forget about your robots for now. They're like some new industrial toy everybody's discovered. You've got much more fundamental things to concern yourself with," he says.

"But you're not taking into account how important they are to us," I tell him. "They're some of our most expensive equipment. We absolutely have to keep them productive."

"Productive with respect to what?" he asks with an edge in his voice.

"Okay, right . . . we have to keep them productive in terms of the goal," I say. "But I need high efficiencies to make those things pay for themselves, and I only get the efficiencies if they're making parts."

Jonah is shaking his head again.

"Alex, you told me in our first meeting that your plant has very good efficiencies overall. If your efficiencies are so good, then why is your plant in trouble?"

He takes a cigar out of his shirt pocket and bites the end off of it.

"Okay, look, I have to care about efficiencies if only for the reason that my management cares about them," I tell him.

"What's more important to your management, Alex: efficiencies or money?" he asks.

"Money, of course. But isn't high efficiency essential to making money?" I ask him.

"Most of the time, your struggle for high efficiencies is taking you in the opposite direction of your goal."

"I don't understand," I say. "And even if I did, my management wouldn't."

But Jonah lights his cigar and says between puffs, "Okay, let's see if I can help you understand with some basic questions and answers. First tell me this: when you see one of your workers standing idle with nothing to do, is that good or bad for the company?"

"It's bad, of course," I say.

"Always?"

I feel this is a trick question.

"Well, we have to do maintenance—"

"No, no, no, I'm talking about a production employee who is idle because there is no product to be worked on."

"Yes, that's always bad," I say.

"Why?"

I chuckle. "Isn't it obvious? Because it's a waste of money! What are we supposed to do, pay people to do nothing? We can't afford to have idle time. Our costs are too high to tolerate it. It's inefficiency, it's low productivity—no matter how you measure it."

He leans forward as if he's going to whisper a big secret to me.

"Let me tell you something," he says. "A plant in which everyone is working all the time is very inefficient."

"Pardon me?"

"You heard me."

"But how can you prove that?" I ask.

He says, "You've already proven it in your own plant. It's right in front of your eyes. But you don't see it."

Now I shake my head. I say, "Jonah, I don't think we're communicating. You see, in my plant, I don't have extra people. The only way we can get products out the door is to keep everyone working constantly."

"Tell me, Alex, do you have excess inventories in your plant?" he asks.

"Yes, we do," I say.

"Do you have a lot of excess inventories?"

"Well . . . yes."

"Do you have *a lot* of a lot of excess inventories?"

"Yeah, okay, we do have a lot of a lot of excess, but what's the point?"

"Do you realize that the only way you can create excess inventories is by having excess manpower?" he says.

I think about it. After a minute, I have to conclude he's right; machines don't set up and run themselves. People had to create the excess inventory.

"What are you suggesting I do?" I ask. "Lay off more people? I'm practically down to a skeleton force now."

"No, I'm not suggesting that you lay off more people. But I am suggesting that you question how you are managing the capacity of your plant. And let me tell you, it is not according to the goal."

Between us, the waiter sets down two elegant silver pots with steam coming out of their spouts. He puts out a pitcher of cream and pours the coffee. While he does this, I find myself staring toward the window. After a few seconds, I feel Jonah reach over and touch my sleeve.

"Here's what's happening," he says. "Out there in the world at large, you've got a market demand for so much of whatever it is you're producing. And inside your company, you've got so many resources, each of which has so much capacity, to fill that demand. Now, before I go on, do you know what I mean by a 'balanced plant'?"

"You mean balancing a production line?" I ask.

He says, "A balanced plant is essentially what every manufacturing manager in the whole western world has struggled to achieve. It's a plant where the capacity of each and every resource is balanced exactly with demand from the market. Do you know why managers try to do this?"

I tell him, "Well, because if we don't have enough capacity, we're cheating ourselves out of potential throughput. And if we have more than enough capacity, we're wasting money. We're missing an opportunity to reduce operational expense."

"Yes, that's exactly what everybody thinks," says Jonah. "And the tendency for most managers is to trim capacity wherever they can, so no resource is idle, and everybody has something to work on."

"Yeah, sure, I know what you're talking about," I say. "We do that at our plant. In fact, it's done at every plant I've ever seen."

"Do you run a balanced plant?" he asks.

"Well, it's as balanced as we can make it. Of course, we've got some machines sitting idle, but generally that's just outdated equipment. As for people, we've trimmed our capacity as much as we can," I explain. "But nobody ever runs a perfectly balanced plant."

"Funny, I don't know of any balanced plants either," he says. "Why do you think it is that nobody after all this time and effort has ever succeeded in running a balanced plant?"

"I can give you a lot of reasons. The number one reason is that conditions are always changing on us," I say.

"No, actually that isn't the number one reason," he says.

"Sure it is! Look at the things I have to contend with—my vendors, for example. We'll be in the middle of a hot order and discover that the vendor sent us a bad batch of parts. Or look at all the variables in my work force—absenteeism, people who don't care about quality, employee turnover, you name it. And then there's the market itself. The market is always changing. So it's no wonder we get too much capacity in one area and not enough in another."

"Alex, the real reason you cannot balance your plant is much more basic than all of those factors you mentioned. All of those are relatively minor."

"Minor?"

"The real reason is that the closer you come to a balanced plant, the closer you are to bankruptcy."

"Come on!" I say. "You've got to be kidding me."

"Look at this obsession with trimming capacity in terms of

the goal," he says. "When you lay off people, do you increase sales?"

"No, of course not," I say.

"Do you reduce your inventory?" he asks.

"No, not by cutting people," I say. "What we do by laying off workers is cut our expenses."

"Yes, exactly," Jonah says. "You improve only one measurement, operational expense."

"Isn't that enough?"

"Alex, the goal is not to reduce operational expense by itself. The goal is not to improve one measurement in isolation. The goal is to reduce operational expense and reduce inventory while simultaneously increasing throughput," says Jonah.

"Fine. I agree with that," I say. "But if we reduce expenses, and inventory and throughput stay the same, aren't we better off?"

"Yes, *if* you do not increase inventory and/or reduce throughput," he says.

"Okay, right. But balancing capacity doesn't affect either one," I say.

"Oh? It doesn't? How do you know that?"

"We just said—"

"I didn't say anything of the sort. I asked you. And you *assumed* that if you trim capacity to balance with market demand you won't affect throughput or inventory," he says. "But, in fact, that assumption—which is practically universal in the western business world—is totally wrong."

"How do you know it's wrong?"

"For one thing, there is a mathematical proof which could clearly show that when capacity is trimmed exactly to marketing demands, no more and no less, throughput goes down, while inventory goes through the roof," he says. "And because inventory goes up, the *carrying cost* of inventory—which is operational expense—goes up. So it's questionable whether you can even fulfill the intended reduction in your total operational expense, the one measurement you expected to improve."

"How can that be?"

"Because of the combinations of two phenomena which are found in every plant," he says. "One phenomenon is called 'dependent events.' Do you know what I mean by that term? I mean that an event, or a series of events, must take place before another can begin . . . the subsequent event *depends* upon the ones prior to it. You follow?"

"Yeah, sure," I say. "But what's the big deal about that?"

"The big deal occurs when dependent events are in combination with another phenomenon called 'statistical fluctuations,'" he says. "Do you know what those are?"

I shrug. "Fluctuations in statistics, right?"

"Let me put it this way," he says. "You know that some types of information can be determined precisely. For instance, if we need to know the seating capacity in this restaurant, we can determine it precisely by counting the number of chairs at each table."

He points around the room.

"But there are other kinds of information we cannot precisely predict. Like how long it will take the waiter to bring us our check. Or how long it will take the chef to make an omelet. Or how many eggs the kitchen will need today. These types of information vary from one instance to the next. They are subject to *statistical fluctuations.*"

"Yeah, but you can generally get an idea of what all those are going to be based on experience," I say.

"But only within a range. Last time, the waiter brought the check in five minutes and 42 seconds. The time before it only took two minutes. And today? Who knows? Could be three, four hours," he says, looking around. "Where the hell is he?"

"Yeah, but if the chef is doing a banquet and he knows how many people are coming and he knows they're all having omelets, then he knows how many eggs he's going to need," I say.

"Exactly?" asks Jonah. "Suppose he drops one on the floor?"

"Okay, so he has a couple extra."

"Most of the factors critical to running your plant successfully cannot be determined precisely ahead of time," he says.

The arm of the waiter comes between us as he puts the totaled check on the table. I pull it to my side of the table.

"All right, I agree," I say. "But in the case of a worker doing the same job day in, day out, those fluctuations average out over a period of time. Frankly, I can't see what either one of those two phenomena have to do with anything."

Jonah stands up, ready to leave.

"I'm not talking about the one or the other alone," he says, "but about the effect of the two of them together. Which is what I want you to think about, because I have to go."

"You're leaving?" I ask.

"I have to," he says.

"Jonah, you can't just run off like this."

"There are clients waiting for me," he says.

"Jonah, I don't have time for riddles. I need answers," I tell him.

He puts his hand on my arm.

"Alex, if I simply told you what to do, ultimately you would fail. You have to gain the understanding for yourself in order to make the rules work," he says.

He shakes my hand.

"Until next time, Alex. Call me when you can tell me what the combination of the two phenomena mean to your plant."

Then he hurries away. Fuming inside, I flag down the waiter and hand him the check and some money. Without waiting for the change, I follow in the direction of Jonah out to the lobby.

I claim my overnight bag from the bellhop at the desk where I checked it, and sling it over my shoulder. As I turn, I see Jonah, still without jacket or tie, talking to a handsome man in a blue pinstripe suit over by the doors to the street. They go through the doors together, and I trudge along a few steps behind them. The man leads Jonah to a black limousine waiting at the curb. As they approach, a chauffeur hops out to open the rear door for them.

I hear the handsome man in the blue pinstripe saying as he gets into the limo behind Jonah, "After the facilities tour, we're scheduled for a meeting with the chairman and several of the board . . ." Waiting inside for them is a silver-haired man who shakes Jonah's hand. The chauffeur closes the door and returns to the wheel. I can see only the vague silhouettes of their heads behind the dark glass as the big car quietly eases into traffic.

I get into a cab.

The drivers asks, "Where to, chief?"

12

There is a guy I heard about in UniCo who came home from work one night, walked in, and said, "Hi, honey, I'm home!" And his greeting echoed back to him from the empty rooms of his house. His wife had taken everything: the kids, the dog, the goldfish, the furniture, the carpets, the appliances, the curtains, the pictures on the wall, the toothpaste, everything. Well, just about everything—actually, she left him two things: his clothes (which were in a heap on the floor of the bedroom by the closet; she had even taken the hangers), and a note written in lipstick on the bathroom mirror which said, "Good-bye, you bastard!"

As I drive down the street to my house, that kind of vision is running through my mind, and has been periodically since last night. Before I pull into the driveway, I look at the lawn for the telltale signs of tracks left by the wheels of a moving van, but the lawn is unmarred.

I park the Mazda in front of the garage. On my way inside, I peek through the glass, Julie's Accord is parked inside, and I look at the sky and silently say, "Thank You."

She's sitting at the kitchen table, her back to me as I come in. I startle her. She stands up right away and turns around. We stare at each other for a second. I can see that the rims of her eyes are red.

"Hi," I say.

"What are you doing home?" Julie asks.

I laugh—not a nice laugh, an exasperated laugh.

"What am *I* doing home? I'm looking for *you!*" I say.

"Well, here I am. Take a good look," she says, frowning at me.

"Yeah, right, here you are now," I say. "But what I want to know is where you were last night."

"I was out," she says.

"All night?"

She's prepared for the question.

"Gee, I'm surprised you even knew I was gone," she says.

"Come on, Julie, let's cut the crap. I must have called the number here a hundred times last night. I was worried sick about you. I tried it again this morning and nobody answered. So I know you were gone all night," I say, "And, by the way, where were the kids?"

"They stayed with friends," she says.

"On a school night?" I ask. "And what about you? Did you stay with a *friend?*"

She puts her hands on her hips.

"Yes, as a matter of fact, I did stay with a friend," she says.

"Man or woman?"

Her eyes get hard on me. She takes a step forward.

"You don't care if I'm home with the kids night after night," she says. "But if I go away for one night, all of a sudden you have to know where I've been, what I've done."

"I just feel you owe me some explanation," I say.

"How many times have you been late, or out of town, or who knows where?" she asks.

"But that's business," I say. "And I always tell you where I've been if you ask. Now I'm asking."

"There's nothing to tell," she says. "All that happened was I went out with Jane."

"Jane?" It takes me a minute to remember her. "You mean your friend from where we used to live? You drove all the way back there?"

"I just had to talk to someone," she says. "By the time we'd finished talking, I'd had too much to drink to drive home. Anyway, I knew the kids were okay until morning. So I just stayed at Jane's."

"Okay, but why? How did this come over you all of a sudden?" I ask her.

"Come over me? All of a sudden? Alex, you go off and leave me night after night. It's no wonder that I'm lonely. Nothing suddenly came over me. Ever since you got into management, your career has come first and everyone else takes whatever is left."

"Julie, I've just tried to make a good living for you and the kids," I tell her.

"Is that all? Then why do you keep taking the promotions?"

"What am I supposed to do, turn them down?"

She doesn't answer.

"Look, I put in the hours because I have to, not because I want to," I tell her.

She still doesn't say anything.

"All right, look: I promise I'll make more time for you and the kids," I say. "Honest, I'll spend more time at home."

"Al, it's not going to work. Even when you're home, you're at the office. Sometimes I've seen the kids tell you something two or three times before you hear them."

"It won't be like that when I get out of the jam I'm in right now," I say.

"Do you hear what you're saying? 'When I get out of the jam I'm in right now.' Do you think it's going to change? You've said all that before, Al. Do you know how many times we've been over this?"

"Okay, you're right. We have been over it a lot of times. But, right now, there's nothing I can do," I say.

She looks up at the sky and says, "Your job has always been on the line. Always. So if you're such a marginal employee, why do they keep giving you promotions and more money?"

I pinch the bridge of my nose.

"How do I make you understand this," I say. "I'm not up for another promotion or pay raise this time. This time it's different. Julie, you have no idea what kind of problems I've got at the plant."

"And you have no idea what it's like here at home," she says.

I say, "Okay, look, I'd like to spend more time at home, but the problem is getting the time."

"I don't need all your time," she says. "But I do need some of it, and so do the kids."

"I know that. But to save this plant, I'm going to have to give it all I've got for the next couple of months."

"Couldn't you at least come home for dinner most of the time?" she asks. "The evenings are when I miss you the most. All of us do. It's empty around here without you, even with the kids for company."

"Nice to know I'm wanted. But sometimes I even need the evenings. I just don't have enough time during the day to get to things like paperwork," I say.

"Why don't you bring the paperwork home," she suggests. "Do it here. If you did that, at least we could see you. And maybe I could even help you with some of it."

I lean back. "I don't know if I'll be able to concentrate, but . . . okay, let's try it."

She smiles. "You mean it?"

"Sure, if it doesn't work, we can talk about it," I say. "Deal?"

"Deal," she says.

I lean toward her and ask, "Want to seal it with a handshake or a kiss?"

She comes around the table and sits on my lap and kisses me.

"You know, I sure missed you last night," I tell her.

"Did you?" she says. "I really missed you too. I had no idea singles bars could be so depressing."

"Singles bars?"

"It was Jane's idea," she says. "Honest."

I shake my head. "I don't want to hear about it."

"But Jane showed me some new dance steps," she says. "And maybe this weekend—"

I give her a squeeze. "If you want to do something this weekend, baby, I'm all yours."

"Great," she says and whispers in my ear, "You know, it's Friday, so . . . why don't we start early?"

She kissed me again.

And I say, "Julie, I'd really love to, but . . ."

"But?"

"I really should check in at the plant," I say.

She stands up. "Okay, but promise me you'll hurry home tonight."

"Promise," I tell her. "Really, it's going to be a great weekend."

13

I open my eyes Saturday morning to see a drab green blur. The blur turns out to be my son, Dave, dressed in his Boy Scout uniform. He is shaking my arm.

"Davey, what are you doing here?" I ask.

He says, "Dad, it's seven o'clock!"

"Seven o'clock? I'm trying to sleep. Aren't you supposed to be watching television or something?"

"We'll be late," he says.

"*We* will be late? For what?"

"For the overnight hike!" he says. "Remember? You promised me I could volunteer you to go along and help the troopmaster."

I mutter something no Boy Scout should ever hear. But Dave isn't fazed.

"Come on. Just get in the shower," he says, as he pulls me out of bed. "I packed your gear last night. Everything's in the car already. We just have to get there by eight."

I manage a last look at Julie, her eyes still shut, and the warm soft mattress as Davey drags me through the door.

An hour and ten minutes later, my son and I arrive at the edge of some forest. Waiting for us is the troop: fifteen boys outfitted in caps, neckerchiefs, merit badges, the works.

Before I have time to say, "Where's the troopmaster?", the other few parents who happen to be lingering with the boys take off in their cars, all pedals to the metal. Looking around, I see that I am the only adult in sight.

"Our troopmaster couldn't make it," says one of the boys.

"How come?"

"He's sick," says another kid next to him.

"Yeah, his hemorrhoids are acting up," says the first. "So it looks like you're in charge now."

"What are we supposed to do, Mr. Rogo?" asks the other kid.

Well, at first I'm a little mad at having all this foisted upon me. But then the idea of having to supervise a bunch of kids doesn't daunt me—after all, I do that every day at the plant. So I gather everyone around. We look at a map and discuss the objectives for this expedition into the perilous wilderness before us.

The plan, I learn, is for the troop to hike through the forest following a blazed trail to someplace called "Devil's Gulch." There we are to bivouac for the evening. In the morning we are to break camp and make our way back to the point of departure, where Mom and Dad are supposed to be waiting for little Freddy and Johnny and friends to walk out of the woods.

First, we have to get to Devil's Gulch, which happens to be about ten miles away. So I line up the troop. They've all got their rucksacks on their backs. Map in hand, I put myself at the front of the line in order to lead the way, and off we go.

The weather is fantastic. The sun is shining through the trees. The skies are blue. It's breezy and the temperature is a little on the cool side, but once we get into the woods, it's just right for walking.

The trail is easy to follow because there are blazes (splotches of yellow paint) on the tree trunks every 10 yards or so. On either side, the undergrowth is thick. We have to hike in single file.

I suppose I'm walking at about two miles per hour, which is about how fast the average person walks. At this rate, I think to myself, we should cover ten miles in about five hours. My watch tells me it's almost 8:30 now. Allowing an hour and a half for breaks and for lunch, we should arrive at Devil's Gulch by three o'clock, no sweat.

After a few minutes, I turn and look back. The column of scouts has spread out to some degree from the close spacing we started with. Instead of a yard or so between boys, there are now larger gaps, some a little larger than others. I keep walking.

But I look back again after a few hundred yards, and the column is stretched out much farther. And a couple of big gaps have appeared. I can barely see the kid at the end of the line.

I decide it's better if I'm at the end of the line instead of at the front. That way I know I'll be able to keep an eye on the whole column, and make sure nobody gets left behind. So I wait for the first boy to catch up to me, and I ask him his name.

"I'm Ron," he says.

"Ron, I want you to lead the column," I tell him, handing over the map. "Just keep following this trail, and set a moderate pace. Okay?"

"Right, Mr. Rogo."

And he sets off at what seems to be a reasonable pace.

"Everybody stay behind Ron!" I call back to the others. "Nobody passes Ron, because he's got the map. Understand?"

Everybody nods, waves. Everybody understands.

I wait by the side of the trail as the troop passes. My son, Davey, goes by talking with a friend who walks close behind him. Now that he's with his buddies, Dave doesn't want to know me. He's too cool for that. Five or six more come along, all of them keeping up without any problems. Then there is a gap, followed by a couple more scouts. After them, another, even larger gap has occurred. I look down the trail. And I see this fat kid. He already looks a little winded. Behind him is the rest of the troop.

"What's your name?" I ask as the fat kid draws closer.

"Herbie," says the fat kid.

"You okay, Herbie?"

"Oh, sure, Mr. Rogo," says Herbie. "Boy, it's hot out, isn't it?"

Herbie continues up the trail and the others follow. Some of them look as if they'd like to go faster, but they can't get around Herbie. I fall in behind the last boy. The line stretches out in front of me, and most of the time, unless we're going over a hill or around a sharp bend in the trail, I can see everybody. The column seems to settle into a comfortable rhythm.

Not that the scenery is boring, but after a while I begin to think about other things. Like Julie, for instance. I really had wanted to spend this weekend with her. But I'd forgotten all about this hiking business with Dave. "Typical of you," I guess she'd say. I don't know how I'm ever going to get the time I need to spend with her. The only saving grace about this hike is that she ought to understand I have to be with Dave.

And then there is the conversation I had with Jonah in New York. I haven't had any time to think about that. I'm rather curious to know what a physics teacher is doing riding around in limousines with corporate heavyweights. Nor do I understand what he was trying to make out of those two items he described. I mean, "dependent events" . . . "statistical fluctuations"—so what? They're both quite mundane.

Obviously we have dependent events in manufacturing. All it means is that one operation has to be done before a second operation can be performed. Parts are made in a sequence of steps. Machine A has to finish Step One before Worker B can proceed with Step Two. All the parts have to be finished before we can assemble the product. The product has to be assembled before we can ship it. And so on.

But you find dependent events in any process, and not just those in a factory. Driving a car requires a sequence of dependent events. So does the hike we're taking now. In order to arrive at Devil's Gulch, a trail has to be walked. Up front, Ron has to walk the trail before Davey can walk it. Davey has to walk the trail before Herbie can walk it. In order for me to walk the trail, the boy in front of me has to walk it first. It's a simple case of dependent events.

And statistical fluctuations?

I look up and notice that the boy in front of me is going a little faster than I have been. He's a few feet farther ahead of me than he was a minute ago. So I take some bigger steps to catch up. Then, for a second, I'm too close to him, so I slow down.

There: if I'd been measuring my stride, I would have recorded statistical fluctuations. But, again, what's the big deal?

If I say that I'm walking at the rate of "two miles per hour," I don't mean I'm walking exactly at a constant rate of two miles per hour every instant. Sometimes I'll be going 2.5 miles per hour; sometimes maybe I'll be walking at only 1.2 miles per hour. The rate is going to fluctuate according to the length and speed of each step. But over time and distance, I should be *averaging* about two miles per hour, more or less.

The same thing happens in the plant. How long does it take to solder the wire leads on a transformer? Well, if you get out your stopwatch and time the operation over and over again, you might find that it takes, let's say, 4.3 minutes on the average. But the actual time on any given instance may range between 2.1 minutes up to 6.4 minutes. And nobody in advance can say, "This one will take 2.1 minutes . . . this one will take 5.8 minutes." Nobody can predict that information.

So what's wrong with that? Nothing as far as I can see. Anyway, we don't have any choice. What else are we going to use in place of an "average" or an "estimate"?

I find I'm almost stepping on the boy in front of me. We've slowed down somewhat. It's because we're climbing a long, fairly steep hill. All of us are backed up behind Herbie.

"Come on, Herpes!" says one of the kids.

Herpes?

"Yeah, Herpes, let's move it," says another.

"Okay, enough of that," I say to the persecutors.

Then Herbie reaches the top. He turns around. His face is red from the climb.

"Atta boy, Herbie!" I say to encourage him. "Let's keep it moving!"

Herbie disappears over the crest. The others continue the climb, and I trudge behind them until I get to the top. Pausing there, I look down the trail.

Holy cow! Where's Ron? He must be half a mile ahead of us. I can see a couple of boys in front of Herbie, and everyone else is lost in the distance. I cup my hands over my mouth.

"HEY! LET'S GO UP THERE! LET'S CLOSE RANKS!" I yell. "DOUBLE TIME! DOUBLE TIME!"

Herbie eases into a trot. The kids behind him start to run. I jog after them. Rucksacks and canteens and sleeping bags are bouncing and shaking with every step. And Herbie—I don't know what this kid is carrying, but it sounds like he's got a junkyard on his back with all the clattering and clanking he makes when he runs. After a couple hundred yards, we still haven't caught up. Herbie is slowing down. The kids are yelling at him to hurry up. I'm huffing and puffing along. Finally I can see Ron off in the distance.

"HEY RON!" I shout. "HOLD UP!"

The call is relayed up the trail by the other boys. Ron, who probably heard the call the first time, turns and looks back. Herbie, seeing relief in sight, slows to a fast walk. And so do the rest of us. As we approach, all heads are turned our way.

"Ron, I thought I told you to set a moderate pace," I say.

"But I did!" he protests.

"Well, let's just all try to stay together next time," I tell them.

"Hey, Mr. Rogo, whadd'ya say we take five?" asks Herbie.

"Okay, let's take a break," I tell them.

Herbie falls over beside the trail, his tongue hanging out. Everyone reaches for canteens. I find the most comfortable log in sight and sit down. After a few minutes, Davey comes over and sits down next to me.

"You're doing great, Dad," he says.

"Thanks. How far do you think we've come?"

"About two miles," he says.

"Is that all?" I ask. "It feels like we ought to be there by now. We must have covered more distance than two miles."

"Not according to the map Ron has," he says.

"Oh," I say. "Well, I guess we'd better get a move on."

The boys are already lining up.

"All right, let's go," I say.

We start out again. The trail is straight here, so I can see everyone. We haven't gone thirty yards before I notice it starting all over again. The line is spreading out; gaps between the boys are widening. Dammit, we're going to be running and stopping all day long if this keeps up. Half the troop is liable to get lost if we can't stay together.

I've got to put an end to this.

The first one I check is Ron. But Ron, indeed, is setting a steady, "average" pace for the troop—a pace nobody should have any trouble with. I look back down the line, and all of the boys are walking at about the same rate as Ron. And Herbie? He's not the problem anymore. Maybe he felt responsible for the last delay, because now he seems to be making a special effort to keep up. He's right on the ass of the kid in front of him.

If we're all walking at about the same pace, why is the distance between Ron, at the front of the line, and me, at the end of the line, increasing?

Statistical fluctuations?

Nah, couldn't be. The fluctuations should be averaging out. We're all moving at about the same speed, so that should mean the distance between any of us will vary somewhat, but will even out over a period of time. The distance between Ron and me should also expand and contract within a certain range, but should average about the same throughout the hike.

But it isn't. As long as each of us is maintaining a normal, moderate pace like Ron, the length of the column is increasing. The gaps between us are expanding.

Except between Herbie and the kid in front of him.

So how is he doing it? I watch him. Every time Herbie gets a step behind, he runs for an extra step. Which means he's actually expending more energy than Ron or the others at the front of the line in order to maintain the same relative speed. I'm wondering how long he'll be able to keep up his walk-run routine.

Yet . . . why can't we all just walk at the same pace as Ron and stay together?

I'm watching the line when something up ahead catches my eye. I see Davey slow down for a few seconds. He's adjusting his packstraps. In front of him, Ron continues onward, oblivious. A gap of ten . . . fifteen . . . twenty feet opens up. Which means the entire line has grown by 20 feet.

That's when I begin to understand what's happening.

Ron is setting the pace. Every time someone moves slower than Ron, the line lengthens. It wouldn't even have to be as obvious as when Dave slowed down. If one of the boys takes a step that's half an inch shorter than the one Ron took, the length of the whole line could be affected.

But what happens when someone moves faster than Ron? Aren't the longer or faster steps supposed to make up for the spreading? Don't the differences average out?

Suppose I walk faster. Can I shorten the length of the line? Well, between me and the kid ahead of me is a gap of about five feet. If he continues walking at the same rate, and if I speed up, I can reduce the gap—and maybe reduce the total length of the column, depending upon what's happening up ahead. But I can only do that until I'm bumping the kid's rucksack (and if I did that he'd sure as hell tell his mother). So I have to slow down to his rate.

Once I've closed the gap between us, I can't go any faster than the rate at which the kid in front of me is going. And he ultimately can't go any faster than the kid in front of him. And so on up the line to Ron. Which means that, except for Ron, each of our speeds depends upon the speeds of those in front of us in the line.

It's starting to make sense. Our hike is a set of dependent events . . . in combination with statistical fluctuations. Each of us is fluctuating in speed, faster and slower. But the ability to go faster than average is restricted. It depends upon all the others ahead of me in the line. So even if I could walk five miles per hour, I couldn't do it if the boy in front of me could only walk two miles per hour. And even if the kid directly in front of me could walk that fast, neither of us could do it unless all the boys in the line were moving at five miles per hour at the same time.

So I've got limits on how fast I can go—both my own (I can only go so fast for so long before I fall over and pant to death) and those of the others on the hike. However, there is no limit on my ability to slow down. Or on anyone else's ability to slow down. Or stop. And if any of us did, the line would extend indefinitely.

What's happening isn't an averaging out of the fluctuations

in our various speeds, but an *accumulation* of the fluctuations. And mostly it's an accumulation of slowness—*because dependency limits the opportunities for higher fluctuations.* And that's why the line is spreading. We can make the line shrink only by having everyone in the back of the line move much faster than Ron's average over some distance.

Looking ahead, I can see that how much distance each of us has to make up tends to be a matter of where we are in the line. Davey only has to make up for his own slower than average fluctuations relative to Ron—that twenty feet or so which is the gap in front of him. But for Herbie to keep the length of the line from growing, he would have to make up for his own fluctuations plus those of all the kids in front of him. And here I am at the end of the line. To make the total length of the line contract, I have to move faster than average for a distance equal to all the excess space between all the boys. I have to make up for the accumulation of all their slowness.

Then I start to wonder what this could mean to me on the job. In the plant, we've definitely got both dependent events and statistical fluctuations. And here on the trail we've got both of them. What if I were to say that this troop of boys is analogous to a manufacturing system . . . sort of a model. In fact, the troop does produce a product; we produce "walk trail." Ron begins production by consuming the unwalked trail before him, which is the equivalent of raw materials. So Ron processes the trail first by walking over it, then Davey has to process it next, followed by the boy behind him, and so on back to Herbie and the others and on to me.

Each of us is like an operation which has to be performed to produce a product in the plant; each of us is one of a set of dependent events. Does it matter what order we're in? Well, somebody has to be first and somebody else has to be last. So we have dependent events no matter if we switch the order of the boys.

I'm the last operation. Only after I have walked the trail is the product "sold," so to speak. And that would have to be our throughput—not the rate at which Ron walks the trail, but the rate at which I do.

What about the amount of trail between Ron and me? It has to be inventory. Ron is consuming raw materials, so the trail the rest of us are walking is inventory until it passes behind me.

And what is operational expense? It's whatever lets us turn inventory into throughput, which in our case would be the energy the boys need to walk. I can't really quantify that for the model, except that I know when I'm getting tired.

If the distance between Ron and me is expanding, it can only mean that inventory is increasing. Throughput is my rate of walking. Which is influenced by the fluctuating rates of the others. Hmmm. So as the slower than average fluctuations accumulate, they work their way back to me. Which means I have to slow down. Which means that, relative to the growth of inventory, throughput for the entire system goes down.

And operational expense? I'm not sure. For UniCo, whenever inventory goes up, carrying costs on the inventory go up as well. Carrying costs are a part of operational expense, so that measurement also must be going up. In terms of the hike, operational expense is increasing any time we hurry to catch up, because we expend more energy than we otherwise would.

Inventory is going up. Throughput is going down. And operational expense is probably increasing.

Is that what's happening in my plant?

Yes, I think it is.

Just then, I look up and see that I'm nearly running into the kid in front of me.

Ah ha! Okay! Here's proof I must have overlooked something in the analogy. The line in front of me is contracting rather than expanding. Everything must be averaging out after all. I'm going to lean to the side and see Ron walking his average two-mile-an-hour pace.

But Ron is not walking the average pace. He's standing still at the edge of the trail.

"How come we're stopping?"

He says, "Time for lunch, Mr. Rogo."

14

"But we're not supposed to be having lunch here," says one of the kids. "We're not supposed to eat until we're farther down the trail, when we reach the Rampage River."

"According to the schedule the troopmaster gave us, we're supposed to eat lunch at 12:00 noon," says Ron.

"And it is now 12:00 noon," Herbie says, pointing to his watch. "So we have to eat lunch."

"But we're supposed to be at Rampage River by now and we're not."

"Who cares?" says Ron. "This is a great spot for lunch. Look around."

Ron has a point. The trail is taking us through a park, and it so happens that we're passing through a picnic area. There are tables, a water pump, garbage cans, barbecue grills—all the necessities. (This is my kind of wilderness I'll have you know.)

"Okay," I say. "Let's just take a vote to see who wants to eat now. Anyone who's hungry, raise your hand."

Everyone raises his hand; it's unanimous. We stop for lunch.

I sit down at one of the tables and ponder a few thoughts as I eat a sandwich. What's bothering me now is that, first of all, there is no real way I could operate a manufacturing plant without having dependent events and statistical fluctuations. I can't get away from that combination. But there must be a way to overcome the effects. I mean, obviously, we'd all go out of business if inventory was always increasing, and throughput was always decreasing.

What if I had a balanced plant, the kind that Jonah was saying managers are constantly trying to achieve, a plant with every resource exactly equal in capacity to demand from the market? In fact, couldn't that be the answer to the problem? If I could get capacity perfectly balanced with demand, wouldn't my excess inventory go away? Wouldn't my shortages of certain parts disappear? And, anyway, how could Jonah be right and everybody else be wrong? Managers have always trimmed capacity to cut costs and increase profits; that's the game.

I'm beginning to think maybe this hiking model has thrown

me off. I mean, sure, it shows me the effect of statistical fluctuations and dependent events in combination. But is it a balanced system? Let's say the demand on us is to walk two miles every hour—no more, no less. Could I adjust the capacity of each kid so he would be able to walk two miles per hour and no faster? If I could, I'd simply keep everyone moving constantly at the pace he should go—by yelling, whip-cracking, money, whatever—and everything would be perfectly balanced.

The problem is how can I realistically trim the capacity of fifteen kids? Maybe I could tie each one's ankles with pieces of rope so that each would only take the same size step. But that's a little kinky. Or maybe I could clone myself fifteen times so I have a troop of Alex Rogos with exactly the same trail-walking capacity. But that isn't practical until we get some advancements in cloning technology. Or maybe I could set up some other kind of model, a more controllable one, to let me see beyond any doubt what goes on.

I'm puzzling over how to do this when I notice a kid sitting at one of the other tables, rolling a pair of dice. I guess he's practicing for his next trip to Vegas or something. I don't mind—although I'm sure he won't get any merit badges for shooting craps —but the dice give me an idea. I get up and go over to him.

"Say, mind if I borrow those for a while?" I ask.

The kid shrugs, then hands them over.

I go back to the table again and roll the dice a couple of times. Yes, indeed: statistical fluctuations. Every time I roll the dice, I get a random number that is predictable only within a certain range, specifically numbers one to six on each die. Now what I need next for the model is a set of dependent events.

After scavenging around for a minute or two, I find a box of match sticks (the strike-anywhere kind), and some bowls from the aluminum mess kit. I set the bowls in a line along the length of the table and put the matches at one end. And this gives me a model of a perfectly balanced system.

While I'm setting this up and figuring out how to operate the model, Dave wanders over with a friend of his. They stand by the table and watch me roll the die and move matches around.

"What are you doing?" asks Dave.

"Well, I'm sort of inventing a game," I say.

"A game? Really?" says his friend. "Can we play it, Mr. Rogo?"

Why not?

"Sure you can," I say.

All of a sudden Dave is interested.

"Hey, can I play too?" he asks.

"Yeah, I guess I'll let you in," I tell him. "In fact, why don't you round up a couple more of the guys to help us do this."

While they go get the others, I figure out the details. The system I've set up is intended to "process" matches. It does this by moving a quantity of match sticks out of their box, and through each of the bowls in succession. The dice determine how many matches can be moved from one bowl to the next. The dice represent the capacity of each resource, each bowl; the set of bowls are my dependent events, my stages of production. Each has exactly the same capacity as the others, but its actual yield will fluctuate somewhat.

In order to keep those fluctuations minimal, however, I decide to use only one of the dice. This allows the fluctuations to range from one to six. So from the first bowl, I can move to the next bowls in line any quantity of matches ranging from a minimum of one to a maximum of six.

Throughput in this system is the speed at which matches come out of the last bowl. Inventory consists of the total number of matches in all of the bowls at any time. And I'm going to assume that market demand is exactly equal to the average number of matches that the system can process. Production capacity of each resource and market demand are perfectly in balance. So that means I now have a model of a perfectly balanced manufacturing plant.

Five of the boys decide to play. Besides Dave, there are Andy, Ben, Chuck, and Evan. Each of them sits behind one of the bowls. I find some paper and a pencil to record what happens. Then I explain what they're supposed to do.

"The idea is to move as many matches as you can from your bowl to the bowl on your right. When it's your turn, you roll the die, and the number that comes up is the number of matches you can move. Got it?"

They all nod. "But you can only move as many matches as you've got in your bowl. So if you roll a five and you only have two matches in your bowl, then you can only move two matches. And if it comes to your turn and you don't have any matches, then naturally you can't move any."

They nod again.

"How many matches do you think we can move through the line each time we go through the cycle?" I ask them.

Perplexity descends over their faces.

"Well, if you're able to move a maximum of six and a minimum of one when it's your turn, what's the average number you ought to be moving?" I ask them.

"Three," says Andy.

"No, it won't be three," I tell them. "The mid-point between one and six isn't three."

I draw some numbers on my paper.

"Here, look," I say, and I show them this:

$$1 \quad 2 \quad 3 \quad 4 \quad 5 \quad 6$$

And I explain that 3.5 is really the average of those six numbers.

"So how many matches do you think each of you should have moved on the average after we've gone through the cycle a number of times?" I ask.

"Three and a half per turn," says Andy.

"And after ten cycles?"

"Thirty-five," says Chuck.

"And after twenty cycles?"

"Seventy," says Ben.

"Okay, let's see if we can do it," I say.

Then I hear a long sigh from the end of the table. Evan looks at me.

"Would you mind if I don't play this game, Mr. Rogo?" he asks.

"How come?"

"Cause I think it's going to be kind of boring," he says.

"Yeah," says Chuck. "Just moving matches around. Like who cares, you know?"

"I think I'd rather go tie some knots," says Evan.

"Tell you what," I say. "Just to make it more interesting, we'll have a reward. Let's say that everybody has a quota of 3.5 matches per turn. Anybody who does better than that, who averages more than 3.5 matches, doesn't have to wash any dishes tonight. But anybody who averages less than 3.5 per turn, has to do extra dishes after dinner."

"Yeah, all right!" says Evan.

"You got it!" says Dave.

They're all excited now. They're practicing rolling the die. Meanwhile, I set up a grid on a sheet of paper. What I plan to do is record the amount that each of them deviates from the average. They all start at zero. If the roll of the die is a 4, 5, or 6 then I'll record—respectively—a gain of .5, 1.5, or 2.5. And if the roll is a 1, 2, or 3 then I'll record a loss of −2.5, −1.5, or −.5 respectively. The deviations, of course, have to be cumulative; if someone is 2.5 above, for example, his starting point on the next turn is 2.5, not zero. That's the way it would happen in the plant.

"Okay, everybody ready?" I ask.

"All set."

I give the die to Andy.

He rolls a two. So he takes two matches from the box and puts them in Ben's bowl. By rolling a two, Andy is down 1.5 from his quota of 3.5 and I note the deviation on the chart.

Ben rolls next and the die comes up as a four.

"Hey, Andy," he says. "I need a couple more matches."

"No, no, no, no," I say. "The game does not work that way. You can only pass the matches that are in your bowl."

"But I've only got two," says Ben.

"Then you can only pass two."

"Oh," says Ben.

And he passes his two matches to Chuck. I record a deviation of −1.5 for him too.

Chuck rolls next. He gets a five. But, again, there are only two matches he can move.

"Hey, this isn't fair!" says Chuck.

"Sure it is," I tell him. "The name of the game is to move matches. If both Andy and Ben had rolled five's, you'd have five matches to pass. But they didn't. So you don't." Chuck gives a dirty look to Andy.

"Next time, roll a bigger number," Chuck says.

"Hey, what could I do!" says Andy.

"Don't worry," Ben says confidently. "We'll catch up."

Chuck passes his measly two matches down to Dave, and I record a deviation of −1.5 for Chuck as well. We watch as Dave rolls the die. His roll is only a one. So he passes one match down to Evan. Then Evan also rolls a one. He takes the one match out of his bowl and puts it on the end of the table. For both Dave and Evan, I write a deviation of −2.5.

"Okay, let's see if we can do better next time," I say.

Andy shakes the die in his hand for what seems like an hour. Everyone is yelling at him to roll. The die goes spinning onto the table. We all look. It's a six.

"All right!"

"Way to go, Andy!"

He takes six match sticks out of the box and hands them to Ben. I record a gain of +2.5 for him, which puts his score at 1.0 on the grid.

Ben takes the die and he too rolls a six. More cheers. He passes all six matches to Chuck. I record the same score for Ben as for Andy.

But Chuck rolls a three. So after he passes three matches to Dave, he still has three left in his bowl. And I note a loss of −0.5 on the chart.

Now Dave rolls the die; it comes up as a six. But he only has four matches to pass—the three that Chuck just passed to him and one from the last round. So he passes four to Evan. I write down a gain of +0.5 for him.

Evan gets a three on the die. So the lone match on the end of the table is joined by three more. Evan still has one left in his bowl. And I record a loss of −0.5 for Evan.

At the end of two rounds, this is what the chart looks like.

	ANDY	BEN	CHUCK	DAVE	EVAN
Turn:	1234567890	1234567890	1234567890	1234567890	1234567890
Roll - - - -	26	46	43	16	13
#Moved	26	26	23	14	13
Inventory:		00	03	10	01

Change +/−	ANDY	BEN	CHUCK	DAVE	EVAN
+2					
+1.5					
+1	*	*			
+0.5					
0					
−1					
−1.5	*	*	*		
−2			*	*	
−2.5				*	*
−3					*
−3.5					

We keep going. The die spins on the table and passes from hand to hand. Matches come out of the box and move from bowl to bowl. Andy's rolls are—what else?—very average, no steady run of high or low numbers. He is able to meet the quota and then some. At the other end of the table, it's a different story.

"Hey, let's keep those matches coming."

"Yeah, we need more down here."

"Keep rolling sixes, Andy."

"It isn't Andy, it's Chuck. Look at him, he's got five."

After four turns, I have to add more numbers—negative numbers—to the bottom of the chart. Not for Andy or for Ben or for Chuck, but for Dave and Evan. For them, it looks like there is no bottom deep enough.

After five rounds, the chart looks like this:

	ANDY	BEN	CHUCK	DAVE	EVAN
Turn:	1234567890	1234567890	1234567890	1234567890	1234567890
Roll - - - -	26425	46152	43225	16351	13641
#Moved	26452	26152	23225	14221	13321
Inventory:		00303	03252	10004	01000

```
Change +/-
 +2.5
 +2
 +1.5          * *
 +1          *               *
 +0.5
  0 - - - - - - - - * - - - - - - - * - - - - - - - - - - - - - - - - - - - -
 -0.5                     *
 -1
 -1.5        *          * *
 -2                          *          *
 -2.5                                   *          *
 -3                                                          *
 -3.5                      * *         *
 -4                                                                   *
 -4.5
 -5                        *          *
 -5.5                                                                 *
 -6
 -6.5
 -7
 -7.5                                 *
 -8                                                                   *
 -8.5
```

"How am I doing, Mr. Rogo?" Evan asks me.

"Well, Evan . . . ever hear the story of the Titanic?"

He looks depressed.

"You've got five rounds left," I tell him. "Maybe you can pull through."

"Yeah, remember the law of averages," says Chuck.

"If I have to wash dishes because you guys didn't give me enough matches . . ." says Evan, letting vague implications of threat hang in the air.

"I'm doing my job up here," says Andy.

"Yeah, what's wrong with you guys down there?" asks Ben.

"Hey, I just now got enough of them to pass," says Dave. "I've hardly had any before."

Indeed, some of the inventory which had been stuck in the first three bowls had finally moved to Dave. But now it gets stuck in Dave's bowl. The couple of higher rolls he had in the first five rounds are averaging out. Now he's getting low rolls just when he has inventory to move.

"C'mon, Dave, gimme some matches," says Evan.

Dave rolls a one.

"Aw, Dave! One match!"

"Andy, you hear what we're having for dinner tonight?" asks Ben.

"I think it's spaghetti," says Andy.

"Ah, man, that'll be a mess to clean up."

"Yeah, glad I won't have to do it," says Andy.

"You just wait," says Evan. "You just wait 'til Dave gets some good numbers for a change."

But it doesn't get any better.

"How are we doing now, Mr. Rogo?" asks Evan.

"I think there's a Brillo pad with your name on it."

"All right! No dishes tonight!" shouts Andy.

After ten rounds, this is how the chart looks . . .

I look at the chart. I still can hardly believe it. It was a balanced system. And yet throughput went down. Inventory went up. And operational expense? If there had been carrying costs on the matches, operational expense would have gone up too.

What if this had been a real plant—with real customers? How many units did we manage to ship? We expected to ship thirty-five. But what was our actual throughput? It was only twenty. About half of what we needed. And it was nowhere near

	ANDY	BEN	CHUCK	DAVE	EVAN
Turn:	1234567890	1234567890	1234567890	1234567890	1234567890
Roll - - - -	2642536452	4615254633	4322561565	1635122132	1364145342
#Moved	2642536452	2615254633	2422561565	1422122132	1332122132
Inventory:		0030313132	0325214510	1000487###	0100000000

```
Change +/-
                      ANDY        BEN       CHUCK       DAVE        EVAN
+5.5                          *
+5
+4.5                                      *
+4                         *  *           *
+3.5                        *             *
+3
+2.5
+2                               *              *
+1.5            *  *             *
+1            *    *          *
+0.5                                      *
  0 - - - - - - *- - - - - - *- - - - - - - - - - - *- - - - - - - - -
-0.5                            *
-1                                   *
-1.5        *            *  *    *
-2                            *       *      *
-2.5                                         *        *
-3                                                    *
-3.5                          *  *  *        *
-4                                                   *
-4.5
-5                            *             *
-5.5                                                      *
-6
-6.5
-7
-7.5                                        *
-8                                                   *
-8.5
-9                                         *
-9.5                                                     *
-10
-10.5                                       *
-11
-11.5                                                     *
-12
-12.5
-13                                        *
-13.5                                      *            *
-14                                                     *
-14.5                                       *
-15
-15.5                                                      *
```

\# Dave's inventory for turns 8,9, and 10 is in double digits, respectively rising to 11 matches, 14 matches, and 17 matches.

the maximum potential of each station. If this had been an actual plant, half of our orders—or more—would have been late. We'd never be able to promise specific delivery dates. And if we did, our credibility with customers would drop through the floor.

All of that sounds familiar, doesn't it?

"Hey, we can't stop now!" Evan is clamoring.

"Yea, let's keep playing," says Dave.

"Okay," says Andy. "What do you want to bet this time? I'll take you on."

"Let's play for who cooks dinner," says Ben.

"Great," says Dave.

"You're on," says Evan.

They roll the die for another twenty rounds, but I run out of paper at the bottom of the page while tracking Dave and Evan. What was I expecting? My initial chart ranged from +6 to −6. I guess I was expecting some fairly regular highs and lows, a normal sine curve. But I didn't get that. Instead, the chart looks like I'm tracing a cross-section of the Grand Canyon. Inventory moves through the system not in manageable flow, but in waves. The mound of matches in Dave's bowl passes to Evan's and onto the table finally—only to be replaced by another accumulating wave. And the system gets further and further behind schedule.

"Want to play again?" asks Andy.

"Yeah, only this time I get your seat," says Evan.

"No way!" says Andy.

Chuck is in the middle shaking his head, already resigned to defeat. Anyway, it's time to head on up the trail again.

"Some game that turned out to be," says Evan.

"Right, some game," I mumble.

15

For a while, I watch the line ahead of me. As usual, the gaps are widening. I shake my head. If I can't even deal with this in a simple hike, how am I going to deal with it in the plant?

What went wrong back there? Why didn't the balanced model work? For about an hour or so, I keep thinking about what happened. Twice I have to stop the troop to let us catch up. Sometime after the second stop, I've fairly well sorted out what happened.

There was no reserve. When the kids downstream in the balanced model got behind, they had no extra capacity to make up for the loss. And as the negative deviations accumulated, they got deeper and deeper in the hole.

Then a long-lost memory from way back in some math class in school comes to mind. It has to do with something called a covariance, the impact of one variable upon others in the same group. A mathematical principle says that in a linear dependency of two or more variables, the fluctuations of the variables down the line will fluctuate around the maximum deviation established by any preceding variables. That explains what happened in the balanced model.

Fine, but what do I do about it?

On the trail, when I see how far behind we are, I can tell everyone to hurry up. Or I can tell Ron to slow down or stop. And we close ranks. Inside a plant, when the departments get behind and work-in-process inventory starts building up, people are shifted around, they're put on overtime, managers start to crack the whip, product moves out the door, and inventories slowly go down again. Yeah, that's it: we run to catch up. (We always run, never stop; the other option, having some workers idle, is taboo.) So why can't we catch up at my plant? It feels like we're always running. We're running so hard we're out of breath.

I look up the trail. Not only are the gaps still occurring, but they're expanding faster than ever! Then I notice something weird. Nobody in the column is stuck on the heels of anybody else. Except me. I'm stuck behind Herbie.

Herbie? What's he doing back here?

I lean to the side so I can see the line better. Ron is no longer leading the troop; he's a third of the way back now. And Davey is ahead of him. I don't know who's leading. I can't see that far. Well, son of a gun. The little bastards changed their marching order on me.

"Herbie, how come you're all the way back here?" I ask.

"Oh, hi, Mr. Rogo," says Herbie as he turns around. "I just thought I'd stay back here with you. This way I won't hold anybody up."

He's walking backwards as he says this.

"Hu-huh, well, that's thoughtful of you. Watch out!"

Herbie trips on a tree root and goes flying onto his backside. I help him up.

"Are you okay?" I ask.

"Yeah, but I guess I'd better walk forwards, huh?" he says. "Kind of hard to talk that way though."

"That's okay, Herbie," I tell him as we start walking again. "You just enjoy the hike. I've got lots to think about."

And that's no lie. Because I think Herbie may have just put me onto something. My guess is that Herbie, unless he's trying very hard, as he was before lunch, is the slowest one in the troop. I mean, he seems like a good kid and everything. He's clearly very conscientious—but he's slower than all the others. (Somebody's got to be, right?) So when Herbie is walking at what I'll loosely call his "optimal" pace—a pace that's comfortable to him —he's going to be moving slower than anybody who happens to be behind him. Like me.

At the moment, Herbie isn't limiting the progress of anyone except me. In fact, all the boys have arranged themselves (deliberately or accidentally, I'm not sure which) in an order that allows every one of them to walk without restriction. As I look up the line, I can't see anybody who is being held back by anybody else. The order in which they've put themselves has placed the fastest kid at the front of the line, and the slowest at the back of the line. In effect, each of them, like Herbie, has found an optimal pace for himself. If this were my plant, it would be as if there were a never-ending supply of work—no idle time.

But look at what's happening: the length of the line is spreading farther and faster than ever before. The gaps between the boys are widening. The closer to the front of the line, the wider the gaps become and the faster they expand.

You can look at it this way, too: Herbie is advancing at his own speed, which happens to be slower than my potential speed. But because of dependency, *my* maximum speed is the rate at which Herbie is walking. My rate is throughput. Herbie's rate governs mine. So Herbie really is determining the maximum throughput.

My head feels as though it's going to take off.

Because, see, it really doesn't matter how fast any *one* of us can go, or does go. Somebody up there, whoever is leading right now, is walking faster than average, say, three miles per hour. So what! Is his speed helping the troop *as a whole* to move faster, to gain more throughput? No way. Each of the other boys down the line is walking a little bit faster than the kid directly behind him. Are any of them helping to move the troop faster? Absolutely not. Herbie is walking at his own slower speed. He is the one who is governing throughput for the troop as a whole.

In fact, whoever is moving the slowest in the troop is the one who will govern throughput. And that person may not always be Herbie. Before lunch, Herbie was walking faster. It really wasn't obvious who was the slowest in the troop. So the role of Herbie—the greatest limit on throughput—was actually floating through the troop; it depended upon who was moving the slowest at a particular time. But overall, Herbie has the least capacity for walking. His rate ultimately determines the troop's rate. Which means—

"Hey, look at this, Mr. Rogo," says Herbie.

He's pointing at a marker made of concrete next to the trail. I take a look. Well, I'll be . . . it's a milestone! A genuine, honest-to-god milestone! How many speeches have I heard where somebody talks about these damn things? And this is the first one I've ever come across. This is what it says:

miles

Hmmm. It must mean there are five miles to walk in both directions. So this must be the mid-point of the hike. Five miles to go.

What time is it?

I check my watch. Gee, it's 2:30 P.M. already. And we left at

8:30 A.M. So subtracting the hour we took for lunch, that means we've covered five miles . . . in five hours?

We aren't moving at two miles per hour. We are moving at the rate of one mile per hour. So with five hours to go . . .

It's going to be DARK by the time we get there.

And Herbie is standing here next to me delaying the throughput of the entire troop.

"Okay, let's go! Let's go!" I tell him.

"All right! All right!" says Herbie, jumping.

What am I going to do?

Rogo, (I'm telling myself in my head), you loser! You can't even manage a troop of Boy Scouts! Up front, you've got some kid who wants to set a speed record. and here you are stuck behind Fat Herbie, the slowest kid in the woods. After an hour, the kid in front—if he's really moving at three miles per hour—is going to be two miles ahead. Which means you're going to have to run two miles to catch up with him.

If this were my plant, Peach wouldn't even give me three months. I'd already be on the street by now. The demand was for us to cover ten miles in five hours, and we've only done half of that. Inventory is racing out of sight. The carrying costs on that inventory would be rising. We'd be ruining the company.

But there really isn't much I can do about Herbie. Maybe I could put him someplace else in the line, but he's not going to move any faster. So it wouldn't make any difference.

Or would it?

"HEY!" I yell forward. "TELL THE KID AT THE FRONT TO STOP WHERE HE IS!"

The boys relay the call up to the front of the column.

"EVERYBODY STAY IN LINE UNTIL WE CATCH UP!" I yell. "DON'T LOSE YOUR PLACE IN THE LINE!"

Fifteen minutes later, the troop is standing in condensed line. I find that Andy is the one who usurped the role of leader. I remind them all to stay in exactly the same place they had when we were walking.

"Okay," I say. "Everybody join hands."

They all look at each other.

"Come on! Just do it!" I tell them. "And don't let go."

Then I take Herbie by the hand and, as if I'm dragging a chain, I go up the trail, snaking past the entire line. Hand in hand, the rest of the troop follows. I pass Andy and keep walking.

And when I'm twice the distance of the line-up, I stop. What I've done is turn the entire troop around so that the boys have exactly the opposite order they had before.

"Now listen up!" I say. "This is the order you're going to stay in until we reach where we're going. Understood? Nobody passes anybody. Everybody just tries to keep up with the person in front of him. Herbie will lead."

Herbie looks shocked and amazed. "Me?"

Everyone else looks aghast too.

"You want *him* to lead?" asks Andy.

"But he's the slowest one!" says another kid.

And I say, "The idea of this hike is not to see who can get there the fastest. The idea is to get there together. We're not a bunch of individuals out here. We're a team. And the team does not arrive in camp until all of us arrive in camp."

So we start off again. And it works. No kidding. Everybody stays together behind Herbie. I've gone to the back of the line so I can keep tabs, and I keep waiting for the gaps to appear, but they don't. In the middle of the line I see someone pause to adjust his pack straps. But as soon as he starts again, we all walk just a little faster and we're caught up. Nobody's out of breath. What a difference!

Of course, it isn't long before the fast kids in the back of the line start their grumbling.

"Hey, Herpes!" yells one of them. "I'm going to sleep back here. Can't you speed it up a little?"

"He's doing the best he can," says the kid behind Herbie, "so lay off him!"

"Mr. Rogo, can't we put somebody faster up front?" asks a kid ahead of me.

"Listen, if you guys want to go faster, then you have to figure out a way to let Herbie go faster," I tell them.

It gets quiet for a few minutes.

Then one of the kids in the rear says, "Hey, Herbie, what have you got in your pack?"

"None of your business!" says Herbie.

But I say, "Okay, let's hold up for a minute."

Herbie stops and turns around. I tell him to come to the back of the line and take off his pack. As he does, I take the pack from him—and nearly drop it.

"Herbie, this thing weighs a ton," I say. "What have you got in here?"

"Nothing much," says Herbie.

I open it up and reach in. Out comes a six-pack of soda. Next are some cans of spaghetti. Then come a box of candy bars, a jar of pickles, and two cans of tuna fish. Beneath a rain coat and rubber boots and a bag of tent stakes, I pull out a large iron skillet. And off to the side is an army-surplus collapsible steel shovel.

"Herbie, why did you ever decide to bring all this along?" I ask.

He looks abashed. "We're supposed to be prepared, you know."

"Okay, let's divide this stuff up," I say.

"I can carry it!" Herbie insists.

"Herbie, look, you've done a great job of lugging this stuff so far. But we have to make you able to move faster," I say. "If we take some of the load off you, you'll be able to do a better job at the front of the line."

Herbie finally seems to understand. Andy takes the iron skillet, and a few of the others pick up a couple of the items I've pulled out of the pack. I take most of it and put it into my own pack, because I'm the biggest. Herbie goes back to the head of the line.

Again we start walking. But this time, Herbie can really move. Relieved of most of the weight in his pack, it's as if he's walking on air. We're flying now, doing twice the speed as a troop that we did before. And we still stay together. Inventory is down. Throughput is up.

Devil's Gulch is lovely in the late afternoon sun. Down in what appears to be the gulch, the Rampage River goes creaming past boulders and outcroppings of rock. Golden rays of sunlight shift through the trees. Birds are tweeting. And off in the distance is the unmistakable melody of high-speed automobile traffic.

"Look!" shouts Andy as he stands atop the promontory, "There's a shopping center out there!"

"Does it have a Burger King?" asks Herbie.

Dave complains, "Hey, this isn't The Wilderness."

"They just don't make wildernesses the way they used to," I

tell him. "Look, we'll have to settle for what we've got. Let's make camp."

The time is now five o'clock. This means that after relieving Herbie of his pack, we covered about four miles in two hours. Herbie was the key to controlling the entire troop.

Tents are erected. A spaghetti dinner is prepared by Dave and Evan. Feeling somewhat guilty because I set up the rules that drove them into their servitude, I give them a hand with cleaning up afterwards.

Dave and I share the same tent that night. We're lying inside it, both of us tired. Dave is quiet for a while. Then he speaks up.

He says, "You know, Dad, I was really proud of you today."

"You were? How come?"

"The way you figured out what was going on and kept everyone together, and put Herbie in front—we'd probably have been on that trail forever if it hadn't been for you," he says. "None of the other guys' parents took any responsibility for anything. But you did."

"Thanks," I tell him. "Actually, I learned a lot of things today."

"You did?"

"Yeah, stuff that I think is going to help me straighten out the plant," I say.

"Really? Like what?"

"Are you sure you want to hear about it?"

"Sure I am," he claims.

We're awake for some time talking about everything. He hangs in there, even asks some questions. By the time we're finished, all we can hear is some snoring from the other tents, a few crickets . . . and the squealing tires of some idiot turning donuts out there on the highway.

16

Davey and I get home around 4:30 on Sunday afternoon. Both of us are tired, but we're feeling pretty good in spite of the miles. After I pull into the driveway, Dave hops out to open the garage door. I ease the Mazda in and go around to open the trunk so we can get our packs.

"I wonder where Mom went," says Dave.

I look over and notice that her car is gone.

"She's probably out shopping or something," I tell Dave.

Inside, Dave stows the camping gear while I go into the bedroom to change clothes. A hot shower is going to feel absolutely terrific. After I wash off the great outdoors, I'm thinking, maybe I'll take everybody out to dinner, get us a good meal as kind of a celebration of the triumphant return of father and son.

A closet door is open in the bedroom. When I reach to shut it, I see that most of Julie's clothes are gone. I stand there for a minute looking at the empty space. Dave comes up behind me.

"Dad?"

I turn.

"This was on the kitchen table. I guess Mom left it."

He hands me a sealed envelope.

"Thanks Dave."

I wait until he's gone to open it. Inside is just a short handwritten note. It says:

Al,

I can't handle always being last in line for you. I need more of you and it's clear now that you won't change. I'm going away for a while. Need to think things over. Sorry to do this to you. I know you're busy.

Yours truly,
Julie

P.S. —I left Sharon with your mother.

When I'm able to move, I put the note in my pocket and go find Davey. I tell him I have to go across town to pick up Sharon, and that he's to stay here. If his mother calls, he's to ask her where she's calling from and get a number where I can call her back. He wants to know if something is wrong. I tell him not to worry and promise to explain when I get back.

I go rocketing to my mother's house. When she opens the door, she starts talking about Julie before I can even say hello.

"Alex, do you know your wife did the strangest thing," she says. "I was making lunch yesterday when the doorbell rang, and when I opened the door Sharon was standing here on the step with her little suitcase. And your wife was in the car at the curb there, but she wouldn't get out and when I went down to talk to her, she drove away."

By now I'm in the door. Sharon runs to greet me from the living room where she is watching television. I pick her up and she gives me a long hug. My mother is still talking.

"What on earth could be wrong with her?" my mother asks me.

"We'll talk about it later," I tell her.

"I just don't understand what—"

"*Later,* okay?"

Then I look at Sharon. Her face is rigid. Her eyes are frozen big. She's terrified.

"So . . . did you have a nice visit with Grandma?" I ask her.

She nods but doesn't say anything.

"What do you say we go home now?"

She looks down at the floor.

"Don't you want to go home?" I ask.

She shrugs her shoulders.

"Do you like it here with Grandma?" my smiling mother asks her.

Sharon starts to cry.

I get Sharon and her suitcase into the car. We start home. After I've driven a couple of blocks, I look over at her. She's like a little statue sitting there staring straight ahead with her red eyes focused on the top of the dashboard. At the next stoplight, I reach over for her and pull her next to me.

She's very quiet for a while, but then she finally looks up at me and whispers, "Is Mommy still mad at me?"

"Mad at you? She isn't mad at you," I tell her.

"Yes she is. She wouldn't talk to me."

"No, no, no, Sharon," I say. "Your mother isn't upset with you. You didn't do anything wrong."

"Then why?" she asks.

I say, "Why don't we wait until we get home. I'll explain it to both you and your brother then."

I think that explaining the situation to both of the kids at the same time turns out to be easier on me than on them. I've always been reasonably adept at maintaining the outward illusion of control in the midst of chaos. I tell them Julie has simply gone away for a little while, maybe only a day or so. She'll be back. She just has to get over a few things that are upsetting and confusing her. I give them all the standard reassurances: your mom still loves you; I still love you; there was nothing that either of you could have done; everything will work out for the best. For the most part, both of them sit there like little rocks. Maybe they're reflecting back what I'm giving them.

We go out and get a pizza for dinner. That normally would be kind of a fun thing. Tonight, it's very quiet. Nobody has anything to say. We mechanically chew and then leave.

When we get back, I make both of the kids do homework for school. I don't know if they do it or not. I go to the phone, and after a long debate with myself, I try to make a couple of calls.

Julie doesn't have any friends in Bearington. None that I know of. So it would be useless to try to call the neighbors. They wouldn't know anything, and the story about us having problems would spread instantly.

Instead, I try calling Jane, the friend from the last place we lived, the one whom Julie claimed to have spent the night with last Thursday. There is no answer at Jane's.

So then I try Julie's parents. I get her father on the phone. After some small talk about the weather and the kids, it's clear he isn't going to make any declarations. I conclude that her parents don't know what's going on. But before I can think of a casual way to end the call and avoid the explanations, her old man asks me, "So is Julie going to talk to us?"

"Ah, well, that's actually why I was calling," I say.

"Oh? Nothing is wrong I hope," he says.

"I'm afraid there is," I say. "She left yesterday while I was on a camping trip with Dave. I was wondering if you had heard from her."

Immediately he's spreading the alarm to Julie's mother. She gets on the phone.

"Why did she leave?" she asks.

"I don't know."

"Well, I know the daughter we raised, and she wouldn't just leave without a very good reason," says Julie's mother.

"She just left me a note saying she had to get away for awhile."

"What did you do to her?" yells her mother.

"Nothing!" I plead, feeling like a liar in the onslaught.

Then her father gets back on the phone and asks if I've talked to the police. He suggests that maybe she was kidnapped. I tell him that's highly unlikely, because my mother saw her drive away and nobody had a gun to her head.

Finally I say, "If you hear from her, would you please have her give me a call? I'm very worried about her."

An hour later, I do call the police. But, as I expected, they won't help unless I have some evidence that something criminal has taken place. I go and put the kids to bed.

Sometime after midnight, I'm staring at the dark bedroom ceiling and I hear a car turning into the driveway. I leap out of bed and run to the window. By the time I get there, the head-lights are arcing back toward the street. It's just a stranger turning around. The car drives away.

17

Monday morning is a disaster.

It starts with Davey trying to make breakfast for himself and Sharon and me. Which is a nice, responsible thing to do, but he totally screws it up. While I'm in the shower, he attempts pancakes. I'm midway through shaving when I hear the fight from the kitchen. I rush down to find Dave and Sharon pushing each other. There is a skillet on the floor with lumps of batter, black on one side and raw on the other, splattered.

"Hey! What's going on?" I shout.

"It's all her fault!" yells Dave pointing at his sister.

"You were burning them!" Sharon says.

"I was not!"

Smoke is fuming off the stove where something spilled. I step over to shut it off.

Sharon appeals to me. "I was just trying to help. But he wouldn't let me." Then she turns to Dave. "Even *I* know how to make pancakes."

"Okay, because both of you want to help, you can help clean up," I say.

When everything is back in some semblance of order, I feed them cold cereal. We eat another meal in silence.

With all the disruption and delay. Sharon misses her school bus. I get Davey out the door, and go looking for her so I can drive her to school. She's lying down on her bed.

"Ready, whenever you are, Miz Rogo."

"I can't go to school," she says.

"Why not?"

"I'm sick."

"Sharon, you have to go to school," I say.

"But I'm sick!" she says.

I go sit down on the edge of the bed.

"I know you're upset. I am too," I tell her. "But these are facts: I have to go to work. I can't stay home with you, and I won't leave you here by yourself. You can go to your grandmother's house for the day. Or you can go to school."

She sits up. I put my arm around her.

After a minute, she says, "I guess I'll go to school."

I give her a squeeze and say, "Atta way, kid. I knew you'd do the right thing."

By the time I get both kids to school and myself to work, it's past nine o'clock. As I walk in, Fran waves a message slip at me. I grab it and read it. It's from Hilton Smyth, marked "urgent" and double underlined.

I call him.

"Well, it's about time," says Hilton. "I tried to reach you an hour ago."

I roll my eyes. "What's the problem, Hilton?"

"Your people are sitting on a hundred sub-assemblies I need," says Smyth.

"Hilton, we're not sitting on anything," I say.

He raises his voice. "Then why aren't they here? I've got a customer order we can't ship because your people dropped the ball!"

"Just give me the particulars, and I'll have somebody look into it," I tell him.

He gives some reference numbers and I write them down.

"Okay, I'll have somebody get back to you."

"You'd better do more than that, pal," says Hilton. "You'd better make sure we get those sub-assemblies by the end of the day—and I mean all 100 pieces, not 87, not 99, but *all* of them. Because I'm not going to have my people do two setups for final assembly on account of your lateness."

"Look, we'll do our best," I tell him, "but I'm not going to make promises."

"Oh? Well, let's just put it this way," he says. "If we don't get 100 sub-assemblies from you today, I'm talking to Peach. And from what I hear you're in enough trouble with him already."

"Listen, *pal,* my status with Bill Peach is none of your damn business," I tell him. "What makes you think you can threaten me?"

The pause is so long I think he's going to hang up on me.

Then he says, "Maybe you ought to read your mail."

"What do you mean by that?"

I can hear him smiling.

"Just get me the sub-assemblies by the end of the day," he says sweetly. "Bye-bye."

I hang up.

"Weird," I mumble.

I talk to Fran. She calls Bob Donovan for me and then notifies the staff that there will be a meeting at ten o'clock. Donovan comes in and I ask him to have an expeditor see what's holding up the job for Smyth's plant. Almost gritting my teeth as I say it, I tell him to make sure the sub-assemblies go out today. After he's gone, I try to forget about the call, but I can't. Finally, I go ask Fran if anything has come in recently that mentions Hilton Smyth. She thinks for a minute, then reaches for a folder.

"This memo just came in on Friday," she says. "It looks like Mr. Smyth got a promotion."

I take the memo she hands me. It's from Bill Peach. It's an announcement that he's named Smyth to the newly-created position of division productivity manager. The appointment is effective at the end of this week. The job description says that all plant managers will now report on a dotted line to Smyth, who will "give special attention to manufacturing-productivity improvement with emphasis on cost reduction."

And I start to sing, "Oh, what a beautiful morning. . . !"

Whatever enthusiasm I expected from the staff with regard to my education over the weekend . . . well, I don't get it. Maybe I thought all I had to do was walk in and open my mouth to reveal my discoveries, and they'd all be instantly converted by the obvious rightness. But it doesn't work that way. We—Lou, Bob, Stacey, and Ralph Nakamura, who runs data processing for the plant—are in the conference room. I'm standing in front next to an easel which holds a big pad of paper, sheet after sheet of which is covered with little diagrams I've drawn during my explanations. I've invested a couple of hours in making those explanations. But now it's almost time for lunch, and they're all just sitting there unimpressed.

Looking down the table at the faces looking back at me, I can see they don't know what to make of what I've told them. Okay, I think I see a faint glimmer of understanding in Stacey's eyes. Bob Donovan is on the fence; he seems to have intuitively grasped some of it. Ralph is not sure what it is I'm really saying. And Lou is frowning at me. One sympathizer, one undecided, one bewildered, and one skeptic.

"Okay, what's the problem?" I ask.

They glance at each other.

"Come on," I say. "This is like I just proved two and two equals four and you don't believe me." I look straight at Lou. "What's the problem you're having?"

Lou sits back and shakes his head. "I don't know, Al. It's just that . . . well, you said how you figured this out by watching a bunch of kids on a hike in the woods."

"So what's wrong with that?"

"Nothing. But how do you know these things are really going on out there in the plant?"

I flip back a few sheets on the easel until I find the one with the names of Jonah's two phenomena written on it.

"Look at this: do we have statistical fluctuations in our operations?" I ask, pointing to the words.

"Yes, we do," he says.

"And do we have dependent events in our plant?" I ask.

"Yes," he says again.

"Then what I've told you has to be right," I say.

"Now hold on a minute," says Bob. "Robots don't have statistical fluctuations. They always work at the same pace. That's one of the reasons we bought the damn things—consistency. And I thought the main reason you went to see this Jonah guy was to find out what to do about the robots."

"It's okay to say that fluctuations in cycle time for a robot would be almost flat while it was working," I tell him. "But we're not dealing just with a robotic operation. Our other operations do have both phenomena. And, remember, the goal isn't to make the robots productive; it's to make the whole system productive. Isn't that right, Lou?"

"Well, Bob may have a point. We've got a lot of automated equipment out there, and the process times ought to be fairly consistent," says Lou.

Stacey turns to him. "But what he's saying—"

Just then the conference room door opens. Fred, one of our expeditors, puts his head into the room and looks at Bob Donovan.

"May I see you for a second?" he asks Bob. "It's about the job for Hilton Smyth."

Bob stands up to leave the room, but I tell Fred to come in. Like it or not, I have to be interested in what's happening on this "crisis" for Hilton Smyth. Fred explains that the job has to go through two more departments before the sub-assemblies are complete and ready for shipment.

"Can we get them out today?" I ask.

"It's going to be close, but we can try," says Fred. "The truck shuttle leaves at five o'clock."

The shuttle is a private trucking service that all the plants in the division use to move parts back and forth.

"Five o'clock is the last run of the day that we can use to reach Smyth's plant," says Bob. "If we don't make that trip, the next shuttle won't be until tomorrow afternoon."

"What has to be done?" I ask.

"Peter Schnell's department has to do some fabricating. Then the pieces have to be welded," says Fred. "We're going to set up one of the robots to do the welds."

"Ah, yes, the robots," I say. "You think we can do it?"

"According to the quotas, Pete's people are supposed to give us the parts for twenty-five units every hour," says Fred. "And I know the robot is capable of welding twenty-five units of this sub-assembly per hour."

Bob asks about moving the pieces to the robot. In a normal situation, the pieces finished by Pete's people probably would be moved to the robot only once a day, or maybe not until the entire batch was finished. We can't wait that long. The robot has to begin its work as soon as possible.

"I'll make arrangements to have a materials handler stop at Pete's department every hour on the hour," says Fred.

"Okay," says Bob. "How soon can Pete start?"

Fred says, "Pete can start on the job at noon, so we've got five hours."

"You know that Pete's people quit at four," says Bob.

"Yeah, I told you it's going to be close," says Fred. "But all we can do is try. That's what you want, isn't it?"

This gives me an idea. I talk to the staff. "You people don't really know what to make of what I told you this morning. But if what I've told you is correct, then we should be able to see the effects occurring out there on the floor. Am I right?"

The heads nod.

"And if we know that Jonah is correct, we'd be pretty stupid to continue running the plant the same way as before—right? So I'm going to let you see for yourselves what's happening. You say Pete's going to start on this at noon?"

"Right," says Fred. "Everyone in that department is at lunch now. They went at eleven-thirty. So they'll start at twelve. And the robot will be set up by one o'clock, when the materials handler will make the first transfer."

I take some paper and a pencil and start sketching a simple schedule.

"The output has to be one hundred pieces by five o'clock— no less than that. Hilton says he won't accept a partial shipment. So if we can't do the whole job, then I don't want us to ship anything," I say. "Now Pete's people are supposed to produce at the rate of twenty-five pieces per hour. But that doesn't mean they'll always have twenty-five at the end of every hour. Sometimes they'll be a few pieces short, sometimes they'll be a few ahead."

I look around; everyone is with me.

"So we've got statistical fluctuations going on," I say. "But we're planning that from noon until four o'clock, Pete's department should have averaged an output of one hundred pieces. The robot, on the other hand, is supposed to be more precise in its output. It will be set up to work at the rate of twenty-five pieces per hour—no more, no less. We also have dependent events, because the robot cannot begin its welding until the materials handler has delivered the pieces from Pete's department."

"The robot can't start until one o'clock," I say, "but by five o'clock when the truck is ready to leave, we want to be loading the last piece into the back. So, expressed in a diagram, this is what is supposed to happen . . ."

I show them the finished schedule, which looks like this:

Demand = 100 pcs.   Quota = 25 pcs. per hour
_____

```
           12 noon 1        2        3        4        5 p.m.
                   [25]
Pete's     --25-- |        [50]
People            | --25-- |        [75]
                           | --25-- |        [100]
                                    | --25-- |

                            [25]
Robot               --25-- |        [50]
                           | --25-- |        [75]
                                    | --25-- |        [100]
                                             | --25-- |
```

"Okay, I want Pete to keep a log of exactly how many parts are actually completed by his department hour by hour," I say. "And I want Fred to keep the same type of log for the robot. And remember: no cheating. We need the real numbers. Okay?"

"Sure, no problem," says Fred.

"By the way, do you actually think we'll be able to ship one hundred pieces today?" I ask.

"I guess it's up to Pete," says Bob. "If he says he can do it, I don't see why not."

"Tell you what," I say to Bob. "I'll bet you ten bucks we don't ship today."

"You serious?" asks Bob.

"Sure I am."

"Okay, you're on," says Bob. "Ten bucks."

While everyone else is at lunch, I call Hilton Smyth. Hilton is at lunch as well, but I leave a message for him. I tell his secretary the sub-assemblies will definitely arrive at his plant tomorrow, but that's the best we can do—unless Hilton wants to pay for a special shipment tonight. (Knowing his concern for holding down costs, I'm sure Hilton won't want to shell out anything extra.)

After that call, I sit back and try to think about my marriage and what to do. Obviously, there has been no news from Julie. I'm mad as hell that she took off—I'm also very worried about her. But what can I do? I can't cruise the streets looking for her. She could be anywhere; I just have to be patient. Eventually I should hear from her. Or her lawyer. Meanwhile, there are two kids who have to be taken care of. Well, for all practical purposes, we'd better make that three kids.

Fran comes into my office with another message slip. She says, "One of the other secretaries just gave me this as I got back from lunch. While you were on the phone, you got a call from David Rogo. Is that your son?"

"Yes, what's the problem?"

"It says, he's worried he won't be able to get into the house after school," she says. "Is your wife gone?"

"Yeah, she's out of town for a few days," I tell her. "Fran, you've got a couple of kids. How do you manage to hold a job and take care of them?"

She laughs. "Well, 'tain't easy. On the other hand, I don't work the long hours you do. If I were you, I'd get some help until she gets back."

When she leaves, I pick up the phone again.

"Hello, Mom? It's Alex."

"Have you heard from Julie yet?" she asks.

"No, I haven't," I say. "Listen, Mom, would you mind staying with me and the kids until Julie gets back?"

At two o'clock I slip out to pick up my mother and take her to the house before the kids get home from school. When I arrive at her house, she's at the door with two suitcases and four cardboard boxes filled with half of her kitchen.

"Mom, we've already got pots and pans at my house," I tell her.

"They're just not the same as mine," she says.

So we load the trunk. I take her and her pots and pans over to the house and unload. She waits for the kids to come home from school, and I race back to the plant.

Around four o'clock, at the end of first shift, I go down to Bob Donovan's office to find out what the story is on Smyth's shipment. He's waiting for me.

"Well, well, well. Good afternoon!" says Bob as I open the door and walk in. "How nice of you to drop by!"

"What are you so happy about?" I ask him.

"I'm always happy when people who owe me money drop by," says Bob.

"Oh, is that right?" I ask him. "What makes you think anybody owes you money?"

Bob holds out his hand and wiggles his fingers. "Come on! Don't tell me you forgot about the bet we made! Ten bucks, remember? I just talked to Pete and his people are indeed going to finish the hundred units of parts. So the robot should have no problem finishing that shipment for Smyth's plant."

"Yeah? Well, if that's true I won't mind losing," I tell him.

"So you concede defeat?"

"No way. Not until those sub-assemblies get on the five o'clock truck," I tell him.

"Suit yourself," says Bob.

"Let's go see what's really going on out there," I say.

We take a walk out on the floor to Pete's office. Before we get there, we pass the robot, who's brightening the area with its weld flashes. Coming the other way are two guys. Just as they pass the welding area, they stop and give a little cheer.

"We beat the robot! We beat the robot!" they say.

"Must be from Pete's department," says Bob.

We smile as we pass them. They didn't really beat anything, of course, but what the hell. They look happy. Bob and I continue on to Pete's office, which is a little steel-sided shack among the machines.

"Hello there," says Pete as we walk in. "We got that rush job done for you today."

"Good, Pete. But do you have that log sheet you were supposed to keep," I ask him.

"Yes, I do," says Pete. "Now where did I put it?"

He sorts through the papers on his desk, talking as he hunts for it.

"You should have seen my people this afternoon. I mean, they really moved. I went around and told them how important this shipment is, and they really put themselves into it. You know how things usually slow down a little at the end of a shift. But today they hustled. They were proud when they walked out of here today."

"Yeah, we noticed," says Bob.

He puts the log sheet down on top of a table in front of us.

"There you are," he says.

We read it.

Demand = 100 pcs.   Quota = 25 pcs. per hour

	12 noon	1	2	3	4	5 p.m.
		19 [−6]				
Pete's	--19--	|	40 [−10]			
People		| --21-	|	68 [−7]		
		-				
			| --28--	|	100 [0]	
				| --32-	|	
				-		

Output = 100 pcs.

"Okay, so you only got nineteen pieces done in the first hour," I say.

"Well, it took us a little longer to get organized, and one guy was late coming back from lunch," says Pete. "But at one o'clock we had a materials handler take the nineteen over to the robot so it could get started."

"Then from one to two, you still missed the quota by four pieces," says Bob.

"Yeah, but so what?" says Pete. "Look what happened from two o'clock to three: we beat the quota by three pieces. Then when I saw we were still behind, I went around and told everyone how important it was for us to get those hundred pieces done by the end of the shift."

"So everyone went a little faster," I say.

"That's right," says Pete. "And we made up for the slow start."

"Yeah, thirty-two pieces in the last hour," says Bob. "So what do you say, Al?"

"Let's go see what's happening with the robot," I say.

At five minutes past five o'clock, the robot is still turning out welded sub-assemblies. Donovan is pacing. Fred walks up.

"Is that truck going to wait?" asks Bob.

"I asked the driver, and he says he can't. He's got other stops to make and if he waits for us, he'll be late all night," says Fred.

Bob turns to the machine. "Well, what the heck is wrong with this stupid robot? It's got all the parts it needs."

I tap him on the shoulder.

"Here," I say. "Look at this."

I show him the sheet of paper on which Fred has been recording the output of the robot. From my shirt pocket, I take out Pete's log and fold the bottom of it so we can put the two pieces of paper together.

Combined, the two of them look like this:

I tell him, "You see, the first hour Pete's people did nineteen pieces. The robot was capable of doing twenty-five, but Pete delivered less than that, so nineteen became the robot's true capacity for that hour."

"Same with the second hour," says Fred. "Pete delivered twenty-one, the robot could only do twenty-one."

Demand = 100 pcs.   Quota = 25 pcs. per hour

	12 noon	1	2	3	4	5 p.m.
		19 [−6]				
Pete's	--19--	|	40[−10]			
People		| --21-	|	68 [−7]		
		-				
			| --28--	|	100 [0]	
				| --32--	|	
			19 [−6]			
Robot	--19--	|	40 [−10]		
			| --21--	|	65 [−10]	
				| --25--	|	90 [−10]
					| --25--	|

Output = 90 pcs.

"Every time Pete's area got behind, it was passed on to the robot," I say. "But when Pete delivered 28 pieces, the robot could still only do twenty-five. That meant that when the final delivery of thirty-two pieces arrived at four o'clock, the robot still had three pieces to work on from the last batch. So it couldn't start on the final batch right away."

"Okay, I see now," says Bob.

Fred says, "You know, the most Pete was ever behind was ten pieces. Kind of funny how that's exactly the number of pieces we ended up short."

"That's the effect of the mathematical principle I was trying to explain this morning," I say. "The maximum deviation of a preceding operation will become the starting point of a subsequent operation."

Bob reaches for his wallet.

"Well, I guess I owe *you* ten bucks," he says to me.

"Tell you what," I say. "Instead of paying me, why don't you give the money to Pete so he can spring for a round of coffee or something for the people in his department—just a little way to say thanks for the extra effort this afternoon."

"Yeah, right, that's a good idea," says Bob. "Listen, sorry we couldn't ship today. Hope it doesn't get us in trouble."

"We can't worry about it now," I tell him. "The gain we made today is that we learned something. But I'll tell you one thing: we've got to take a close look at our incentives here."

"How come?" asks Bob.

"Don't you see? It didn't matter that Pete got his hundred pieces done, because we still couldn't ship," I say. "But Pete and his people thought they were heroes. Ordinarily, *we* might have thought the same thing. That isn't right."

18

When I get home that evening, both of the kids greet me at the door. My mother is in the background, with steam pouring out of the kitchen. I presume it has something to do with dinner and that she has everything under control. In front of me, Sharon's face is beaming up at me.

"Guess what!" she says.

"I give up," I say.

"Mommy called on the phone," Sharon says.

"She did!" I say.

I glance up at my mother. She shakes her head.

"Davey answered the phone," she says. "I didn't talk to her."

I look down at Sharon. "So what did Mommy say?"

"She said she loved Davey and me," says Sharon.

"And she said she would be away for a while," adds Davey. "But that we shouldn't worry about her."

"Did she say when she would be coming back?" I ask.

"I asked her that," says Davey. "But she said she couldn't say right now."

"Did you get a phone number so I can call her back?" I ask him.

He looks down at the floor.

"David! You were supposed to ask her for the number if she called!"

He mumbles, "I did, but . . . she didn't want to give it to me."

"Oh," I say.

"Sorry, Dad."

"It's okay, Dave. Thanks for trying."

"Why don't we all sit down to dinner," my mother says cheerily.

This time the meal is not silent. My mother talks, and she does her best to cheer us up. She tells us stories about the Depression and how lucky we are to have food to eat.

Tuesday morning is a little bit more normal. Joining efforts, my mother and I manage to get the kids to school and me to work on time. By 8:30, Bob, Stacey, Lou, and Ralph are in my office, and we're talking about what happened yesterday. Today, I find them much more attentive. Maybe it's because they've seen the proof of the idea take place on their own turf, so to speak.

"This combination of dependency and fluctuations is what we're up against every day," I tell them. "I think it explains why we have so many late orders."

Lou and Ralph are examining the two charts we made yesterday. "What would have happened if the second operation hadn't been a robot, if it had been some kind of job with people?" asks Lou.

"We would have had another set of statistical fluctuations to complicate things," I say. "Don't forget we only had two operations here. You can imagine what happens when we've got dependency running through ten or fifteen operations, each with its own set of fluctuations, just to make one part. And some of our products involve hundreds of parts."

Stacey is troubled. She asks, "Then how can we ever control what's going on out there?"

I say, "That's the billion-dollar question: how can we control the fifty-thousand or—who knows?—maybe it's fifty-million variables which exist in this plant?"

"We'd have to buy a new super computer just to keep track of all of them," says Ralph.

I say, "A new computer wouldn't save us. Data management alone isn't going to give us more control."

"What about longer lead times?" asks Bob.

"Oh, you really think longer lead time would have guaranteed our ability to ship that order to Hilton Smyth's plant?" I ask him. "How long had we already known about that order before yesterday, Bob?"

Bob wiggles back and forth. "Hey, all I'm saying is that we'd have some slop in there to make up for the delays."

Then Stacey says, "Longer lead times increase inventory, Bob. And that isn't the goal."

"Okay, I know that," Bob is saying. "I'm not fighting you. The only reason I mention the lead times is I want to know what we do about all this."

Everybody turns to me.

I say, "This much is clear to me. We have to change the way we think about production capacity. We cannot measure the capacity of a resource in isolation. Its true productive capacity depends upon where it is in the plant. And trying to level capacity with demand to minimize expenses has really screwed us up. We shouldn't be trying to do that at all."

"But that's what everybody else does," says Bob.

"Yes, everybody does. Or claims to. As we now can see, it's a stupid thing to try," I say.

"So how do other manufacturers survive?" asks Lou.

I tell him I was wondering that myself. What I suspect is that as a plant comes close to being balanced through the efforts of engineers and managers doing the wrong things, events head toward a crisis and the plant is very quickly *un* balanced by shifting workers or by overtime or by calling back some people from layoff. The survival incentive overrides false beliefs.

"Okay, but again, what are we going to do?" asks Bob. "We can't hire without division approval. And we've even got a policy against overtime."

"Maybe it's time to call Jonah again," says Stacey.

And I say, "I think maybe you're right."

It takes Fran half an hour to locate the area of the world where Jonah happens to be today, and another hour passes before Jonah can get to the phone to talk to us. As soon as he's on the line, I have another secretary round up the staff again and corral them in my office so we can hear him on a speaker phone. While they're coming in, I tell Jonah about the hike with Herbie where I discovered the meaning of what he was telling me, and what we've learned about the effects of the two phenomena in the plant.

"What we know now," I tell him, "is that we shouldn't be looking at each local area and trying to trim it. We should be trying to optimize the whole system. Some resources have to have more capacity than others. The ones at the end of the line should have more than the ones at the beginning—sometimes a lot more. Am I right?"

"You're on the money," says Jonah.

"Good. Glad to hear we're getting somewhere," I say. "Only the reason I called is, we need to know where to go from here."

He says, "What you have to do next, Alex, is distinguish between two types of resources in your plant. One type is what I call a bottleneck resource. The other is, very simply, a non-bottleneck resource."

I whisper to everybody to start taking some notes on this.

"A bottleneck," Jonah continues, "is any resource whose capacity is equal to or *less than* the demand placed upon it. And a non-bottleneck is any resource whose capacity is greater than the demand placed on it. Got that?"

"Right," I tell him.

"Once you have recognized these two types of resources," says Jonah, "you will begin to see vast implications."

"But, Jonah, where does market demand come in?" Stacey asks. "There has to be some relationship between demand and capacity."

He says, "Yes, but as you already know, you should not balance *capacity* with demand. What you need to do instead is balance the *flow of product* through the plant with demand from the market. This, in fact, is the first of nine rules that express the relationships between bottlenecks and non-bottlenecks and how you should manage your plant. So let me repeat it for you: Balance flow, not capacity."

Stacey is still puzzled. She says, "I'm not sure I understand. Where do the bottlenecks and non-bottlenecks come into the picture?"

Jonah says, "Let me ask you: which of the two types of resources determines the effective capacity of the plant?"

"It would have to be the bottleneck," she says.

I say, "That's right. It's like the kid on that hike last weekend —Herbie. He had the least capacity and he was the one who actually determined how fast the troop as a whole could move."

"So where should you balance the floor?" asks Jonah.

"Oh, I see," says Stacey. "The idea is to make the flow through the bottleneck equal to demand from the market."

"Basically, yes, you've got it," says Jonah. "Actually, the flow should be a tiny bit less than the demand."

"How come?" asks Lou.

"Because if you keep it equal to demand and the market demand goes down, you'll lose money," says Jonah. "But that's a fine point. Speaking fundamentally, the bottleneck flow should be on a par with demand."

Bob Donovan is now making various noises, trying to get into the conversation.

"Excuse me, but I thought bottlenecks were bad," says Bob. "They ought to be eliminated where possible, right?"

"No, bottlenecks are not necessarily bad—or good," says Jonah, "they are simply a reality. What I am suggesting is that where they exist, you must then use them to control the flow through the system and into the market."

That makes sense to me as I'm listening, because I'm remembering how I used Herbie to control the troop during the hike.

"Now I have to run," says Jonah, "because you caught me during a ten-minute break in a presentation."

I jump in. "Jonah, before you go—!"

"Yes?"

"What's our next step?"

He says, "Well, first of all, does your plant have any bottlenecks?"

"We don't know," I tell him.

"Then that's your next step," he says. "You have to find this out, because it makes an enormous difference in how you manage your resources."

"How do we find the bottlenecks?" says Stacey.

"It's very simple, but it would take a few minutes to explain. Look, try to figure that out for yourselves," says Jonah. "It's really easy to do if you think about it first."

I say, "Okay, but. . . ."

"Good-bye for now," he says. "Call me when you know if you have a bottleneck."

The speaker phone issues a click, followed by a fuzzy hum.

"Well . . . what now?" asks Lou.

"I guess we look at all our resources," I say, "and compare them against market demand. If we find one in which demand is greater than capacity, then we'll know we've got a bottleneck."

"What happens if we find one?" asks Stacey.

"I guess the best thing to do would be what I did to the scout troop," I say. "We adjust capacity so the bottleneck is at the front of production."

"My question," Lou says, "is what happens if our resource with the least capacity in fact has a capacity greater than what market demand calls for?"

"Then I guess we'd have something like a bottle without a neck," I say.

"But there would still be limits," says Stacey. "The bottle would still have walls. But they'd be greater than the market demand."

"And if that's the case?" asks Lou.

"I don't know," I tell him. "I guess the first thing to do is find out if we've got a bottleneck."

"So we go look for Herbie," says Ralph. "If he's out there."

"Yeah, quick, before we talk ourselves to death," says Bob.

I walk into the conference room a few days later and there's paper everywhere. The main table is covered with computer print-outs and binders. Over in the corner, a data terminal has been installed; next to it, a printer is churning out even more paper. The wastebaskets are full. So are all the ashtrays. The litter of white styrofoam coffee cups, empty sugar packets and creamer containers, napkins, candy bar and cracker wrappers, and so on is scattered about. What has happened is the place has been turned into our headquarters in the search for Herbie. We have not found him yet. And we're getting tired.

Sitting at the far end of the main table is Ralph Nakamura. He and his data processing people, and the system data base they manage, are essential to the search.

Ralph does not look happy as I come in. He's running his skinny fingers through his thinning black hair.

"This isn't the way it's supposed to be," he's saying to Stacey and Bob.

"Ahh, perfect timing," says Ralph when he sees me. "Do you know what we just did?"

"You found Herbie?" I say.

Ralph says, "No, we just spent two and a half hours calculating the demand for machines that don't exist."

"Why'd you do that?"

Ralph starts to sputter. Then Bob stops him.

"Wait, wait, wait a minute. Let me explain," says Bob. "What happened was they came across some routings which still listed some of the old milling machines as being part of the processing. We don't use them—"

"Not only don't we use them, just found out we sold them a year ago," says Ralph.

"Everybody down in that department knows those machines aren't there anymore, so it's never been a problem," says Bob.

So it goes. We're trying to calculate demand for every resource, every piece of equipment, in the plant. Jonah had said a bottleneck is any resource which is equal to or less than the market demand placed on it. To find out if we've got one then, we concluded we first would have to know the total market demand for products coming out of this plant. And, second, we would have to find out how much time each resource has to contribute toward filling the demand. If the number of available hours for production (discounting maintenance time for machines, lunch and breaks for people, and so on) for the resource is equal to or less than the hours demanded, then we know we've found our Herbie.

Getting a fix on the total market demand is a matter of pulling together data which we have on hand anyway—the existing backlog of customer orders, and the forecast for new product and spare parts. It's the complete product mix for the entire plant, including what we "sell" to other plants and divisions in the company.

Having done that, we're now in the process of calculating the hours each "work center" has to contribute. We're defining a work center as any group of the same resources. Ten welders with the same skills constitute a work center. Four identical machines constitute another. The four machinists who set up and run the machines are still another, and so on. Dividing the total of work center hours needed, by the number of resources in it, gives us the relative effort per resource, a standard we can use for comparison.

Yesterday, for instance, we found the demand for injection molding machines is about 260 hours a month for all the injection molded parts that they have to process. The available time for those machines is about 280 hours per month, per resource. So that means we still have reserve capacity on those machines.

But the more we get into this, the more we're finding that the accuracy of our data is less than perfect. We're coming up with bills of material that don't match the routings, routings that don't have the current run-times—or the correct machines, as we just found out—and so on.

"The problem is, we've been under the gun so much that a lot of the updating has just fallen by the wayside," says Stacey.

"Hell, with engineering changes, shifting labor around, and all that happening all the time, it's just plain tough to keep up with it no matter what," says Bob.

Ralph shakes his head. "To double-check and update every piece of data relevant to this plant could take months!"

"Or years," mumbles Bob.

I sit down and close my eyes for a second. When I open my eyes, they're all looking at me.

"Obviously, we're not going to have time for that," I say. "We've only got ten weeks now to make something happen before Peach blows the whistle. I know we're on the right track, but we're still just limping along here. We've got to accept the fact we're not going to have perfect data to work with."

Ralph says, "Then I have to remind you of the old data processing aphorism: Garbage in, garbage out."

"Wait a minute," I say. "Maybe we're being a little too methodical. Searching a data base isn't the only way to find answers. Can't we come up with some other faster way to isolate the bottleneck—or at least identify the candidates? When I think back to the model of the boys on the hike, it was obvious who the slower kids were on the trail. Doesn't anybody have any hunches where the Herbie might be in the plant?"

"But we don't even know if we've got one yet," says Stacey.

Bob has his hands on his hips. His mouth is half open as if he might say something. Finally, he does.

"Hell, I've been at this plant for more than twenty years. After that much time, I know where the problems usually seem to start," he says. "I think I could put together a list of areas where we might be short on capacity; at least that would narrow the focus for us. It might save some time."

Stacey turns to him. "You know, you just gave me an idea. If we talk to the expeditors. They could probably tell us which parts they're missing most of the time, and in which departments they usually go to look for them."

"What good is that going to do?" asks Ralph.

"The parts most frequently in short supply are probably the ones that would pass through a bottleneck," she says. "And the department where the expeditors go to look for them is probably where we'll find our Herbie."

I sit up in my seat. "Yeah, that makes a lot of sense."

I stand up and start to pace.

"And I'll tell you something *I* just thought of," I say. "Out on the trail, you could tell the slower kids by the gaps in the line. The slower the kid, the greater the distance between him and the kid in front of him. In terms of the analogy, those gaps were inventory."

Bob, Ralph, and Stacey stare at me.

"Don't you see?" I ask them. "If we've got a Herbie, it's probably going to have a huge pile of work-in-process sitting in front of it."

"Yeah, but we got huge piles all over the place out there," says Bob.

"Then we find the biggest one," I say.

"Right! That's got to be another sure sign," says Stacey.

I turn and ask, "What do you think, Ralph?"

"Well, it all sounds worth a try," says Ralph. "Once you've narrowed the field to maybe three of four work centers, it won't take long for us to check your findings against the historical data just to be sure."

Bob looks at Ralph and says in a kidding voice, "Yeah, well, we've all seen how good that is."

But Ralph doesn't take it in a kidding way. He looks embarrassed.

"Hey, I can only work with what I've got," he says. "What do you want me to do?"

"Okay, the important thing is that we have new methods to try," I say. "Let's not waste time pinning the blame on bad data. Let's get to work."

Fueled by the energy of new ideas, we go to work, and the search goes quickly . . . so quickly, in fact, that what we discover makes me feel as though we've run ourselves straight into a wall.

"This is it. Hello, Herbie," says Bob.

In front of us is the NCX-10.

"Are you sure this is a bottleneck?" I ask.

"There's some of the proof," he says as he points to the stacks of work-in-process inventory nearby—weeks of backlog according to the report Ralph and Stacey put together and which we reviewed about an hour ago.

"We talked to the expeditors," says Bob. "They say we're always waiting for parts from this machine. Supervisors say the same. And the guy who runs this area got himself a set of earplugs to keep him from going deaf from all the bitching he gets from everyone."

"But this is supposed to be one of our most efficient pieces of equipment," I say.

"It is," says Bob. "It's the lowest-cost, highest-rate means we have of producing these particular parts."

"So why is this a bottleneck?"

"This is the only one like it we've got," he says.

"Yes, I know that," I say, and I stare at him until he explains.

"See, this machine here is only about two years old. Before we installed it, we used other machines to do what it does. But this machine can do all the operations that used to take three different machines," says Bob.

He tells me about how they used to process these parts using the three separate types of machines. In one typical instance, the process times per part were something like two minutes on the first machine, eight minutes on the second, and four minutes on the third—a grand total of fourteen minutes per part. But the new NCX-10 machine can do all three processes in ten minutes per part.

I say, "You're telling me we're saving four minutes per part. Doesn't that mean we're producing more parts per hour than we were? How come we've got so much inventory stacked up for this thing?"

"With the old way, we had more machines," he says. "We had two of the first type, five of the second type, and three of the third type."

I nod, understanding now. "So you could do more parts, even though it took you longer per part. Then why did we buy the NCX-10?"

"Each of the other machines had to have a machinist to run it," Bob says. "The NCX-10 only needs two guys on it for setups. Like I said, it's the lowest cost way for us to produce these parts."

I take a slow walk all the way around the machine.

"We do run this thing three shifts, don't we?" I ask Bob.

"Well, we just started to again. It took a while to find a replacement for Tony, the setup guy on third shift who quit."

"Oh, yeah . . ." I say. Man, Peach really did it to us that day. I ask, "Bob, how long does it take to train new people on this machine?"

"About six months," he says.

I shake my head.

"That's a big part of the problem, Al. We train somebody and after a couple of years they can go elsewhere and make a few dollars more with somebody else," says Bob. "And we can't seem to attract anybody good with the wages we offer."

"Well why don't we pay more for people on this equipment?"

"The union," says Bob. "We'd get complaints, and the union would want us to up the pay-grade for all the setup people."

I take a last look.

"Okay, so much for this," I say.

But that isn't all. The two of us walk to the other side of the plant where Bob gives me a second introduction.

"Meet Herbie Number Two: the heat-treat department," says Bob.

This one looks more like what you might think of in terms of an industrial Herbie. It's dirty. It's hot. It's ugly. It's dull. And it's indispensable.

Heat-treat basically is a pair of furnaces . . . a couple of grimy, dingy, steel boxes, the insides of which are lined with ceramic blocks. Gas burners raise the internal temperatures to the 1500-degree-Fahrenheit range.

Certain parts, after they've been machined or cold-worked or whatever at ordinary temperatures, can't be worked on anymore until they've been treated with heat for an extended period of time. Most often, we need to soften the metal, which becomes very hard and brittle during processing, so it can have more machining done to it.

So the furnace operators put in the parts, from a dozen or less to a couple of hundred, then they fire up the thing and cook the parts in there for a long time—anywhere from six hours to sixteen hours. And afterwards, the parts always have to go through a further cool-down to air temperature outside the furnace. We lose a lot of time on this process.

"What's the problem here—we need bigger furnaces?" I ask.

Bob says, "Well . . . yes and no. Most of the time these furnaces are running half empty."

"How come?"

"It's the expeditors who seem to cause the problem," he says. "They're always running over here and having us run five of this part or a dozen of that part just so they can have enough to assemble a shipment. So we end up having fifty parts wait while we heat-treat a handful. I mean, this operation is run like a barbershop—take a number and stand in line."

"So we're not running full batches."

"Yeah, sometimes we are. But sometimes even if we do a full batch in number, it's not enough to fill the furnace."

"The batches are too small?"

"Or too big in size, and we have to run a second heat to handle the pieces that wouldn't fit in the first. It just never seems to work out," says Bob. "You know, a couple of years ago, there was a proposal to add a third furnace, on account of the problems."

"What happened to it?"

"It was killed at the division level. They wouldn't authorize the funds because of low efficiencies. They told us to use the capacity we've got. Then maybe they'd talk expansion. Besides, there was all kinds of noise about how we've got to save energy and how another furnace would burn twice as much fuel and all that."

"Okay, but if we filled the furnace every time, would we have enough capacity to meet demand?" I ask.

Bob laughs.

"I don't know. We've never done it that way before."

Once upon a time, I had an idea for doing to the plant essentially what I did with the boys on the hike. I thought the best thing to do would be to reorganize everything so the resource with the least capacity would be first in the routings. All other resources would have gradual increases in capacity to make up for the statistical fluctuations passed on through dependency.

Well, the staff and I meet right after Bob and I get back to the office, and it's pretty obvious, awfully damn quick, that my grand plan for the perfect *un* balanced plant with Herbie in front is just not going to fly.

"From a production standpoint, we can't do it," says Stacey.

"There is just no way we can move even one Herbie—let alone two—to the front of production," Bob says. "The sequence of operations has to stay the way it is. There's nothing we can do about it."

"Okay, I already can see that," I say.

"We're stuck with a set of dependent events," says Lou.

As I listen to them, I get that old familiar feeling which comes whenever a lot of work and energy are about to go down the tubes. It's kind of like watching a tire go flat.

I say, "Okay, if we can't do anything to change their position in the sequence, then maybe we can increase their capacities. We'll make them into non-bottlenecks."

Stacey asks, "But what about the step-up in capacity from beginning to end?"

"We'll reorganize . . . we'll decrease capacity at the head of production and increase it each stage on through," I suggest.

"Al, we're not just talking about moving people around. How can we add capacity without adding equipment?" asks Bob. "And if we're talking about equipment, we're getting ourselves into some major capital. A second furnace on heat-treat, and possibly a second n/c machine . . . brother, you're talking megabucks."

"The bottom line," says Lou, "is that we don't have the money. If we think we can go to Peach and ask him for *excess* capacity for a plant that currently isn't making money in the middle of one of the worst years in the company's history . . . well, excuse my French, but we're out of our goddamned minds."

19

My mother and the kids and I are having dinner that evening when Mom says to me, "Aren't you going to eat your peas, Alex?"

I tell her, "Mom, I'm an adult now. It's my option whether or not to eat my peas."

She looks hurt.

I say, "Sorry. I'm a little depressed tonight."

"What's wrong, Dad?" asks Davey.

"Well . . . it's kind of complicated," I say. "Let's just finish dinner. I've got to leave for the airport in a few minutes."

"Are you going away?" asks Sharon.

"No, I'm just going to pick up somebody," I say.

"Is it Mommy?" asks Sharon.

"No, not Mommy. I wish it could be."

"Alex, tell your children what's bothering you," says my mother. "It affects them, too."

I look at the kids and realize my mother's right. I say, "We found out we've got some problems at the plant which we might not be able to solve."

"What about the man you called?" she asks. "Can't you talk to him?"

"You mean Jonah? That's who I'm picking up at the airport," I say. "But I'm not sure even Jonah's help will do any good."

Hearing this, Dave is shocked. He says, "You mean . . . all that stuff we learned about on the hike, about Herbie setting the speed for the whole troop and all that—none of that was true?"

"Of course it's still true, Dave," I tell him. "The problem is, we discovered we've got *two* Herbies at the plant, and they're right where we don't want them. It would be as if we couldn't rearrange the boys on the trail and Herbie had a twin brother—and now they're both stuck in the middle of the line. They're holding everything up. We can't move them. We've got piles and piles of inventory stacked up in front of them. I don't know what we can do."

Mom says, "Well, if they can't do the work, you'll just have to let them go."

"It's not people; it's equipment," I explain. "We can't fire machines. And, anyway, what they do is essential. We couldn't produce most of our products without these two operations."

"So why don't you make them go faster?" asks Sharon.

"Sure, Dad," says Davey. "Remember what happened on the hike when you took Herbie's pack from him? Maybe you could do something kind of like that in the plant."

"Yeah, but it's not quite that simple," I say.

Mom says, "Alex, I know you'll do the best you can. If you've got these two slow pokes holding everything up, you'll just have to keep after them and make sure they don't waste any more time."

I say, "Yeah, well, I've got to run. Don't wait up for me. I'll see you in the morning."

Waiting at the gate, I watch Jonah's plane taxi up to the terminal. I talked to him in Boston this afternoon just before he was leaving for Los Angeles. I told him I wanted to thank him for his advice, but that the situation at the plant was impossible so far as we could see.

"Alex, how do you know it's impossible?" he asked.

I told him, "We've only got two months left before my boss goes to the board of directors with his recommendation. If we had more time, maybe we could do something, but with only two months. . . ."

"Two months is still enough time to show an improvement," he said. "But you have to learn how to run your plant by its constraints."

"Jonah, we've analyzed the situation thoroughly—"

He said, "Alex, there are two ways that the ideas I'm giving you won't work. One is if there isn't any demand for the products your plant makes."

"No, we have a demand, although it's shrinking as our prices go up and service deteriorates," I said. "But we still have a sizeable backlog of orders."

"I also can't help you if you're determined not to change. Have you made up your mind to do nothing and let the plant close?"

"It's not that we want to give up," I told him. "It's that we don't see any other possibilities."

"Okay then. Have you tried to take some of the load off the bottlenecks by using other resources?" he asked.

"You mean offloading? We can't. These are the only two resources of their type in the plant."

He paused for a moment and finally he said, "All right, one more question: Does Bearington have an airport?"

And so here he is tonight, walking out of Gate Two. He changed his flight to Los Angeles to make a stop here for the evening. I walk up to him and shake his hand.

"How was your flight?" I ask him.

"Have you ever spent time in a sardine can?" he says, then adds, "I shouldn't complain. I'm still breathing."

"Well, thanks for coming," I tell him. "I appreciate you changing your plans, although I'm still not sure you can help us."

"Alex, having a bottleneck—"

"Two bottlenecks," I remind him.

"Having *two* bottlenecks doesn't mean you can't make money," he says. "Quite the contrary, in fact. Most manufacturing plants do not have bottlenecks. They have enormous excess capacity. But they should have them—one on every part they make."

He reads the puzzled look on my face.

"You don't understand, but you will," he said. "Now I want you to give me as much background on your plant as you can."

All the way from the airport, I talk non-stop about our predicament. When we reach the plant, I park the Mazda in front of the offices. Waiting for us inside are Bob, Lou, Stacey and Ralph. They're standing around the vacant receptionist's desk. Everyone is cordial, but as I make the introductions I can tell the staff is waiting to see if this Jonah guy—who bears no resemblance to any consultant they've ever seen walk through the door—really knows what he's doing. Jonah stands in front of them and begins to pace as he talks.

"Alex called me today because you perceive a problem with the bottlenecks you've discovered in your plant," says Jonah. "Actually, you are experiencing a combination of several problems. But first things first. From what Alex has told me, your most immediate need is to increase throughput and improve your cash flow. Am I right?"

"That sure would be a big help," says Lou. "How do you think we might be able to do that?"

"Your bottlenecks are not maintaining a flow sufficient to meet demand and make money," he says. "So there is only one thing to do. We have to find more capacity."

"But we don't have the money for more capacity," says Lou.

"Or the time to install it," says Bob.

"I'm not talking about more capacity from one end of the plant to the other," says Jonah. "To increase the capacity of the plant is to increase the capacity of *only* the bottlenecks."

"You mean make them into non-bottlenecks," says Stacey.

"No," he says. "Absolutely not. The bottlenecks stay bottlenecks. What we must do is find enough capacity for the bottlenecks to become more equal to demand."

"Where're we going to find it?" asks Bob. "You mean it's just layin' around out there?"

"In effect, yes," says Jonah. "If you are like most manufacturers, you will have capacity that is *hidden* from you because some of your thinking is incorrect. And I suggest that first of all we go into your plant and see for ourselves exactly how you are managing your two bottlenecks."

"Why not," I say. "After all, no one visits this plant and escapes without a tour."

The six of us put on the safety glasses and hats and go into the plant. Jonah and I head the column as we walk through the double doors into the orange light. It's about halfway into second shift now and somewhat quieter than it is on day turn. That's good because it lets us hear each other better when we talk. I point out various stages of production to Jonah as we walk. I notice Jonah's eyes measuring the stacks of inventory piled everywhere. I try to hurry us along.

"This is our NCX-10 n/c machine," I tell Jonah as we arrive at the big machine.

"And this is your bottleneck, correct?" asks Jonah.

"One of them," I say.

"Can you tell me why isn't it working right now?" asks Jonah.

Indeed, the NCX-10 is stopped at the moment.

I say, "Well . . . ah, good question. Bob, why isn't the NCX-10 running?"

Bob glances at his watch.

"Probably because the set-up people went on break about ten minutes ago," says Bob. "They should be back in about twenty minutes."

"There is a clause in our union contract which stipulates there must be a half-hour break after every four hours of work," I explain to Jonah.

He asks, "But why should they take their break now instead of when the machine is running?"

Bob says, "Because it was eight o'clock and—"

Jonah holds up his hands and says, "Wait a minute. On any *non*-bottleneck machine in your plant, no problem. Because, after all, some percentage of a non-bottleneck's time *should* be idle. So who cares when those people take their breaks? It's no big deal. But on a bottleneck? It's exactly the opposite."

He points to the NCX-10 and says, "You have on this machine only so many hours available for production—what is it . . . 600, 700 hours?"

"It's around 585 hours a month," says Ralph.

"Whatever is available, the demand is even greater," says Jonah. "If you lose one of those hours, or even half of it, you have lost it forever. You cannot recover it someplace else in the system. Your throughput for the entire plant will be lower by whatever amount the bottleneck produces in that time. And that makes an enormously expensive lunch break."

"But we have a union to deal with," says Bob.

Jonah says, "So talk to them. They have a stake in this plant. They're not stupid. But you have to make them understand."

Yeah, I'm thinking; that's easier said than done. On the other hand . . .

Jonah is walking around the NCX-10 now, but he's not just looking at it alone. He's looking at other equipment in the plant. He comes back to us.

"You've told me this is the only machine of its type in the plant," says Jonah, "But this is a relatively new machine. Where are the older machines that this one replaced? Do you still have those?"

Bob says vaguely, "Well, some of them we do. Some of them we got rid of. They were practically antiques."

"Do you have at least one of each type of the older machines necessary to do what this X-what-ever-it-is machine does?" Jonah asks.

Lou edges in and and says, "Excuse me, but you're not actually suggesting we use that old equipment, are you?"

"If it's still operational, then yes, I might suggest it," says Jonah.

Lou's eyes blink.

He says, "Well, I'm not sure what that would do to our cost profile. But I have to tell you that those old machines are going to be much more expensive to operate."

Jonah says, "We'll deal with that directly. First, I just want to know if you have the machines or not."

For the answer, we turn to Bob—who chuckles.

"Sorry to disappoint you all," he says, "but we got rid of an entire class of machine that we'd need to supplement the NCX-10."

"Why did we go do a dumb thing like that?" I ask.

Bob says, "We needed the floor space for that new pen to hold inventory."

I say, "Oh."

"It seemed like a good idea at the time," says Stacey.

Moving right along to heat-treat, we gather in front of the furnaces.

The first thing Jonah does is look at the stacks of parts and ask, "Are you sure all this inventory requires heat-treat?"

"Oh, absolutely," says Bob.

"There are no alternatives in the processing ahead of this department that would prevent the need for heat-treat on at least some of these parts?" he asks.

We all look at each other.

"I guess we'd have to consult with engineering," I say. Bob rolls his eyes.

"What's the matter?" I ask.

"Let's just say our friends in engineering aren't as responsive as they could be," says Bob. "They're not too happy about changing requirements. Their attitude is usually, 'Do it this way because we said so.'"

To Jonah, I say, "I'm afraid he does have a point. Even if we can get them to cooperate, it might take a month of Sundays for them to approve it."

Jonah says, "Okay, let me ask you this: are there vendors in the area who can heat-treat parts for you?"

"There are," says Stacey, "but going outside would increase our cost-per-part."

The expression on Jonah's face says he's getting a little bored with this stonewalling. He points at the mountains of parts.

"How much money is represented in that pile?" he asks.

Lou says, "I don't know . . . maybe ten or fifteen thousand dollars in parts."

"No, it isn't *thousands* of dollars, not if this is a bottleneck," says Jonah, "Think again. It's considerably more."

Stacey says, "I can go dig up the records if you like, but the cost won't be much more than what Lou said. At the most, I'd guess we've got about twenty thousands dollars in material—"

"No, no," says Jonah. "I'm not just talking about the cost of materials. How many products are you going to sell to customers as soon as you can process this entire pile?"

The staff and I talk among ourselves for a moment.

"It's kind of hard to say," says Bob.

"We're not sure all the parts in that pile would translate into immediate sales," says Stacey.

"Oh really? You are making your bottlenecks work on parts that will not contribute to throughput?" asks Jonah.

"Well . . . some of them become spare parts or they go into finished goods inventory. Eventually it becomes throughput," says Lou.

"*Eventually,*" says Jonah. "And, meanwhile, how big did you say your backlog of overdue orders is?"

I explain to him that sometimes we inflate the batch quantities to improve efficiency.

"Tell me again how this improves your efficiency," says Jonah.

I feel myself starting to turn red with the memory of earlier conversations.

"Okay, never mind that for now," says Jonah. "Let's concern ourselves strictly with throughput. I'll put my question differently: how many products are you *unable* to ship because you are missing the parts in that pile?"

That's easier to determine because we know what our backlog is. I tell him how many millions we've got in backlog and about what percent of that is held up on account of bottleneck parts.

"And if you could finish the parts in that pile, you could assemble and ship the product?" he asks.

"Sure, no problem," says Bob.

"And what is the selling price of each unit?"

"About a thousand dollars a unit on the average," says Lou, "although it varies, of course."

"Then we are not dealing with ten or fifteen or even twenty thousand dollars here," says Jonah. "Because we are dealing with how many parts in that pile?"

"Perhaps, a thousand," says Stacey.

"And each part means you can ship a product?"

"Generally, yes," she says.

"And each product shipped means a thousand dollars," says Jonah. "A thousand units times a thousand dollars is how much money?"

In unison, our faces turn toward the mountain.

"One million dollars," I say with awe.

"On one condition!" says Jonah. "That you get these parts in and out of heat-treat and shipped as a finished product before your customers get tired of waiting and go elsewhere!"

He looks at us, his eyes shifting from face to face.

"Can you afford to rule out any possibility," he asks, "especially one that is as easy to invoke as a change in policy?"

Everyone is quiet.

"By the way, I'll tell you more about how to look at the costs in a moment. But one more thing," says Jonah. "I want to know where you do quality inspection on bottleneck parts."

I explain to him that most inspection is done prior to final assembly.

"Show me," says Jonah.

So we go to an area where we do quality inspections. Jonah asks about bottleneck parts that we reject. Immediately, Bob points to a pallet stacked with shiny steel parts. On top of them is a pink sheet of paper, which indicates rejection by Quality Control, or Q.C. as it's known. Bob picks up the job jacket and reads the forms inside.

"I'm not sure what's wrong with these, but they must be defective for some reason," says Bob.

Jonah asks, "Did these parts come through a bottleneck?"

"Yeah, they did," says Bob.

"Do you realize what the rejection by Q.C. has done to you?" asks Jonah.

"It means we have to scrap about a hundred parts," says Bob.

"No, think again," says Jonah. "These are *bottleneck* parts."

It dawns on me what he's getting at.

"We lost the time on the bottleneck," I say.

Jonah whirls toward me.

"Exactly right!" he says. "And what does lost time on a bottleneck mean? It means you have lost throughput."

"But you're not saying we should ignore quality, are you?" asks Bob.

"Absolutely not. You can't make money for long without a quality product," says Jonah. "But I am suggesting you use quality control in a different way."

I ask, "You mean we should put Q.C. in front of the bottlenecks?"

Jonah raises a finger and says, "Very perceptive of you. Make sure the bottleneck works only on good parts by weeding out the ones that are defective. If you scrap a part before it reaches the bottleneck, all you have lost is a scrapped part. But if you scrap the part after it's passed the bottleneck, you have lost time that cannot be recovered."

"Suppose we get sub-standard quality downstream from the bottleneck?" says Stacey.

"That's another aspect of the same idea," says Jonah. "Be sure the process controls on bottleneck parts are very good, so these parts don't become defective in later processing. Are you with me?"

Bob says, "Just one question: where do we get the inspectors?"

"What's wrong with shifting the ones you already have to the bottlenecks?" asks Jonah.

"That's something we can think about," I tell him.

"Good. Let's go back to the offices," says Jonah.

We go back to the office building and meet in the conference room.

"I want to be absolutely sure you understand the importance of the bottlenecks," says Jonah. "Every time a bottleneck finishes a part, you are making it possible to ship a finished product. And how much does that mean to you in sales?"

"It averages around a thousand dollars a unit," says Lou.

"And you're worried about spending a dollar or two at the bottlenecks to make them more productive?" he asks. "First of all, what do you think the cost of, let's say, the X machine is for one hour?"

Lou says, "That's well established. It costs us $32.50 per hour."

"And heat-treat?"

"That's $21 per hour," says Lou.

"Both of those amounts are incorrect," says Jonah.

"But our cost data—"

"The numbers are wrong, not because you have made a calculating error, but because the costs were determined as if these work centers existed in isolation," says Jonah. "Let me explain: when I was a physicist, people would come to me from time to time with problems in mathematics they couldn't solve. They wanted me to check their numbers for them. But after a while I learned not to waste my time checking the numbers—because the numbers were almost always right. However, if I checked the *assumptions,* they were almost always wrong."

Jonah pulls a cigar out of his pocket and lights it with a match.

"That's what's going on here," he says between puffs. "You have calculated the cost of operating these two works centers according to standard accounting procedures . . . *without* considering the fact that both are bottlenecks."

"How does that change their costs?" asks Lou.

"What you have learned is that the capacity of the plant is equal to the capacity of its bottlenecks," says Jonah. "Whatever the bottlenecks produce in an hour is the equivalent of what the plant produces in an hour. So . . . an hour lost at a bottleneck is an hour lost for the entire system."

"Right, we're with you," says Lou.

"Then how much would it cost for this entire plant to be idle for one hour?" asks Jonah.

"I really can't say, but it would be very expensive," admits Lou.

"Tell me something," asks Jonah. "How much does it cost you to operate your plant each month?"

Lou says, "Our total operating expense is around $1.6 million per month."

"And let's just take the X machine as an example," he says. "How many hours a month did you say it's available for production?"

"About 585," says Ralph.

"The actual cost of a bottleneck is the total expense of the system divided by the number of hours the bottleneck produces," says Jonah. "What does this make it?"

Lou takes out his calculator from his coat pocket and punches in the numbers.

"That's $2,735," says Lou. "Now wait a minute. Is that right?"

"Yes, it's right," says Jonah. "If your bottlenecks are not working, you haven't just lost $32 or $21. The true cost is the cost of an hour of the entire system. And that's twenty seven *hundred* dollars."

Lou is flabbergasted.

"That puts a different perspective on it," says Stacey.

"Of course it does," says Jonah. "And with that in mind, how do we optimize the use of the bottlenecks? There are two principal themes on which you need to concentrate . . .

"First, make sure the bottlenecks' time is not wasted," he says. "How is the time of a bottleneck wasted? One way is for it to be sitting idle during a lunch break. Another is for it to be processing parts which are already defective—or which will become defective through a careless worker or poor process control. A third way to waste a bottleneck's time is to make it work on parts you don't need."

"You mean spare parts?" asks Bob.

"I mean anything that isn't within the current demand," he says. "Because what happens when you build inventory now that you won't sell for months in the future? You are sacrificing present money for future money; the question is, can your cash flow sustain it? In your case, absolutely not."

"He's right," admits Lou.

"Then make the bottlenecks work only on what will contribute to throughput *today* . . . not nine months from now," says Jonah. "That's one way to increase the capacity of the bottlenecks. The other way you increase bottleneck capacity is to take some of the load off the bottlenecks and give it to non-bottlenecks."

I ask, "Yeah, but how do we do that?"

"That's why I was asking those questions when we were out in the plant," he says. "Do all of the parts have to be processed by the bottleneck? If not, the ones which don't can be shifted to non-bottlenecks for processing. And the result is you gain capacity on your bottleneck. A second question: do you have other machines to do the same process? If you have the machines, or if you have a vendor with the right equipment, you can offload from the bottleneck. And, again, you gain capacity which enables you to increase throughput."

I come into the kitchen for breakfast the next morning and sit down to a big steaming bowl of my mother's oatmeal . . . which I have hated ever since I was a kid. I'm staring at the oatmeal (and the oatmeal is staring back) when Mom/Grandma asks, "So how did everything go last night?"

I say, "Well, actually, you and the kids were on the right track at dinner."

"We were?" asks Dave.

"We need to make the Herbies go faster," I say. "And last night Jonah pointed out some ways to do that. So we learned a lot."

"Well, now, isn't that good news," says my mother.

She pours a cup of coffee for herself and sits down at the table. It's quiet for a moment. Then I notice that Mom and the kids are eyeing each other.

"Something wrong?" I ask.

"Their mother called again last night while you were gone," says my mother.

Julie has been calling the kids regularly since she left. But for whatever reason of her own, she still won't tell them where she is. I'm debating whether to hire a private detective to find out where she's hiding.

"Sharon says she heard something when she was on the phone talking," says my mother.

I look at Sharon.

"You know that music Grandpa always listens to?" she says.

I say, "You mean Grandpa Barnett?"

"Uh-huh, you know," she says, "the music that puts you to sleep, with the—what are they called?"

"Violins," says Dave.

"Right, the violins," says Sharon. "Well, when Mom wasn't talking, I heard that on the phone last night."

"I heard 'em too," says Dave.

"Really?" I say. "That's very interesting. Thank you both for noticing that. Maybe I'll give Grandma and Grandpa Barnett another call today."

I finish my coffee and stand up.

"Alex, you haven't even touched your oatmeal," says Mom.

I lean down and kiss her on the cheek. "Sorry, I'm late for school."

I wave to the kids and hurry to grab my briefcase.

"Well, I'll just have to save it so you can eat it tomorrow," says my mother.

20

Driving to the plant, I pass the motel where Jonah stayed last night. I know he's long gone—he had a 6:30 A.M. flight to catch. I offered to pick him up this morning and drive him to the airport, but (lucky for me) he refused and said he'd take a cab.

As soon as I get to the office, I tell Fran to set up a meeting with the staff. Meanwhile, I start to write down a list of the actions Jonah suggested last night. But Julie comes to mind and won't leave. I close my office door and sit down at my desk. I find the number for Julie's parents and dial it.

The first day after Julie left, her parents called to ask me if I had heard anything. They haven't called back since. A day or two ago, I tried getting in touch with them to find out if *they* had heard anything. I called in the afternoon and I talked to Julie's mother, Ada. She said she didn't know where Julie was. Even then, I didn't quite believe her.

Now Ada answers again.

"Hi, this is Alex," I tell her. "Let me talk to Julie."

Ada is flustered. "Well, um, ah . . . she isn't here."

"Yes, she is."

I hear Ada sigh.

"She *is* there, isn't she," I say.

Finally Ada says, "She does not want to talk to you."

"How long, Ada? How long has she been there? Were you lying to me even that Sunday night when I called?"

"No, we were not *lying* to you," she says indignantly. "We had no idea where she was. She was with her friend, Jane, for a few days."

"Sure, and what about the other day when I called?"

"Julie simply asked me not to say where she was," says Ada, "and I shouldn't even be telling you now. She wants to be by herself for a while."

"Ada, I need to speak with her," I say.

"She will not come to the phone," says Ada.

"How do you know until you've asked?"

The phone on Ada's end is put down on the table. Footsteps fade away and return a minute later.

"She says she'll call you when she's ready," says Ada.

"What does that mean?"

"If you hadn't neglected her all these years, you wouldn't be in this situation," she says.

"Ada—"

"Good-bye," she says.

She hangs up the phone. I try calling back right away, but there is no answer. After a few minutes, I force my mind back to getting ready to talk to the staff.

At ten o'clock, the meeting starts in my office.

"I'd like to know what you think about what you heard last night," I say. "Lou, what was your reaction?"

Lou says, "Well . . . I just couldn't believe what he was saying about an hour of a bottleneck. I went home last night and thought it over to see if it all made sense. And, actually, we were wrong about a lost hour of a bottleneck costing $2,700."

"We were?" I ask.

"Only eighty percent of our products flow through the bottlenecks," says Lou as he takes a piece of note paper from his shirt pocket. "So the truer cost ought to be eighty percent of our operating expense, and that comes to $2,188 an hour—not $2,735."

"Oh," I say. "I suppose you're right."

Then Lou smiles.

"Nevertheless," he says, "I have to admit it was quite an eye-opener to look at the situation from that perspective."

"I agree," I say. "What about the rest of you?"

I go from person to person around the office asking for reactions, and we're all pretty much in agreement. Even so, Bob seems hesitant about committing to some of the changes Jonah was talking about. And Ralph isn't sure yet where he fits in. But Stacey is a strong advocate.

She sums up, saying, "I think it makes enough sense to risk the changes."

"Although I'm nervous about anything that increases operating expense at this point in time," says Lou, "I agree with Stacey. As Jonah said, we may face a bigger risk just staying on the path we've been following."

Bob raises one of his meaty hands in preparation for a comment.

"Okay, but some of what Jonah talked about will be easier and faster to make happen than the rest," he says. "Why don't we go ahead with the easier things right away and see what kind of effect they have while we're developing the others."

I tell him, "That sounds reasonable. What would you do first?"

"I think I'd wanna move the Q.C. inspection points first, to check parts going into the bottlenecks," says Bob. "The other Q.C. measures will take a little time, but we can have an inspector checking pre-bottleneck parts in no time—by the end of today if you want."

I nod. "Good. What about new rules for lunch breaks?"

"We might have a squawk or two from the union," he says.

I shake my head. "I think they'll go along with it. Work out the details and I'll talk to O'Donnell."

Bob makes a note on the paper pad on his lap. I stand up and step around the desk to emphasize what I'm about to say.

"One of the questions Jonah raised last night really struck home for me," I tell them. "Why are we making the bottlenecks work on inventory that won't increase throughput?"

Bob looks at Stacey, and she looks back at him.

"That's a good question," she says.

Bob says, "We made the decision—"

"I know the decision," I say. "Build inventory to maintain efficiencies." But our problem is not efficiencies. Our problem is our backlog of overdue orders. And it's very visible to our customers and to division management. We positively must do something to improve our due-date performance, and Jonah has given us the insight on what that something has to be.

"Until now, we've expedited orders on the basis of who's screamed the loudest," I say. "From now on, late orders should get first priority over the others. An order that's two weeks late gets priority over an order that's one week late, and so on."

"We've tried that from time to time in the past," says Stacey.

"Yes, but the key this time is we make sure the *bottlenecks* are processing parts for those late orders according to the same priority," I say.

"That's the sane approach to the problem, Al," says Bob, "Now how do we make it happen?"

"We have to find out which inventory en route to the bottlenecks is needed for late orders and which is simply going to end up in a warehouse. So here's what we need to do," I say. "Ralph, I want you to make us a list of all the overdue orders. Have them ranked in priority ranging from the most days overdue to the least days overdue. How soon can you have that for us?"

"Well, that in itself won't take very long," he says. "The problem is we've got the monthlies to run."

I shake my head. "Nothing is more important to us right now than making the bottlenecks more productive. We need that list as soon as possible, because once you've got it, I want you to work with Stacey and her people in inventory control—find out what parts still have to be processed by either of the bottlenecks to complete those orders."

I turn to Stacey.

"After you know which parts are missing, get together with Bob and schedule the bottlenecks to start working on the parts for the latest order first, the next latest, and so on."

"What about the parts that don't go through either one of the bottlenecks?" asks Bob.

"I'm not going to worry about those at the moment," I tell him. "Let's work on the assumption that anything not needing to go through a bottleneck is either waiting in front of assembly already, or will be by the time the bottleneck parts arrive."

Bob nods.

"Everybody got it?" I ask. "Nothing else takes priority over this. We don't have time to take a step back and do some kind of headquarters number where everyone takes six months to think about it. We know what we have to do. Let's get it done."

That evening, I'm driving along the Interstate. Around sunset, I'm looking around at the rooftops of suburban houses to either side of the highway. A sign goes by which says I'm two miles from the exit to Forest Grove. Julie's parents live in Forest Grove. I take that exit.

Neither the Barnetts nor Julie know I'm coming. I told my mother not to tell the kids. I simply hopped in the car after work and headed down here. I've had enough of this hide-and-seek game she's playing.

From a four-lane highway, I turn onto a smooth blacktop street which winds through a quiet neighborhood. It's a nice neighborhood. The homes are unquestionably expensive and the lawns without exception are immaculate. The streets are lined with trees just getting the new leaves of spring. They are brilliant green in the golden setting sun.

I see the house halfway down the street. It's the two-story brick colonial painted white. It has shutters. The shutters are made of aluminum and have no hinges; they are non-functional but traditional. This is where Julie grew up.

I park the Mazda by the curb in front of the house. I look up the driveway, and sure enough, there is Julie's Accord in front of the garage.

Before I have reached the front door, it opens. Ada Barnett is standing behind the screen. I see her hand reach down and click the screen door lock as I approach.

"Hello," I say.

"I told you she doesn't want to talk to you," says Ada.

"Will you just ask her please?" I ask. "She *is* my wife."

"If you want to talk to Julie, you can do it through her lawyer," says Ada.

She starts to close the door.

I say, "Ada, I am not leaving until I talk to your daughter."

"If you don't leave, I will call the police to have you removed from our property," says Ada Barnett.

"Then I will wait in my car," I say. "You don't own the street."

The door closes. I walk across the lawn and over the sidewalk, and get in the Mazda. I sit there and stare at the house. Every so often, I notice the curtains move behind the window glass of the Barnett house. After about forty five minutes, the sun has set and I'm seriously wondering how long I can sit here when the front door opens again.

Julie walks out. She's wearing jeans and sneakers and a sweater. The jeans and sneakers make her look young. She reminds me of a teenager meeting a boyfriend her parents disapprove of. She comes across the lawn and I get out of the car. When she's about ten feet away she stops, as if she's worried about getting too close, where I might grab her, pull her into the car, and drive like the wind to my tent in the desert or something. We look each other over. I slide my hands into my pockets.

For openers, I say, "So . . . how have you been?"

"If you want to know the truth," she says, "I've been rotten. How have you been?"

"Worried about you."

She glances away. I slap the roof of the Mazda.

"Let's go for a ride," I say.

"No, I can't," she says.

"How about a walk then?" I ask.

"Alex, just tell me what you want, okay?" she says.

"I want to know why you're doing this!"

"Because I don't know if I want to be married to you anymore," she says. "Isn't that obvious?"

"Okay, can't we talk about it?"

She says nothing.

"Come on," I say. "Let's take that walk—just once around the block. Unless you want to give the neighbors lots to talk about."

Julie looks around at the houses and realizes we're a spectacle. Awkwardly, she steps toward me. I hold out my hand. She doesn't take it, but we turn together and begin a stroll down the sidewalk. I wave to the Barnett house and note the flurry of a curtain. Julie and I walk a hundred feet or so in the twilight before we say anything. At last I break the silence.

"Look, I'm sorry about what happened that weekend," I tell her. "But what else could I do? Davey expected me—"

"It wasn't because you went on the hike with Davey," she says. "That was just the last straw. All of a sudden, I just couldn't stand it anymore. I had to get away."

"Julie, why didn't you at least let me know where you were?"

"Listen," she says. "I went away from you so I could be alone."

Hesitantly, I ask, "So . . . do you want a divorce?"

"I don't know yet," she says.

"Well, when will you know?"

"Al, this has been a very mixed up time for me," she says. "I don't know what to do. I can't decide anything. My mother tells me one thing. My father tells me something else. My friends tell me something else. Everyone except me knows what I should do."

"You went off to be by yourself to make a decision that's going to affect both of us as well as our kids. And you're listening to everyone except the three other people whose lives are going to be screwed up if you don't come back," I say.

"This is something I need to figure out on my own, away from the pressures of you three."

"All I'm suggesting is that we talk about what's bothering you."

She sighs in exasperation and says, "Al, we've been over it a million times already!"

"Okay, look, just tell me this: are you having an affair?"

Julie stops. We have reached the corner.

She says coldly, "I think I've gone far enough with you."

I stand there for a moment as she turns and heads back toward her parents' house. I catch up with her.

I say, "Well? Are you or aren't you?"

"Of course I'm not having an affair!" she yells. "Do you think I'd be staying with my *parents* if I were having an affair?"

A man who is walking his dog turns and stares at us. Julie and I stride past him in stiff silence.

I whisper to Julie, "I just had to know . . . that's all."

"If you think I'd leave my children just to go have a fling with some stranger, you have no understanding of who I am," she says.

I feel as if she'd slapped my face.

"Julie, I'm sorry," I tell her. "That kind of thing sometimes happens, and I just needed to make sure of what's going on."

She slows her walk. I put my hand on her shoulder. She brushes it off.

"Al, I've been unhappy for a long time," she says. "And I'll tell you something: I feel guilty about it. I feel as though I don't have a right to be unhappy. I just know I am."

With irritation, I see we're back in front of her parents' house. The walk was too short. Ada is standing in plain view at the window. Julie and I stop. I lean against the rear fender of the Mazda.

"Why don't you pack your things and come home with me," I suggest, but she's shaking her head before I've even finished the sentence.

"No, I'm not ready to do that," she says.

"Okay, look," I say. "The choice is this: You stay away and we get a divorce. Or we get back together and struggle to make the marriage work. The longer you stay away, the more we're going to drift apart from each other and toward a divorce. And if we get a divorce, you know what's going to happen. We've seen it happen over and over to our friends. Do you really want that? Come on, come home. I promise we can make it better."

She shakes her head. "I can't, Al. I've heard too many promises before."

I say, "Then you want a divorce?"

Julie says, "I told you, I don't know!"

"Okay," I say finally. "I can't make up your mind for you. Maybe it is your decision. All I can say is I want you back. I'm sure that's what the kids want too. Give me a call when you know what *you* want."

"That was exactly what I planned to do, Al."

I get into the Mazda and start the engine. Rolling down the window, I look up at her as she stands on the sidewalk next to the car.

"You know, I do happen to love you," I tell her.

This finally melts her. She comes to the car and leans down. Reaching through the window, I take her hand for a moment. She kisses me. Then without a word she stands up and walks away; halfway across the lawn, she breaks into a run. I watch her until she's disappeared through the door. Then I shake my head, put the car into gear, and drive away.

21

I'm home by ten o'clock that night. Depressed, but home. Rummaging through the refrigerator, I attempt to find dinner, but have to settle for cold spaghetti and some leftover peas. Washing it down with some leftover vodka, I dine in dejection.

I'm wondering while I'm eating what I'm going to do if Julie doesn't come back. If I don't have a wife, do I start to date women again? Where would I meet them? I have a sudden vision of myself standing in the bar of the Bearington Holiday Inn, attempting to be sexy while asking strange females, "What's your sign?"

Is *that* my fate? My God. And anyway, do lines like that even work these days? Did they ever?

I must know *somebody* to go out with.

For a while, I sit there thinking of all the available women I know. Who would go out with me? Whom would I want to go out with? It doesn't take long to exhaust the list. Then one woman comes to mind. Getting up from my chair, I go to the phone and spend about five minutes staring at it.

Should I?

Nervously, I dial the number. I hang up before it rings. I stare at the phone some more. Oh, what the hell! All she can do is say no, right? I dial the number again. It rings about ten times before anyone answers.

"Hello." It's her father.

"May I speak to Julie please."

Pause. "Just a minute."

The moments pass.

"Hello?" says Julie.

"Hi, it's me."

"Al?"

I say, "Yeah, listen, I know it's late, but I just want to ask you something."

"If it has to do with getting a divorce or coming home—"

"No, no, no," I tell her. "I was just wondering if while you're making up your mind, there would be any harm in us seeing each other once in a while."

She says, "Well . . . I guess not."

"Good. What are you doing Saturday night?" I ask.

There is a moment of silence as the smile forms on her face. Amused, she asks, "Are you asking me for a date?"

"Yes, I am."

Long pause.

I say, "So would you like to go out with me?"

"Yes, I'd like that a lot," she says finally.

"Great. How about I see you at 7:30?"

"I'll be ready," she says.

The next morning in the conference room, we've got the two supervisors of the bottlenecks with us. By "us," I mean Stacey, Bob, Ralph and me. Ted Spencer is the supervisor responsible for the heat-treat furnaces. He's an older guy with hair that looks like steel wool and a body like a steel file. We've got him and Mario DeMonte, supervisor of the machining center with the NCX-10. Mario is as old as Ted, but plumper.

Stacey and Ralph both have red eyes. Before we sat down, they told me about the work that went into this morning's meeting.

Getting the list of overdue orders was easy. The computer listed them and sorted them according to lateness. Nothing to it, didn't even take a minute. But then they had to go over the bills of material for each of the orders and find out which parts are done by the bottlenecks. And they had to establish whether there was inventory to make those parts. That took most of the night.

We all have our own photocopies of a hand-written list Ralph has had prepared. Listed in the print-out is a grand total of sixty seven records, our total backlog of overdue orders. They have been sorted from most-days-past-due to least-days. The worst one, at the top of the list, is an order that is fifty eight days beyond the delivery date promised by marketing. The best are one day late; there are three of those orders.

"We did some checking," says Ralph. "And about ninety percent of the current overdues have parts that flow through one or both of the bottleneck operations. Of those, about eighty five percent are held up at assembly because we're waiting for those parts to arrive before we can build and ship."

"So it's obvious those parts get first priority," I explain to the two supervisors.

Then Ralph says, "We went ahead and made a list for both heat-treat and the NCX-10 as to which parts they each have to process and in what order—again, the same sequence of latest order to least late. In a day or two we can generate the list by computer and stop burning the midnight oil."

"Fantastic, Ralph. I think both you and Stacey have done a super job," I tell him. Then I turn to Ted and Mario. "Now, all you gentlemen have to do is have your foremen start at the top of the list and work their way down."

"That sounds easy enough," says Ted. "I think we can handle that."

"You know, we may have to go track some of these down," says Mario.

"So you'll have to do some digging through the inventory," says Stacey. "What's the problem?"

Mario frowns and says, "No problem. You just want us to do what's on this list, right?"

"Yep, it's that simple," I say. "I don't want to see either of you working on something not on that list. If the expeditors give you any problem, tell them to come see me. And be sure you stick to the sequence we've given you."

Ted and Mario both nod.

I turn to Stacey and say, "You do understand how important it is for the expeditors not to interfere with this priority list, don't you?"

Stacey says, "Okay, but you have to promise me you won't change it because of pressure from marketing."

"My word of honor," I tell her. Then I say to Ted and Mario, "In all seriousness, I hope you two guys know that heat-treat and the NCX-10 are the most important processes in the whole plant. How well you manage those two could very well determine whether this plant has a future."

"We'll do our best," says Ted.

"I can assure you that they will," says Bob Donovan.

Right after that meeting, I go down the hall to the personnel relations for a meeting with Mike O'Donnell, the union local president. When I walk in, my personnel manager, Scott Dolin, is gripping the armrests of his chair with white knuckles, while O'Donnell is talking at the top of his voice.

"What's the problem here?" I ask.

"You know very well what the problem is: your new lunch rules in heat-treat and n/c machining," says O'Donnell. "They're in violation of the contract. I refer you to Section Seven, Paragraph Four . . ."

I say, "Okay, wait a minute, Mike. It's time we gave the union an update on the situation of the plant."

For the rest of the morning I describe for him the situation the plant is in. Then I tell him some of what we've discovered and explain why the changes are necessary.

Wrapping up, I say, "You understand, don't you, that it's probably only going to affect about twenty people at the most?"

He shakes his head.

"Look, I appreciate you trying to explain all this," he says. "But we got a contract. Now if we look the other way on one thing, what's to say you won't start changing whatever else you don't like?"

I say, "Mike, in all honesty, I can't tell you that down the road aways, we won't need to make other changes. But we're ultimately talking about jobs. I'm not asking for cuts in wages or concessions on benefits. But I am asking for flexibility. We have to have the leeway necessary to make changes that will allow the plant to make money. Or, very simply, there may not be a plant in a few months."

"Sounds like scare tactics to me," he says finally.

"Mike, all I can say is, if you want to wait a couple of months to see if I'm just trying to scare everyone, it'll be too late."

O'Donnell is quiet for a moment.

Finally, he says, "I'll have to think about it, talk it over and all that. We'll get back to you."

By early afternoon, I can't stand it anymore. I'm anxious to find out how the new priority system is working. I try calling Bob Donovan, but he's out in the plant. So I decide to go have a look for myself.

The first place I check is the NCX-10. But when I get to the machine, there's nobody to ask. Being an automated machine, it runs a lot of the time with nobody tending it. The problem is that when I walk up, the damn thing is just sitting there. It isn't running and nobody is doing a set-up. I get mad.

I go find Mario.

"Why the hell isn't that machine working?" I ask him.

He checks with the foreman. Finally he walks back to me.

"We don't have the materials," he says.

"What do you mean, *you don't have materials,*" I shout. "What do you call these stacks of steel everywhere?"

"But you told us to work according to what's on the list," says Mario.

"You mean you finished all the late parts?"

"No, they did the first two batches of parts," says Mario. "When they got to the third part on the list, they looked all around and couldn't find the materials for it in the queue. So we're shut down until they turn up."

I'm ready to strangle him.

"That's what you wanted us to do, right?" says Mario. "You wanted us to do only what was on the list and in the same order as listed, didn't you? Isn't that what you said?"

Finally I say, "Yes, that is what I said. But didn't it occur to you that if you couldn't do one item on the list you should go on to the next?"

Mario looks helpless.

"Well, where the hell are the materials you need?" I ask him.

"I have no idea," he says. "They could be any of half-a-dozen places. But I think Bob Donovan might have somebody looking for them already."

"Okay, look," I tell him. "You have the setup people get this machine ready for whatever is the *next* part on that list for which you do have the materials. And keep this hunk of junk running."

"Yes sir," says Mario.

Fuming mad, I start back to the office to have Donovan paged, so I can find out what went wrong. Halfway there, I pass some lathes and there he is, talking to Otto the foreman. I don't know how civil the tone is. Otto appears to be dismayed by Bob's presence. I stop and stand there waiting for Bob to finish and notice me. Which happens directly. Otto walks over and calls his machinists together. Bob comes over to me.

I say, "You know about what's going on—"

"Yes, I know," he says. "That's why I'm here."

"What's the problem?"

"Nothing, no problem," he says. "Just standard operating procedure."

It turns out, as Bob explains to me, that the parts they were waiting for at the NCX-10 have been sitting there for about a week. Otto has been running other batches of parts. He didn't know about the importance of the parts destined for the NCX-10. To him they looked like any other batch—and a rather unimportant one judging from the size. When Bob got here, they were in the middle of a big, long run. Otto didn't want to stop . . . until Donovan explained it to him, that is.

"Dammit, Al, it's just like before," Bob says. "They get set up and they start running one thing, and then they have to break in the middle so we can finish something else. It's the same damn thing!"

"Now hold on," I say. "Let's think about this for a second."

Bob shakes his head. "What is there to think about?"

"Let's just try to reason this through," I say. "What was the problem?"

"The parts didn't arrive at the NCX-10, which meant the operators couldn't run the batch they were supposed to be running," says Bob in kind of a sing-song way.

"And the cause was that the bottleneck parts were held up by this non-bottleneck machine running non-bottleneck parts," I say. "Now we've got to ask ourselves why that happened."

"The guy in charge here was just trying to stay busy, that's all," says Bob.

"Right. Because if he didn't stay busy, someone like you would come along and jump all over him," I say.

"Yeah, and if I didn't, then someone like you would jump all over me," says Bob.

"Okay, granted. But even though this guy was busy, he wasn't helping to move toward the goal," I say.

"Well . . ."

"He wasn't, Bob! Look," I say. I point to the parts destined for the NCX-10. "We need those parts now, not tomorrow. The non-bottleneck parts we may not need for weeks, or even months —maybe never. So by continuing to run the non-bottleneck parts, this guy was actually interfering with our ability to get an order out the door and make money."

"But he didn't know any better," says Bob.

"Exactly. He couldn't distinguish between an important batch of parts and an unimportant one," I say. "Why not?"

"Nobody told him."

"Until you came along," I say. "But you can't be everywhere, and this same kind of thing is going to happen again. So how do we communicate to everybody in the plant which parts are important?"

"I guess we need some kind of system," says Bob.

"Fine. Let's go work on one right away so we don't have to keep putting up with this crap," I say. "And before we do anything else, let's make sure that people at both of the bottlenecks know to keep working on the order with the highest priority number on the list."

Bob has a final chat with Otto to make sure he knows what to do with the parts. Then the two of us head for the bottlenecks.

Finally we're walking back to the office. Glancing at Bob's face, I can tell he's still bothered by what happened.

"What's wrong? You look unconvinced about all this," I say.

"Al, what's going to happen if we repeatedly have people break up process runs to run parts for the bottlenecks?" he asks.

"We should be able to avoid idle time on the bottlenecks," I say.

"But what's going to happen to our costs on the other 98 percent of the work centers we got here?" he asks.

"Right now, don't worry about it. Let's just keep the bottlenecks busy," I say. "Look, I'm convinced you did the right thing back there. Aren't you?"

"Maybe I did the right thing," he says, "but I had to break all the rules to do it."

"Then the rules had to be broken," I say. "And maybe they weren't good rules to begin with. You know we've always had to break up process runs for expediency to get orders shipped. The difference between then and now is that now we know to do it ahead of time, before the external pressure comes. We've got to have faith in what we know."

Bob nods in agreement. But I know he'll only believe the proof. Maybe I'm the same, if I'm honest about it.

A few days pass while we develop a system to cure the problem. But at eight o'clock on Friday morning, at the beginning of first shift, I'm in the cafeteria watching the employees wander in. With me is Bob Donovan.

After our earlier misunderstanding, I decided that the more people who know about the bottlenecks and how important they are, the better off we'll be. We're holding fifteen-minute meetings with everyone working in the plant, both foremen and hourly people. This afternoon, we'll do the same thing with people working second shift, and I'll come in late tonight to talk to the third shift as well. When we've got everybody this morning, I get up in front of them and talk.

"All of you know that this plant has been in a downward slide for some time. What you don't know is that we're in the position to begin to change that," I tell them. "You're here in this meeting because we're introducing a new system today . . . a system which we think will make the plant more productive than it's been in the past. In the next few minutes, I'm going to explain briefly some of the background that made us develop this new system. And then Bob Donovan is going to tell you how it works."

Trying to keep meetings to fifteen minutes doesn't give us the time to tell them very much. But using the analogy of an hourglass, I do explain briefly about the bottlenecks and why we have to give priority to parts on the heat-treat and NCX-10 routings. For the things I can't take time to tell them, there is going to be a newsletter, which will replace the old plant employee paper, and which will report developments and progress in the plant.

Anyway, I turn over the microphone to Donovan and he tells them how we're going to prioritize all materials in the plant so everybody knows what to work on.

"By the end of today, all work-in-process on the floor will be marked by a tag with a number on it," he says and holds up some samples. "The tag will be one of two colors: red or green.

"A red marker means the work attached to it has first priority. The red tags go on any materials needing to be processed by a bottleneck. When a batch of parts with that color marker arrives at your work station, you are to work on them right away."

Bob explains what we mean by "right away." If the employee is working on a different job, it's okay to finish what he's doing, as long as it doesn't take more than half an hour. Before an hour has passed, certainly, the red-tagged parts should be getting attention.

"If you are in the middle of a setup, break the setup immediately and get ready for the red parts. When you've finished the bottleneck parts, you can go back to what you were doing before.

"The second color is green. When there is a choice between working on parts with a red marker and parts with a green marker, you work on the parts with the red marker first. So far, most of the work-in-process out there will be marked by green. Even so, you work on green orders only if you don't have any red ones in queue.

"That explains the priority of the colors. But what happens when you've got two batches of the same color? Each tag will have a number marked on it. You should always work on the materials with the lowest number."

Donovan explains some of the details and answers a couple of questions, after which I wrap it up.

I tell them, "This meeting was my idea. I decided to take you away from your jobs, mostly because I wanted everyone to hear the same message at the same time, so that—I hope—you'll have a better understanding of what's going on. But another reason is that I know it's been a long time since most of you have heard any good news about the plant. What you've just heard about is a beginning. Even so, the future of this plant and the security of your jobs will only be assured when we start making money again. The most important thing you can do is to work with us . . . and, together, we'll all be working to keep this plant working."

Late that afternoon, my phone rings.

"Hi, this is O'Donnell. Go ahead with the new policy on lunch and coffee breaks. We won't challenge it."

I relay the news to Donovan. And with these small victories, the week ends.

At 7:29 on Saturday evening, I park the washed, waxed, buffed and vacuumed Mazda in the Barnett driveway. I reach for the bouquet of flowers beside me on the seat, and step out onto the lawn wearing my new courting duds. At 7:30, I ring the doorbell.

Julie opens the door.

"Well, don't you look nice," she says.

"So do you," I tell her.

And she does.

There are a few stiff minutes spent talking with her parents. Mr. Barnett asks how everything is going at the plant. I tell him it looks like we may be on our way to a recovery, and mention the new priority system and what it will do for the NCX-10 and heat-treat. Both of her parents look at me blankly.

"Shall we go?" suggests Julie.

Joking, I tell Julie's mother, "I'll have her home by ten o'clock."

"Good," says Mrs. Barnett. "We'll be waiting."

22

"There you have it," says Ralph.

"Not bad," says Stacey.

"Not bad? It's a lot better than not bad," says Bob.

"We must be doing something right," says Stacey.

"Yeah, but it isn't enough," I mutter.

A week has passed. We're grouped around a computer terminal in the conference room. Ralph has extracted from the computer a list of overdue orders that we shipped last week.

"Isn't enough? At least it's progress," says Stacey. "We shipped twelve orders last week. For this plant, that's not bad. And they were our twelve most overdue orders."

"By the way, our worst overdue order is now only forty four days late," says Ralph. "As you may recall, the worst one used to be fifty eight days."

"All right!" says Donovan.

I step back to the table and sit down.

Their enthusiasm is somewhat justified. The new system of tagging all the batches according to priority and routing has been working fairly well. The bottlenecks are getting their parts promptly. In fact, the piles of inventory in front of them have grown. Following bottleneck processing, the red-tagged parts have been getting to final assembly faster. It's as if we've created an "express lane" through the plant for bottleneck parts.

After putting Q.C. in front of the bottlenecks, we discovered that about five percent of the parts going into the NCX-10 and about seven percent going into heat-treat did not conform to quality requirements. If those percentages hold true in the future, we'll effectively have gained that time for additional throughput.

The new policy of having people cover the bottlenecks on lunch breaks has also gone into effect. We're not sure how much we've gained from that, because we didn't know how much we were losing before. At least we're doing the right thing now. But I have heard reports that from time to time the NCX-10 is idle—and it happens when there is nobody on break. Donovan is supposed to be looking into the causes.

The combination of these has allowed us to ship our most critical orders and to ship a few more of them than normal. But I know we're not going fast enough. A few weeks ago we were limping along; now we're walking, but we ought to be jogging.

Glancing back toward the monitor, I see the eyes are upon me.

"Listen . . . I know we've taken a step in the right direction," I explain. "But we have to accelerate the progress. It's good that we got twelve shipments out last week. But we're still having some customer orders become past due. It's not as many, I'll grant you, but we still have to do better. We really shouldn't have *any* late orders."

Everyone walks away from the computer and joins me around the table. Bob Donovan starts telling me how they're planning some refinements on what we've already done.

I say, "Bob, those are fine, but they're minor. How are we coming on the other suggestions Jonah made?"

Bob glances away.

"Well . . . we're looking into them," he says.

I say, "I want recommendations on offloading the bottlenecks ready for our Wednesday staff meeting."

Bob nods, but says nothing.

"You'll have them for us?" I ask.

"Whatever it takes," he says.

That afternoon in my office, I have a meeting with Elroy Langston, our Q.C. manager, and Barbara Penn, who handles employee communications. Barbara writes the newsletters, which are now explaining the background and reasons for the changes taking place in the plant. Last week, we distributed the first issue. I put her together with Langston to have her work on a new project.

After parts exit the bottlenecks, they often tend to look almost identical to the parts going *into* the bottlenecks. Only a close examination by a trained eye will detect the difference in some cases. The problem is how to make it easy for the employee to tell the two apart . . . and to make it possible for the employee to treat the post-bottleneck parts so more of them make it to assembly and are shipped as quality products. Langston and Penn are in my office to talk about what they've come up with.

"We already have the red tags," says Penn. "So that tells us the part is on a bottleneck routing. What we need is a simple way to show people the parts they need to treat with special attention —the ones they need to treat like gold."

"That's a suitable comparison," I tell her.

She says, "So what if we simply mark the tags with pieces of yellow tape after the parts are finished by the bottlenecks. The tape would tell people on sight that these are the parts you treat like gold. In conjunction with this, I'll do an internal promotion to spread the word about what the tape means. For media, we might use some sort of bulletin board poster, an announcement that the foremen would read to the hourly people, maybe a banner which would hang in the plant—those kinds of things."

"As long as the tape can be added without slowing down the bottlenecks, that sounds fine," I say.

"I'm sure we can find a way to do it so it doesn't interfere," says Langston.

"Good," I say. "One other concern of mine is that I don't want this to be just a lot of promotion."

"That's perfectly understood," says Langston with a smile. "Right now, we're systematically identifying the causes of quality problems on the bottlenecks and in subsequent processing. Once we know where to aim, we'll be having specific procedures developed for bottleneck-routed parts and processes. And once they're established, we'll set up training sessions so people can learn those procedures. But that's obviously going to take some time. For the short term, we're specifying that the existing procedures be double-checked for accuracy on the bottleneck routes."

We talk that over for a few minutes, but basically all of it seems sound to me. I tell them to proceed full speed and to keep me informed of what's happening.

"Nice job," I say to both of them as they stand up to leave. "By the way, Roy, I thought Bob Donovan was going to sit in on this meeting."

"That man is hard to catch these days," says Langston. "But I'll brief him on what we talked about."

Just then, the phone rings. Reaching with one hand to answer it, I wave to Langston and Penn with the other as they walk out the door.

"Hi, this is Donovan."

"It's too late to call in sick," I tell him. "Don't you know you just missed a meeting?"

THE GOAL

That doesn't faze him.

"Al, have I got something to show you!" says Bob. "Got time to take a little walk?"

"Yeah, I guess so. What's this all about?"

"Well . . . I'll tell you when you get here," says Bob. "Meet me on the receiving dock."

I walk down to the dock, where I see Bob; he's standing there waving to me as if I might miss him. Which would be impossible. There is a flat-bed truck backed up to the dock, and in the middle of the bed is a large object on a skid. The object is covered by a gray canvas tarp which has ropes tying it down. A couple of guys are working with an overhead crane to move the thing off of the truck. They're raising it into the air as I walk up to Bob. He cups his hands around his mouth.

"Easy there," Bob calls as he watches the big gray thing sway back and forth.

Slowly, the crane maneuvers the cargo back from the truck and lowers it safely to the concrete floor. The workers release the hoist chains. Bob walks over and has them untie the ropes holding down the canvas.

"We'll have it off in a minute," Bob assures me.

I stand there patiently, but Bob can't refrain from helping. When all the ropes are untied, Donovan takes hold of the tarp and, with a flair of gusto, flings it off of what it's concealing.

"Ta-da!" he says as he stands back and gestures to what has to be one of the oldest pieces of equipment I've ever seen.

"What the hell is it?" I ask.

"It's a Zmegma," he says.

He takes a rag and wipes off some of the grime.

"They don't build 'em like this anymore," he says.

"I'm very glad to hear that," I say.

"Al," he says, "the Zmegma is just the machine we need!"

"That looks like it might have been state-of-the-art for 1942. How's it going to help us?"

"Well . . . I admit it ain't no match for the NCX-10. But if you take this baby right here," he says patting the Zmegma, "and one of those Screwmeisters over there," he says pointing across the way, "and that other machine off in the corner, together they can do all the things the NCX-10 can do."

I glance around at the different machines. All of them are old and idle. I step closer to the Zmegma to look it over.

"So this must be one of the machines you told Jonah we sold to make way for the inventory holding pen," I say.

"You got it," he says.

"It's practically an antique. All of them are," I say, referring to the other machines. "Are you sure they can give us acceptable quality?"

"It isn't automated equipment, so with human error we might have a few more mistakes," says Bob. "But if you want capacity, this is a quick way to get it."

I smile. "It's looking better and better. Where did you find this thing?"

"I called a buddy of mine this morning up at our South End plant," he says. "He told me he still had a couple of these sitting around and he'd have no problem parting with one of them. So I grabbed a guy from maintenance and we took a ride up to have a look."

I ask him, "What did it cost us?"

"The rental fee on the truck to haul it down here," says Bob. "The guy at South End told us just to go ahead and take it. He'll write it off as scrap. With all the paperwork he'd have to do, it was too much trouble to sell it to us."

"Does it still work?"

"It did before we left," says Bob. "Let's find out."

The maintenance man connects the power cable to an outlet on a nearby steel column. Bob reaches for the power switch and hits the ON button. For a second, nothing happens. Then we hear the slow, gathering whirr from somewhere in the guts of the old machine. Poofs of dust blow out of the antique fan housing. Bob turns to me with a dumb grin on his big face.

"Guess we're in business," he says.

23

Rain is beating at the windows of my office. Outside, the world is gray and blurred. It's the middle of a middle-of-the-week morning. In front of me are some so-called "Productivity Bulletins" put out by Hilton Smyth which I've come across in my in-basket. I haven't been able to make myself read past the first paragraph of the one on top. Instead, I'm gazing at the rain and pondering the situation with my wife.

Julie and I went out on our "date" that Saturday night, and we actually had a good time. It was nothing exotic. We went to a movie, we got a bite to eat afterwards, and for the heck of it we took a drive through the park on the way home. Very tame. But it was exactly what we needed. It was good just to *relax* with her. I admit that at first I felt kind of like we were back in high school or something. But, after a while, I decided that wasn't such a bad feeling. I brought her back to her parents at two in the morning, and we made out in the driveway until her old man turned on the porch light.

Since that night, we've continued to see each other. A couple of times last week, I made the drive up to see her. Once, we met halfway at a restaurant. I've been dragging myself to work in the morning, but with no complaints. We've had fun together.

By some unspoken agreement, neither of us talk about divorce or marriage. The subject has only come up once, which happened when we talked about the kids and agreed they should stay with Julie and her folks as soon as school ends. I tried then to push us into some answers, but the old argument syndrome began to brew quickly, and I backed off to preserve the peace.

It's a strange state of limbo we're in. It almost feels the way it did before we got married and "settled down." Only now, we're both quite familiar to each other. And there is this storm which has gone south for a while, but which is sure to swing back someday.

A soft tap at the door interrupts this meditation. I see Fran's face peeking around the edge of the door.

"Ted Spencer is outside," she says. "He says he needs to talk to you about something."

"What about?"

Fran steps into the office and closes the door behind her. She quickly comes over to my desk and whispers to me.

"I don't know, but I heard on the grapevine that he had an argument with Ralph Nakamura about an hour ago," she says.

"Oh," I say. "Okay, thanks for the warning. Send him in."

A moment later Ted Spencer comes in. He looks mad. I ask him what's happening down in heat-treat.

He says, "Al, you've got to get that computer guy off my back."

"You mean Ralph? What have you got against him?"

"He's trying to turn me into some kind of clerk or something," says Ted. "He's been coming around and asking all kinds of dumb questions. Now he wants me to keep some kind of special records on what happens in heat-treat."

"What kind of records?" I ask.

"I don't know . . . he wants me to keep a detailed log of everything that goes in and out of the furnaces . . . the times we put 'em in, the times we take 'em out, how much time between heats, all that stuff," says Ted. "And I've got too much to do to be bothered with all that. In addition to heat-treat, I've got three other work centers I'm responsible for."

"Why does he want this time log?" I ask.

"How should I know? I mean, we've already got enough paperwork to satisfy anybody, as far as I'm concerned," says Ted. "I think Ralph just wants to play games with numbers. If he's got the time for it, then fine, let him do it in his own department. I've got the productivity of *my* department to worry about."

Wanting to end this, I nod to him. "Okay, I hear you. Let me look into it."

"Will you keep him out of my area?" asks Ted.

"I'll let you know, Ted."

After he's gone, I have Fran track down Ralph Nakamura for me. What's puzzling me is that Ralph is not what you'd call an abrasive person, and yet he sure seems to have made Ted very upset.

"You wanted to see me?" asks Ralph from the door.

"Yeah, come on in and sit down," I say to him.

He seats himself in front of my desk.

"So tell me what you did to light Ted Spencer's fuse," I say to him.

Ralph rolls his eyes and says, "All I wanted from him was to keep an accurate record of the actual times for each heat of parts in the furnace. I thought it was a simple enough request."

"What prompted you to ask him?"

"I had a couple of reasons," says Ralph. "One of them is that the data we have on heat-treat seems to be very inaccurate. And if what you say is true, that this operation is so vital to the plant, then it seems to me we ought to have valid statistics on it."

"What makes you think our data is so inaccurate?" I ask.

"Because after I saw the total on last week's shipments I was kind of bothered by something. A few days ago on my own, I did some projections of how many shipments we would actually be able to make last week based on the output of parts from the bottlenecks. According to those projections, we should have been able to do about eighteen to twenty shipments instead of twelve. The projections were so far off that I figured at first I must have made a big mistake. So I took a closer look, double-checked my math and couldn't find anything wrong. Then I saw that the estimates for the NCX-10 were within the ballpark. But for heat-treat, there was a big difference."

"And that's what made you think that the data base must be in error," I say.

"Right," he says. "So I went down to talk to Spencer. And, ah. . . ."

"And what?"

"Well, I noticed some funny things were happening," he says. "He was kind of tight-lipped when I started asking him questions. Finally, I just happened to ask him when the parts that were being treated in the furnace at the moment were going to be finished. I thought I'd get a time on an actual heat by myself, just to see if we were close to the standard. He said the parts could come out at around 3 P.M. So I went away, and came back at three. But nobody was around. I waited for about ten minutes, then went to look for Ted. When I found him, he said he had the furnace helpers working somewhere else and they'd get around to unloading the furnace in a little while. I didn't think much about it. Then around 5:30, as I was leaving for the day, I decided I'd go by the furnace to ask what time the parts had actually come out. But the same parts were still in there."

"Two-and-a-half hours after they *could* have come out, they hadn't been unloaded?" I ask.

"That's right," says Ralph. "So I found Sammy, the second-shift foreman down there, and asked him what was going on. He told me he was short-handed that night, and they'd get to it later. He said it didn't hurt the parts to stay in the furnace. While I was there, he shut off the burners, but I found out later that the parts didn't come out until about eight o'clock. I didn't mean to start trouble, but I'd thought if we recorded the actual times per heat, we'd at least have some realistic figures to use for estimating. You see, I asked some of the hourly people down there and they told me those kinds of delays happen a lot in heat-treat."

"No kidding," I say. "Ralph . . . I want you to take all the measurements down there that you need. Don't worry about Ted. And do the same thing on the NCX-10."

"Well, I'd like to, but it's kind of a chore," he says. "That's why I wanted Ted and the others just to jot down the times and all."

I say, "Okay, we'll take care of that. And, ah . . . thanks very much."

"You're welcome," he says.

"By the way, what was the other reason?" I ask him. "You mentioned you had more than one."

"Oh, well, it's probably not that important."

"No, tell me," I say.

"I don't really know if we can do it or not," says Ralph, "but it occurred to me we might find a way to use the bottlenecks to predict when we'll be able to ship an order."

I contemplate that possibility.

"Sounds interesting," I tell him. "Let me know what you come up with."

Bob Donovan's ears are on fire by the time I've finished telling him what Ralph discovered about heat-treat on his own. I'm very upset about this. He's sitting in a chair in my office while I walk in circles in front of him.

But when I'm done, Bob tells me, "Al, the trouble is there is nothing for the guys down there to do while heat-treat is cookin' the parts. You load up one of the damn furnaces, shut the doors, and that's it for six or eight hours, or however long it takes. What are they supposed to do? Stand around and twiddle their thumbs?"

"I don't care what they do between times as long as they get the parts in and out of the furnace pronto," I say. "We could have done almost another batch of parts in the five hours of waiting for people to finish what they were doing elsewhere and change loads."

"All right," says Bob. "How about this: we loan the people to other areas while the parts cook, but as soon as the time is up, we make sure we call them back immediately so—"

"No, because what's going to happen is everybody will be very conscientious about it for two days, and then it'll slip back to the way it is now," I say. "I want people at those furnaces standing by, ready to load and unload twenty-four hours a day, seven days a week. The first ones I want assigned there are foremen who are responsible full-time for what happens down there. And tell Ted Spencer that the next time I see him, he'd better know what's going on in heat-treat or I'll kick his ass."

"You bet," says Bob. "But you know you're talking about two, maybe three people per shift."

"Is that all?" I ask. "Don't you remember what lost time on a bottleneck costs us?"

"Okay, I'm with you," he says. "Tell you the truth, what Ralph found out about heat-treat is a lot like what I found out on my own about those rumors of idle time on the NCX-10."

"What's going on there?"

Bob tells me that, indeed, it's true the NCX-10 is sitting idle for as much as half an hour or more at a time. But the problem is not lunch breaks. If the NCX-10 is being set up and lunch time rolls around, the two guys stay until the setup is completed. Or, if the setup is a long one, they spell each other, so one goes and eats while the other continues with the setup. We're covered fine during breaks. But if the machine stops, say, in the middle of the afternoon, it may sit there for twenty, thirty, forty minutes or so before anyone gets around to starting a new setup. The reason is the setup people are busy with *other* machines, with non-bottle-necks.

"Then let's do the same thing on the NCX-10 as I want to do on heat-treat," I tell Bob. "Let's get a machinist and a helper and have them permanently stationed at the NCX-10. When it stops, they can get to work on it immediately."

"That's just dandy with me," says Bob. "But you know how it's going to look on paper. It's going to seem like we increased the direct labor content of the parts coming out of heat-treat and the NCX-10."

I slump into the chair behind my desk.

"Let's fight one battle at a time," I say.

The next morning, Bob comes to the staff meeting with his recommendations. They basically consist of four actions. The first two concern what he and I talked about the day before—dedicating a machinist and helper to the NCX-10, and stationing a foreman and two workers at the heat-treat furnaces. The assignments would apply to all three shifts. The other two recommendations concern offloading the bottlenecks. Bob has determined if we could activate one each of these old machines—the Zmegma and the two others—just one shift a day, we could add eighteen percent to the output of parts of the type produced by the NCX-10. Last of all, is that we take some of the parts queued at heat-treat and send them out to the vendor across town.

As he's presenting these, I'm wondering what Lou is going to say. As it happens, Lou offers little resistance.

"Knowing what we know now," says Lou, "it's perfectly legitimate for us to assign people to the bottlenecks if it will increase our throughput. We can certainly justify the cost if it increases sales—and thereby increases cash flow. My question is, where are you going to get the people?"

Bob says we could call them back from layoff.

"No, you can't. See, the problem we have," says Lou, "is that the division has a recall freeze in effect. We can't recall without their approval."

"Do we have people in the plant who can do these jobs?" asks Stacey.

"You mean steal people from other areas?" asks Bob.

"Sure," I say. "Take people from the non-bottlenecks. By definition, they have excess capacity anyway."

Bob thinks about it for a minute. Then he explains that finding helpers for heat-treat is no big deal. And we do have some old machinists, who haven't been laid off because of seniority, who are qualified to run the Zmegma and the other two machines. Establishing a two-person set-up crew on the NCX-10, however, has him worried.

"Who's going to set up the other machines?" he asks.

"The helpers on the other machines know enough to set up their own equipment," I say.

"Well, I guess we can try it," says Bob. "But what happens if stealing people turns non-bottlenecks into bottlenecks?"

I tell him, "The important thing is to maintain the flow. If we take a worker away, and we can't maintain the flow, then we'll put the worker back and steal a body from someplace else. And if we still can't keep the flow going, then we'll have no choice but to go to a division and insist that we either go to overtime or call a few people back from layoff."

"Okay," says Bob. "I'll go for it."

Lou gives us his blessing.

"Good. Let's do it," I say. "And, Bob, make sure the people you pick are good. From now on, we put only our best people to work on the bottlenecks."

And so it is done.

The NCX-10 gets a dedicated setup crew. The Zmegma and the other machines go to work. The outfit across town is only too glad to take our surplus parts for heat-treating. And in our own heat-treat department, two people per shift are assigned to stand by, ready to load and unload parts from the furnaces. Donovan juggles the work-center responsibilities so heat-treat has a foreman there at all times.

For a foreman, heat-treat seems like a very small kingdom, not much of a prize. There is nothing intrinsically attractive about running that operation, and having only two people to manage makes it seem like no big deal. To prevent it from seeming like a demotion to them, I make a point to go down there periodically on each of the shifts. In talking to the foreman, I drop some rather direct hints that the rewards will be great for anyone who can improve the output of heat-treated parts.

Shortly thereafter, some amazing things happen. Very early one morning, I'm down there at the end of third shift. A young guy named Mike Haley is the foreman. He's a big black man whose arms always look as though they're going to burst the sleeves on his shirts. We've noticed that over the past week he's pushed about ten percent more parts through heat-treat on his shift than the others have. Records are not usually set on third shift, and we're starting to wonder if it's Mike's biceps that are doing the trick. Anyway, I go down there to try to learn what he's doing.

As I walk up, I see the two helpers are not just standing around with nothing to do. They're moving parts. In front of the furnaces are two tightly organized stacks of work-in-process, which the helpers are building. I call Mike over and ask him what they're doing.

"They're getting ready," he says.

"What do you mean?"

"They're getting ready for when we have to load one of the furnaces again," he says. "The parts in each stack are all treated at the same temperature."

"So you're splitting and overlapping some batches," I say.

"Sure," he says. "I know we're not really supposed to do that, but you need the parts, right?"

"Sure, no problem. You're still doing the treating according to the priority system?" I ask.

"Oh, yeah," he says. "Come here. Let me show you."

Mike leads me past the control console for the furnaces to a worn old battleship of a desk. He finds the computer print-out for the week's most important overdue orders.

"See, look at number 22," he says pointing to it. "We need fifty of the high stress RB-dash-11's. They get treated at a 1200–degree temperature cycle. But fifty of them won't fill up the furnace. So we look down and what do we see here but item number 31, which calls for 300 fitted retaining rings. Those also take a 1200–degree cycle."

"So you'll fill up the furnace with as many of the retaining rings after you've loaded the fifty of the first item," I say.

"Yeah, that's it," says Mike. "Only we do the sorting and stacking in advance so we can load the furnace faster."

"That's good thinking," I tell him.

"Well, we could do even better if I could get someone to listen to an idea I got," he says.

"What do you have in mind?"

"Well, right now, it takes anywhere up to an hour or so to change a furnace load using the crane or doing it by hand. We could cut that down to a couple of minutes if we had a better system." He points to the furnaces. "Each one of those has a table which the parts sit on. They slide in and out on rollers. If we could get some steel plate and maybe a little help from engineering, we could make those tables interchangeable. That way we could stack a load of parts in advance and switch loads with the use of a forklift. If it saves us a couple of hours a day, that means we can do an extra heat of parts over the course of a week."

I look from the furnaces back to Mike. I say, "Mike, I want you to take tomorrow night off. We'll get one of the other foremen to cover for you."

"Sounds good to me," he says with a grin. "How come?"

"Because the day after tomorrow, I want you on day turn. I'm going to have Bob Donovan put you together with an I.E. to write up these procedures formally, so we can start using them round the clock," I tell him. "You keep that mind of yours working. We need it."

Later that morning, Donovan happens by my office.

"Hi, there," he says.

"Well, hello," I tell him. "Did you get my note on Haley?"

"It's being taken care of," says Bob.

"Good. And let's make sure he gets some more money out of this whenever the wage freeze is lifted," I say.

"Okay," says Bob as a smile spreads across his face. Then he leans against the doorway.

"Something else?" I ask.

"Got good news for you," says Bob.

"How good?"

"Remember when Jonah asked us if all the parts going through heat-treat really needed it?"

I tell him I remember.

"I just found out that in three cases, it wasn't engineering that specified heat-treat. It was us," says Bob.

"What do you mean?"

He explains that about five years ago some group of hot-shots were trying to improve the efficiencies of several of the machining centers. To speed up the processing, the cutting tool "bite" was increased. So on each pass, instead of shaving a chip that was a millimeter thick, the tool took off three millimeters. But increasing the amount of metal taken off on each pass made the metal brittle. And this necessitated heat-treating.

"The thing is, the machines we made more efficient happen to be non-bottlenecks," says Bob. "We have enough capacity on them to slow down and still meet demand. And if we go back to the slower processing, we don't need the heat-treat. Which means we can take about twenty percent of the current load off the furnaces."

"Sounds fantastic," I tell him. "What about getting it approved by engineering?"

"That's the beauty of it," says Bob. "*We* were the ones who initiated the change five years ago."

"So if it was our option to begin with," I say, "we can change it back any time we want."

"Right! We don't need to get an engineering change order, because we already have an approved procedure on the books," says Bob.

He leaves shortly with my blessing to implement the change as soon as possible. I sit there marveling that we're going to *reduce* the efficiency of some operations and make the entire plant more productive. They'd never believe it on the fifteenth floor.

24

It's a Friday afternoon. Out in the parking lot, the people on first shift are getting into their cars to go home. There is the usual congestion at the gate. I'm in my office—minding my own business—when suddenly, from through the half-open door . . . BAM!

Something ricochets off the ceiling tiles. I jump to my feet, check myself for wounds and, finding none, search the carpet for the offending missile. It's a champagne cork.

There is laughing outside my door. In the next instant, it seems as though everyone is in my office. There is Stacey, Bob Donovan (who holds the bottle from which the cork came), Ralph, Fran, a couple of the secretaries, and a swarm of other people—even Lou joins us. Fran hands me one of the styrofoam coffee cups she's dispensing to everyone. Bob fills it from the bottle.

"What's this all about?" I ask.

"I'll tell you in the toast I'm going to make as soon as everyone has something to swallow," says Bob.

More bottles are opened—there is a case of this stuff—and when all the cups are filled, Bob lifts his own.

"Here's to a new plant record in shipments of product," he says. "Lou went through the records for us and discovered that until now the best this place has ever done in a month was thirty-one orders shipped at value of about two million dollars. This month we topped that. We shipped fifty-seven customer orders with a value of . . . well, in round numbers, we'll call it a cool three million."

"Not only did we ship more product," says Stacey, "but, having just calculated our inventory levels, I am pleased to report that between last month and now, we've had a twelve percent net decline in work-in-process inventory."

"Well, then, let's drink to making money!" I say.

And we do.

"Mmmmm . . . industrial strength champagne," says Stacey.

"Very distinctive," says Ralph to Bob. "Did you pick this out yourself?"

"Keep drinking. It gets better," says Donovan.

I'm just about to hazard a second cup when I notice Fran beside me.

"Mr. Rogo?"

"Yes."

"Bill Peach is on the line," says Fran.

I shake my head wondering what the hell it's going to be this time.

"I'll take it at your desk, Fran."

I go out there and punch the blinking button on my phone and pick it up.

"Yes, Bill, what can I do for you?"

"I was just talking to Johnny Jons," says Peach.

I automatically grab a pencil and pull over a pad of paper to take down the particulars on whatever order is causing us grief. I wait for Peach to continue, but he doesn't say anything for a second.

"What's the problem?" I ask him.

"No problem," says Peach. "Actually he was very happy."

"Really? What about?"

"He mentioned you've been coming through lately for him on a lot of late customer orders," says Peach. "Some kind of special effort I guess."

"Well, yes and no. We're doing a few things a little differently now," I say.

"Well, whatever. The reason I called is I know how I'm always on your case when things go wrong, Al, so I just wanted to tell you thanks from me and Jons for doing something right," says Peach.

"Thanks, Bill," I tell him. "Thanks for calling."

"Thankyouthankyouthankyouthankyouthankyou," I'm blithering to Stacey as she parks her car in my driveway. "You are a truly wonderful person for driving me home . . . and I truly meant that truly."

"Don't mention it," she says. "I'm glad we had something to celebrate."

She shuts off the engine. I look up at my house, which is dark except for one light. I had the good sense earlier to call my mother and tell her not to hold dinner for me. That was smart because the celebration continued onward and outward after

Peach's call. About half of the original group went to dinner together. Lou and Ralph threw in the towel early. But Donovan, Stacey and I—along with three or four die-hards—went to a bar after we ate and we had a good time. Now it is 1:30 and I am blissfully stinko.

The Mazda for safety's sake, it still parked behind the bar. Stacey, who switched to club soda a couple of hours ago, has generously played chauffeur to Bob and me. About ten minutes ago, we nudged Donovan through his kitchen door where he stood there bewildered for a moment before bidding us a good evening. If he remembers, Donovan is supposed to enlist his wife later today to drive us over to the bar and retrieve our vehicles.

Stacey gets out of the car and comes around and opens my door so I can spill myself onto the driveway. Standing up on uncertain legs, I steady myself against the car.

"I've never seen you smile so much," says Stacey.

"I've got a lot to smile about," I tell her.

"Wish you could be this happy in staff meetings," she says.

"Henceforth, I shall smile continuously through all staff meetings," I proclaim.

"Come on, I'll make sure you get to the door," she says.

With her hands around my arm to steady me, she guides me up the front walk to the door.

When we're at the door, I ask her, "How about some coffee?"

"No, thanks," she says. "It's late and I'd better get home."

"Sure?"

"Absolutely."

I fumble with the keys, find the lock, and the door swings open to a dark living room. I turn to Stacey and extend my hand.

"Thank you for a wonderful evening," I tell her. "I had a swell time."

Then as we're shaking hands, I for some reason step backwards, trip over the doorstep and lose all my balance.

"Woops!"

The next thing I know Stacey and I are sprawled on the floor together. Fortunately—or maybe not as it turns out—Stacey thinks this is colossally funny. She's laughing so hard, tears start to roll down her cheeks. And so I start laughing too. Both of us are rolling on the floor with laughter—when the lights come on.

"You bastard!"

I look up, my eyes adjusting to the sudden light, and there she is.

"Julie? What are you doing here?"

Without answering, she's now stomping through the kitchen. As I get to my feet and stagger after her, the door to the garage opens. The light switch in the garage clicks. I see her in silhouette for half a second.

"Julie! Wait a minute!"

I hear the garage door rumbling open as I attempt to follow her. As I go into the garage, she's already getting into her car. The door slams. I zig-zag closer, wildly waving my arms. The engine starts.

"I sit here waiting for you all night, putting up with your mother for six hours," she yells through the rolled-down window, "and you come home drunk with some floozy!"

"But Stacey isn't a floozy, she's—"

Accelerating to about thirty miles per hours in reverse, Julie backs out of the garage, down the driveway (narrowly missing Stacey's car) and into the street. I'm left standing there in the light of the garage. The tires of her car chirp upon the asphalt.

She's gone.

On Saturday morning, I wake up and groan a couple of times. The first groan is from the hangover. The second groan is from the memory of what happened.

When I'm able, I get dressed and venture into the kitchen in quest of coffee. My mother is there.

"You know your wife was here last night," says my mother as I pour my first cup.

So then I find out what happened. Julie showed up just after I called here last night. She had driven over on impulse, because she had missed me and she had wanted to see the kids. She apparently wanted to surprise me, which she did.

Later, I call the Barnett's number. Ada gives me the routine of "She doesn't want to talk to you anymore."

When I get to the plant on Monday, Fran tells me Stacey has been looking for me since she arrived this morning. I have just settled in behind my desk when Stacey appears at the door.

"Hi. Can we talk?" she asks.

"Sure. Come on in," I say.

She seems disturbed about something. She's avoiding my eyes as she sits down.

I say, "Listen, about Friday night, I'm sorry about what happened when you dropped me off."

Stacey says, "It's okay. Did your wife come back?"

"Uh, well, no, she didn't. She's staying with her parents for a little while," I say.

"Was it just because of me?" she asks.

"No, we've been having some problems lately."

"Al, I still feel kind of responsible," she says. "Look, why don't I talk to her."

"No, you don't have to do that," I say.

"Really, I think I ought to talk to her," says Stacey. "What's her number?"

I finally admit to myself it might be worth a try. So I give the Barnett's number to Stacey. She writes it down, and promises to call sometime today. Then she continues to sit there.

"Was there something else?" I ask.

"I'm afraid there is," she says.

She pauses.

"So what is it?"

"I don't think you're going to like this," she says. "But I'm pretty sure about it . . ."

"Stacey," I say. *"What?"*

"The bottlenecks have spread."

"What do you mean 'the bottlenecks have spread'?" I ask. "Is there a disease out there or something?"

"No, what I mean is we have a new bottleneck—or maybe even more than one; I'm not sure yet. Here, let me show you," she says as she comes around the side of the desk with some computer print-outs she's brought. "These are listings of parts that are queued up at final assembly."

She goes over the lists with me. As always, the bottleneck parts are still in short supply. But lately there have been shortages of some *non*-bottleneck parts as well.

She says, "Last week we had a case in which we had to build an order for 200 DBD-50's. Out of 172 different parts, we were missing 17. Only one of them was a red-tagged part. The rest were green tags. The red part came out of heat-treat on Thursday and was ready by Friday morning. But the others are still missing."

I lean back in my chair and pinch the bridge of my nose.

"Dammit, what the hell is going on out there? I had assumed the parts that have to go through a bottleneck would reach assembly last. Is there a materials shortage on those green-tagged parts? Some kind of vendor problem?" I ask her.

Stacey shakes her head. "No, I haven't had any problems with purchasing. And none of the parts have any processing by outside contractors. The problem is definitely internal. That's why I really think we have one or more new bottlenecks."

I get up from my desk, walk around the office.

"Maybe with the increase in throughput, we've loaded the plant to a level that we've run out of capacity on some other resources in addition to heat-treat and the NCX-10," Stacey suggests quietly.

I nod. Yes, that sounds like a possibility. With the bottlenecks more productive now, our throughput has gone up and our backlog is declining. But making the bottlenecks more productive has put more demand on the other work centers. If the demand on another work center has gone above one hundred percent, then we've created a *new* bottleneck.

Of the ceiling, I ask, "Does this mean we're going to have to go through the whole process of finding the bottlenecks all over again? Just when it seemed like we were on our way out of this mess. . . ."

Stacey folds the print-outs.

I tell her, "Okay, look, I want you to find out everything you can—exactly which parts, how many, what products are affected, which routings they're on, how often they're missing, all that stuff. Meanwhile, I'm going to try to get hold of Jonah to see what he has to say about all this."

After Stacey leaves, and Fran does the calling to locate Jonah, I stand by the window in my office and stare at the lawn while I think. I took it as a good sign that inventory levels had declined after we implemented the new measures to make the bottlenecks more productive. A month ago we were *wading* through parts on the non-bottleneck routings. There were piles and piles, and the piles kept growing. But some of the stocks have dwindled over the past couple of weeks of product assembly. Last week, for the first time since I've been at this plant, you could actually walk over to the assembly line without having to turn sideways to squeeze between the stacks and bins of inventory. I thought it was good. But now this happens.

"Mr. Rogo," says Fran through the intercom speaker. "I've got him on the line."

I pick up the phone. "Jonah? Hi. Listen, we've got trouble here."

"What's wrong?" he asks.

After I tell him the symptoms, Jonah asks what we've done since his visit. So I relate all the history to him—putting Q.C. in front of the bottlenecks, training people to give special care to bottleneck parts, activating the three machines to supplement the NCX-10, the new lunch rules, assigning certain people to work only at the bottlenecks, increasing the batch sizes going into heat-treat, implementing the new priority system in the plant. . . .

"New priority system?" asks Jonah.

"Right," I say, and then I explain about the red tags and green tags, and how the system works.

Jonah says, "Maybe I'd better come have another look."

I'm at home that night when the phone rings.

"Hi," says Julie's voice when I answer.

"Hi."

"I owe you an apology. I'm sorry about what happened on Friday night," she says. "Stacey called me here. Al, I'm really embarrassed. I completely misunderstood."

"Yeah, well . . . it seems to me there's a lot of misunderstanding between us lately," I say.

"All I can say is I'm sorry. I drove down thinking you'd be glad to see me."

"I would have been if you'd stayed," I say. "In fact, if I'd known you were coming, I would have come home after work."

"I know I should have called," she says, "but I was just in one of those moods."

"I guess you shouldn't have waited for me," I tell her.

She says, "I just kept thinking you'd be home any minute. And the whole time, your mother kept giving me the evil eye. Finally she and the kids went to bed, and about an hour later I fell asleep on the sofa and slept until you came in."

"Well . . . you want to be friends again?"

I can hear her relief.

"Yes, I would," she says. "When will I see you?"

I suggest we try Friday all over again. She says she can't wait that long. We compromise on Wednesday.

25

Déjà vu. At the airport next morning, I again greet Jonah as he walks out of Gate Two.

By ten o'clock, we're in the conference room at the plant. Sitting around the table are Lou, Bob, Ralph and Stacey. Jonah paces in front of us.

"Let's start with some basic questions," he says. "First of all, have you determined exactly which parts are giving you the problem?"

Stacey, who is sitting at the table with a veritable fortress of paper around her and looking as if she's ready for a siege, holds up a list.

She says, "Yes, we've identified them. In fact, I spent last night tracking them down and double checking the data with what's on the floor out there. Turns out the problem covers thirty parts."

Jonah asks, "Are you sure you released the materials for them?"

"Oh, yes," says Stacey. "No problem there. They've been released according to schedule. But they're not reaching final assembly. They're stuck in front of our new bottleneck."

"Wait a minute. How do you *know* it's really a bottleneck?" asks Jonah.

She says, "Well, since the parts are held up, I just figured it had to be . . ."

"Before we jump to conclusions, let's invest half an hour to go into the plant so we can find out what's happening," Jonah says.

So we parade into the plant, and a few minutes later we're standing in front of a group of milling machines. Off to one side are big stacks of inventory marked with green tags. Stacey stands there and points out the parts that are needed in final assembly. Most of the missing parts are right here and all bear green tags. Bob calls over the foreman, a hefty guy by the name of Jake, and introduces him to Jonah.

"Yeah, all them parts been sittin' here for about two, three weeks or more," says Jake.

"But we need them now," I say. "How come they're not being worked on?"

Jake shrugs his shoulders. "You know which ones you want, we'll do 'em right now. But that goes against them rules you set up in that there priority system."

He points to some other skids of materials nearby.

"You see over there?" says Jake. "They all got red tags. We got to do all of 'em before we touch the stuff with green tags. That's what you told us, right?"

Uh-huh. It's becoming clear what's been happening.

"You mean," says Stacey, "that while the materials with green tags have been building up, you've been spending all your time on the parts bound for the bottlenecks."

"Yeah, well, most of it," says Jake. "Hey, like we only got so many hours in a day, you know what I mean?"

"How much of your work is on bottleneck parts?" asks Jonah.

"Maybe seventy-five or eighty percent," says Jake. "See, everything that goes to heat-treat or the NCX-10 has to pass through here first. As long as the red parts keep coming—and they haven't let up one bit since that new system started—we just don't have the time to work on very many of the green-tag parts."

There is a moment of silence. I look from the parts to the machines and back to Jake again.

"What the hell do we do now?" asks Donovan in echo to my own thoughts. "Do we switch tags? Make the missing parts red instead of green?"

I throw up my hands in frustration and say, "I guess the only solution is to expedite."

"No, actually, that is not the solution at all," Jonah says, "because if you resort to expediting now, you'll have to expedite all the time, and the situation will only get worse."

"But what else can we do?" asks Stacey.

Jonah says, "First, I want us to go look at the bottlenecks, because there is another aspect to the problem."

Before we can see the NCX-10, we see the inventory. It's stacked as high as the biggest forklift can reach. It's not just a mountain, but a mountain with many peaks. The piles here are even bigger than before we identified the machine as a bottleneck. And tied to every bin, hanging from every pallet of parts is a red tag. Somewhere behind it all, its own hugeness obscured from our view, is the NCX-10.

"How do we get there from here?" asks Ralph, looking for a path through the inventory.

"Here, let me show you," says Bob.

And he leads us through the maze of materials until we reach the machine.

Gazing at all the work-in-process around us, Jonah says to us, "You know, I would guess, just from looking at it, that you have at least a month or more of work lined-up here for this machine. And I bet if we went to heat-treat we would find the same situation. Tell me, do you know why you have such a huge pile of inventory here?"

"Because everyone ahead of this machine is giving first priority to red parts," I suggest.

"Yes, that's part of the reason," says Jonah. "But why is so much inventory coming through the plant to get stuck here?"

Nobody answers.

"Okay, I see I'm going to have to explain some of the basic relationships between bottlenecks and non-bottlenecks," says Jonah. Then he looks at me and says, "By the way, do you remember when I told you that a plant in which everyone is working all the time is very *in* efficient? Now you'll see exactly what I was talking about."

Jonah walks over to the nearby Q.C. station and takes a piece of chalk the inspectors use to mark defects on the parts they reject. He kneels down to the concrete floor and points to the NCX-10.

"Here is your bottleneck," he says, "the X-what-ever-it-is machine. We'll simply call it 'X.' "

He writes an X on the floor. Then he gestures to the other machines back down the aisle.

"And feeding parts to X are various non-bottleneck machines and workers," he says. "Because we designated the bottleneck as X, we'll refer to these non-bottlenecks as 'Y' resources. Now, for the sake of simplicity, let's just consider one non-bottleneck in combination with one bottleneck . . ."

With the chalk, he writes on the floor:

$$Y \longrightarrow X$$

Product parts are what join the two in a relationship with each other, Jonah explains, and the arrow obviously indicates the flow of parts from one to the other. He adds that we can consider *any* non-bottleneck feeding parts to X, because no matter which one we choose, its inventory must be processed at some subsequent point in time by X.

"By the definition of a non-bottleneck, we know that Y has extra capacity. Because of its extra capacity, we also know that Y will be faster in filling the demand than X," says Jonah. "Let's say both X and Y have 600 hours a month available for production. Because it is a bottleneck, you will need all 600 hours of the X machine to meet demand. But let's say you need only 450 hours a month, or 75 percent, of Y to keep the flow equal to demand. What happens when Y has worked its 450 hours? Do you let it sit idle?"

Bob says, "No, we'll find something else for it to do."

"But Y has already satisfied market demand," says Jonah.

Bob says, "Well, then we let it get a head start on next month's work."

"And if there is nothing for it to work on?" asks Jonah.

Bob says, "Then we'll have to release more materials."

"And *that* is the problem," says Jonah. "Because what happens to those extra hours of production from Y? Well, that inventory has to go somewhere. Y is faster than X. And by keeping Y active, the flow of parts to X must be greater than the flow of parts leaving X. Which means . . ."

He walks over to the work-in-process mountain and makes a sweeping gesture.

"You end up with all this in front of the X machine," he says. "And when you're pushing in more material than the system can convert into throughput, what are you getting?"

"Excess inventory," says Stacey.

"Exactly," says Jonah. "But what about another combination? What happens when X is feeding parts to Y?"

Jonah writes that on the floor with the chalk like this . . .

$$X \dashrightarrow Y$$

"How much of Y's 600 hours can be used productively here?" asks Jonah.

"Only 450 hours again," says Stacey.

"That's right," says Jonah. "If Y is depending exclusively upon X to feed it inventory, the maximum number of hours it can work is determined by the output of X. And 600 hours from X equates to 450 hours for Y. After working those hours, Y will be starved for inventory to process. Which, by the way, is quite acceptable."

"Wait a minute," I say. "We have bottlenecks feeding non-bottlenecks here in the plant. For instance, whatever leaves the NCX-10 will be processed by a non-bottleneck."

"From other non-bottlenecks you mean. And do you know what happens when you keep Y active that way?" asks Jonah. "Look at this."

He draws a third diagram on the floor with the chalk.

$$Y \rightarrow A$$
$$X \rightarrow S$$
$$S$$
$$E$$
$$M$$
$$B$$
$$L$$
$$Y$$

In this case, Jonah explains, some parts do not flow through a bottleneck; their processing is done only by a non-bottleneck and the flow is directly from Y to assembly. The other parts *do* flow through a bottleneck, and they are on the X route to assembly where they are mated to the Y parts into a finished product.

In a real situation, the Y route probably would consist of one non-bottleneck feeding another non-bottleneck, feeding yet another non-bottleneck, and so on, to final assembly. The X route might have a series of non-bottlenecks feeding a bottleneck, which in turn feeds a chain of more non-bottlenecks. In our case, Jonah says, we've got a group of non-bottleneck machines downstream from X which can process parts from either the X or the Y route.

"But to keep it simple, I've diagrammed the combination with the fewest number of elements—one X and one Y. No matter how many non-bottlenecks are in the system, the result of activating Y just to keep it busy is the same. So let's say you keep both X and Y working continuously for every available hour. How efficient would the system be?"

"Super efficient," says Bob.

"No, you're wrong," says Jonah. "Because what happens when all this inventory from Y reaches final assembly?"

Bob shrugs and says, "We build the orders and ship them."

"How can you?" asks Jonah. "Eighty percent of your products require at least one part from a bottleneck. What are you going to substitute for the bottleneck part that hasn't shown up yet?"

Bob scratches his head and says, "Oh, yeah . . . I forgot."

"So if we can't assemble," says Stacey, "we get piles of inventory again. Only this time the excess inventory doesn't accumulate in front of a bottleneck; it stacks up in front of final assembly."

"Yeah," says Lou, "and another million bucks sits still just to keep the wheels turning."

And Jonah says, "You see? Once more, the non-bottleneck does not determine throughput, even if it works twenty-hour hours a day."

Bob asks, "Okay, but what about that twenty percent of products *without* any bottleneck parts? We can still get high efficiencies with them."

"You think so?" asks Jonah.

On the floor he diagrams it like this . . .

$$Y \rightarrow PRODUCT\ A$$
$$X \rightarrow PRODUCT\ B$$

This time, he says, the X and Y operate independently of one another. They are each filling separate marketing demands.

"How much of Y's 600 hours can the system use here?" asks Jonah.

"All of 'em," says Bob.

"Absolutely not," says Jonah. "Sure, at first glance it looks as if we can use one hundred percent of Y, but think again."

"We can only use as much as the market demand can absorb," I say.

"Correct. By definition, Y has excess capacity," says Jonah. "So if you work Y to the maximum, you once again get excess inventory. And this time you end up, not with excess work-in-process, but with excess finished goods. The constraint here is not in production. The constraint is marketing's ability to sell."

As he says this, I'm thinking to myself about the finished goods we've got crammed into warehouses. At least two-thirds of those inventories are products made entirely with non-bottleneck parts. By running non-bottlenecks for "efficiency," we've built inventories far in excess of demand. And what about the remaining third of our finished goods? They have bottleneck parts, but most of those products have been sitting on the shelf now for a couple of years. They're obsolete. Out of 1,500 or so units in stock, we're lucky if we can sell ten a month. Just about all of the *competitive* products with bottleneck parts are sold virtually as soon as they come out of final assembly. A few of them sit in the warehouse a day or two before they go to the customer, but due to the backlog, not many.

I look at Jonah. To the four diagrams on the floor, he has now added numbers so that together they look like this . . .

1) $Y \rightarrow X$ 3) $Y \rightarrow A$ 4) $Y \rightarrow$ PRODUCT A
              $X \rightarrow S$ $X \rightarrow$ PRODUCT B
2) $X \rightarrow Y$ S
                   E
                   M
                   B
                   L
                   Y

Jonah says, "We've examined four linear combinations involving X and Y. Now, of course, we can create endless combinations of X and Y. But the four in front of us are fundamental enough that we don't have to go any further. Because if we use these like building blocks, we can represent *any* manufacturing situation. We don't have to look at trillions of combinations of X and Y to find what is universally true in all of them; we can generalize the truth simply by identifying what happens in each of these four cases. Can you tell me what you have noticed to be similar in all of them?"

Stacey points out immediately that in no case does Y ever determine throughput for the system. Whenever it's possible to activate Y above the level of X, doing so results only in excess inventory, not in greater throughput.

"Yes, and if we follow that thought to a logical conclusion," says Jonah, "we can form a simple rule which will be true in every case: the level of utilization of a non-bottleneck is not determined by its own potential, but by some other constraint in the system."

He points to the NCX-10.

"A major constraint here in your system is this machine," says Jonah. "When you make a non-bottleneck do more work than this machine, you are not increasing productivity. On the contrary, you are doing exactly the opposite. You are creating excess inventory, which is against the goal."

"But what are we supposed to do?" asks Bob. "If we don't keep our people working, we'll have idle time, and idle time will lower our efficiencies."

"*So what?*" asks Jonah.

Donovan is taken aback. "Beg pardon, but how the hell can you say that?"

"Just take a look behind you," says Jonah. "Take a look at the monster you've made. It did not create itself. You have created this mountain of inventory with your own decisions. And why? Because of the wrong assumption that you must make the work-ers produce one hundred percent of the time, or else get rid of them to 'save' money."

Lou says, "Well, granted that maybe one hundred percent is unrealistic. We just ask for some acceptable percentage, say, ninety percent."

"Why is ninety percent acceptable?" asks Jonah. "Why not sixty percent, or twenty-five? The numbers are meaningless un-less they are based upon the constraints of the system. With enough raw materials, you can keep one worker busy from now until retirement. But *should* you do it? Not if you want to make money."

Then Ralph suggests, "What you're saying is that making an employee work and profiting from that work are two different things."

"Yes, and that's a very close approximation of the second rule we can logically derive from the four combinations of X and Y we talked about," says Jonah. "Putting it precisely, activating a resource and utilizing a resource are not synonymous."

He explains that in both rules, "utilizing" a resource means making use of the resource in a way that moves the system toward the goal. "Activating" a resource is like pressing the ON switch of a machine; it runs whether or not there is any benefit to be derived from the work it's doing. So, really, activating a non-bottleneck to its maximum is an act of maximum stupidity.

"And the implication of these rules is that we must *not* seek to optimize every resource in the system," says Jonah. "A system of local optimums is not an optimum system at all; it is a very inefficient system."

"Okay," I say, "but how does knowing this help us get the missing parts unstuck at the milling machines and moved to final assembly?"

Jonah says, "Think about the build-up of inventory both here and at your milling machines in terms of these two rules we just talked about."

"I think I see the cause of the problem," Stacey says, "We're releasing material faster than the bottlenecks can process it."

"Yes," says Jonah. "You are sending work onto the floor whenever *non*-bottlenecks are running out of work to do."

I say, "Granted, but the milling machines are a bottleneck."

Jonah shakes his head and says, "No, they are not—as evidenced by all this excess inventory behind you. You see, the milling machines are not intrinsically a bottleneck. *You* have turned them into one."

He tells us that with an increase in throughput, it is possible to create new bottlenecks. But most plants have so much extra capacity that it takes an enormous increase in throughput before this happens. We've only had a twenty percent increase. When I had talked to him by phone, he thought it unlikely a new bottleneck would have occurred.

What happened was that even as throughput increased, we continued loading the plant with inventory as if we expected to keep all our workers fully activated. This increased the load dumped upon the milling machines and pushed them beyond their capacity. The first-priority, red-tagged parts were processed, but the green-tagged parts piled up. So not only did we get excess inventory at the NCX-10 and at heat-treat, but due to the volume of bottleneck parts, we clogged the flow at another work center and prevented non-bottleneck parts from reaching assembly.

When he's finished, I say, "All right, I see now the error of our ways. Can you tell us what we should do to correct the problem?"

"I want you all to think about it as we walk back to your conference room and then we'll talk about what you should do," says Jonah. "The solution is fairly simple."

26

Just how simple the solution is doesn't become apparent to me until I'm home that night. I'm sitting at the kitchen table with a pad of paper and a pencil thinking about what was suggested today when Sharon comes in.

"Hi," she says as she sits down.

"Hi," I say back. "What's up?"

"Not much," she says. "Just wondered what you were doing."

"I'm working," I tell her.

"Can I help?" she asks.

"Well . . . I don't know," I say. "It's kind of technical. I think you'll probably be bored by it."

"Oh," she says. "Does that mean you want me to leave?"

Guilt strikes.

"No, not if you want to stay," I tell her. "Do you want to try to solve a problem?"

"Okay," she says, brightening.

I say, "All right. Let me think of how to put this to you. Do you know about the scout hike Dave and I were on?"

"She doesn't, but I do!" says Dave, racing into the kitchen. He skids to a stop on the smooth floor and says, "Sharon doesn't know anything about the hike. But I can help you."

I say, "Son, I think there is a career for you in sales."

Sharon indignantly says, "Yes, I *do* know about the hike."

"You weren't even there," says Dave.

"I've heard everybody talk about it," she says.

"Okay, *both* of you can work on this," I say. "Here's the problem: We've got a line of kids on a hike in the woods. In the middle of the line, we've got Herbie. We've already taken the pack off Herbie's back to help him go faster, but he's still the slowest. Everybody wants to go faster than Herbie. But if that happens, the line will spread out and some of the kids will get lost. For one reason or another, we can't move Herbie from the middle of the line. Now, how do we keep the line from spreading?"

They both become thoughtful.

I say, "All right, now both of you go into the other room. I'll give you ten minutes, and then we'll see which one of you comes up with the best idea to keep everyone together in the line."

"What does the winner get?" asks Dave.

"Well . . . anything within reason."

"Anything?" asks Sharon.

"Within reason," I repeat.

So they leave and I get about ten minutes of peace and quiet. Then I see the two faces looking around the corner.

"Ready?" I ask.

They come in and sit down at the kitchen table with me.

"Want to hear my idea?" asks Sharon.

"My idea is better," says Dave.

"It is not!" she tells him.

"Okay, enough!" I say. "What's your idea, Sharon?"

Sharon says, "A drummer."

"Pardon me?"

"You know . . . like in a parade," she says.

"Oh, I know what you mean," I say, realizing what she has in mind. "There aren't any gaps in a parade. Everybody is marching in step."

Sharon beams. Dave gives her a dirty look.

"So everybody's marching in step . . . to a beat," I say, thinking out loud. "Sure. But how do you keep the people in front of Herbie from setting a faster pace?"

"You have Herbie beat the drum," says Sharon.

I think about it and say, "Yeah, that's not bad."

"But my idea is better," says Dave.

I turn to him. "Okay, wise guy, what's your idea?"

"Tie ropes to everyone," says Dave.

"Ropes?"

"You know, like mountain climbers," he says. "You tie everyone together at the waist with one long rope. So, that way, no one could get left behind, and nobody could speed up without everybody speeding up."

I say, "Hmmm . . . that's very good."

It would mean that the line—which would translate to the total inventory in the plant—could never be longer than the rope. And the rope, of course, could be of a pre-determined length, which means we could control it with precision. Everyone would have to walk at the same speed. I look at Dave, a little in awe of his creativity.

"Come to think of it, the rope makes it sound like having physical links between all the equipment," I tell him, "which is like an assembly line."

"Yeah, an assembly line," says Dave. "Didn't you tell me once that an assembly line is supposed to be the best way to make things?"

"Well, yes, it's the most efficient way to manufacture," I say. "In fact, we use that approach when we do the final assembly for most of our products. The problem is that an assembly line won't work throughout the whole plant."

"Oh," says Dave.

"But those are both good ideas you two thought up," I tell them. "In fact, if we changed each of your ideas just a little bit we'd almost have the solution suggested to us today."

"Like how?" asks Sharon.

"See, to keep the line from spreading, it actually wouldn't be necessary to keep everyone marching to exactly the same step or to keep everyone tied to the rope," I tell them. "What we really have to do is just keep the kid at the front of the line from walking faster than Herbie. If we can do that, then everybody will stay together."

"So we just tie the rope from Herbie to the kid at the front," says Dave.

"Or, maybe Herbie and the boy at the front of the line have signals," says Sharon. "When the boy in front goes too fast, Herbie tells him to wait or slow down."

"That's right," I say. "Both of you figured it out."

"So what do we *both* win?" asks Sharon.

"What do you want?" I ask. "A pizza with everything? A night at the movies?"

They're quiet for a moment.

"The movies sound good," says Sharon, "but what I'd really like is if you could get Mom to come home again."

Now it gets very quiet.

Dave says finally, "But if you can't, we'll understand."

"Well, I'm doing my best," I say. "Meanwhile, how about the movies?"

After the kids have gone to bed, I sit up wondering for the hundredth time whether Julie will come back. Compared with my marital difficulties, the inventory problem at the plant seems simple—or at least it seems simple now. I guess every problem is easy once you've figured it out.

We are, in effect, going to do what my two kids came up with. The Herbies (the bottlenecks) are going to tell us when to let more inventory into the system—except we're going to use the aid of computers instead of drums and ropes.

After we returned to the conference room in the office building today, we started talking, and we all agreed that we're obviously releasing too much material. We don't need five or six weeks of inventory in front of the bottleneck to keep it productive.

"If we can withhold materials for red parts, instead of pushing them out there as soon as the first non-bottleneck has nothing to do," said Stacey, "the milling machines will then have time to work on the green parts. And the parts we're missing will reach assembly with no problem."

Jonah nodded and said, "That's right. What you have to do is find a way to release the material for the red parts according to the rate at which the bottlenecks need material—and strictly at that rate."

Then I said, "Fine, but how do we time each release of material so it arrives at the bottleneck when it's needed?"

Stacey said, "I'm not sure, but I see what you're worried about. We don't want the opposite problem of no work in front of the bottleneck."

"Hell, we got at least a month before that happens, even if we released no more red tags from today on," said Bob. "But I know what you mean. If we idle the bottleneck, we lose throughput."

"What we need," I said, "is some kind of signal to link the bottlenecks with the release-of-materials schedule."

Then Ralph, to my surprise, spoke up and said, "Excuse me, this is just a thought. But maybe we can predict when to release material by some kind of system based on the data we've kept on both the bottlenecks."

I asked him what he was getting at.

He said, "Well, since we started keeping data on the bottlenecks, I've been noticing I'm able to predict several weeks in advance what each bottleneck will be working on at a particular time. See, as long as I know exactly what's in queue, I just take the average setup and process times for each type of part, and I'm able to calculate when each batch should clear the bottleneck. Because we're only dealing with one work center, with much less dependency, we can average the statistical fluctuations and get a better degree of accuracy."

Ralph went on to say that he knows from observation it takes about two weeks, plus or minus a day or two, for material to reach the bottlenecks from the first operations.

"So by adding two weeks to the setup and process times of what's in queue at the bottleneck," said Ralph, "I know how long it will take until the bottleneck is actually working on material we release. And as each batch leaves the bottleneck, we can update our information and calculate a date when Stacey should release more red-tag material."

Jonah looked at Ralph and said, "that's excellent!"

"Ralph," I said, "that's terrific. How accurate do you really think we can be with this?"

"I'd say we'd be accurate to within plus or minus a day," he said. "So if we keep, say, a three-day stock of work-in-process in front of each bottleneck, we should be safe."

Everyone was telling Ralph how impressed they were when Jonah said, "But, in fact, Ralph, you can do much more than that with the same information."

"Like what?" asked Ralph.

Jonah said, "You can also attack the inventory problems in front of assembly."

"You mean we not only can do something about excess inventory on the bottleneck parts, but on the non-bottleneck parts as well?" I asked.

"Exactly," said Jonah.

But Ralph said, "Sorry, folks, I'm not sure how I'd do that."

Then Jonah explained it to him—and all of us. If Ralph can determine a schedule for releasing red-tag materials based on the bottlenecks, he can also determine a schedule for final assembly. Once he knows when the bottleneck parts will reach final assembly, he can calculate backwards and determine the release of the non-bottleneck materials along each of their routes. In this way, the bottlenecks will be determining the release of all the materials in the plant.

I said, "You know, that's going to produce the same effect as moving the bottlenecks to the head of production, which is what I'd intended for us to do."

"Yeah, it sounds good," said Ralph. "But I have to warn you, I can't say how long it'll take before I can do all that. I mean, I can have schedule for the red-tagged materials worked out in a fairly short order. The rest of it will take awhile."

"Aw, come on, Ralphie," said Bob, "a computer wiz like you ought to be able to crank that out in no time."

"I can crank something out in no time," said Ralph, "but I'm not going to promise it'll work."

I told him, "Relax; as long as we ease the load on the milling machines, we'll be okay for the short haul. That'll give you the time to get something basic in place."

"You may feel you have the time now to relax," said Jonah, "but I have to catch a plane for Chicago in thirty-five minutes."

"Oh, shit," I muttered, automatically glancing at my watch. "I guess we'd better move."

It was not a graceful parting. Jonah and I ran out of the building, and I broke numerous speed limits—without incident—getting him to the airport.

"I have, shall we say, a special interest in plants like yours," said Jonah. "So I'd appreciate it if you'd keep me informed of what happens."

"Sure," I told him. "No problem. In fact, I'd planned on it."

"Good," said Jonah. "I'll be talking to you."

And with that he was out of the car and, with a wave, was sprinting through the terminal doors. I didn't get a call, so I suppose he made it.

When I go to work the next morning, we have a meeting about how to implement this approach. But before we can get down to talking about it, Bob Donovan starts waving a red flag at us.

"You know, we could be walking into a big problem," says Bob.

"What's that?" I ask.

"What happens if efficiencies all over the plant go down?" he asks.

I say, "Well, I think that's a risk we'll have to take."

"Yeah, but it sounds like we're going to have a lot of people idle around here if we do this," says Bob.

"Yeah, we might have some people idle from time to time," I admit.

"So are we just supposed to let everyone stand around out there?" asks Bob.

"Why not?" asks Stacey. "Once the somebody is already on the payroll, it doesn't cost us any more to have him be idle. Whether somebody produces parts or waits a few minutes doesn't increase our operating expense. But excess inventory . . . now *that* ties up a lot of money."

"Okay," says Bob, "but what about the reporting system? Seems to me that at the end of the month, when old Bill Peach is ready to decide if we stay open or if we close down, he's not going to be awfully positive about us if he sees our efficiencies have taken a dive. I hear they do tend to frown upon that at headquarters."

There is quiet in the room. Then Lou says, "He does have a point, Al."

I listen to the hum of the air conditioning for a moment.

"All right, look," I say finally. "If we *don't* go ahead with a system to withhold inventory and release it according to the bottlenecks, we'll be missing a major opportunity to improve performance and save the plant. And I'm not about to stand by and let that happen just to maintain a standard that obviously has more impact on middle management politics than it does on the bottom line. I say we go ahead with this. And if efficiencies drop, let them."

After those brave words, so reminiscent of Admiral Farragut and his Damn-the-Torpedoes speech, the others are a little misty-eyed.

"And, ah, Bob," I tell Donovan, "if there *is* a lot of idle time out there, don't hassle anybody—just make damn sure it doesn't show up in the efficiency reports next month, okay?"

"Gotcha, boss."

27

". . . Let me say in conclusion that had it not been for the increase in revenue generated last month by the Bearington plant and its products, the UniWare Division's losses would have continued for the seventh consecutive month. All of the other manufacturing operations in the division reported only marginal gains in performance or sustained losses. Despite the improvement at Bearington and the fact that as a result the division recorded its first operating profit of this year, we have a long way to go before we are back on solid financial footing."

Having said that, Ethan Frost gets the nod from Bill Peach and sits down. I'm sitting halfway down a long table where all the plant managers are gathered. On Peach's right is Hilton Smyth, who happens to be glowering at me in the aftermath of Frost's tribute to my plant. I relax in my chair and for a moment allow myself to contemplate the view through the broad plateglass window, a sunny city on an early summer day.

May has ended. Aside from the problem with the shortages of non-bottleneck parts, which have now gone away, it's been an excellent month. We're now timing the release of all materials according to a new system Ralph Nakamura developed, which is keyed to the speed of the bottlenecks. He's got a data terminal now at both of the bottlenecks, so as inventory is processed, the latest information can be fed directly into the plant data base. With the new system we're beginning to see excellent results.

Ralph did a little experimenting with the system and soon discovered we can predict within a day, more or less, when a shipment will leave the plant. Based on this, we've been able to put together a report to marketing listing all customer orders and dates when they will be shipped. (I don't know if anybody in marketing really believes that report, but so far it's been highly accurate.)

"Rogo," says Peach, "because you seem to be the only one among us who has improved to any degree, we'll let you start the round of reports."

I open up the cover of my report and launch into a presentation of the highlights. By almost every standard, we've had a good month. Inventory levels have fallen and are continuing to fall rapidly. Withholding some materials has meant we're no longer choking on work-in-process. Parts are reaching the bottle-necks when they're supposed to, and the flow through the plant is much smoother than before.

And what happened to efficiencies? Well, they did fall ini-tially as we began to withhold raw material from the floor, but not as much as we had been afraid they would—it turns out we were consuming excess inventory. But with the rate of shipments up dramatically, that excess has melted quickly. And now that we're beginning to resume releases of materials to non-bottlenecks again, efficiencies are on their way back up. Donovan has even told me confidentially he thinks the real numbers in the future will be almost the same as before.

The best news is we've wiped out our backlog of overdue orders. Amazing as it seems, we're completely caught up. So cus-tomer service has improved. Throughput is up. We're on our way back. It's too bad the standard report we've prepared can't begin to tell the full story of what's really going on.

When I've finished, I look up the table and see Hilton Smyth whispering something to Bill Peach. There is quiet around the table for a moment. Then Bill nods to Hilton and talks to me.

"Good job, Al," Bill says stiffly.

Through with me, Bill asks another manager to deliver his report. I sit back, irritated slightly that Peach wasn't more posi-tive, that he didn't put more praise on me the way Frost had indicated he should. I came in here feeling as though we'd really turned the plant around. And I guess I expected a little more than a "good job," a pat on the head.

But then I have to remind myself that Peach doesn't know the extent of the change. Should he know? Should we be telling him? Lou has asked me about this. And I've told him, no; let's hold off for a while.

We could go to Bill Peach and make a presentation to him, put all our cards on the table and let him decide. In fact, that's exactly what we will do eventually. But not yet. And I think I have a good reason.

I've worked with Bill Peach for a lot of years; I know him pretty well. He's a smart man—but he is not an innovator. A couple of years ago, he might have let us run with this for a while. Not today. I have a feeling if we go to him now, he'll put on his hard nose and tell me to run the plant by the cost accounting methods he believes in.

I have to bide my time until I can go to him with a solid case that my way (Jonah's way, really) is the one that truly works. It's too early for that. We've broken too many rules to tell him the full story now.

But will we have the time? That's what I keep asking myself. Peach hasn't voluntarily lifted the threat to close the plant. I thought he might say something (publicly or privately) after this report, but he hasn't. I look at him at the end of the table. He seems distracted, not like himself. The others talk and he seems only half interested. Hilton seems to cue him on what to say. What's with him?

The meeting breaks up about an hour after lunch, and by then I've decided to have a private talk with Peach if I can get it. I follow him out into the corridor from the conference room and ask him. He invites me into his office.

"So when are you going to let us off the hook?" I ask him after the door is closed.

Bill sits down in a big upholstered chair and I take the one opposite him. Without the desk between us, it's a nice little intimate chat.

Bill looks straight at me and says, "What makes you think I'm going to?"

"Bearington is on its way back," I tell him. "We can make that plant make money for the division."

"Can you?" he asks. "Look, Al, you've had a good month. That's a step in the right direction. But can you give us a second good month? And a third and fourth? That's what I'm waiting to see."

"We'll give them to you," I say to him.

"I'm going to be frank," says Peach. "I'm not yet convinced this hasn't been just a flash in the pan, so to speak. You had a huge overdue backlog. It was inevitable you'd ship it eventually. What have you done to reduce costs? Nothing that I can see. It's going to take a ten or fifteen percent reduction in operating expense to make the plant profitable for the long term."

I feel my heart sink. Finally, I say, "Bill, if next month we turn in another improvement, will you at least delay the recommendation to close the plant?"

He shakes his head. "It'll have to be a bigger improvement than what you gave us in this past period."

"How big?"

"Just give me fifteen percent more on the bottom line than you did this month," he says.

I nod. "I think we can do that," I say—and note the split second of shock blink into Peach's face.

Then he says, "Fine. If you can deliver that, and keep delivering it, we'll keep Bearington open."

I smile. If I do this for you, I'm thinking, you'd be an idiot to close us.

Peach stands, our chat concluded.

I fly the Mazda up the entrance ramp to the Interstate with the accelerator floored and the radio turned up loud. The adrenalin is pumping. The thoughts in my head are racing faster than the car.

Two months ago I figured I might be sending out my resume by now. But Peach just said if we turned in another good month he'd let the plant stay open. We're almost there. We just might be able to pull this off. Just one more month.

But fifteen percent?

We've been eating up our backlog of orders at a terrific rate. And by doing so we've been able to ship a tremendous volume of product—tremendous by any comparison: last month, last quarter, last year. It's given us a big surge of income, and it's looked fantastic on the books. But now that we've shipped all the overdues, and we're putting out new orders much faster than before. . . .

The thought creeps up on me that I'm in really big trouble. Where the hell am I going to get the orders that will give me an extra fifteen percent?

Peach isn't just asking for another good month; he's demanding an incredible month. He hasn't promised anything; I have—and probably too much. I'm trying to remember the orders scheduled for the coming weeks and attempting to calculate in my head if we're going to have the volume of business necessary for the bottom-line increase Peach wants to see. I have a scary feeling it won't be enough.

Okay, I can ship ahead of schedule. I can take the orders

scheduled for the first week or two of July and ship them in June instead.

But what am I going to do after that? I'm going to be putting us into a huge hole in which we have nothing else to do. *We need more business.*

I wonder where Jonah is these days.

Glancing down at the speedometer, I find to my surprise that I'm zipping along at eighty. I slow down. I loosen my tie. No sense killing myself trying to get back to the plant. It occurs to me, in fact, that by the time I get back to the plant it'll be time to go home.

Just about then, I pass a sign saying I'm two miles from the interchange that would put me on the highway to Forest Grove. Well, why not? I haven't seen Julie or the kids in a couple of days. Since the end of school, the kids have been staying with Julie and her parents.

I take the interchange and get off at the next exit. At a gas station on the corner, I make a call to the office. Fran answers and I tell her two things: First, pass the word to Bob, Stacey, Ralph, and Lou that the meeting went well for us. And, second, I tell her not to expect me to come in this afternoon.

When I get to the Barnett's house, I get a nice welcome. I spend quite a while just talking to Sharon and Dave. Then Julie suggests we go for a walk together. It's a fine summer afternoon outside.

As I'm hugging Sharon to say goodbye, she whispers in my ear, "Daddy, when are we all going to go home together?"

"Real soon, I hope," I tell her.

Despite the assurance I gave her, Sharon's question doesn't go away. I've been wondering the same thing myself.

Julie and I go to the park, and after walking for awhile, we sit down on a bench by the river. We sit without saying anything for a while. She asks me if something is wrong. I tell her about Sharon's question.

"She asks me that all the time," says Julie.

"She does? What do you tell her?"

Julie says, "I tell her we'll be going home real soon."

I laugh. "That's what I said to her. Do you really mean that?"

She's quiet for a second. Finally, she smiles at me and says sincerely, "You've been a lot of fun to be around in the last few weeks."

"Thanks. The feeling is mutual," I say.

She takes my hand and says, "But . . . I'm sorry, Al. I'm still worried about coming home."

"Why? We're getting along a lot better now," I say, "What's the problem?"

"Look, we've had some good times for a change. And that's fine. I've really needed this time with you," she says. "But if we go back to living together, you know what's going to happen don't you? Everything will be fine for about two days. But a week from now we'll be having the same arguments. And a month later, or six months, or a year from now . . . well, you know what I mean."

I sigh. "Julie, was it that bad living with me?"

"Al, it wasn't *bad*," she says. "It was just . . . I don't know. You weren't paying any attention to me."

"But I was having all kinds of problems in my job. I was really in over my head for awhile. What did you expect from me?"

"More than what I was getting," Julie says. "You know, when I was growing up, my father always came home from work at the same time. The whole family always ate together. He spent the evenings at home. With you, I never know what's going on."

"You can't compare me to your father," I say. "He's a dentist. After the last tooth of the day is filled, he can lock up and go home. My business isn't like that."

"Alex, the problem is *you* are not like that," she says. "Other people go to work and come home at regular times."

"Yes, you're partially right. I am not like other people," I admit. "When I get involved in something, I really get involved. And maybe that has to do with the way *I* was brought up. Look at my family—we hardly ever ate together. Somebody always had to be minding the store. It was my father's rule: the business was what fed us, so it came first. We all understood that and we all worked together."

"So what does that prove except our families were different?" she asks. "I'm telling you about something that bothered me so much and for so long that I wasn't even sure if I loved you anymore."

"So what makes you sure you love me now?"

"Do you want another fight?" she asks.

I look the other way.

"No, I don't want to fight," I tell her.

I hear her sigh. Then she says, "You see? Nothing has changed . . . has it."

Neither of us says a word for quite awhile. Julie gets up and walks over to the river. It looks for a second as if she might run away. She doesn't. She comes back again and sits down on the bench.

She says to me, "When I was eighteen, I had everything planned—college, a teaching degree, marriage, a house, children. In that order. All the decisions were made. I knew what china pattern I wanted. I knew the names I wanted for the kids. I knew what the house should look like and what color the rug should be. Everything was certain. And it was so important that I have it all. But now . . . I have it all, only it's different somehow. None of it seems to matter."

"Julie, why does your life have to conform to this . . . this perfect image you have in your head?" I ask her. "Do you even know *why* you want the things you do?"

"Because that's how I grew up," she says. "And what about you? Why do you have to have this big career? Why do you feel compelled to work twenty-four hours a day?"

Silence.

Then she says, "I'm sorry. I'm just very confused."

"No, that's okay," I say. "It was a good question. I have no idea why I wouldn't be satisfied being a grocer, or a nine-to-five office worker."

"Al, why don't we just try to forget all this," she suggests.

"No, I don't think so," I tell her. "I think we should do the opposite. We ought to start asking a few more questions."

Julie gives me a skeptical look and asks, "Like what?"

"Like what is our marriage supposed to do for us?" I ask her. "My idea of the goal of a marriage is not living in a perfect house where everything happens according to a clock. Is that the goal for you?"

"All I'm asking for is a little dependability from my husband," she says. "And what's all this about a *goal?* When you're married, you're just married. There is no goal."

"Then why be married?" I ask.

"You get married because of commitment . . . because of

love . . . because of all the reasons everybody else does," she says. "Alex, you're asking a lot of dumb questions."

"Whether they're dumb or smart, I'm asking them because we've been living together for fifteen years and we have no clear understanding of what our marriage is supposed to do . . . or become . . . or anything!" I sputter. "We're just coasting along, doing 'what everyone else does.' And it turns out the two of us have some very different assumptions of what our lives are supposed to be like."

"My parents have been married for thirty-seven years," she says, "and they never asked any questions. Nobody ever asks 'What is the goal of a marriage?' People just get married because they're in love."

"Oh. Well, that explains everything, doesn't it," I say.

"Al, please don't ask these questions," she says. "They don't have any answers. And if we keep talking this way, we're going to ruin everything. If this is your way of saying you're having second thoughts about us—"

"Julie, I'm not having second thoughts about you. But you're the one who can't figure out what's wrong with us. Maybe if you tried to think about this logically instead of simply comparing us to the characters in a romance novel—"

"I do not read romance novels," she says.

"Then where did you get your ideas about how a marriage is supposed to be?" I ask her.

She says nothing.

"All I'm saying is we ought to throw away for the moment all the pre-conceptions we have about our marriage, and just take a look at how we are right now," I tell her. "Then we ought to figure out what we want to have happen and go in that direction."

But Julie doesn't seem to be listening. She stands up.

"I think it's time we walked back," she says.

On the way back to the Barnett house, we're as silent as two icebergs in January, the two of us drifting together. I look at one side of the street; Julie looks at the opposite. When we walk through the door, Mrs. Barnett invites me to stay for dinner, but I say I've got to be going. I say goodbye to the kids, give Julie a wave and leave.

I'm getting into the Mazda when I hear her come running after me.

"Will I see you again on Saturday?" she asks.

I smile a little "Yeah, sure. Sounds good."

She says, "I'm sorry about what happened."

"I guess we'll just have to keep trying until we get it right."

We both start smiling. Then we do some of that nice stuff that makes an argument almost worth the agony.

28

I get home just as the sun is starting to set. The sky is rosy pink. As I'm unlocking the kitchen door, I hear the phone ringing inside. I rush in to grab it.

"Good morning," says Jonah.

"Morning?" Outside the window, the sun is almost below the horizon. I laugh. "I'm watching the sun set. Where are *you* calling from?"

"Singapore," he says.

"Oh."

"By the way, from my hotel I'm watching the sun *rise*," Jonah says. "Alex, I wouldn't have called you at home, but I'm not going to be able to talk to you again for a few weeks."

"Why not?"

"Well, it's a long story and I can't go into it now," he says. "But I'm sure we'll have a chance to discuss it some time."

"I see. . . ." I wonder what's going on, but say, "That's too bad. It puts me in a kind of a bind, because I was just about to ask for your help again."

"Has something gone wrong?" he asks.

"No," I tell him. "Everything is generally going very well from an operations standpoint. But I just had a meeting with my division vice president, and I was told the plant has to show an even bigger improvement."

"You're still not making money?" he asks.

I say, "Yes, we are making money again, but we need to accelerate the improvement to save the plant from being shut down."

I hear the trace of a chuckle on the other end of the line, and Jonah says, "If I were you, I wouldn't worry too much about being shut down."

"Well, from what the head of the division has told me, the possibility of a shut-down is real," I tell him. "And until he says otherwise, I can't afford to take this lightly."

"Alex, if you want to improve the plant even more, I'm with you all the way," Jonah says. "And since I won't have the opportunity to speak to you for awhile, let's talk about it now. Bring me up to date on what's happening."

So I do. Then, wondering if we've reached some theoretical limit by now, I ask him if there is anything else we can try.

"Anything else?" he says. "Believe me, we have only begun. Now, here's what I suggest. . . ."

Early the next morning, I'm in my office at the plant considering what Jonah told me. Outside is the dawn of the day he's already seen in Singapore. Stepping out to get a cup of coffee, I find Stacey at the coffee machine.

"Hello there," she says. "I hear everything went fairly well for us at headquarters yesterday."

"Well, not bad," I say. "I'm afraid we still have a way to go before we convince Peach we're good for the long term. But I talked to Jonah last night."

"Did you tell him about our progress?" she asks.

"Yes," I say. "And he suggested we try what he called 'the next logical step.' "

I see her face take on a nervous grin. "What's that?"

"Cut our batch sizes in half on non-bottlenecks," I say.

Stacy takes a step back as she thinks about this. "But why?" she asks.

I say with a smile, "Because in the end we'll make more money."

"I don't understand," she says. "How is that going to help us?"

"Hey, Stacey, you're in charge of inventory control," I tell her. "You tell me what would happen if we cut our batch sizes in half."

Thinking, she sips her coffee for a moment. Her brow compresses in concentration. Then she says, "If we cut our batch sizes in half, then I guess that at any one time we'd have half the work-in-process on the floor. I guess that means we'd only need half the investment in work-in-process to keep the plant working. If we could work it out with our vendors, we could conceivably cut all our inventories in half, and by cutting our inventories in half, we reduce the amount of cash tied up at any one time, which eases the pressure on cash flow."

I'm nodding each time she says a sentence, and finally I say, "That's right. That's *one* set of benefits."

She says, "But to reap those benefits fully, we'd have to have our suppliers increase the frequency of deliveries to us and reduce the quantity of each delivery. That's going to take some negotiating through purchasing, and I'm not sure all the vendors will go for it."

I tell her, "That's something we can work on. Eventually they'll go for it because it's to their advantage as well as ours."

"But if we go to smaller batch sizes," she says, squinting at me in cynicism, "doesn't that mean we'll have to have more set-ups on equipment?"

"Sure," I say, "don't worry about it."

"Don't—?"

"Yeah, don't worry about it."

"But Donovan—"

"Donovan will do just fine, even with more setups," I say. "And, meanwhile, there is *another* set of benefits, aside from what you said, that we can have almost immediately."

"What's that?" she asks.

"You really want to know?"

"Sure, I do."

"Good. You set up a meeting with the other functions and I'll tell everyone at the same time."

For dumping that little chore of the meeting arrangements on her, Stacey pays me back in kind by setting the meeting for noon at the most expensive restaurant in town—with lunch bill-able to *my* expense number, of course.

"What could I do?" she asks as we sit down at the table. "It was the only time everybody was available, right, Bob?"

"Right," says Bob.

I'm not mad. Given the quality and quantity of work these people have done recently, I can't complain about picking up the tab for lunch. I get right down to telling everybody what Stacey and I had talked about this morning, and lead up to the other set of benefits.

Part of what Jonah told me last night over the phone had to do with the time a piece of material spends inside a plant. If you consider the total time from the moment the material comes into the plant to the minute it goes out the door as part of a finished product, you can divide that time into four elements.

One of them is setup, the time the part spends waiting for a resource, while the resource is preparing itself to work on the part.

Another is process time, which is the amount of time the part spends being modified into a new, more valuable form.

A third element is queue time, which is the time the part spends in line for a resource while the resource is busy working on something else ahead of it.

The fourth element is wait time, which is the time the part waits, not for a resource, but for another part so they can be assembled together.

As Jonah pointed out last night, setup and process are a small portion of the total elapsed time for any part. But queue and wait often consume large amounts of time—in fact, the majority of the elapsed total that the part spends inside the plant.

For parts that are going through *bottlenecks,* queue is the dominant portion. The part is stuck in front of the bottleneck for a long time. For parts that are only going through *non-bottlenecks,* wait is dominant, because they are waiting in front of assembly for parts that are coming from the bottlenecks. Which means that in each case, the bottlenecks are what dictate this elapsed time. Which, in turn, means the bottlenecks dictate inventory as well as throughput.

We have been setting batch sizes according to an economical batch quantity (or EBQ) formula. Last night, Jonah told me that although he didn't have time over the phone to go into all the reasons, EBQ has a number of flawed assumptions underlying it. Instead, he asked me to consider what would happen if we cut batch sizes by half from their present quantities.

If we reduce batch sizes by half, we also reduce by half the time it will take to process a batch. That means we reduce queue and wait by half as well. Reduce those by half, and we reduce by about half the total time parts spend in the plant. Reduce the time parts spend in the plant, and. . . .

"Our total lead time condenses," I explain. "And with less time spent sitting in a pile, the speed of the flow of parts increases."

"And with faster turn-around on orders, customers get their orders faster," says Lou.

"Not only that," says Stacey, "but with shorter lead times we can respond faster."

"That's right!" I say. "If we can respond to the market faster, we get an advantage in the marketplace."

"That means more customers come to us because we can deliver faster," says Lou.

"Our sales increase!" I say.

"And so do our bonuses!" says Stacey.

"Whoa! Whoa now! Hold up here a minute!" says Bob.

"What's the matter?" I ask him.

"What about setup time?" he says. "You can batch sizes in half, you double the number of setups. What about direct labor? We got to save on setups to keep down costs."

"Okay, I knew this would come up," I tell them. "Now look, it's time we think about this carefully. Jonah told me last night that there was a corresponding rule to the one about an hour lost at a bottleneck. You remember that? An hour lost at a bottleneck is an hour lost for the entire system."

"Yeah, I remember," Bob says.

I say, "The rule he gave me last night is that an hour saved at a non-bottleneck is a mirage."

"A *mirage!*" he says. "What do you mean, an hour saved at a non-bottleneck is a mirage? An hour saved is an hour saved!"

"No, it isn't," I tell him. "Since we began withholding materials from the floor until the bottlenecks are ready for them, the non-bottlenecks now have idle time. It's perfectly okay to have more setups on non-bottlenecks, because all we're doing is cutting into time the machines would spend being idle. Saving setups at a non-bottleneck doesn't make the system one bit more productive. The time and money saved is an illusion. Even if we double the number of setups, it won't consume all the idle time."

"Okay, okay," says Bob. "I guess I can see what you mean."

"Now Jonah said, first of all, to cut the batch sizes in half. Then he suggested I go immediately to marketing and convince them to conduct a new campaign which will promise customers earlier deliveries."

"Can we do it?" asks Lou.

I tell them, "Already, our lead times have condensed considerably over what they were before thanks to the priority system and making the bottlenecks more productive. We have reduced lead time of about three to four months down to two months or even less. If we cut our batch sizes in half, how fast do you think we can respond?"

There is an eternity of hemming and hawing while this is debated.

Finally, Bob admits, "Okay, if we cut batch sizes in half, then that means it ought to take half the time it does now. So instead of six to eight weeks, it should take about four weeks . . . maybe even three weeks in a lot of cases."

"Suppose I go to marketing and tell them to promise customers deliveries in three weeks?" I say.

"Whoa! Hold on!" says Bob.

"Yeah, give us a break!" says Stacey.

"All right, four weeks then," I say. "That's reasonable, isn't it?"

"Sounds reasonable to me," says Ralph.

"Well . . . okay," says Stacey.

"I think we should risk it," says Lou.

"So are you willing to commit to this with us?" I ask Bob.

Bob sits back and says, "Well . . . I'm all for bigger bonuses. What the hell. Let's try it."

Friday morning finds the Mazda and me again hustling up the Interstate toward headquarters. I hit town just as the sun hits the glass of the UniCo building and reflects a blinding glare. Kind of pretty actually. For a moment, it takes my mind off my nerves. I've got a meeting scheduled with Johnny Jons in his office. When I called, he was quite willing to see me, but sounded less than enthusiastic about what I said I'd like to talk about. I feel there's a lot riding on my ability to convince him to go along with what we want to do. So I've found myself biting a fingernail or two during the trip.

Jons doesn't really have a desk in his office. He has a sheet of glass on chrome legs. I guess that's so that everyone can get a good look at his Gucci loafers and silk socks—which he exposes as he leans back in this chair, interweaves his fingers and puts them behind his head.

He says, "So . . . how is everything going?"

"Everything is going very well right now," I say. "In fact, that's why I wanted to talk to you."

Jons immediately dons an impassive face.

"All right, listen," I tell him, "I'm going to lay my cards out for you. I'm not exaggerating when I say everything is going well. It is. We've worked off our backlog of overdue orders, as you know. At the beginning of last week, the plant began producing strictly to meet projected due dates."

Jons nods and says, "Yes, I've noticed my phone hasn't been ringing lately with complaints from customers missing their orders."

"My point," I tell him, "is that we've really turned the plant around. Here, look at this."

From my breifcase, I take the latest list of customer orders. Among other things, it shows the due dates promised, along with the dates when Ralph expected shipment, and the dates the products were actually shipped.

"You see," I tell Jons as he studies the list on the glass top of his table, "we can predict to within twenty-four hours one way or the other when an order will leave the plant."

"Yes, I've seen something like this floating around," says Jons. "These are the dates?"

"Of course."

"This is impressive," says Jons.

"As you can see by comparing a few recently shipped orders with ones of a month or so before, our production lead times have condensed dramatically. Four months' lead time is no longer a holy number with us. From the day you sign the contract with the customer to the day we ship, the current average is about two months. Now, tell me, do you think that could help us in the marketplace?"

"Sure it could," says Jons.

"Then how about *four weeks?*"

"*What?* Al, don't be ridiculous," says Jons. "Four weeks!"

"We can do it."

"Come on!" he says. "Last winter, when demand for every damn thing we make was way down, we were promising delivery in four months, and it was taking six! Now you're telling me you can go from contract to finished product in four weeks?"

"I wouldn't be here talking to you if we couldn't," I tell him, hoping desperately that we're right.

Jons snorts, unconvinced.

"Johnny, the truth is I need more business," I tell him. "With our overdues gone, and our current backlog declining, I've got to get more work into my plant. Now we both know the business is out there; it's just that the competition is getting more of it than we are."

Jons looks at me through narrowed eyes. "You can really

turn around an order of 200 Model 12's or 300 DBD-50's in four weeks?"

"Try me," I tell him. "Get me five orders—hell, get me *ten* orders—and I'll prove it to you."

"And what happens to our credibility if you can't come through?" he asks.

Flustered, I look down through the glass table.

"Johnny," I say, "I'll make a bet with you. If I don't deliver in four weeks, I'll buy you a brand new pair of Guccis."

He laughs, shakes his head and finally says, "Okay, you're on. I'll pass the word to the salespeople that on all your products, we're offering terms of factory shipment in six weeks."

I start to protest. Jons holds up a hand.

"I know you're confident," he says. "And if you ship any new orders in less than five weeks, I'll buy *you* a new pair of shoes."

29

A full moon is shining through the bedroom window and into my eyes. The night is still. I look at the clock beside me, which says it's 4:20 A.M. Next to me in bed, Julie is sleeping.

Resting on my elbow, I look down at Julie. With her dark hair spilled out on the white pillow, she looks nice sleeping in the moonlight. I watch her for a while. I wonder what her dreams are like.

When I woke up, I was having a nightmare. It was about the plant. I was running up and down the aisles and Bill Peach was chasing me in his crimson Mercedes. Every time he was about to run me over, I'd duck between a couple of machines or hop on a passing forklift. He was yelling at me from the window about my bottom line not being good enough. Finally he trapped me in the shipping department. I had my back against stacks of cardboard cartons, and the Mercedes was racing toward me at a hundred miles an hour. I tried to shield my eyes from the blinding head-lights. Just as Peach was about to get me, I woke up and discovered that the headlights were moonbeams on my face.

Now I'm too much awake, and too aware of the problem I was trying to forget this past evening with Julie for me to fall back to sleep. Not wanting to awaken Julie with my restlessness, I slip out of bed.

The house is all ours tonight. We started out this evening with nothing particular to do, when we remembered we had a whole house in Bearington with nobody in it to bother us. So we bought a bottle of wine, some cheese and a loaf of bread, came here and got comfortable.

From the living room window where I stand in the dark looking out, it seems as though the whole world is asleep except me. I'm angry with myself at not being able to sleep. But I can't let go of what's on my mind.

Yesterday we had a staff meeting. There was some good news —and some bad news. Actually, there was a lot of good news. High among the headlines were the new contracts marketing has been winning for us. We've picked up about half-a-dozen new orders since I talked to Johnny. More good news was the fact that efficiencies have gone up, not down, as a result of what we've been doing in the plant. After we began withholding the release of materials and timing the releases according to the completed processing of heat-treat and the NCX-10, efficiencies dipped somewhat. But that was because we were consuming excess inventories. When the excess inventories were exhausted—which happened quickly as a result of the increase in throughput—efficiencies came back up again.

Then, two weeks ago, we implemented the new smaller batch sizes. When we cut batch sizes in half for non-bottlenecks, efficiencies stayed solid, and now it seems as though we're keeping the work force even more occupied than before.

That's because a really terrific thing has happened. Before we reduced batch sizes, it wasn't uncommon for a work center to be forced idle because it didn't have anything to process—even though we were wading through excess inventory. It was usually because the idle work center had to wait for the one preceding it to finish a large batch of some item. Unless told otherwise by an expeditor, the materials handlers would wait until an entire batch was completed before moving it. In fact, that's still the case. But now that the batches are smaller, the parts are ready to be moved to the next work station *sooner* than they were before.

What we had been doing many times was turning a non-bottleneck into a temporary bottleneck. This was forcing other work centers downstream from it to be idle, which reflected poorly on efficiencies. Now, even though we've recognized that non-bottlenecks have to be idle periodically, there is actually *less* idle time than before. Since we cut batch sizes, work is flowing through the plant more smoothly than ever. And it's weird, but the idle time we do have is less noticeable. It's spread out in shorter segments. Instead of people hanging around with nothing to do for a couple of hours, now they'll have maybe a few ten- to twenty-minute waits through the day for the same volume of work. From everybody's standpoint, that's much better.

Still more good news is that inventories are at their lowest ever in the plant. It's almost shocking to walk out into the plant now. Those stacks and piles of parts and sub-assemblies have shrunk to half their former size. It's as if a fleet of trucks had come and hauled everything away. Which is, in fact, about what happened. We've shipped the excess inventory as finished product. Of course, the notable part of the story is that we haven't filled the plant back up again by dumping new work-in-process on the floor. The only work-in-process out there now is for current demand.

But then there's the bad news. Which is what I'm thinking about when I hear footsteps on the carpet behind me in the dark.

"Al?"

"Yeah."

"How come you're out here in the dark?"

"Can't sleep."

"What's wrong?"

"Nothing."

"Then why don't you come back to bed?"

"I'm just thinking about some things."

It's quiet for a second. For a moment, I think she's gone away. Then I feel her beside me.

"Is it the plant?" she asks.

"Yeah."

"But I thought everything was getting better," she says. "What's wrong?"

"It has to do with our cost measurement," I tell her.

She sits down beside me.

"Why don't you tell me about it," she says.

"Sure you want to hear about it?" I ask.

"Yes, I do."

So I tell her: the cost of parts looks as though it's gone up because of the additional setups necessitated by the smaller batch sizes.

"Oh," she says. "I guess that's bad, right?"

"Politically speaking, yes," I tell her. "Financially speaking, it doesn't make a damn bit of difference."

"How come?" she asks.

"Well . . . do you know why it looks like the cost has gone up?" I ask her.

"No, not at all," she says.

I get up to switch on a lamp and find a piece of paper and pencil.

I tell her, "Okay, I'll give you an example. Suppose we have a batch of 100 parts. The time to set up the machine is 2 hours, or 120 minutes. And the process time per part is 5 minutes. So we've invested per part 5 minutes *plus* 2 hours of set-up divided by 100. It comes to 1.2 minutes of set-up per part. According to the accountants, the cost of the part is based upon direct labor of 6.2 minutes.

"Now if we cut the batch in half, we still have the same amount of set-up time. But it's spread over 50 parts instead of 100. So now we've got 5 minutes of process time, plus 2.4 minutes of set-up for a grand total of 7.4 minutes of direct labor. And the calculations are all based on the cost of direct labor."

Then I explain the way costs are calculated. First, there is the raw material cost. Then there is the cost of direct labor. And finally there is "burden," which essentially works out to be cost of the direct labor multiplied by a factor, in our case, of about three. So on paper, if the direct labor goes up, the burden also goes up.

"So with more set-ups, the cost of making parts goes up," says Julie.

"It *looks* that way," I tell her, "but in fact it hasn't really done anything to our actual expenses. We haven't added more people to the payroll. We haven't added any additional cost by doing more set-ups. In fact, the cost of parts has gone down since we began the smaller batch sizes."

"Down? How come?"

"Because we've reduced inventory and increased the amount of money we're bringing in through sales," I explain. "So the same burden, the same direct labor cost is now spread over more *product*. By making and selling more product for the same cost, our operating expense has gone down, not up."

"How could the measurement be wrong?" she asks.

I say, "The measurement assumes that all of the workers in the plant are always going to be fully occupied, and therefore, in order to do more set-ups, you have to hire more people. That isn't true."

"What are you going to do?" she asks me.

I look up at the window. The sun is now over the roof of my neighbor's house. I reach over for her hand.

"What am I going to do? I'm going to take you out to breakfast."

When I get to the office, Lou walks in.

"More bad news for me?" I joke.

He says, "Look . . . I think I can help you out on this cost of products thing."

"Yeah? Like how?"

"I can change the base we're using for determining the cost of parts. Instead of using the cost factor of the past twelve months, which is what I'm supposed to be doing, we can use the past two months. That will help us, because for the past two months, we've had big increases in throughput."

"Yeah," I say, sensing the possibilities. "Yeah, that might work. And actually the past two months are a lot more representative of what's really going on here than what happened last year."

Lou leans from side to side. He says, "We-l-l-l, yes, that's true. But according to accounting policy, it's not valid."

"Okay, but we have a good excuse," I say. "The plant *is* different now. We're really a hell of a lot better than we were."

"Al, the problem is Ethan Frost will never buy it," says Lou.

"Then why did you suggest it?"

"Frost won't buy it *if* he knows about it," says Lou.

I nod slowly. "I see."

"I can give you something that will slide through on the first glance," says Lou. "But if Frost and his assistants at division do any checking, they'll see through it in no time."

"You're saying we could end up in very hot water," I say.

"Yeah, but if you want to take a chance. . . ." says Lou.

"It could give us a couple more months to really show what we can do," I say, finishing the thought for him.

I get up and walk around for a minute turning this over in my mind.

Finally I look at Lou and say, "There is no way I can show Peach an increase in the cost of parts and convince him the plant is better off this month than last. If he sees these numbers and gets the idea our costs are going up, we'll be in hot water anyway."

"So you want to try it?" Lou asks.

"Sure."

"All right," he says. "Remember, if we get caught—"

"Don't worry. I'll practice my tap dancing."

As Lou is on his way out, Fran buzzes me to say Johnny Jons is on my line. I pick up the phone.

"Hello there," I tell him, We're practically old pals by now; I've been on the phone with him just about every day—and sometimes three or four times a day—for the past few weeks. "What can I do for you today?"

"Remember our dear friend Bucky Burnside?" says Jons.

"How could I forget good ole Bucky," I say. "Is he still complaining about us?"

"No, not anymore," says Jons. "At the moment, in fact, we don't even have a single active contract with Burnside's people. That's the reason I'm calling. For the first time in months, they've expressed interest in buying something from us again."

"What are they interested in?"

"Model 12's," he says. "They need a thousand units."

"Terrific!"

"Maybe not," says Jons. "They need the whole order by the end of the month."

"That's only about two weeks away," I say.

"I know," says Jons. "The sales rep on this already checked with the warehouse. Turns out we've only got about fifty of the Model 12's in stock."

He's telling me, of course, we'll have to manufacture the other 950 by the end of the month if we want the business.

"Well . . . Johnny, look, I know I told you I wanted business, and you've pulled in some nice contracts since I talked to you," I say. "But a thousand Model 12's in two weeks is asking a lot."

He says, "Al, to tell you the truth, I didn't really think we could do anything with this one when I called. But I thought I'd let you know about it, just in case you knew something I didn't. After all, a thousand units means a little over a million dollars in sales to us."

"Yes, I realize that," I say. "Look, what's going on that they need these things so fast?"

He tells me he did some digging and found out that the order had originally gone to our number-one competitor, who makes a product similar to the Model 12. The competitor had had the order on its books for about five months. But they hadn't filled it yet, and this week it became clear they would not be able to meet the due date.

"My guess is that Burnside turned to us, because they've heard about us offering such fast turn-around to everyone else," he says. "Frankly, I think they're desperate. And, hell, if there is any way we can pull this off, it'd sure be a good way for us to save face with them."

"Well, I don't know. I'd like that business back again, too, but. . . ."

"The real kick in the head is if we had only had the foresight to build a finished goods inventory of Model 12's while we had those slow sales months, we could have made this sale," he says.

I have to smile to myself, because at the beginning of the year I might have agreed with that.

"It's too bad," Johnny is saying. "Aside from the initial business, it could have been a big opportunity for us."

"How big?"

"Strong hints have been dropped that if we can come through on this one, we could become their preferred supplier," says Jons.

I'm quiet for a moment.

"All right. You really want this, don't you?" I ask him.

"So bad I can taste it," he says. "But if it's impossible. . . ."

"When do you have to let them know?" I ask.

"Probably sometime today, or tomorrow at the latest," he says. "Why? Do you think we can really do it?"

"Maybe there's a way. Let me see how we stand and I'll give you a call back," I tell him.

As soon as I get off the phone with Jons, I round up Bob, Stacey, and Ralph for a meeting in my office, and when we're all together I tell him what Jons told me.

"Ordinarily, I would think this is out of the question," I say. "But before we say no, let's think about it."

Everybody looks at me with the certain knowledge this is going to be a waste of time.

I say, "Let's just see what we can do, okay?"

For the rest of the morning, we're busy with this. We go over the bill of material. Stacey checks on raw materials inventories. Ralph does a quick estimate of how long it will take to produce a thousand units after the materials are on hand. By eleven o'clock, he has calculated that the bottlenecks can turn out parts for the Model 12 at the rate of about one-hundred per day.

"So, yes, it would be technically feasible for us to take the order," says Ralph. "But that's only if we work on nothing else for two weeks except the thousand units for Burnside."

"No, I don't want to do that," I tell him, thinking about us screwing up relations with a dozen customers just to please one. "Let's try something else."

"Like what?" asks Bob, who is sitting there with us, looking about as enthusiastic as a bump on a log.

I say, "A few weeks ago, we cut our batch sizes by half, and the result was we could condense the time inventory spends in the plant, which also gave us an increase in throughput. What if we cut the batch sizes by half *again?*"

Ralph says, "Gee, I hadn't thought of that."

Bob leans forward. "Cut them again? Sorry, Al, but I don't see how the heck that can help us, not with the volume we're already committed to."

"You know," says Ralph, "we have quite a few orders we'd planned to ship ahead of their due dates. We could re-schedule some of those in the priority system so they'd ship when promised instead of early. That could give us more time available on the bottlenecks, and it wouldn't hurt anybody."

"Good point, Ralph," I tell him.

"But, hell, we still can't get a thousand units done no-how," drawls Bob. "Not in two weeks."

I say, "Well, then, if we cut the batch sizes, how many units *can* we do in two weeks and still ship our current orders on time."

Bob pulls on his chin and says, "I guess we could look into it."

"I'll see what I can find out," says Ralph, standing so he can leave and go back to his computer.

His interest finally piqued, Bob says, "Maybe I'd better go with you so we can noodle this thing out together."

While Ralph and Bob are wrestling with this new possibility, Stacey enters with news about inventories. She's ascertained we can obtain all the materials we need either from our own stocks or from vendors within a few days, with one exception.

"The electronic control modules for the Model 12 are a problem," says Stacey. "We don't have enough of this type in stock. And we don't have the technology to build them in-house. *But* we've located a vendor in California who has them. Unfortunately, the vendor can't promise a shipment of that quantity in less than four to six weeks, including shipping. I'd say we might as well forget it."

"Wait a minute, Stacey; we're thinking about a little change in strategy. How many modules could they give us per week?" I ask her. "And how soon could they ship the first week's quantity to us?"

"I don't know, but doing it that way, we might not be able to get a volume discount," says Stacey.

"Why not?" I ask. "We'd be committing to the same thousand units—it's just that we'd be staggering the shipments."

"Well, then there's the added shipping cost," she says.

"Stacey, we're talking a million dollars in business here," I tell her.

"Okay, but they'll take at least three days to a week to get here by truck," she says.

"So why can't we have them shipped air freight?" I ask. "They're not very big parts."

"Well. . . ." says Stacey.

"Look into it, but I doubt if the air freight bill is going to eat up the profit on a million-dollar sale," I tell her. "And if we can't get these parts, we can't get the sale."

"All right. I'll see what they can do," she says.

At the end of the day, the details are still being sweated out, but we know enough for me to place a call to Jons.

"I've got a deal on those Model 12's for you to relay to Burnside," I say.

"Really?" says Jons excitedly. "You want to take the business?"

"Under certain conditions," I tell him. "First of all, there is no way we can deliver the full thousand units in two weeks. But we can ship 250 per week to them for four weeks."

"Well, okay, they might go for that," says Jons, "but when can you start shipping?"

"Two weeks from the day they give us the order," I say.

"Are you sure about this?" asks Johnny.

"The units will ship when we say they will," I tell him.

"You're that confident?"

"Yes."

"Okay, okay. I'll call them and see if they're interested. But, Al, I just hope what you're telling me is real, because I don't want to go through all the hassles we had before with these people."

A couple of hours later, my phone rings at home.

"Al? We got it! We got the order!" shouts Jons into my right ear.

And in my left ear, I hear a million bucks rung up on the cash register.

"You know what?" Jons is saying. "They even like the smaller shipments *better* than getting all thousand units at once!"

I tell him, "Okay, great, I'll get the ball rolling right away. You can tell them that two weeks from today, we'll ship the first 250."

30

At the beginning of the new month, we have a staff meeting. Everyone is present except Lou. Bob tells me he'll be in shortly. I sit down and fidget. To get the meeting rolling while we're waiting for Lou, I ask about shipments.

"How is Burnside's order coming along?" I ask.

"The first shipment went out as scheduled," says Donovan.

"How about the rest of it?" I ask.

"No problems to speak of," says Stacey. "The control boxes were a day late, but there was time enough for us to assemble without delaying the shipment. We got this week's batch from the vendor on time."

I say, "Good. What's the latest on the smaller batches?"

"The flow through the shop is even better now," says Bob.

"Excellent," I say.

Just then Lou comes into the meeting. He's late because he was finishing the figures for this month. He sits down and looks straight at me.

"Well?" I ask. "Did we get our fifteen percent?"

"No," he says, "we got seventeen percent, thanks in part to Burnside. And the coming month looks just fine."

Then he goes into a wrap-up of how we performed through the second quarter. We're now solidly in the black. Inventories are about forty percent of what they were three months ago. Throughput has doubled.

"Well, we've come a long way, haven't we?" I ask.

Sitting on my desk when I get back from lunch the next day are two crisp, white envelopes with the UniWare Division logo in the upper left corner. I open one and unfold the stiff stationery. The body of the letter is only two short paragraphs, with Bill Peach's signature on the bottom. It's congratulating us on the Burnside business. Tearing open the other, I find it too is from Peach. It too is short and to the point. It formally directs me to prepare for a performance review of the plant, which is to be held at headquarters.

The smile I had from reading the first letter broadens. Three months ago, that second letter would have dunked me into dread, because although it doesn't say so directly, I presume the review will be the occasion for determining the future of the plant. I was expecting some kind of formal evaluation. And now I am no longer dreading it—on the contrary, I welcome it. What do we have to worry about? Hell, this is an opportunity to show what we've done!

Throughput is going up as marketing spreads the word about us to other customers. Inventories are a fraction of what they were and still falling. With more business and more parts over which to spread the costs, operating expense is down. We're making money.

The following week, I'm away from the plant for two days with my personnel manager, Scott Dolin. We're at an off-site, very confidential meeting in St. Louis with the division's labor relations group and the other plant managers. Most of the discussion is about winning wage concessions from the various unions. It's a frustrating session for me—at Bearington, we don't particularly need to lower wages. So I'm less than enthusiastic about much of the strategy suggested, knowing it could lead to problems with the union, which could lead to a strike, which could kill the progress we've been making with customers. Aside from all that, the meeting is poorly run and ends with very little decided. I return to Bearington.

About four in the afternoon, I walk through the doors of the office building. The receptionist flags me down as I pass. She tells me Bob Donovan has asked to see me the moment I arrive. I have Bob paged and he comes hurrying into my office a few minutes later.

"What's up, Bob?" I ask.

"Hilton Symth," he says. "He was here in the plant today."

"He was *here?*" I ask. "Why?"

Bob shakes his head and says, "Remember the videotape about robots that was in the works a couple of months ago?"

"That was killed," I say.

"Well, it was reincarnated," says Bob. "Only now it's Hilton, because he's productivity manager for the division, doing the speech instead of Granby. I was having a cup of coffee out of the machine over by C-aisle this morning when I see this T.V. crew come trooping along. By the time I found out what they were doing here, Hilton Smyth is standing at my elbow."

"Didn't anybody here know they were coming?" I ask.

He tells me Barbara Penn, our employee communicator, knew about it.

"And she didn't think to *tell anybody?*" I say.

"See, the whole thing was re-scheduled on short notice," says Bob. "Since you and Scott weren't around, she went ahead on her own, cleared it with the union, and made all the arrangements. She sent around a memo, but nobody got a copy until this morning."

"Nothing like initiative," I mutter.

He goes on to tell me about how Hilton's crew proceeded to set up in front of one of the robots—not the welding types, but another kind of robot which stacks materials. It soon became obvious there was a problem, however: the robot didn't have anything to do. There was no inventory for it, and no work on its way.

In a videotape about productivity, the robot, of course, could not simply sit there in the background and do nothing. It had to be *producing*. So for an hour, Donovan and a couple of assistants searched every corner of the plant for something the robot could manipulate. Meanwhile, Smyth became bored with the wait, so he started wandering around, and it wasn't long before he noticed a few things.

"When we got back with the materials, Hilton started asking all kinds of things about our batch sizes," says Bob. "I didn't know what to tell him, because I wasn't sure what you've said up at headquarters and, uh . . . well, I just thought you ought to know."

I feel my stomach twisting. Just then the phone rings. I pick it up at my desk. It's Ethan Frost at headquarters. He tells me he's just had a talk with Hilton Smyth. I excuse myself to Bob, and he leaves. When he's gone and the door is shut, I talk to Frost for a couple of minutes and afterwards go down to see Lou.

I walk though the door and start to tap dance.

Two days later, an audit team from headquarters arrives at the plant. The team is headed by the division's assistant controller, Neil Cravitz, a fiftyish man who has the most bone-crushing handshake and the most humorless stare of anyone I've ever met.

They march in and take over the conference room. In hardly any time at all, they've found we changed the base for determining the cost of products.

"This is highly irregular," says Cravitz, peering at us over the tops of his glasses as he looks up from the spreadsheets.

Lou stammers that, okay, maybe it wasn't exactly according to policy, but we had valid reasons for basing costs on a current two-month period.

I added, "It's actually a more truthful representation this way,"

"Sorry, Mr. Rogo," says Cravitz. "We have to observe standard policy."

"But the plant *is* different now!"

Around the table, all five accountants are frowning at Lou and me. I finally shake my head. There is no sense attempting to appeal to them. All they know are their accounting standards.

The audit team recalculates the numbers, and it now looks as if our costs have gone up. When they leave, I try to head them off by calling Peach before they can return, but Peach is unexpectedly out of town. I try Frost, but he's gone too. One of the secretaries offers to put me through to Smyth, who seems to be the only manager in the offices, but I ungracefully decline.

For a week, I wait for the blast from headquarters. But it never comes. Lou gets a rebuke from Frost in the form of a memo warning him to stick to approved policy, and a formal order to redo our quarterly report according to the old cost standards and to submit it before the review. From Peach, there is nothing.

I'm in the middle of a meeting with Lou over our *revised* monthly report early one afternoon. I'm crestfallen. With the numbers based on the old cost factor, we're not going to make our fifteen percent. We're only going to record a 12.8 percent increase on the bottom line, not the seventeen percent Lou originally calculated.

"Lou, can't we massage this a little more?" I'm pleading.

He shakes his head. "From now on, Frost is going to be scrutinizing everything we submit. I can't do any better than what you see now."

Just then I become aware of this sound outside the offices that's getting louder and louder.

Wuppa-wuppa-wuppa-wuppa-wuppa-wuppa-wuppa-wuppa.

I look at Lou and he looks at me.

"Is that a helicopter?" I ask.

Lou goes to the window and looks out.

"Sure is, and it's landing on our lawn!" he says.

I get to the window just as it touches down. Dust and brown grass clippings are whirling in the prop wash around this sleek red and white helicopter. With the blades still twirling down to a stop, the door opens and two men get out.

"That first one looks like Johnny Jons," says Lou.

"It *is* Johnny Jons," I say.

"Who's the other guy?" asks Lou.

I'm not sure. I watch them cross the lawn and start to walk through the parking lot. Something about the girth and the striding, arrogant swagger of the huge, white-haired second man triggers the recollection of a distant meeting. It dawns on me who he is.

"Oh, god," I say.

"I didn't think He needed a helicopter to get around," says Lou.

"It's worse than God," I say, "It's Bucky Burnside!"

Before Lou can utter another word, I'm running for the door. I dash around the corner and into Stacey's office. She, along with her secretary and some people she's meeting with, are all at the window. Everybody is watching the damn helicopter.

"Stacey, quick, I need to talk to you right now!"

She comes over to the door and I pull her into the hallway.

"What's the status on Burnside's Model 12's?" I ask her.

"The last shipment went out two days ago."

"It was on time?"

"Sure," she says. "It went out the door with no problems, just like the previous shipments."

I'm running again, mumbling "thanks" over my shoulder to her.

"Donovan!"

He's not in his office. I stop at his secretary's desk.

"Where's Bob?" I ask her.

"I think he went to the men's room," she says.

I go sprinting in that direction. Bursting through the door, I find Bob washing his hands.

"On Burnside's order," I ask him, "were there any quality problems?"

"No," says Bob, startled to see me. "Nothing I know about."

"Were there *any* problems on that order?" I ask him.

He reaches for a paper towel and dries his hands. "No, the whole thing came off like clockwork."

I fall back against the wall. "Then what the hell is he doing here?"

"Is *who* doing here?" asks Bob.

"Burnside," I tell him. "He just landed in a helicopter with Johnny Jons."

"What?"

"Come with me," I tell him.

We go to the receptionist, but nobody is in the waiting area.

"Did Mr. Jons come through here just now with a customer?" I ask her.

She says, "The two men in the helicopter? No I watched them and they went past here and into the plant."

Bob and I hustle side by side down the corridor and through the double doors, into the orange light and production din of the plant. One of the supervisors sees us from across the aisle and, without being asked, points in the direction Jons and Burnside took. As we head down the aisle, I spot them ahead of us.

Burnside is walking up to every employee he sees and he's *shaking hands* with each of them. Honest! He's shaking hands, clapping them on the arm, saying things to them. And he's smiling.

Jons is walking with him. He's doing the same thing. As soon as Burnside lets go of a hand, Jons shakes it as well. They're pumping everybody in sight.

Finally, Jons sees us approaching, taps Burnside on the shoulder, and says something to him. Burnside dons this big grin and comes striding up to me with his hand extended.

"Here's the man I especially want to congratulate," says Burnside in a growling kind of voice. "I was saving the best for last, but you beat me to it. How are you?"

"Fine, just fine, Mr. Burnside," I tell him.

"Rogo, I came down here because I want to shake the hand of every employee in your whole plant," growls Burnside. "That was a hell of job this plant did on our order. A hell of a good job! Those other bastards had the order for five months and still couldn't get it down, and here your people finish the whole thing in five weeks. Must have been an incredible effort!"

Before I can say anything, Jons jumps into the conversation and says, "Bucky and I were having lunch today, and I was telling him how you pulled out all the stops for him, how everybody down here really gave it everything they had."

I say, "Ah . . . yeah, we just did our best."

"Mind if I go ahead?" asks Burnside, intending to continue down the aisle.

"No, not at all," I say.

"Won't hurt your efficiency, will it?" asks Burnside.

"Not one bit," I tell him. "You go right ahead."

I turn to Donovan then and out of the corner of my mouth say, "Get Barbara Penn down here right away with the camera she uses for the employee news. And tell her to bring lots of film."

Donovan goes trotting off to the offices, and Jons and I follow Bucky up and down the aisles, the three of us shaking hands with one and all.

Johnny, I notice, is virtually atwitter with excitement. When Burnside is far enough ahead that he can't hear us, he turns to me and asks, "What's your shoe size?"

"Ten and a half," I tell him. "Why?"

"I owe you a pair of shoes," says Jons.

I say, "That's okay, Johnny; don't worry about it."

"Al, I'm telling you, we're meeting with Burnside's people next week on a long-term contract for Model 12's—10,000 units a year!"

The number just about sends me reeling backwards.

"And I'm calling in my whole department when I get back," Jons continues as we walk. "We're going to do a new campaign pushing everything you make down here, because this is the only plant we've got in this damn division that can ship a quality product on time. With your lead times, Al, we're going to blow everybody out of the market! Thanks to you, we've finally got a winner."

I'm beaming. "Thanks Johnny. But, as it turned out, Burnside's order didn't take any extra effort at all."

"Shhhh! Don't let Burnside know," Johnny says.

Behind me, I hear two hourly guys talking.

"What was that all about?" asks one.

"Beats me," says the other. "Guess we musta done somthin' right."

On the eve of the plant performance review, with presentation rehearsed and ten copies of our report in hand, and with nothing more to do except imagine what could go wrong, I call Julie.

"Hi," I tell her. "Listen, I have to be at headquarters for a meeting tomorrow morning. And because Forest Grove is more or less on the way, I'd like to come up and be with you tonight. What do you think?"

"Sure, it sounds great," she says.

So I leave work a little early and hit the highway.

As I head up the Interstate, Bearington is spread out to my left. The "Buy Me!" sign on top of the high-rise office building is still in place. Living and breathing within the range of my sight are 30,000 people who have no idea that one small but important part of the town's economic future will be decided tomorrow. Most of them haven't the slightest interest in the plant or what we've done here—except if UniWare closes us, they'll be mad and scared. And if we stay open? Nobody will care. Nobody will even know what we went through.

Well, win or lose, I know I did my best.

When I get to Julie's parents' house, Sharon and Dave run up to the car. After getting out of my suit and into some "off-duty" clothes, I spend about an hour throwing a frisbee to the two kids. When they've exhausted me, Julie has the idea the two of us should go out to dinner. I get the feeling she wants to talk to me. I clean up a little and off we go. As we're driving along, we pass the park.

"Al, why don't we stop for awhile," says Julie.

"How come?" I ask.

"The last time we were here we never finished our walk," she says.

So I pull over. We get out and walk. By and by, we come to the bench by the river, and the two of us sit down.

"What's your meeting about tomorrow?" she asks.

"It's a plant performance review," I say. "The division will decide the future of the plant."

"Oh. What do you think they'll say?"

"We didn't quite make what I promised Bill Peach," I say. "One set of numbers doesn't look as good as it truly is because of the cost-of-products standards. You remember me telling you about some of that, don't you?"

She nods, I shake my head momentarily, still angry at what happened as a result of the audit.

"But even with that, we still had a good month. It just doesn't show up as the fantastic month we really had," I tell her.

"You don't think they'd still close the plant, do you?" she asks.

"I don't think so," I say. "A person would have to be an idiot to condemn us just because of an increase in cost of products. Even with screwed-up measurements, we're making money."

She reaches over to take my hand and says, "It was nice of you to take me out to breakfast that morning."

I smile and say, "After listening to me ramble on at five o'clock in the morning, you deserved it."

"When you talked to me then, it made me realize how little I know about what you do," she says. "I wish you had told me more over the years."

I shrug. "I don't know why I haven't, I guess I thought you wouldn't want to hear it. Or I didn't want to burden you with it."

"Well, I should have asked you more questions," she says.

"I'm sure I didn't give you many opportunities by working those long hours."

"When you weren't coming home those days before I left, I really took it personally," she says. "I couldn't believe it didn't have something to do with me. Deep down, I thought you must be using it as an excuse to stay away from me."

"No, absolutely not, Julie. When all those crises were occurring, I just kept thinking you *must* know how important they were," I tell her. "I'm sorry. I should have told you more."

She squeezes my hand.

"I've been thinking about some of the things you said about our marriage when we were sitting here last time," she says. "I have to say you're right. For a long time, we *have* just been coasting along. In fact, we were drifting apart. I've watched you get more and more wrapped up in your job as the years have gone by. And to compensate for losing you, I got wrapped up in things like decorating the house and spending my time with friends. We lost sight of what was important."

I look at her in the sunlight. The awful frosting in her hair which she had when I came home the day the NCX-10 went down is finally gone. It's grown out. Her hair is thick and straight again, and all the same dark brown.

She says, "Al, the one thing I definitely know now is that I want more of you, not less. That's always been the problem for me."

She turns to me with her blue eyes, and I get a long-lost feeling about her.

"I finally figured out why I haven't wanted to go back to Bearington with you," she says. "And it isn't just the town, although I don't like it very much there. It's that since we've been living apart, we've actually spent more time being together. I mean, when we were living in the same house, I felt as though you took me for granted. Now you bring me flowers. You go out of your way to be with me. You take time to do things with me and the kids. Al, it's been nice. I know it can't go on this way forever—I think my parents are getting a little tired of the arrangement—but I haven't wanted it to end."

I start to feel very good.

I say, "At least we're sure we don't want to say good-bye."

"Al, I don't know exactly what our goal is, or ought to be, but I think we know there must be some kind of need between us," she says. "I know I want Sharon and Dave to grow up to be good people. And I want us to give each other what we need."

I put my arm around her.

"For starters, that sounds worth shooting for," I tell her. "Look, it's probably easier said than done, but I can certainly try to keep from taking you for granted. I'd like you to come home, but unfortunately, the pressures that caused all the problems are still going to be there. They're just not going to go away. I can't ignore my job."

"I've never asked you to," she says. "Just don't ignore me or the kids. And I'll really try to understand your work."

I smile.

"You remember a long time ago, after we got married and we both had jobs, how we'd come home and just talk to each other for a couple of hours, and sympathize with each other about the trials and tribulations we'd suffered during the day?" I ask. "That was nice."

"But then there were babies," says Julie. "And, later, you started putting in extra hours at work."

"Yeah, we got out of the habit," I tell her. "What do you say we make a point to do that again?"

"That sounds terrific," she says. "Look, Al, I know that leaving you must have seemed selfish on my part. I just went crazy for a little while. I'm sorry—"

"No, you don't have to be sorry," I tell her. "I should have been paying attention."

"But I'll try to make it up to you," she says. Then she smiles briefly and adds, "Since we're walking down memory lane, maybe you remember the first fight we had, how we promised afterwards we'd always try to look at a situation from the other's point of view as well as our own. Well, I think for the past couple of years we haven't been doing that very often. I'm willing to try it again if you are."

"I am too," I say.

There is a long hug.

"So . . . you want to get married?" I ask her.

She leans back in my arms and says, "I'll try anything twice."

"You know, don't you, it's not going to be perfect," I tell her. "You know we're still going to have fights."

"And I'll probably be selfish about you from time to time," she says.

"What the hell," I tell her, "Let's go to Vegas and find a justice of the peace."

She laughs, "Are you serious?"

"Well, I can't go tonight," I say. "I've got that meeting in the morning. How about tomorrow night?"

"You are serious!"

"All I've been doing since you left is putting my paycheck in the bank. After tomorrow it'll definitely be time to blow some of it."

Julie smiles. "Okay, big spender. Let's do it."

31

The next morning on the fifteenth floor of the UniCo building, I walk into the conference room at a few minutes before ten o'clock. Sitting at the far end of the long table is Hilton Smyth and sitting next to him is Neil Cravitz. Flanking them are various staff people.

I say, "Good morning."

Hilton looks up at me without a smile and says, "If you close the door, we can begin."

"Wait a minute. Bill Peach isn't here yet," I say. "We're going to wait for him, aren't we?"

"Bill's not coming. He's involved in some negotiations," says Smyth.

"Then I would like this review to be postponed until he's available," I tell him.

Smyth's eyes get steely.

"Bill specifically told me to conduct this and to pass along my recommendation to him," says Smyth. "So if you want to make a case for your plant, I suggest you get started. Otherwise, we'll have to draw our own conclusions from your report. And with that increase in cost of products Neil has told me about, it sounds to me as if you have a little explaining to do. I, for one, would particularly like to know why you are not observing proper procedures for determining economical batch quantities."

I pace in front of them a moment before answering. The fuse to my anger has started a slow burn. I try to put it out and think about what this means. I don't like the situation one bit. Peach damn well *ought* to be here. And I was expecting to be making my presentation to Frost, not his assistant. But from the sound of it, Hilton may have set himself up with Peach to be my judge, jury, and possibly, executioner. I decide the safest bet is to talk.

"Fine," I say finally. "But before I go into my presentation of what has been happening at my plant, let me ask you a question. Is it the goal of the UniWare Division to reduce costs?"

"Of course it is," says Hilton impatiently.

"No, actually, that is not the goal," I tell them. "The goal of UniWare is to make money. Agreed?"

Cravitz sits up in his chair and says, "That's true."

Hilton gives me a tentative nod.

I say, "I'm going to demonstrate to you that regardless of what our costs look like according to standard measurements, my plant has never been in a better position to make money."

And so it begins.

An hour and a half later, I'm midway through an explanation of the effects of the bottlenecks upon inventory and throughput when Hilton stops me.

"Okay, you've taken a lot of time to tell us all this, and I personally can't see the significance," says Hilton. "Maybe at your plant you did have a couple of bottlenecks and you discovered what they were. Well, I mean *bravo* and all that, but when I was a plant manager we dealt with bottlenecks wandering everywhere."

"Hilton, we're dealing with fundamental assumptions that are wrong," I tell him.

"I can't see that you're dealing with anything fundamental," says Hilton. "It's at best simple common sense, and I'm being charitable at that."

"No, it's more than just common sense. Because we're doing things every day that are in direct contradiction to the established rules most people use in manufacturing," I tell him.

"Such as?" asks Cravitz.

"According to the cost-accounting rules that everybody has used in the past, we're supposed to balance capacity with demand first, then try to maintain the flow," I say. "But instead we shouldn't be trying to balance capacity at all; we need excess capacity. The rule we should be following is to balance the *flow* with demand, not the capacity.

"*Two,* the incentives we usually offer are based on the assumption that the level of utilization of any worker is determined by his own potential," I tell them. "That's totally false because of dependency. For any resource that is not a bottleneck, the level of activity from which the system is able to profit is not determined by its individual potential but by some other constraint within the system."

Hilton says impatiently, "What's the difference? When somebody is working, we're getting use out of him."

"No, and that's a *third* assumption that's wrong," I say.

"We've assumed that utilization and activation are the same. Activating a resource and utilizing a resource are not synonymous."

And the argument goes on.

I say an hour lost at a bottleneck is an hour out of the entire system. *Hilton* says an hour lost at a bottleneck is just an hour lost of that resource.

I say an hour saved at a non-bottleneck is worthless. *Hilton* says an hour saved at a non-bottleneck is an hour saved at that resource.

"All this talk about bottlenecks," says Hilton. "Bottlenecks temporarily limit throughput. Maybe your plant is proof of that. But they have little impact upon inventory."

"It's completely the opposite, Hilton," I say. "Bottlenecks govern both throughput and inventory. And I'll tell you what my plant really has shown: it's proved our performance measurements are wrong."

Cravitz drops the pen he's holding and it rolls noisily on the table.

"Then how are we to evaluate the performance of our operations?" asks Cravitz.

"By the bottom line," I tell him. "And based upon that evaluation, my plant has now become the best in the UniWare Division, and possibly the best in its industry. We're making money when none of the others are."

"Temporarily you may be making money. But if you're really running your plant this way, I can't possibly see how your plant can be profitable for very long," says Hilton.

I start to speak, but Hilton raises his voice and talks over me.

"The fact of the matter is that your cost-of-products measurement increased," says Hilton. "And when costs go up, profits have to go down. It's that simple. And that's the basis of what I'll be putting into my report to Bill Peach."

Afterwards, I find myself alone in the room. Messrs. Smyth and Cravitz have gone. I'm staring into my open briefcase—then with a fist, I slam it shut.

I'm muttering to myself something about their pigheadedness as I exit the conference room and go to the elevators. I press the "down" button. But when the elevator arrives, I'm not there. I'm walking back up the corridor again, and I'm heading for the corner office.

Bill's secretary, Meg, watches me approach. I stride up to her desk, where she's sorting paper clips.

"I need to see Bill," I tell her.

"Go right in. He's waiting for you," she says.

"Hello, Al," he greets me as I enter his office. "I knew you wouldn't leave without seeing me. Take a seat."

As I approach his desk I start to talk, "Hilton Smyth is going to submit a negative report about my plant, and I feel that as my manager you should hear me out before you come to any conclusions."

"Go ahead, tell me all about it. Sit down, we're not in a rush."

I continue to talk. Bill puts his elbows on the desktop and his fingers together in front of his face. When I finally stop he says, "And you explained all of this to Hilton?"

"In great detail."

"And what was his response?" he asks.

"He basically refused to listen. He continues to claim that as long as cost of products increase, profits eventually have to go down."

Bill looks straight into my eyes and asks, "Don't you think he has a point?"

"No, I don't. As long as I keep my operating expenses under control and Johnny Jons is happy, I don't see how profits can help but continue to go up."

"Fine," he says, and buzzes Meg. "Can you call Hilton, Nathan, and Johnny Jons in here please."

"What's going on?" I ask him.

"Don't worry, just wait and see," he says calmly.

It's not long before they all enter the room and take seats.

"Hilton," Bill turns to him, "you heard Alex's report this morning. You've also seen all the financial results. As the productivity manager of the division, and as a fellow plant manager, what's your recommendation?"

"I think that Alex should be called to order," he says in a formal voice. "And I think that immediate actions should be taken in his plant before it's too late. The productivity in Alex's plant is deteriorating, cost of products is going up, and proper procedures are not being followed. I think that immediate actions are in order."

Ethan Frost clears his throat, and when we all look at him

he says, "And what about the fact that in the last two months that plant has turned profits rather than losses, while releasing a lot of cash for the division?"

"That is only a temporary phenomenon," Hilton states. "We must expect big losses in the very near future."

"Johnny, do you have anything to add?" Bill asks.

"Yes, certainly. Alex's plant is the only one that can produce miracles—to deliver what the client needs in a surprisingly short time. You've all heard about Burnside's visit. With such a plant backing up sales, they can really go out and blast the market."

"Yes, but at what price?" Hilton reacts. "Cutting batches to far below optimum size. Devoting the entire plant to one order. Do you know the long-term ramifications?"

"But I haven't devoted the plant to one order!" I can't contain my anger. "As a matter of fact, I haven't got any past-due orders. All my clients are pleased."

"Miracles exist only in fairy tales," Hilton says cynically.

Nobody says a word. At last I cannot hold back, "So what's the verdict—is my plant going to be closed?"

"No," says Bill. "Not at all. Do you think we're such bad managers that we would close a gold mine?"

I sigh in relief. Only now do I notice I've been holding my breath.

"As manager of productivity of the division," Hilton says with a red face, "I feel it's my duty to protest."

Bill ignores him, and turning to Ethan and Johnny he asks, "Shall we tell them now, or wait until Monday?"

They both laugh.

"Hilton, this morning I asked you to sit in for me because we were meeting with Granby. Two months from now the three of us are moving up the ladder, to head the group. Granby left it to us to decide who will be the next manager of the division. I think that the three of us have decided. Congratulations, Alex; you will be the one to replace me."

When I return to the plant, Fran hands me a message "It's from Bill Peach. What's going on?"

"Call everybody. I have some good news," I smile.

Bill's message is: "I recommend you use these two months to prepare yourself. You still have a lot to learn, hotshot."

At last I'm able to reach Jonah in New York and fill him in on the latest developments. Although pleased for me, he does not seem surprised.

"And all this time I just worried about saving my one plant," I tell him. "Now it seems that I'm ending up with three."

"Good luck," says Jonah. "Keep up the good work."

Hurriedly, before he hangs up I ask in a desperate voice, "I'm afraid that luck will not be enough; I'm out of my depth. Can't you come down and help me?" I haven't spent two hours tracking down Jonah just to hear his congratulations. Frankly, I'm terrified at the prospect of my new job. It's one thing to handle a production plant, but handling a division of three plants does not mean just three times the work, it also means responsibility for product design and marketing.

"Even if I had the time, I don't think it's a good idea," I hear his disappointing answer.

"Why not? It seemed to work fine so far."

"Alex," he says in a stern voice, "as you climb up the ladder and your responsibilities grow, you should learn to rely more and more on yourself. Asking me to come now will lead to the opposite; it will increase the dependency."

I refuse to see his point. "Can't you continue to teach me?"

"Yes, I can," he answers. "But first you should find out exactly what it is that you want to learn. Call me then."

I don't give up easily. "I want to learn how to run an efficient division, isn't it obvious?"

"In the past you wanted to learn how to run an efficient plant," Jonah sounds impatient. "Now you want to learn how to run an efficient division. We both know that it will not end here. What *is* it that you want to learn? Can you spell it out?"

"Actually, I guess that I want to learn how to manage—a plant, a division, a company, any type or size organization." After a second of hesitation I add, "It wouldn't be bad to learn how to manage my life, but I'm afraid that would be asking for too much."

"Why too much?" says Jonah to my surprise. "I think that every sensible person should want to learn how to manage his or her life."

"Great, when can we start?" I ask eagerly.

"Now. Your first assignment is to find out what techniques are needed for effective management."

"What?" I ask in a choked voice.

"Come on, I didn't ask you to develop them, just to determine clearly what they should be. Call me when you have the answer. And Alex, congratulations on your promotion."

32

"I'm really proud of you. Three more steps like that and we will have made it. Shall we drink to it?"

Julie's forced enthusiasm strikes a responding chord inside me. "No, I don't think so." I refuse the toast, an event which, as you can imagine, is not very common.

Julie doesn't say a word. She just slowly lowers her drink, leans slightly forward, and looks directly into my eyes. It's quite apparent that she is waiting for some explanation.

Under the pressure I start to talk slowly, trying to verbalize my rambling thoughts. "Julie, I really don't think that we should toast it, at least not in the way you make it sound, like toasting an empty victory. Somehow I feel that you were right all along—what is this promotion if not just winning a point in the rat race?"

"Hmm," is her only response.

My wife can express herself very clearly without even opening her mouth—which is definitely not the case for me. Here I am, rambling all over the place . . . 'Rat race' . . . 'Empty victory.' What on earth am I talking about? But still, why do I feel it's inappropriate to toast my promotion?

"The family paid too big a price for this promotion," I finally say.

"Alex you're being too hard on yourself. This crisis was about to explode one way or the other."

She continues, "I gave it a lot of thought and let's face it, if you had given up, the feeling of failure would have spoiled every good part of our marriage. I think you should be proud of this promotion. You didn't step on anybody to get it; you won it fair and square."

A chill goes down my back as I remember it. I was in deep trouble. My plant was under a real threat of being closed down; over six hundred people were about to join the already long unemployment lines; my career was one inch from being kissed by limbo; and on top of all that, the unbelievable hours I was putting in at work had pushed our marriage to the brink of going down the tube. In short, I was about to change from a bright, rising star into an ordinary bum.

But I didn't give up. Against all odds I continued to fight. And I was not alone. Jonah introduced me to his common-sense (and thus very controversial) approach to managing a company. It made a lot of sense, so my team enthusiastically backed me up. And it was fun, real fun. Let me tell you, the last few months were quite stormy. I think that we violated almost every rule of corporate America. But we made it. We turned the plant around. So much so that it saved the entire division. Now, Julie and I are sitting in this fancy restaurant celebrating. I'm going to head the division, which means relocation—a fact that probably contributes a lot to Julie's supportive mood.

Raising my glass I say confidently, "Julie, let's drink to my promotion. Not as a step toward the tip of the pyramid, but let's drink to what it *really* means—positive reassurance to our exciting, worthwhile journey."

A broad smile is spreading over Julie's face and our glasses make a clear, gentle sound.

We turn to our menus, in a good mood. "It's your celebration as much as it is mine," I say generously. After a while, and in a more somber tone I continue, "Actually, it's much more Jonah's achievement than mine."

"You know Alex, it's so typical of you," Julie says apparently disturbed. "You worked so hard and now you want to give the credit to somebody else?"

"Julie, I'm serious. Jonah is the one who gave me all the answers, I was just the instrument. As much as I would like to think otherwise, that's the plain, bare truth."

"No, it's far from the truth."

I turn nervously in my chair, "But . . ."

"Alex, stop this nonsense," Julie says in a firm voice. "Artificial modesty doesn't suit you." She raises her hand to prevent me from answering and firmly continues, "Nobody handed you solutions on a silver platter. Tell me, Mr. Rogo, how many nights did you sweat until you succeeded in finding the answers?"

"Quite a few," I admit with a smile.

"You see!" Julie tries to close the subject.

"No, I don't see," I laugh. "I'm very well aware that Jonah didn't simply give me the answers. As a matter of fact, during those long nights, (and days), considerable time was spent cursing him for just that. But, come on, Julie, the fact that he elected to present them in the form of very pointed questions doesn't change a thing."

Rather than continuing, Julie calls the waiter and starts to order. She's right. This line of discussion will just ruin a pleasant evening.

It's not until I'm busy with my delicious veal parmesan that my thoughts start to crystallize. What was the nature of the answers, the solutions, that Jonah caused us to develop? They all had one thing in common. They all made common sense, and at the same time, they flew directly in the face of everything I'd ever learned. Would we have had the courage to try to implement them if it weren't for the fact that we'd had to sweat to construct them? Most probably not. If it weren't for the conviction that we gained in the struggle—for the ownership that we developed in the process—I don't think we'd actually have had the guts to put our solutions into practice.

Still deep in thought, I raise my eyes from the plate and examine Julie's face. It's as if she was waiting for me all this time.

"How come you didn't think of it yourselves?" I hear her asking. "To me your answers look like plain, common sense. Why couldn't you do it without Jonah's guiding questions?"

"Good question, very good question. Frankly, I doubt I know the answer."

"Alex, don't tell me you haven't thought about it."

"Yes, I have," I admit. "All of us, back in the plant, had the same question. The solutions look trivial, but the fact is that for years we've done the exact opposite. Moreover, the other plants still insist on sticking to the old, devastating ways. Probably Mark Twain was right saying that 'common sense is not common at all' or something similar."

"That's not an answer to my question." She doesn't let me off the hook.

"Just bear with me," I plead. "I really don't know. I'm not sure that I even know the meaning of 'common sense'. What do you think we mean when we refer to something as 'common sense'?"

"It's unfair to answer a question with a question." She refuses my apparent attempt to turn the table.

"Why not?" I try again.

She doesn't allow her lips to move.

"Okay," I give up. "The best that I have come up with so far is to recognize that we refer to something as common sense only if it is in line with our own intuition."

She nods her head in approval.

"Which only helps to intensify your question," I continue. "It only means that when we recognize something as common sense, it must be that, at least intuitively, we knew it all along. Why is there so often the need for an external trigger to help us realize something that we already knew intuitively?"

"That was my question!"

"Yes, darling, I know. Probably these intuitive conclusions are masked by something else, something that's not common sense."

"What could that be?"

"Probably common practice."

"Makes sense," she smiles and turns to finish her dinner.

"I must admit," I say after a while, "that Jonah's way of leading to the answers through asking questions, his 'Socratic approach,' is very effective at peeling away the layers—the thick layers—of common practice. I tried to explain the answers to others, who needed them as badly as we did, but got nowhere. As a matter of fact, if it hadn't been for Ethan Frost's appreciation of our improvements to the bottom line, my approach might have led to some very undesirable results.

"You know," I continue, "it's amazing how deeply ingrained those things are that we've been told and practiced, but never spent the time to think about on our own. 'Don't give the answers, just ask the questions!' I'll have to practice *that*."

Julie doesn't look too enthused.

"What's the matter?" I ask.

"Nothing," she says.

" 'Don't give the answers,' definitely makes sense," I try to convince her. "Spelling out the answers when you are trying to convince someone who blindly follows the common practice is totally ineffective. Actually there are only two possibilities, either you are not understood, or you *are* understood."

"You don't say?"

"In the first case, no real harm has been done, people are just going to ignore you. The second case might be much worse, people might understand you. They'll take your message as something worse than criticism."

"What is worse than criticism?" she asks innocently.

"Constructive criticism." I smile gloomily, remembering the harsh responses of Hilton Smyth and that Cravitz fellow. "You have a point, but it's below the belt. People will never forgive you for that."

"Alex, you don't have to convince me that when I want to persuade somebody—especially my husband—that giving answers is not the way. I'm simply not convinced that only asking questions is much better."

I think about it. She is right. Whenever I tried just to ask questions it was interpreted as patronizing, or even worse, that I was simply negative.

"It looks like one should think twice before charging the tall windmills of common practice." I conclude gloomily.

Julie busies herself with the delicious cheesecake our waiter is placing in front of us. I do the same.

When the coffee's served I gather enough stamina to continue the conversation. "Julie, is it really so bad? I don't recall giving you a lot of grief."

"Are you kidding? Not only are you stubborn like a Southern mule, you had to go and pass on these genes to your kids. I bet you gave Jonah a hard time as well."

I think about it for a short while. "No Julie, with Jonah somehow it was different. You see, whenever I'm talking with Jonah, I have the distinct feeling that not only is he ready with his questions, he's also ready with my questions. It must be that the Socratic method is much more than just asking questions. One thing I can tell you, improvising with this method is hazardous, believe me, I've tried. It's like throwing a sharpened boomerang."

Then it dawns on me. Here's the answer. This is the technique that I should ask Jonah to teach me: how to persuade other people, how to peel away the layers of common practice, how to overcome the resistance to change.

I tell Julie about my last telephone conversation with Jonah.

"That's very interesting," she says at last. "You definitely need to learn how to manage your life better. But sweetheart," she laughs, "be careful, remember what happened to Socrates. He was forced to drink poison."

"I don't intend to give Jonah any poison," I say, still very excited. "Julie, let me tell you, whenever Jonah and I talked about my troubles at the plant, I always felt he anticipated my response. It actually bothered me for quite some time."

"Why?"

"When did he have the time to learn so much? I'm not talking about theories, I'm talking about his intimate understanding of how the wheels are really turning in a plant. As far as I know, he never worked one day of his life in industry. He's a physicist. I can't believe that a scientist, sitting in his ivory tower, can know so much about the detailed realities of the shop floor. Something doesn't match.

"Alex, if that's the case, it seems that you should ask Jonah to teach you something more than just the Socratic method."

33

Lou is my first and most important target. If I'm unable to persuade him to join me, I'm basically lost. It's not going to be easy. He's very close to retirement and I know to what extent he's involved in his community. I take a deep breath and walk into his office. "Hey Lou, is it a good time?"

"Good as any. How can I help you?"

Perfect opening, but somehow I don't have the guts to go straight to the point. "I was just wondering about your forecast for the next two months," I say. "Do you see any problem in us reaching and maintaining the fifteen percent net profit? Not that it's crucial any more," I hurriedly add, "but I'd hate giving Hilton Smyth even the slightest opening to hiss, 'I told you so.'"

"You can sleep tight. According to my calculations we'll easily cross the twenty percent net profit for the next two months."

"What!" I can hardly believe my ears. "Lou, what's the matter with you? Since when do you believe marketing's chronically optimistic outlook?"

"Alex, a lot has happened to me recently, but believing marketing is not one of them. Actually, my forecast is based on a slight decline in incoming orders."

"So how did you pull this rabbit out of your hat?"

"Have a seat, it'll take me some time to explain. I have something important to tell you," he says.

It's clear that I'm going to hear about another devious accounting trick. "All right, let's hear it."

I make myself comfortable while Lou shuffles papers. After two minutes I lose my patience, "Well, Lou?"

"Alex, we blamed the distorted way in which product costs are calculated for giving the appearance that our net profit was only twelve point eight percent, rather than over seventeen percent as we believed was the case. I know that you were furious about it, but what I've found out is that there's an even bigger accounting distortion. It's tied to the way that we evaluate inventory, but it's hard for me to explain. Maybe I'll try to do it through the balance sheet."

He pauses again. This time I wait patiently.

"Maybe I should start with a question," he says. "Do you agree that inventory is a liability?"

"Of course, everybody knows that. And even if we didn't know it, the last few months have shown to what extent inventory is a liability. Do you think we could have pulled off this fast response to orders if the floor had been as jammed up as before? And haven't you noticed that quality has improved, and overtime has gone down—not to mention that we hardly ever have to expedite today!"

"Yeah," he says, still looking at his papers. "Inventory is definitely a liability, but under what heading are we forced to report it on the balance sheet?"

"Holy cow, Lou!" I jump to my feet. "I knew that the financial measurements were remote from reality, but to that extent— to report liabilities under the heading of assets? I never realized the full implications . . . Tell me, what are the bottom line ramifications?"

"Bigger than you think, Alex. I've checked and rechecked it, but the numbers do talk. You see, we're evaluating inventory according to the cost to produce the goods. These costs include not only the money we pay for the raw materials, but also the value added in production.

"You know what we have done in the last few months. Donovan has worked only on things that we have orders for. Stacey has released material accordingly. We've drained about fifty percent of the work in process from the plant, and about twenty-five percent from finished goods. We've saved a lot by not purchasing new materials to replace this excess inventory, and the cash figures show it clearly. But on our books, the assets represented by inventory went down, since they were only partially compensated for by the cash we didn't have to pay out. In this period, when we were reducing inventory, all the difference between the product cost and the material cost of the reduced inventory showed up as a net loss."

I swallow hard. "Lou, you're telling me that we were penalized for doing the right thing? That reducing the excess inventory was interpreted by our books as a loss?"

"Yes," he replies, still looking at his papers.

"Well tell me, what was the impact—in numbers?"

"Our actual net profit was well over twenty percent in each of the last three months," he says flatly.

I stare at him. I can't believe my ears.

"But look at the good side," he says sheepishly, "now that the inventory has stabilized at a new, low level, this effect won't disturb us any longer."

"Thank you very much," I say sarcastically and turn to leave.

When I reach the door I turn around and ask him, "When did you discover this phenomena? When did you find out that we were turning much more profit than the targeted fifteen percent?"

"A week ago."

"So why didn't you tell me? I could have used these facts very effectively in the plant review."

"No Alex, you couldn't have used them at all, it just would have confused your story. You see, everyone evaluates inventory this way, it's even required by the tax authorities. You didn't stand a chance. But I did discuss it at length with Ethan Frost; he understood it perfectly."

"So that's what happened, you fox. Now I understand why Ethan became so supportive," I say, sitting back down.

When we've finished grinning at each other, Lou says in a quiet voice, "Alex, I have another issue."

"Another bomb?"

"You might call it that, but it's sort of a personal matter. Ethan told me that he's going with Bill Peach to the group. I know that you will need a good divisional controller, someone who has experience in the more diverse subjects that are dealt with at the division level. I'm just one year from retirement; everything that I know is old-fashioned. So . . ."

Here it comes, I say to myself. I must stop him before he states that he doesn't want to come with me. Once he says it, it'll be much harder to change his mind.

"Lou, wait," I interrupt him. "Look at the work that we've done in the last few months. Don't you think . . ."

"That's exactly what I was about to bring up," he interrupts me in turn. "Look at it from my point of view. All my life I've gathered numbers and compiled reports. I've seen myself as somebody who has to supply the data, as an impartial, objective observer. But the last few months have shown me to what extent I was wrong. I wasn't an objective observer; I was following, almost blindly, some erroneous procedures without understanding the far-reaching, devastating ramifications.

"I've given it a lot of thought lately. We need financial measurements for sure—but we don't need them for their own sake. We need them for two different reasons. One is control; knowing to what extent a company is achieving its goal of making money. The other reason is probably even more important; measurements should induce the parts to do what's good for the organization as a whole. What's become apparent to me is that neither of these two objectives is being met.

"For example, this conversation we just had. We knew very well that the plant had drastically improved, but the distorted measurements have almost condemned us. I'm submitting efficiency reports, product-cost reports, and now we both know to what extent they just lead workers and management alike to do what's bad for the company."

I've never heard Lou talk for so long. I agree with everything he just said, but I'm totally confused. I don't know what he's getting at.

"Alex, I can't stop here. I can't retire now. Do me a personal favor, take me with you. I want the opportunity to devise a new measurement system, one that'll correct the system we have now, so that it *will* do what we expect it to do. So that a controller can be proud of his job. I don't know if I'll succeed, but at least give me the chance."

What am I supposed to say? I stand up and stretch out my hand. "It's a deal."

Back at my desk I ask Fran to call Bob Donovan in. With Lou on one side and Bob on the other, I'll be free to concentrate on the two areas I know the least, engineering and marketing.

What am I going to do about marketing? The only person I appreciate in that department is Johnny Jons; no wonder Bill has decided to take him along.

The phone rings. It's Bob.

"Hey Al, I'm sitting with Stacey and Ralph, we're really cooking. Can you join us?"

"How long will it take?" I ask.

"No way to tell. Probably 'til the end of the day."

"In that case, I'll pass. But Bob, we need to talk. Can you get away for a few minutes?"

"Sure, no problem."

And in no time, he enters my office. "What's up, boss?"

I decide to give it to him straight, "How'd you like to be responsible for all production of the division?"

The only thing he manages to say is a long "Wow." He puts his big body in a chair, looks at me, and doesn't say any more.

"Well, Bob, surprised?"

"You bet."

I go to pour us coffee and he starts to talk to my back. "Alex, I don't want that job. Not now. You know, a month ago I would have grabbed the offer with both hands. It's way beyond what I expected."

Puzzled, I turn around, a cup in each hand. "What's the matter Bob, afraid?"

"You know better than that."

"So what happened in the past month to change your perspective?"

"Burnside."

"You mean he made you a better offer?"

He fills the room with his booming laughter. "No, Alex, nothing like that. What gave me a new perspective was the way we handled Burnside's urgent order. I learned so much from how we handled that case that I would rather stay in this plant and develop it further."

Surprises all around me. I thought I knew these people. I expected it would be impossible to convince Lou, and he almost begged me for the job. I didn't expect any problems with Bob, and he just declined my offer. It's really annoying.

"You'd better explain," I hand him his cup.

Bob's chair squeaks in protest as he fidgets. If I were staying here longer, I would have ordered a more massive chair just for him.

"Haven't you noticed how unique the events of Burnside's order were?" he says at last.

"Yes, of course. I've never heard of the president of a company going to thank the workers of a vendor."

"Yeah, yeah, that too. But look at the whole chain of events. Johnny called you with an impossible client wish. He didn't believe it could be done, and neither did the client. And on the surface, it was impossible. But we looked into it. We considered the bottleneck availability, we considered the vendor limitations, and we came back with something pretty unusual.

"We didn't say a flat no, or a flat yes, and then miss the due date by a mile, as we used to do. We re-engineered the deal; we came back with a counter-offer that was feasible and that the client liked even more than his original request."

"Yes," I say, "it was good work. Especially considering what came out after that. But that was a peculiar set of circumstances."

"It was peculiar because normally we don't take the initiative —but maybe there's a way to make it standard. Don't you see? We actually engineered a sale. We—in the plant, in production—engineered a sale."

I think about it. He's right. Now I start to see where he's heading.

Bob, probably misinterpreting my silence, says, "For you it's not a big deal, you always looked at production and sales as two links in the same chain. But look at me. All the time I'm buried out on the shop floor, thinking that my responsibility is to put out fires, and viewing the sales department as snake oil salesmen, spreading unrealistic promises to our clients. For me, this event was a revelation.

"Look, we give sales a rigid lead time for each product. So if it's not in finished goods, those are the numbers they should use to promise to clients. Yeah, they deviate from it, but not by much. Maybe there should be another way. Maybe the quoted lead times should be done case by case, according to the load on the bottlenecks. And maybe we shouldn't regard the quantities required as if we have to supply them in one shot.

"Alex, I'd like to look into it more. Actually, that's what Stacey, Ralph, and I are doing right now. We were looking for you, you should join us. It's pretty exciting."

It certainly sounds it, but I can't allow myself to get sucked in right now. I have to continue with preparations for my next job. "Tell me again what you are up to," I finally say.

"We want to make production a dominant force in getting good sales. Sales which will fit both the client's needs and the plant's capabilities like a glove. Exactly as we did in Burnside's case. But you see, for that I have to be *here*, in the plant. As long as we don't understand it in full, as long we don't develop the new procedures, we have to be intimately involved with all the details."

"So what you want to do is to find those procedures. I see. This is interesting—but Bob, that's not like you. Since when have you been interested in such things?"

"Since you came and forced us to rethink the way we were doing stuff. Do you think somebody needs better proof than what's happened here in the past months? Here we were, running things like we'd always done it—by the seat of our pants, slowly but surely sinking. And then we took the time and re-examined it from basic principles. And look at how many sacred cows we've had to slaughter! Worker efficiency—whoops, out the window. Optimum batch sizes—there it goes. Releasing work just because we have the material and the people—that's gone as well. And I can go on and on. But look at the result. If I hadn't seen it myself, I wouldn't believe it.

"Yeah, Alex, I want to stay here and continue what you've started. I want to be the new plant manager. You caused us to change almost every rule in production. You forced us to view production as a means to satisfy sales. I want to change the role production is playing in getting sales."

"Fine with me. But Bob, when you nail those procedures," and to myself I add, 'if,' "will you consider taking on responsibility for all the plants in the division?"

"You bet, boss. I'll teach 'em a trick or two."

"Let's drink to it," I say. And we toast with our coffee.

"Who do you suggest should take your place?" I ask him. "Frankly, I'm not impressed with any of your superintendents."

"Unfortunately, I agree with you. The best would be Stacey, but I don't give it much chance she'd take it."

"Why don't we ask her. You know what? Let's call both Stacey and Ralph in and discuss your idea."

"So, at last you found him," Stacey says to Bob, as she and Ralph enter the room, each loaded with papers.

"Yes, Stacey," I answer. "And it definitely looks like a promising idea. But before that, there's another thing that we'd like to discuss with you. We've just agreed that Bob will take my place as plant manager. How about you taking his place as production manager?"

"Congratulations, Bob." They both shake his hand. "That's no surprise."

Since Stacey hasn't answered my question, I continue, "Think about it, you don't have to answer now. We know that you love your job and that you don't want the burden of all the personnel problems that go with being a production manager, but we both think that you'd do a fantastic job."

"You bet," Bob adds his two cents.

She looks calmly at me, and says, "Last night I was lying in bed, praying. I was praying that this job would be offered to me."

"Done," Bob shouts quickly.

"Now that you've accepted," I say to Stacey, "can you tell us why you want this job so badly?"

"Looks like being a material manager," Bob booms, "is starting to be boring around this plant—not enough expediting, not enough rush calls. . . . I didn't know that you liked that type of excitement."

"No, I didn't, and I don't. That's why I was so happy with our new method, timing the release of material according to the bottlenecks' consumption. But you know my fear, what happens if new bottlenecks pop up?

"What my people and I have done is to examine daily the queues in front of the assembly and in front of the bottlenecks— we call them 'buffers.' We check just to be sure that everything that's scheduled to be worked on is there—that there are no 'holes.' We thought that if a new bottleneck pops up it would immediately show up as a hole in at least one of these buffers. It took us some time to perfect this technique, but now it's working smoothly.

"You see, whenever there's a hole in a buffer—and I'm not talking about just the work that's supposed to be done on a given day, but the work for two or three days down the road—we go and check in which work center the materials are stuck. And then . . ."

"And then you expedite!" Bob jumps in.

"No, nothing of the sort. We don't break setups, or light a fire. We just point out to the foreman of that work center which job we would prefer he gets to next."

"That's very interesting," I say.

"Yeah. And it became even more interesting when we realized that we were visiting the same six or seven work centers every time. They're not bottlenecks, but the sequence in which they perform their jobs became very important. We call them 'capacity constraint resources,' CCR for short."

"Yeah, I know all about it. Those foremen have become almost dependent on your people to prioritize their work," Bob says. "But Stacey, you're not answering our question."

"I'm coming to it. See, these holes have become more and more dangerous lately—sometimes to the extent that assembly has to deviate significantly from their scheduled sequence. And it's become apparent that the foremen of the CCRs have more and more difficulty supplying on time. Ralph was telling me that these work centers still have enough capacity, and maybe on the average he's right, but I'm afraid that any additional increase in sales will throw us into chaos."

So here's a bomb, ticking below our feet, and I didn't even realize it. I'm pressing so hard on marketing to bring more sales, and according to what Stacey's just revealed that might blow up the whole plant. I'm still trying to digest it when she continues.

"Don't you realize that we've concentrated our improvement efforts too narrowly? We tried so hard to improve our bottlenecks, when what we should do is improve the CCRs as well. Otherwise we'll run into an 'inter-active' bottleneck situation.

"See, the key is not in the hands of the materials people. If interactive bottlenecks emerge, chaos is inevitable; we'll have to expedite all over the place."

"So what are you suggesting?" I ask.

"The key is in the hands of production. These techniques to manage the buffers should not be used just to track missing parts while there is still time, they should be used mainly to focus our local improvement efforts. We must guarantee that the improvements on the CCRs will always be sufficient to prevent them from becoming bottlenecks.

"Alex, Bob, that's why I want this job so badly. I want to make sure that the material manager's job will continue to be boring. I want to demonstrate how local improvements should be managed. And I want to show all of you how much more throughput we can squeeze from the same resources."

"What about you Ralph, it's your turn to surprise me."

"What do you mean?" he says in his quiet voice.

"It looks like everyone around here has a pet project. What ace are you hiding up your sleeve?"

He smiles gently, "No aces, just a wish."

We all look at him encouragingly.

"I've started to like my job. I feel like I'm part of a team."

We all nod in approval.

"It's not just me and the computer anymore, trying to fiddle with inaccurate or untimely data. People really need me now, and I feel like I'm contributing. But you know what? I think that the change, at least as it relates to my function, is very fundamental. What I'm holding in my files is data. What you are usually asking for is information. I always regarded information as those sections of the data which are needed in order to make a decision—and for that, let me admit it, for most decisions my data was simply unsuitable. Remember the time we were trying to find the bottlenecks?" He looks at each of us in turn. "It took me four days to admit that I simply couldn't find the answer. What I started to realize is that information is something else. Information is the answer to the question asked. The more I am able to do it, the more a part of the team I become.

"This bottleneck concept has really helped me to move along these lines. Let's face it, today the plant obeys a schedule that's released from the computer.

"What's my wish, you ask? I want to develop a system that'll help in what Bob wants to do, that will help to shrink drastically the time and effort needed to engineer a sale, as he calls it. I want to develop a system to help Stacey manage the buffers, and even to help in managing the local improvements. I want to develop a system to help Lou measure, in a much more beneficial way, the local performance. You see, like everyone else, I have my dreams."

34

It's quite late, the kids are already fast asleep. Julie and I are sitting in the kitchen; we're each holding a warm cup of tea in our hands. I tell her about what happened today at the plant. She seems to be more than mildly interested; she actually claims that she finds it fascinating.

I love it. Rehashing the day's events with Julie really helps me to digest it all.

"So what do you think?" I ask her at last.

"I'm starting to see what Jonah meant when he warned you about increasing the dependency," she replies.

That makes me think for a while, but I still can't see the connection. "What do you mean?"

"Maybe I'm wrong, but you gave me the impression that you're not too sure that Lou'll be able to come up with a good, new measurement system."

"That's right," I smile.

"Is a new measurement system important for you?"

"Are you kidding? I don't know of another single thing which is as important as that."

"So if it weren't for Jonah's refusal to continue giving you pointed questions, am I right in assuming that you'd be on the phone right now, trying to squeeze more hints from him?"

"Most probably," I admit. "It's certainly important enough."

"And what about Bob's idea," she continues. "Do you regard that as something important?"

"If he pulls it off it'll be a revolution. It'll guarantee that we take a big share of the market. Definitely our problem with getting more sales will be over."

"And how much hope do you have that he'll be able to do it?"

"Not much, I'm afraid. Ah. I see your point. Yeah, I would have run to Jonah with these questions as well. And the same with the issues that Stacey and Ralph have raised, each one of them is essential."

"And how many more things will pop up when you start to manage the division?"

"You're right, Julie. And Jonah is also right. I felt it today as well. When each one of them spelled out their immediate dream in such a tangible form, I wondered what mine is. The only thing that kept popping into my mind is that I must learn how to manage. But where on earth am I going to find the answer to Jonah's question: What are the techniques needed for management? I don't know, Julie. What do you think I should do now?"

"All the people back at the plant owe you a lot," she says, stroking my hair. "They're proud of you, and rightfully so. You've created quite a team. But this team is going to be broken up in two months when we go to the division. Why don't you spend the time that's left sitting with them and going over your question. They'll have ample time after you're gone to work on their problems. Anyhow, it'll be much easier for them to achieve what they want to achieve if you have the management techniques."

I look at her in silence. Here is my real, true advisor.

So I've done what my advisor suggested. I gathered them all together and explained that if each of them wants to be free to concentrate on his pet project the division must be well run, and in order for the division to be well run the division manager must know what he is doing. And since I, frankly, don't have the foggiest idea of how to run a division they had better put their brains to helping me. Thus, we are going to devote the afternoons—provided of course that no special emergency comes up—to help me analyze how the division should be run.

I decide to start the meeting with the most naive questions. Initially they might think that I've lost all my self confidence, but I must expose to them the magnitude of the problem I'm about to face. Otherwise I'm going to end up, at best, with some fragmented, vague suggestions.

"What are the first things I should do when I assume my new position?" I ask them.

They look at each other, and then Bob says, "I'd start by visiting Hilton Smyth's plant."

After the laughter dies, Lou says that I should first meet with my staff; "you know most of them but you've never worked closely with them."

"What is the purpose of these meetings?" I innocently ask.

If this question had been asked under any other circumstances they would have taken it as a clear indication of a total lack of managerial knowledge. As it is they play the game.

"Basically you should do general fact finding first," Lou answers.

"You know," Bob adds, "like where the entrance is, where the toilets are . . ."

"I do think that meeting the people is important," Stacey interrupts the laughter. "Financial numbers only reveal a small fraction of the picture. You have to find out what the people think is going on. What do they see as problems? Where do we stand vis-a-vis the clients?"

"Who has a grudge against whom?" Bob contributes, and then in a more serious tone. "You also have to get a sense of the local politics."

"And then?"

"And then," Bob continues. "I'd probably take a tour of the various production facilities, visit some of the big clients, and probably even some suppliers. You've got to get the full picture."

Maintaining my poker face I ask, "And then?"

At last I've succeeded to provoke them, since both Stacey and Bob answer vehemently, "And then you'll take it from there!"

How easy it is to give advice when the responsibility is on someone else's shoulders. Okay wise guys, it's time to turn the table, and in a calm voice I say, "Yes, what you suggested just now is the usual line of action one takes when he is told to 'go there and fix it.' Let me play it back for you, but in a more schematic way. Where are the colored markers?"

I grab a red marker and turn to the white board.

"The first step, as you all have pointed out, is fact finding. I hold a staff meeting and what do I find? Oh, here we find fact A," and I draw a nice red circle. "And here are three somewhat smaller circles. And here is a tiny one and there are two which are overlapping. Now let's talk with another manager, this is very helpful. You see, this circle, he claims, is not as big as we were led to believe. And here, in the left upper corner are two more biggies. Now, someone else reveals to us that some rectangles exist. We check, and yes, he's right. Here there is one and here and here and here. We're making progress, the picture starts to unfold."

What they actually see is how the white board is getting the measles. It looks like one of the drawings my kids used to bring home from kindergarten.

I don't think they got the message, they just seem confused; so I decide to continue a little more bluntly. "It's about time to talk with another manager, we must get a sense of the local politics. Oh, this is very interesting, there are also green circles, and even some green stars. Here's an unidentified shape—never mind, we'll address it later. Now, let's tour the production facilities, visit clients, and even some suppliers. We're bound to reveal many more interesting facts." As I talk the board is filled with overlapping shapes.

"Now that we have the full picture, we can take it from here," I finally conclude and put the markers down. "Well?"

The board looks like a nightmare in Technicolor. I take a deep breath and pick up the phone to order more coffee.

Nobody says a word, not even Bob.

"Let's make it less personal," I say after a while. "Suppose that we are a committee that's been given the ungrateful task of 'find out what's going on.' How do you suggest we should start?"

They all smile. Somehow pretending that we're a committee makes us feel much better. "The safety of being part of a herd," I think to myself; the blame will not be aimed at anyone in particular.

"Ralph, will you volunteer to describe the committee's actions?"

"They would probably start in the same way—fact finding. And as you so vividly demonstrated, they would end up in the same colorful ditch. But Alex, is there any other way to start? How can you do anything sensible without knowing what's going on, without having the data?" Ralph is true to his profession; for him, knowing what's going on is equivalent to having the data neatly stored in his computer files.

Bob points to the white board and chuckles, "You call this mess knowing what's going on? Alex, come on. We all know that this nonsense of fact finding will continue until our committee runs out of ideas for gathering further facts."

"Or they run out of time," Stacey adds with a bitter smile.

"Yes, of course," Bob accepts, and turning to everybody he finishes his questions, "What do you think that we, acting as a committee, would do next? We know a committee can't submit this mess."

They all laugh nervously. I'm really pleased. They've finally started to realize the problem that I'm facing.

"What are they going to do now?" Stacey muses. "They'll probably try to arrange this monstrous pile of facts in some order."

"Most likely," Lou agrees. "Sooner or later one of the committee members will suggest organizing the shapes according to their relative size."

"I don't think so," Bob disagrees. "Determining the relative size of different shapes is quite difficult. They will probably decide to organize them according to the type of shapes." Lou doesn't seem to accept this, and so Bob explains, "They can arrange the data by circles, rectangles, and stars."

"What are they going to do with those four arbitrary shapes?" Ralph asks.

"Probably they'll be put in a class of their own, the exceptions."

"Yes, of course," Ralph agrees. "The major reason for the constant reprogramming are those exceptions that keep popping up."

"No, I have a better idea," Lou says stubbornly. "They'll probably arrange them by color; in this way there will be no ambiguity. Tell you what." He continues when he realizes that Bob is about to object, "Let's arrange them first by color, within color by shape, and within each subclass we'll arrange them by size. This way everybody will be happy." Count on Lou to find an acceptable compromise.

"It's a marvelous idea," Ralph picks up the ball. "Now we can submit our findings in the form of tables and histograms. It will be a very impressive report, especially once I pump up the graphics package. Minimum two hundred pages, guaranteed."

"Yes, an impressive, in-depth survey," I say sarcastically. We all sit silently, absorbing the bitter lesson we've just taught ourselves.

"You know," I say after a while, "It's much worse than just wasting time producing useless, pompous reports. This overconcern about the 'proper way to arrange things' manifests itself in other harmful ways."

"What do you mean?" Lou asks me.

"I mean the merry-go-round that we're all too familiar with; arranging the company according to product lines and then changing it according to functional capabilities—and vice versa. Deciding that the company is wasting too much money on duplicated efforts and thus moving to a more centralized mode. Ten years later, we want to encourage entrepreneurship and we move back to decentralization. Almost every big company is oscillating, every five to ten years from centralization to decentralization, and then back again."

"Yeah," says Bob. "As a president of a company, when you don't know what to do, when things are not going well, you can always shuffle the cards—reorganize." Mockingly he continues, "That will do it! This reorganization will solve all our problems!"

We stare at each other. If it weren't so painfully true, we might laugh.

"Bob," I say at last. "This isn't funny. The only somewhat practical ideas I had in mind for what I should do as the new division manager were all based on reorganizing the division."

"Oh, no," they all groan.

"O.K. then," and I turn back to the white board, which is not so white any more. "What is one supposed to do with this pile of colored shapes, except to arrange them in some order? Dealing directly with the pile is obviously totally impractical. Arranging the facts according to some order, classification, must be the first step. Maybe we can proceed from there in a different way than writing reports or rearranging the company, but the first step definitely must be to put some order into the mess."

As I continue to look at the board, a new question starts to bother me; "In how many ways can one arrange the assembled facts?"

"Obviously, we can arrange them by color," Lou answers.

"Or by size," Stacey adds.

"Or by shape." Bob doesn't give up on his suggestion.

"Any other possibilities?" I ask.

"Yes, of course," Ralph says. "We can divide the board by an imaginary grid and arrange the shapes according to their coordinates." When he sees our puzzled looks he clarifies, "It'll give us the ability to construct many different arrangements based on the shapes' relative position on the board."

"What a great idea," Bob says sarcastically. "You know what, I'd rather use the dart technique—throw a dart and start arranging the shapes according to the order in which we nail 'em. All these methods have just as much meaning. At least my last suggestion offers some satisfaction."

"O.K. fellows," I say firmly. "Bob's last suggestion has really clarified what we're dealing with here. We're dealing with the fact that we haven't got any idea of what we're doing. If we're just looking for some arbitrary order, and we can choose among so many possibilities, then what's the point in putting so much effort in collecting so much data? What do we gain from it, except the ability to impress people with some thick reports or to throw the company into another reorganization in order to hide from the fact that we don't really understand what we're doing? This avenue of first collecting data, getting familiar with the facts, seems to lead us nowhere. It's nothing more than an exercise in futility. Come on, we need another way to attack the issue. Any suggestions?"

When nobody answers, I say, "Enough for today. We'll continue tomorrow—same time, same place."

35

"Well, anybody got anything good, any breakthroughs?" I try to start the meeting off as cheerfully as possible. It's not exactly how I feel; I spent the whole night tossing in my bed, searching for any opening, which I never did find.

"I think that I have one," Stacey speaks up. "Not exactly a breakthrough, but . . ."

"Wait," says Ralph.

Ralph interrupting. That's new.

In an apologetic tone he explains, "Before we go off on a different angle, I'd like to return to where we were yesterday. I think we were too hasty in our decision that classification of data can't lead to something good. May I?"

"Sure," Stacey says, almost in relief.

"Well," Ralph fidgets, apparently uncomfortable, "as you know, or maybe you don't, I minored in chemistry in college. I don't know much about it, but one story stuck in my mind. Last night I looked back at my notes from class and I think you'll find it interesting as well. It's a story about a remarkable Russian named Mendeleev, and it happened less than one hundred fifty years ago."

Noticing that he grabbed our attention, he becomes more confident. Ralph is a family man and has three little children, so he's probably used to telling stories.

"Right from the start, in the days of ancient Greece, people postulated that underlying the phenomenal variety of materials there must be a simple set of elements from which all other substances are composed."

As he gets into his story his voice becomes rich with undertones.

"The Greeks naively assumed that the elements were air, earth, water and . . ."

"Fire," Bob completes the list.

"Correct," says Ralph.

What a wasted talent. He's a real story teller, I think to myself. Who would have suspected it?

"Since then, as you know, people have proven that earth is

not a basic element but actually composed of many different more basic minerals. Air is composed of different types of gases, and even water is a composition of more basic elements, hydrogen and oxygen. The kiss of death to the naive Greece approach came at the end of the eighteenth century, when Lavoisier showed that fire is not a substance but rather a process, the process of attachment to oxygen."

"Over many years, out of the chemists' mammoth work, the more basic elements emerged and by the middle of the nineteenth century, sixty-three elements had been identified. The situation actually resembled our colored board. Many circles, rectangles, stars, and other shapes, in many colors and sizes filled the area with no apparent order. A real mess."

"Many tried to organize the elements but no one succeeded in offering anything that was not immediately dismissed as a futile arbitrary exercise. It got to the point that most chemists gave up on the possibility of finding any generic order and concentrated their efforts on finding more hard facts regarding the combination of the elements to create other, more complicated materials."

"Makes sense," Bob remarks. "I like practical people."

"Yes Bob," Ralph smiles at him, "But there was one professor who claimed that in his eyes it resembled dealing with the leaves while nobody had found yet the trunk."

"Good point," says Lou.

"So this peculiar Russian professor who, by the way, taught in Paris, decided to concentrate on revealing the underlying order governing the elements. How would you go about it?"

"Shape is out of the question," Stacey says, looking at Bob.

"Why? What do you have against shapes?" Bob demands.

"Out of the question," she repeats. "Some of the elements are gases, some are liquids."

"Yeah, you're right." Being Bob he continues, "But what about color? You like colors, don't you? Some gases have colors, like green chlorine, and we can say that the others have transparent colors."

"Nice try," Ralph says, ignoring their apparent attempt to ridicule his story. "Unfortunately some elements do not have a decisive color. Take pure carbon, for example. It appears as black graphite, or more rarely as a sparkling diamond."

"I prefer diamonds," Stacey jokes.

We all laugh, then responding to Ralph's gesture I give it a try. "We probably have to look for a more numerical measure. This way we'll be able to arrange the elements without being criticized for subjective preferences."

"Very good," says Ralph. He's probably mistaken us for his kids. "What do you suggest as a suitable measure?" he asks me.

"I didn't take chemistry," I reply, "not even as a minor. How would I know?" But since I don't want to offend Ralph I continue, "Maybe something like specific gravity, electrical conductivity, or something more fancy like the number of calories absorbed or released when the element is combining with a reference element like oxygen."

"Not bad, not bad at all. Mendeleev took basically the same approach. He chose to use a quantitative measurement that was known for each element and which didn't change as a function of the temperature or the state of the substance. It was the quantity known as atomic weight, which represents the ratio between the weight of one atom of the given element and the weight of one atom of the lightest element, hydrogen. This number provided Mendeleev with a unique numerical identifier for each element."

"Big deal," Bob can't hold himself. "Exactly as I suspected, now he could organize all the elements according to their ascending atomic weights, like soldiers in a line. But what good does it do? What practical things can possibly come out of it? Like I said, children playing with lead soldiers, pretending that they do very important work."

"Not so fast," Ralph responds. "If Mendeleev had stopped here, I would accept your criticism, but he took it a step further. He didn't arrange the elements in a line. He had noticed that each seventh soldier represents basically the same chemical behavior, though with increased intensity. Thus he organized the elements in a table with seven columns.

"In this way all the elements were displayed according to ascending atomic weight, and in each column you find elements with the same chemical behavior in ascending intensity. For example, in the first column of his table stood lithium, which is the lightest of all metals, and which, when put into water, becomes warm. Right below it is sodium, which when put into water, flames. Then the next one in the same column is potassium, which reacts even more violently to water. The last one is cesium which flames even in regular air."

"Very nice, but as I suspected it's nothing more than child's play. What are the practical implications?" Down-to-earth Bob.

"There were practical ramifications," Ralph answers. "You see, when Mendeleev constructed his table, not all the elements were already found. This caused some holes in his table that he reacted to by 'inventing' the appropriate missing elements. His classification gave him the ability to predict their weight and other properties. You must agree that's a real achievement."

"How was it accepted by the other scientists of his time?" I ask, curious. "Inventing new elements must have been received with some skepticism."

"Skepticism is an understatement. Mendeleev became the laughing stock of the entire community. Especially when his table was not as neatly arranged as I described it to you. Hydrogen was floating there above the table, not actually in any column, and some rows didn't have one element in their seventh column, but a hodgepodge of several elements crowded into one spot."

"So what happened at the end?" Stacey impatiently asks. "Did his predictions come true?"

"Yes," says Ralph, "and with surprising accuracy. It took some years, but while he was still alive all the elements that Mendeleev predicted were found. The last of the elements that he 'invented' was found sixteen years later. He had predicted it would be a dark gray metal. It was. He predicted that its atomic weight would be about 72; in reality it was 72.32. Its specific gravity he thought would be about 5.5, and it was 5.47."

"I bet nobody laughed at him then."

"Certainly not. The attitude switched to admiration and his periodic table is regarded by students of chemistry today as basic as the ten commandments."

"I'm still not impressed," my stubborn replacement says.

I feel obliged to remark, "The biggest benefit was probably the fact that due to Mendeleev's table people didn't have to waste time looking for more elements." And turning to Bob I say "You see, the classification helped in determining, once and for all, how many elements do exist. Putting any new element in the table would have upset the clear order."

Ralph coughs in embarrassment, "Sorry Alex but that's not the case. Only ten years after the table was fully accepted, several new elements were discovered, the noble gases. It turned out that the table should have been constructed to have eight columns, not seven."

"Just as I've said," Bob jumps in a triumphant voice. "Even when it works you still can't trust it."

"Calm down, Bob. You must admit that Ralph's story has a lot of merit for us. I suggest that we ask ourselves what's the difference between Mendeleev's classification of the chemical elements and our many attempts to arrange the colored shapes in order? Why was his so powerful and ours so arbitrary?"

"That's just it," says Ralph, "Ours were arbitrary, and his was . . ."

"Was what? Not arbitrary?" Lou completes his sentence.

"Forget it." Ralph agrees. "That's not a serious answer. I'm just playing with words."

"What exactly do we mean by arbitrary, and not arbitrary?" I raise the question.

Since nobody answers I continue, "Actually, what are we looking for? We're looking to arrange the facts in some order. What type of order are we seeking? An arbitrary order that we superimpose externally on the facts, or are we trying to reveal an intrinsic order, an order that already exists there?"

"You're absolutely right," Ralph is getting excited, "Mendeleev definitely revealed an intrinsic order. He didn't reveal the reason for that order, that had to wait for another fifty years, when the internal structure of the atoms was found, but he definitely revealed the intrinsic order. That's why his classification was so powerful. Any other classification that just tries to superimpose some order, any order, on the given facts is useful in only one sense—it gives the ability to present the facts in a sequence, tables, or graphs. In other words, helpful in preparing useless, thick reports.

"You see," he continues enthusiastically, "we, in our attempts to arrange the colored shapes, didn't reveal any intrinsic order. Simply because in that arbitrary collection there was no intrinsic order to be revealed. That's why all our attempts were arbitrary, all futile to the same extent."

"Yes, Ralph," Lou says in a cold tone, "But that doesn't mean that in other cases, where intrinsic order does exist, like in managing a division, we can't fool ourselves in the same way. We can always procrastinate by wasting our time playing with some artificial, external order. Let's face it, what do you think Alex and I would have done with the pile of facts that we suggested he gather. Judging by what we've done for so long here in the plant, probably just that—playing a lot of games with numbers and words. The question is what are we going to do differently now? Anybody got an answer?"

Looking at Ralph sunk in his chair I say, "If we could reveal the intrinsic order of the events in the division, that would certainly be of tremendous help."

"Yes," Lou says, "But how does one go about revealing the intrinsic order?"

"How can one identify an intrinsic order even when he stumbles on it?" Bob adds.

After a while Lou says, "Probably in order to answer this question we should ask a more basic one: What provides the intrinsic order among various facts? Looking at the elements that Mendeleev had to deal with, they all seemed different. Some were metals and some gases, some yellow and some black, no two were identical. Yes, there were some that exhibited similarities, but that's also the case for the arbitrary shapes that Alex drew on the board."

They continue to argue but I'm not listening any more. I'm stuck on Lou's question, "How does one go about revealing the intrinsic order?" He asked it as if it were a rhetorical question, as if the obvious answer is that it is impossible. But scientists do reveal the intrinsic order of things . . . and Jonah is a scientist.

"Suppose that it is possible," I break into the conversation, "suppose that a technique to reveal the intrinsic order does exist? Wouldn't such a technique be a powerful management tool?"

"Without a doubt," says Lou. "But what's the point in daydreaming?"

"And what happened to you today?" I ask Julie, after I've told her the day's events in detail.

"I spent some time in the library. Do you know that Socrates didn't write anything? Socrates' dialogues actually were written by his pupil, Plato. The librarian here is a very pleasant woman, I like her a lot. Anyhow, she recommended some of the dialogues and I've started to read them."

I can't hold my surprise, "You read philosophy! What for, isn't it boring?"

She grins at me, "You were talking about the Socratic

method as a method to persuade other people. I wouldn't touch philosophy with a ten foot pole, but to learn a method to persuade my stubborn husband and kids—for that I'm willing to sweat."

"So you started to read philosophy," I'm still trying to digest it.

"You make it sound like a punishment," she laughs. "Alex, did you ever read the dialogues of Socrates?"

"No."

"They're not too bad. They're actually written like stories. They're quite interesting."

"How many have you read so far?" I ask.

"I'm still slaving on the first one, *Protagoras*."

"It'll be interesting to hear your opinion tomorrow." I say skeptically. "If it's still positive, maybe I'll read it, too."

"Yeah, when pigs fly," she says. Before I can answer, she stands up, "Let's hit the sack."

I yawn and join her.

36

We're getting started a little late since Stacey and Bob have to deal with some problematic orders. I wonder what's really happening; are we drifting back into trouble? Is Stacey's warning about her Capacity Constraint Resources starting to materialize? She was concerned about any increase in sales and, for sure, sales are slowly but constantly on the rise. I dismiss these thoughts; it's just the natural friction that should be expected when your material manager moves her responsibilities to her replacement. I decided not to interfere; if it evolves into something serious they won't hesitate to tell me.

This is not going to be easy. We all are action-oriented and searching for basic procedures is almost against our nature, no matter how much Bob tells me that he's been transformed.

So when, at last, they all take seats I remind them about the issue on the table. If we want the same movement that we've succeeded in starting here to happen in the entire division, we have to clarify for ourselves what we actually have done—in a generic sense. Repeating the specific actions won't work. Not only are the plants very different from each other; how can one fight local efficiencies in sales, or cut batches in product design?

Stacey is the only one who has something to offer and her idea is simple. If Jonah forced us to start by asking, 'what is the goal of the company', Stacey suggests that we start by asking, 'what is our goal'—not as individuals, but as managers.

We don't like it. It's too theoretical. Bob yawns, looks bored. Lou responds to my unspoken request and volunteers to play the game.

With a smile he says, "This is trivial. If the goal of our company is 'to make more money now as well as in the future,' then our job is to try and move our division to achieve that goal."

"Can you do it?" Stacey asks. "If the goal includes the word 'more', can we achieve the goal?"

"I see what you mean," Lou responds, still smiling. "No, of course we can't achieve a goal that is open-ended. What we'll have to do is to try and move the division toward that goal. And you are right, Stacey, it's not a one-shot effort, we have to constantly strive toward it. Let me rephrase my initial answer." And in his punctuating voice, emphasizing each word, he concludes, "A good job will be to start our division on a process of on-going improvement."

Turning to me, Stacey says, "You asked for an idea of how to tackle the subject? I think that we should proceed from here."

"How?" Donovan echoes the question that everybody is thinking.

"I don't know," is Stacey's answer. When she sees Bob's expression she says defensively, "I didn't claim to have a breakthrough, just an idea."

"Thank you Stacey," I say, and turning to the rest I point to the white board that nobody has bothered to erase yet. "We must admit that it is a different angle from the one we had so far."

We are stuck. Donovan's question is certainly in place. So I try to gain some momentum by cleaning the board and writing in big letters "A process of on-going improvement."

It doesn't help much. We sit in silence for a while staring at the board.

"Comments?" I ask at last. And, as expected, it's Bob who voices everybody's feeling.

"I'm sick and tired of these big words. Everywhere I go, I hear the same thing." He stands up, goes to the board, and mimicking a first grade teacher he intones "A process . . . of . . . on-going . . . improvement."

Sitting back down he adds, "Even if I wanted to forget it I can't. Hilton Smyth's memos are all spotted with this phrase. By the way Alex, these memos keep on coming, and more often than before. In the name of savings, at least saving paper, can't you do something to stop it?"

"In due time. But let's keep at it. If nothing comes out of these discussions, then the only useful thing that I will be able to do as the division manager will be to stop some memos. Come on Bob, spit out your frustrations."

It doesn't take much to encourage Bob to voice his true opinion. "Every plant in our company, has already launched at least four or five of those pain-in-the-neck improvement projects. If you ask me, they lead only to indigestion problems. You go down there, to the floor, and mention a new improvement project and you'll see the response. People have already developed allergies to the phrase."

"So, what are you suggesting should be done?" I pour some more fuel on his flames.

"To do what we have done here," he roars back. "We, here, have not done any of these. We have not launched even one formal improvement project. But look at what we have achieved. No talks, no big words, but if you ask me, what we've achieved here is the real thing."

"You're right," I try to calm the volcano that I have awakened. "But Bob, if we want to do the same in the entire division we must pinpoint what exactly the difference is between what we have done and what everyone else has tried to do."

"We haven't launched so many improvement projects," he says.

"That is not accurate," Stacey responds. "We have taken many initiatives: in shop floor procedures, in measurements, in quality, in local processes, not to mention the changes that we have made in the way we release material to production." Raising her hand to stop Bob from interrupting, she concludes: "True, we didn't call them improvement projects, but I don't believe the crucial difference is that we didn't bother to title them."

"So why do you think we have succeeded where so many have failed?" I ask her.

"Simple," Bob jumps in. "They talked, we did."

"Who is playing with words now," I shut him off.

"I think that the key," Stacey says in a thoughtful tone, "is in the different way we interpreted the word 'improvement'."

"What do you mean?" I ask her.

"She is absolutely right!" Lou beams. "It's all a matter of measurements."

"For an accountant," Bob speaks to the room, "Everything is a matter of measurements."

Lou stands up and starts to pace the room. I rarely see him so excited.

We wait.

At last he turns to the board and writes:

THROUGHPUT   INVENTORY   OPERATING EXPENSE

Then he turns back to us and says, "Everywhere, improvement was interpreted as almost synonymous to cost savings. People are concentrating on reducing operating expenses as if it's the most important measurement."

"Not even that," Bob interrupts. "We were busy reducing costs that didn't have any impact on reducing operating expenses."

"Correct," Lou continues. "But the important thing is that we, in our plant, have switched to regard throughput as the most important measurement. Improvement for us is not so much to reduce costs but to increase throughput."

"You are right," Stacey agrees. "The entire bottleneck concept is not geared to decrease operating expense, it's focused on increasing throughput."

"What you are telling us," I say slowly, trying to digest it, "is that we have switched the scale of importance."

"That's precisely what it is," Lou says. "In the past, cost was the most important, throughput was second, and inventory was a remote third." Smiling at me he adds, "To the extent that we regarded it as assets. Our new scale is different. Throughput is most important, then inventory—due to its impact on throughput and only then, at the tail, comes operating expenses. And our numbers certainly confirm it," Lou provides the evidence. "Throughput and inventory had changed by several tens of percent while operating expenses went down by less than two percent."

"This is a very important lesson," I say. "What you claim is that we have moved from the 'cost world' into the 'throughput world'."

After a minute of silence I continue, "You know what, it really highlights another problem. Changing the measurements' scale of importance, moving from one world into another, is without a doubt a culture change. Let's face it, that is exactly what we had to go through, a culture change. But how are we going to take the division through such a change?"

I go to pour myself another cup of coffee. Bob joins me. "You know, Alex, something is still missing. I have the feeling that the entire approach we took was different."

"In what way?" I ask.

"I don't know. But one thing I can tell you, we haven't declared any improvement project, they grow from the need. Somehow it was always obvious what the next step should be."

"I guess so."

We spend good time. We bring up the actions we took and verify that each one actually has been guided by our new scale. Bob is very quiet until he jumps to his feet.

"I nailed the bastard!" he shouts, "I have it!"

He goes to the board, grabs a marker and put a heavy circle around the word 'improvement.' "Process of on-going improvement," he booms. "Lou and his fixation on measurements forced us to concentrate on the last word. Don't you realize that the real sneaky SOB is the first one?" and he draws several circles around the word 'process.'

"If Lou has a fixation about measurements," I say somewhat irritated, "then you certainly have a fixation about processes. Let's hope your fixation will turn up to be as useful as his."

"Sure thing, boss. I knew that the way we handled it was different. That it wasn't just a matter of scales."

He returned to his seat still beaming.

"Do you care to elaborate?" Stacey inquires in a soft voice.

"You haven't got it?" Bob is surprised.

"Neither did we." We all looked perplexed.

He looks around and when he realizes that we are serious he asks, "What is a process? We all know. It's a sequence of steps to be followed. Correct?"

"Yes . . ."

"So, will anybody tell me what the process is that we should follow? What is the process mentioned in our 'process of on-going improvement'? Do you think that launching several improvement projects is a process? We haven't done that, we have followed a process. That's what we have done."

"He's right," says Ralph in his quiet voice.

I stand up and shake Bob's hand. Everybody is smiling at him.

Then Lou asks, "What process have we followed?"

Bob doesn't hurry to answer. At last he says, "I don't know, but we definitely followed a process."

To save embarrassment I hurriedly say, "Let's find it. If we followed it, it shouldn't be too difficult to find. Let's think, what is the first thing we did?"

Before anybody has a chance to answer Ralph says, "You know, these two things are connected."

"What things?"

"In the 'cost world' as Alex called it, we are concerned primarily with cost. Cost is drained everywhere, everything cost us money. We had viewed our complex organization as if it were composed out of many links and each link is important to control."

"Will you please get to the point?" Bob asks impatiently.

"Let him talk," Stacey is no less impatient.

Ralph ignores them both and calmly continues, "It's like measuring a chain according to its weight. Every link is important. Of course, if the links are very different from each other then we use the principle of the twenty-eighty rule. Twenty percent of the variables are responsible for eighty percent of the result. The mere fact that we all know the Pareto principle shows us to what extent Lou is right, the extent to which we all were in the cost world."

Stacey puts her hand on Bob's to prevent him from interfering.

"We recognize that the scale has to be changed," Ralph continues. "We choose throughput as the most important measurement. Where do we achieve throughput? At each link? No. Only at the end of all operations. You see, Bob, deciding that throughput is number one is like changing from considering weight to considering strength."

"I don't see a thing," is Bob's response.

Ralph doesn't let go, "What determines the strength of a chain?" he asks Bob.

"The weakest link, wise guy."

"So if you want to improve the strength of the chain, what must your first step be?"

"To find the weakest link. To identify the bottleneck!" Bob pats him on the back. "That's it! What a guy!" And he pats him again.

Ralph looks a little bent, but he is glowing. As a matter of fact, we all are.

After that it was easy. Relatively easy. It wasn't too long before the process was written clearly on the board:

STEP 1. Identify the system's bottlenecks.
(After all it wasn't too difficult to identify the oven and the NCX10 as the bottlenecks of the plant.)

STEP 2. Decide how to exploit the bottlenecks.
(That was fun. Realizing that those machines should not take a lunch break, etc.)

STEP 3. Subordinate everything else to the above decision.
(Making sure that everything marches to the tune of the constraints. The red and green tags.)

STEP 4. Elevate the system's bottlenecks.
(Bringing back the old Zmegma, switching back to old, less "effective" routings. . . .)

STEP 5. If, in a previous step, a bottleneck has been broken go back to step 1.

I look at the board. It's so simple. Plain common sense. I'm wondering, and not for the first time, how come we didn't see it before, when Stacey speaks up.

"Bob is right, we certainly followed this process, and we cycled through it more than once—even the nature of the bottlenecks we had to deal with changed."

"What do you mean by the 'nature of the bottlenecks?'" I ask.

"I mean a major change," she says. "You know, something serious like the bottleneck changing from being a machine to being something totally different, like insufficient market demand. Each time that we've gone through this five-step cycle the nature of the bottleneck has changed. First the bottlenecks were the oven and the NCX10, then it was the material release system —remember the last time when Jonah was here?—then it was the market, and I'm afraid that very soon it'll be back in production."

"You're right," I say. And then, "It's a little odd to call the market or the system of material release a bottleneck. Why don't we change the word, to . . ."

"Constraint?" Stacey suggests.

We correct it on the board. Then we just sit there admiring our work.

"What am I going to do to continue the momentum?" I ask Julie.

"Never satisfied, huh?" and then she adds passionately,

"Alex, why do you drive yourself so hard? Aren't the five steps that you developed enough of an achievement for one day?"

"Of course it's enough. It's more than enough. Finding the process that everybody is looking for, the way to proceed systematically on the line of on-going improvement, is quite an achievement. But Julie, I'm talking about something else. How can we continue to improve the plant rapidly?"

"What's the problem? It seems that everything is sailing forward quite smoothly."

I sigh, "Not exactly, Julie. I can't push aggressively for more orders because we're afraid that any additional sales will create more bottlenecks and throw us back into the nightmare of expediting. On the other hand, I can't ask for a major expansion in hiring or machines; the existing bottom line results don't justify it yet."

"My impatient husband," she laughs. "It looks like you simply have to sit tight and wait until the plant generates enough money to justify more investments. In any event darling, very shortly it will be Donovan's headache. It's about time you allowed others to worry."

"Maybe you're right," I say, not totally convinced.

37

"Something is wrong," Ralph says after we've made ourselves comfortable. "Something is still missing."

"What?" Bob says aggressively, all geared up to protect our new creation.

"If step 3 is right . . ." Ralph is speaking very slowly, "if we have to subordinate everything to the decision that we made on the constraint, then . . ."

"Come on Ralph," Bob says. "What's all this 'if we have to subordinate'? Is there any doubt that we must subordinate the non-constraints to the constraints? What are the schedules that you generate on your computers if not the act of subordinating everything to our decision about the bottlenecks' work?"

"I don't doubt that," Ralph says apologetically. "But when the nature of the constraint has changed, one would expect to see a major change in the way we operate all non-constraints."

"That makes sense," Stacey says encouragingly. "So what is bothering you?"

"I don't recall that we did such changes."

"He's right," Bob says in a low voice. "I don't recall it either."

"We didn't," I confirm after a while.

"Maybe we should have?" Bob says in a thoughtful voice.

"Let's examine it," I say. And then, "When was the first time the constraint changed?"

"It happened when some green-tag parts started arriving at assembly too late," Stacey says without hesitation. "Remember our fear that new bottlenecks were popping up?"

"Yes," I say. "And then Jonah came and showed us it wasn't new bottlenecks, but that the constraint had shifted to being the way we released work to the plant."

"I still remember the shock," Bob comments, "of restricting the release of material, even though the people had practically nothing else to work on."

"And our fear that 'efficiencies' would drop," Lou comments. "In retrospect, I'm amazed that we had the courage to do it."

"We did it because it made perfect sense," I say. "Reality certainly proved us right. So Ralph, in that case at least, we did affect all the non-constraints. Should we move on?"

Ralph doesn't answer.

"Something's still troubling you?" I inquire.

"Yes," he says, "but I can't put my finger on it."

I wait for him.

Finally Stacey says, "What's the problem, Ralph? You, Bob, and I generated the work list for the constraints. Then you had the computer generate release dates for all material, based on that list. We definitely changed the way we operated a non-constraint, that is, if we consider the computer as a non-constraint."

Ralph laughs nervously.

"Then," Stacey continues, "I made my people obey those computer lists. That was a major change in the way they operate —especially when you consider how much pressure the foremen put on them to supply them with work."

"But you must admit the biggest change was on the shop floor," Bob contributes. "It was very difficult for most people to swallow that we really meant they shouldn't work all the time. Don't forget that the fear of layoffs was hanging heavily above us."

"I guess it's all right," Ralph gives up.

"What did we do with the method we were using?" Lou asks. "You know, the green and red tags."

"Nothing," Stacey replies. "Why should we do anything about it?"

"Thank you, Lou," Ralph says. "That is exactly what was bothering me." Turning to Stacey he adds, "Do you remember the reason for using those tags in the first place? We wanted to establish clear priorities. We wanted each worker to know what is important and must be worked on immediately, and what is less important."

"That's right," she says. "That's exactly why we did it. Oh, I see what you mean. Now—not like in the past when we released stuff just to provide work—now whatever we release to the floor is basically of the same importance. Let me think for a minute."

We all do.

"Oh shit," she moans.

"What's the matter?" Bob asks.

"I just realized the impact that those darn tags have on our operation."

"Well?" Bob presses her.

"I'm embarrassed," she says. "I've been complaining about our problems with the six or seven capacity constraint resources, I raised all the red flags, I've gone as far as to demand that incoming orders be restricted. And now I see that I've created the problem with my own hands."

"Fill us in, Stacey," I request. "You're way ahead of us."

"Of course. You see, when do the green and red tags have an impact? Only when a work center has a queue, when the worker has to choose between two different jobs that are waiting; then he always works on the red tag first."

"So?"

"The largest queues," Stacey goes on, "are in front of the bottlenecks, but there the tags are irrelevant. The other place where we have relatively high queues is in front of the capacity constraint resources. These resources supply some parts to the bottlenecks, red-tag parts, but they work on many more green-tag parts, parts that go to assembly not through the bottlenecks. Today they do the red-tag parts first. This naturally delays the arrival of the green parts to assembly. We catch it when it is pretty late, when holes are already evident in the assembly buffer. Then, and only then, we go and change the priorities at those work centers. Basically, we restore the importance of the green parts."

"So what you're telling us," Bob cannot contain his surprise, "is that if you just eliminate the tags, it will be much better?"

"Yes, that's what I'm saying. If we eliminate the tags and we instruct the workers to work according to the sequence in which the parts arrive—first come, first done—the parts will be done in the right sequence, fewer holes will be created in the buffers, my people will not have to track where the material is stuck, and . . ."

"And the foreman will not have to constantly reshuffle priorities." Bob completes her sentence.

I try to confirm what I heard. "Stacey, are you positive that your warning about those constraint resources was just a false alarm? Can we safely take more orders?"

"I think so," she says. "It explains one of my biggest mysteries, why there are so few holes in the bottlenecks' buffers, while there are more and more in the assembly buffer. By the way fellows, the fact that there are more and more holes indicates that eventually we will run into the problem of insufficient capacity, but not right now. I'll take care of those tags immediately. You won't see them tomorrow."

"Well, this discussion was very beneficial," I conclude. "Let's carry on. When was the second constraint broken?"

"When we started shipping everything much ahead of time," Bob answers. "Shipping three weeks earlier is a clear indication that the constraint is no longer in production but in the market. Lack of sufficient orders limited the plant from making more money."

"Correct," Lou confirms. "What do you think: did we do anything different on the non-constraints?"

"Not me," says Bob.

"Me neither," echoes Ralph. "Hey, wait a minute. How come we continue to release material according to the oven and the NCX10 if they are no longer the constraints?"

We look at each other. Really, how come?

"Something even funnier is going on. How come my computer shows that these two work centers are still a constraint, that they are constantly loaded to one hundred percent?"

I turn my eyes to Stacey, "Do you know what's going on?"

"I'm afraid I do," she admits. "It's definitely not my day."

"And all this time I wondered why our finished goods were not depleting at a faster rate," I say.

"Will one of you tell us what's going on?" Bob says impatiently.

"Go ahead, Stacey."

"Come on fellas, don't look at me like that. After operating for so long with mountains of finished goods, wouldn't anybody do the same?"

"Do what?" Bob is lost. "Will you please stop talking in riddles?"

"We all knew how important it was to make the bottlenecks work all the time." Stacey starts at last to explain. "Remember, 'An hour lost on the bottleneck is an hour lost for the entire plant.' So, when I realized that the load on the bottlenecks was dropping, I issued orders for products to be on the shelf, in stock. Stupid, I know now, but at least at the moment our finished goods are balanced to roughly six weeks. No more of that awful situation where we hold mountains of some products and not even one single unit of others."

"That's good," Lou says. "It means we can easily deplete it. Alex be careful not to do it too fast, remember the bottom-line ramifications."

It's Stacey's turn to be puzzled. "Why shouldn't we get rid of the finished products as fast as possible?" she asks.

"Never mind," I impatiently say. "Lou can, and should, explain it to all of you later. Right now we should correct our five-step process. Now we all know to what extent Ralph was right, something is definitely missing."

"Can I correct it?" Stacey says sheepishly, and goes to the board.

When she returns to her seat the board has the following:

1. IDENTIFY the system's constraint(s).
2. Decide how to EXPLOIT the system's constraint(s).
3. SUBORDINATE everything else to the above decision.
4. ELEVATE the system's constraint(s).
5. WARNING!!!! If in the previous steps a constraint has been broken, go back to step 1, but do not allow INERTIA to cause a system's constraint.

Examining the board, Lou moans, "It's much worse than I thought."

"On the contrary," I'm surprised. "It's much better than I thought."

We look at each other. "You first," I say. "Why do you claim that it's much worse?"

"Because I've lost my only guideline."

When he realizes that we don't get it, he elaborates; "All the changes that we made so far, all the sacred cows that we had to slaughter, had one thing in common, they all stem from cost accounting. Local efficiencies, optimum batch sizes, product cost, inventory evaluations, all came from the same source. I didn't have much problem with it. As a controller I questioned cost accounting validity for a long time. Remember, it's the invention of the beginning of the century when conditions were much different from today. As a matter of fact, I started to have a very good guideline; if it comes from cost accounting it must be wrong."

"Very good guideline," I smile. "But what is your problem?"

"Don't you see, the problem is much bigger; it's not only cost accounting. We put on the green and red tags not because of cost accounting, but because we realized the importance of the bottle-necks. Stacey created orders for finished goods because of our new understanding, because she wanted to make sure that the bottlenecks' capacity will not be wasted. I thought that it takes a lot of time to develop inertia. What I now see is that it takes less than one month."

"Yes, you are right," I say gloomily. "Whenever the con-straint is broken it changes conditions to the extent that it is very dangerous to extrapolate from the past."

"As a matter of fact," Stacey adds, "even the things that we put in place in order to elevate the constraint must be reexam-ined."

"How can we do it?" Bob asks. "It's impossible to question everything every time."

"Something is still missing," Ralph summarizes.

Something definitely is still missing.

"Alex, it's your turn to explain," Lou says.

"Explain what?"

"Why did you claim that it's much better?"

I smile. It's about time for some good news.

"Fellows, what stopped us from once again taking another jump on the bottom line? Nothing, except for the conviction that we don't have enough capacity. Well, now we know differently. Now we know that we have a lot of spare capacity."

How much spare capacity do we actually have?

"Stacey, how much of the current load on the oven and the NCX10 is due to the fictitious orders?"

"Roughly twenty percent," she says quietly.

"Marvelous," I rub my hands together. "We have enough capacity to really take the market. I'd better drive to headquar-ters tomorrow morning and have a heart-to-heart talk with Johnny Jons. Lou, I'll definitely need you. On second thought, Ralph, will you join us? And bring your computer with you, we're going to show them something."

38

It is six o'clock in the morning when I pick up Lou and Ralph at the plant. We (I) decided that it will be best, since picking them up at their houses would mean I would have had to leave home close to five. In any event, we're probably not going to spend more than a few hours at headquarters so it's reasonable to assume that we'll be back to work in the afternoon.

We hardly talk. Ralph, in the back seat, is busy with his laptop computer. Lou probably thinks that he's still in bed. I drive on automatic pilot. That is, my mind is busy constructing imaginary conversations with Johnny Jons. I somehow have to convince him to get many more orders for our plant.

Yesterday, in the heat of discovering the amount of free capacity that we have, I looked only on the bright side. Now I wonder if I'm not just asking for miracles.

I recheck the numbers in my head. In order to fill our capacity Johnny will have to come up with over ten million dollars of additional sales. It is totally unrealistic that he holds so much up his sleeve.

So, squeezing, begging, and pleading techniques will not help. We'll have to come up with some innovative ideas. Well, the truth is that so far I haven't been able to come up with any. Let's hope Johnny has some clever ideas; he's the one who is supposed to be the expert in sales.

"I want you to meet Dick Pashky," Johnny Jons says as we enter the small conference room. "He's one of my best people. Dedicated, professional, and above all he's full of innovative approaches. I thought it would be a good idea for you to get to know him. Do you mind if he joins us?"

"On the contrary," I smile. "We need some innovative ideas. You see, what I want is for you to get my plant additional business —ten million dollars' worth."

Johnny bursts out laughing. "Jokers, all of you in production are wonderful jokers. Dick, what did I tell you? It's not easy to deal with plant managers. One is asking me to persuade his client to pay a ten percent increase in price, another wants me to get rid of a pile of old junk for full price, but Alex, you're the best—ten million dollars!"

He continues to laugh, but I don't join in.

"Johnny, put on your thinking cap. You must find more orders for my plant, ten million dollars more."

He stops laughing and looks at me, "You are serious. Alex, what's happened to you? You know how tough it is to get more business these days; it's dog eat dog out there. Everybody is cutting each other's throats for the smallest order and you're talking about ten million dollars more?"

I don't hurry to respond. I lean back in my seat and look at him. Finally I say, "Listen Johnny, you know that my plant has improved. What you don't know is to what extent it's improved. We're now capable of delivering everything within two weeks. We've demonstrated that we never miss an order, not even by one day. Our quality has improved to the extent that I'm sure we're the best in the market. We are very responsive, very quick, and above all, very reliable. This is not a sales pitch, it's the truth."

"Alex, I know all this. I hear it from the best source, from my clients. But that doesn't mean that I can immediately turn it into cash. Sales take time, credibility is not built overnight, it's a gradual process. And by the way, you shouldn't complain; I'm bringing you more and more sales. Be patient and don't press for miracles."

"I have twenty percent spare capacity." I say, letting this sentence hang in the air.

From the lack of response I understand that Johnny doesn't see the relevance.

"I need twenty percent more sales," I translate for him.

"Alex, orders are not apples hanging from trees. I can't just go out and pick some for you."

"There must be orders that you decline, because the quality requirement is too high or because the client is asking for unreasonably short delivery times or something. Get me those orders."

"You probably don't know how bad the economy is," he sighs. "Today I accept any order, anything that moves. I know that a lot of dancing will be required later, but the current pressure is simply too high."

"If the competition is so fierce and the economy is so bad,"

Lou says in his quiet voice, "then it must be that clients are pressing for lower prices."

"Pressing is not the word. Squeezing is much more appropriate. Can you imagine, and this is just between us, in some cases I'm forced to accept business for practically zero margin."

I start to see the light at the end of the tunnel.

"Johnny, do they sometimes demand prices that are lower than our cost?"

"Sometimes? All the time."

"And what do you do?" I continue.

"What can I do?" he laughs. "I try to explain the best I can. Sometimes it even works."

I swallow hard and say, "I'm ready to accept orders for ten percent below cost."

Johnny doesn't hurry to answer. His peoples' bonuses are based on total sales dollars. Finally he says, "Forget it."

"Why?"

He doesn't answer. I persist, "Why should I forget it?"

"Because it's stupid, because it doesn't make any business sense," he says in a hard voice, and then softer, "Alex, I don't know what tricks you have in mind but let me tell you, all those tricks have a very short life span before they explode in your face. Why do you want to ruin a promising career? You've done an outstanding job, why go and mess it up? Besides, if we lower prices for one client, it's just a matter of time until the others find out and demand the same. What then?"

He has a point. The last argument shows that the light at the end of the tunnel was just a train.

Help comes from an unexpected side.

"Djangler is not connected to our regular customers," Dick says hesitantly. "Besides, with the quantities he's asking for, we can always claim we gave him a volume discount."

"Forget it," Johnny is practically shouting. "That bastard is asking us to give him the goods for basically nothing, not to mention that he wants us to ship to France at our expense."

Turning to me he says, "This French guy has chutzpah, it's unbelievable. We negotiated for three months. We established each other's credibility, we agreed on terms and conditions. It all takes time. He asked for every technical detail that you can imagine, and we're not talking about one or two products, it's for almost the entire range. All this time not even a peep about prices. At the end, just two days ago, when everything is agreed, he faxes me that our prices are not acceptable and sends his counter offer. I was expecting the usual thing, asking for price reductions of ten percent, maybe fifteen percent considering the large quantities that he is willing to buy, but no, these Europeans probably have a different perception. For example, Model Twelve, the one that you pulled such a miracle on. Our price is nine hundred and ninety-two dollars. We sell it to Burnside for eight hundred and twenty-seven dollars; they're a big client and they consume very large quantities of this particular product. The bastard had the nerve to offer seven hundred and one dollars. Did you hear that! Seven hundred and one dollars. Now you understand?"

I turn to Ralph, "What's our material cost for Model Twelve?"

"Three hundred thirty-four dollars and seven cents," Lou answers without any hesitation.

"Johnny, are you sure that accepting this order will not have any impact on our domestic clients?"

"Not unless we go out, and sing it from the rooftops. On this point Dick is right, no impact. But the whole idea is ridiculous. Why are we wasting our time?"

I look at Lou, he nods.

"We'll take it," I say.

When Johnny doesn't respond, I repeat, "We'll take it."

"Can you explain what is going on?" he finally says, between gritted teeth.

"It's very simple," I answer. "I told you that I have spare capacity. If we take this order, the only out-of-pocket cost to produce these products will be the cost of the materials. We'll get seven hundred and one dollars, and we'll pay three hundred and thirty-four dollars. That's three hundred seventy-eight dollars to the bottom line per unit."

"It's three hundred sixty-six ninety-three per unit, and you forgot the freight," Lou corrects me.

"Thank you. How much is the air freight per unit?" I ask Johnny.

"I don't remember, but it's not more than thirty bucks."

"Can we see the details of that deal?" I ask him. "What I'm particularly interested in is the products, the quantities per month, and the prices."

Johnny gives me a long look and then turns to Dick, "Bring it."

Once Dick is on his way, Johnny says in a puzzled voice, "I don't get it. You want to sell in Europe for a price that is much less than what we get here, even less than the production cost, and you still claim that you'll make a lot of money? Lou, you're a controller, does it make sense to you?"

"Yes," Lou says.

Seeing the miserable expression on Johnny's face, I jump in before Lou has a chance to explain. Financial calculations, showing the fallacy of the 'product cost' concept won't help, it will just confuse Johnny even more than he's confused now. I decide to approach it from another angle.

"Johnny, where do you prefer to buy a Japanese camera, in Tokyo or in Manhattan?"

"In Manhattan, of course."

"Why?"

"Because in Manhattan it's cheaper, everybody knows that," Johnny says confidently, here he's on solid ground. "I know a place on Forty-seventh Street where you can get a real bargain— half price compared to what they asked me to pay in Tokyo."

"Why do you think it is cheaper in Manhattan?" I ask, and then answer my own question, "Ah, we know, transportation prices must be negative."

We all laugh.

"O.K. Alex. You've convinced me. I still don't understand but if it's good for the Japanese, it must be profitable."

We work on the numbers for almost three hours. It's a good thing that I brought both Ralph and Lou.

We calculate the load that this large deal will place on the bottlenecks—no problem. We check the impact on each of the seven problematic work centers—two might reach the dangerous zone, but we can manage. Then we calculate the financial impact —impressive. Very impressive. At last we're ready.

"Johnny, I have one more question. What guarantees that the European manufacturers won't start a price war?"

"What do you care," Johnny brushes the issue aside. "With such ridiculous prices I'm going to lock in Monsieur Djangler for at least one year."

"Not good enough," I say.

"Now you're really getting difficult. I knew that this was too good to be true."

"That's not the point, Johnny. I want to use this deal as a beachhead to penetrate Europe. We can't afford a price war. We must come up with something else besides price, something that will make it very difficult to compete with us. Tell me, what's the average supply time in Europe?"

"About the same as here, eight to twelve weeks," he answers.

"Good. Promise your Monsieur that if he commits to the quantities per year, we'll deliver any reasonable quantity within three weeks of receiving his fax."

In astonishment he asks, "Are you serious?"

"Dead serious. And by the way, I can start to deliver immediately. I have whatever's needed for the first shipment in stock."

"I guess it's your neck," he sighs. "What the heck, in any event you will have full responsibility very shortly. If I don't hear from you, I'll fax him tomorrow. Consider it a done deal."

Only after we pull out of the parking lot do we let ourselves go; it takes us more than fifteen minutes to settle down. That is, Lou and Ralph dive into polishing the numbers. From time to time they come up with a slight correction, usually not more than a few hundred dollars. Compared to the total deal it's not significant at all. But Lou finds it relaxing.

I don't let it bother me. I sing at the top of my voice.

It takes us more than half the way home until they are satisfied. Lou announces the final number. The contribution to the net profit of the plant is an impressive seven digits, a fact that doesn't deter him from specifying it down to the last cent.

"Quite a profitable deal," I say. "And to think that Johnny was about to drop it. . . . What a strange world."

"One thing for sure," Lou concludes. "You can't rely on marketing people to solve the marketing problems. They're captured by old, devastating, common practices to an even larger extent than production.

"Try to imagine," he continues, "the reaction of people when I start to explain to them they are the ones who believe too much in cost accounting."

"Yes, I sigh. "Judging from today I shouldn't expect much help from these guys. Even though, you know, there might be something in Dick."

"Hard to tell," he comments. "Especially when Johnny is holding him so tightly under his thumb. Alex, how are you going to do it?"

"Do what?"

"Change the entire division?"

That puts an end to my euphoria. Damn you Lou, why did you have to bring it up?

"God have mercy on me," I say. "Yesterday we were talking about inertia. We were complaining about the inertia that we have. Compare it to the inertia that we are going to face in the division."

Ralph laughs, Lou groans, and I feel pity for myself.

This week, even though we made such impressive progress, one thing was definitely proven—I'm still managing by the seat of my pants.

Take yesterday, for example. If it weren't for Ralph's instinct that something was missing, we wouldn't even have noticed the huge, open opportunities. Or today. How close was I to giving up? If it hadn't been for Lou putting us on the right track . . . .

I must find out just what are the management techniques I should master. It's simply too risky not to. I must concentrate on it. I even know where to begin. . . .

Maybe I was holding the key all along. What did I say to Julie in the restaurant? My own words echo in my head: "When did Jonah have the time to learn so much? As far as I know he never worked one day of his life in industry. He's a physicist. I can't believe that a scientist, sitting in his ivory tower, can know so much about the detailed realities of the shop floor."

And then, the idea of 'scientist' came up again, when Lou and Ralph were arguing about the usefulness of classifying data. And I myself supplied the answer: How does one go about revealing the intrinsic order? Lou asked it as if it is a rhetorical question, as if the obvious answer is that it is impossible. But scientists do reveal the intrinsic order of things . . . and Jonah is a scientist.

Somewhere in the scientific method lies the answer for the needed management techniques. It is obvious. But what can I do? I cannot read a book in physics, I don't know enough mathematics to get through even the first page.

But maybe I don't need it. Jonah stressed that he wasn't

asking me to develop the methods, just to determine clearly what they should be. Maybe popular science books would be sufficient? At least I should give it a try.

I should go to the library and start digging. The first modern physicist was Newton, that's probably the place to start.

I'm sitting in my office, my feet up on the desk and staring blankly into the room.

The entire morning, I got only two calls—both from Johnny Jons. First he called to inform me that the deal with the French is signed. He was very proud of the fact that he negotiated a better deal than expected; in return for the flexibility and immediacy of our response to their future requests, he succeeded in squeezing slightly higher prices.

The second time he wanted to know if he could approach our domestic clients with the same concept. That is, to shoot for a long-term contract where only the overall yearly quantities are fixed, and we promise three weeks' delivery for any specific request.

I assured him that we don't have any problem responding, and encouraged him to go ahead.

He's excited. I'm far from it.

Everybody is busy. Launching this huge new deal has made them really busy. I'm the only one who has nothing to do. I feel redundant. Where are the days of the telephone ringing off the hook, when I had to run from one important issue to the other, when there were not enough hours in the day?

All those calls and meetings were fire fighting. I remind myself. No fires, no fighting. Now, everything is running smoothly—almost too smoothly.

Actually, what bothers me is that I know what I should be doing. I need to guarantee that the current situation will continue, that things are thought out in advance so fires will not break out. But this means finding the answer to Jonah's question.

I stand up and leave. On my way out I say to Fran, "In the unlikely event that anyone needs me, I'll be at the public library."

"Enough for today," I say and close the book. I stand up and stretch, "Julie, join me for a cup of tea?"

"Good idea, I'll be with you in a minute."

"You're really into it," I comment as she joins me at the kitchen table.

"Yeah, it's fascinating."

I hand her a steaming cup. "What can be so fascinating about ancient Greek philosophy?" I wonder aloud.

"It's not what you think," she laughs. "These dialogues of Socrates are really interesting."

"If you say so," I don't try to disguise my skepticism.

"Alex, your perceptions are all wrong, it's not at all like what you think."

"So what is it?" I ask.

"Well, It's hard to explain," she hedges. "Why don't you try to read them yourself?"

"Maybe one day I will," I say, "but for the moment I've enough reading to do."

She takes a sip from her cup. "Did you find what you're looking for?"

"Not exactly," I admit. "Reading popular science books doesn't lead you directly to management techniques. But I've started to see something interesting."

"Yes?" she says encouragingly.

"It's how physicists approach a subject; it's so vastly different from what we do in business. They don't start by collecting as much data as possible. On the contrary, they start with one phenomenon, some fact of life, almost randomly chosen, and then they raise a hypothesis: a speculation of a plausible cause for the existence of that fact. And here's the interesting part. It all seems to be based on one key relationship: IF . . . THEN."

Somehow this last sentence causes Julie to straighten up in her chair. "Keep going," she says intensely.

"What they actually do is to derive the unavoidable results logically from their hypothesis. They say: IF the hypothesis is right THEN logically another fact must also exist. With these logical derivations they open up a whole spectrum of other effects. Of course the major effort is to verify whether or not the predicted effects do exist. As more and more predictions are verified, it becomes more obvious that the underlying hypothesis is correct. To read, for example, how Newton did it for the law of gravity is fascinating."

"Why?" she asks, as if she knows the answer but is anxious to hear it from me.

"Things start to be connected to each other. Things that we never thought were related start to be strongly connected to each other. One single common cause is the reason for a very large spectrum of different effects. You know Julie, it's like order is built out of chaos. What can be more beautiful than that?"

With glittering eyes she asks, "Do you know what you have just described? The Socratic dialogues. They're done in exactly the same way, through exactly the same relationship, IF . . . THEN. Maybe the only difference is that the facts do not concern material but human behavior."

"Interesting, very interesting. Come to think about it," I say, "my field, management, involves both material and people behavior. If the same method can be used for each then it's probably the basis for Jonah's techniques."

She thinks about it for a while. "You're probably right. But if you are then I'm willing to bet that when Jonah starts to teach you those techniques you'll find that they are much more than techniques. They must be thinking processes."

We each dive into our thoughts.

"Where do we take it from here?"

"I don't know," I answer. "Frankly, I don't think that all this reading really gets me closer to answering Jonah's question. Remember what he said? 'I'm not asking you to develop the management techniques, only to determine what they should be.' I'm afraid I'm trying to jump to the next step, to develop them. Determining the management techniques must come from the need itself, from examining how I currently operate and then trying to find out how I should operate."

39

"Any messages?" I ask Fran.

"Yes," she answers, to my surprise. "From Bill Peach. He wants to talk to you."

I get him on the phone. "Hey Bill, what's up?"

"I just received your numbers for last month," he says. "Congratulations hotshot, you definitely made your point. I've never seen anything even remotely close to this."

"Thank you," I say pleased. "By the way, what are the results at Hilton Smyth's plant?"

"You must turn the dagger, huh?" he laughs. "As you predicted, Hilton is not doing too well. His indicators continue to improve, but his bottom line continues to sink into the red."

I cannot contain myself, "I told you that those indicators are based on local optimum and that they have nothing to do with the global picture."

"I know, I know," he sighs. "As a matter of fact, I think that I knew it all along, but I guess an old mule like me needs to see the proof in black and red. Well, I think that I've finally seen it."

"It's about time," I think to myself but to the phone I say, "So what's next?"

"This is actually why I called you, Alex. I spent the entire day yesterday with Ethan Frost. It seems that he's in agreement with you, but I can't understand what he is talking about." Bill sounds quite desperate. "There was a time that I thought I understood all this mumbo jumbo of 'cost of goods sold' and variances, but after yesterday, it's obvious that I don't. I need someone who can explain it to me in straight terms, someone like you. You do understand all this, don't you?"

"I think I do," I answer. "Actually it is very simple. It's all a matter of. . . ."

"No, no," he interrupts me. "Not on the phone. Besides, you have to come here anyway—only one month left, you should get familiar with the details of your new job."

"Tomorrow morning okay?"

"No problem," he answers. "And Alex, you have to explain to me what you've done to Johnny Jons. He goes around claiming that we can make a lot of money if we sell below what it costs us to produce. That is pure baloney."

I laugh, "See you tomorrow."

Bill Peach abandoning his precious indicators? This is something I have to tell everyone; they'll never believe it. I go to Donovan's office, but he's not there, nor is Stacey. They must be on the floor. I ask Fran to locate them. In the meantime I'm going to Lou to tell him the news.

Stacey reaches me there. "Hey boss, we have some problems here. Can we come in half an hour?"

"No rush," I say. "It's not so important, take your time."

"I don't agree," she says. "I'm afraid that it is important."

"What are you talking about?"

"It probably has started," she answers. "Bob and I will be in your office in half an hour. Okay?"

"Okay," I say, quite puzzled.

"Lou, do you know what's going on?" I ask.

"No." he says. "Unless of course, you're referring to the fact that Stacey and Bob have been busy for the last week, playing expeditors."

"They are?"

"To make a long story short," Bob concludes the briefing of the last hour, "already twelve work centers are on unplanned overtime."

"The situation is out of control," Stacey continues. "Yesterday one order was not shipped on time, today three more will be delayed for sure. According to Ralph, we're going downhill from there. He claims that before the end of the month we'll miss the shipping dates on about twenty percent of our orders, and not by just one or two days."

I'm looking at my phone. It won't take more than a few days and this monster will ring off the hook with furious complaints. It's one thing to be consistently bad; the clients are used to it and they protect themselves by stocks or time buffers. But now we have spoiled them, they are already used to our good performance.

This is much worse than I've imagined. It might ruin the plant.

How did it happen? Where did I go astray?

"How come?" I ask them.

"I told you," Bob says. "Order no. 49318 is stuck because of . . ."

"No Bob," Stacey stops him. "It's not the details that are important. We should look for the core problem. Alex, I think that we simply accepted more orders than we can process."

"That's obvious," I say. "But how come? I thought we checked that the bottlenecks have enough capacity. We also checked your seven other problematic work centers. Did we make a mistake in the calculations?"

"Probably," Bob answers.

"Not likely," is Stacey's response. "We checked and double checked it."

"So?"

"So, I don't know," Bob says. "But it doesn't matter. We have to do something now, and fast."

"Yes, but what?" I'm a little impatient. "As long as we don't know what caused the situation, the best we can do is to throw punches in all directions. That was our old mode of operation. I had hoped that we learned better."

I accept their lack of response as agreement and continue, "Let's call Lou and Ralph and move into the conference room. We must put our heads together to figure out what is really going on."

"Let's get the facts straight," Lou says after less than fifteen minutes. "Bob, are you convinced that you need to keep using so much overtime?"

"The efforts of the last few days have convinced me that even with overtime we are going to miss due dates," Bob answers.

"I see," Lou doesn't look too happy. "Ralph, are you convinced that at the end of the month, in spite of the overtime, we are going to be late on many orders?"

"If we don't find a smart way to solve this mess, without a doubt," Ralph answers confidently. "I can't tell you the dollar amount, that depends on Bob and Stacey's decisions of how much overtime to use and which orders to expedite. But it is in the neighborhood of over a million dollars."

"That's bad," Lou says. "I'll have to redo my forecast."

I throw him a murderous look. That is the major damage that he sees? Redo the forecast!

"Can we address the real issue?" I say in a freezing voice. They all turn to me waiting.

"Listening again to what you're saying, I don't see a major problem," I say. "It is obvious that we tried to swallow more than we can chew. What we have to do is to determine by how much and then compensate. It is as simple as that."

Lou nods his head in approval. Bob, Ralph, and Stacey continue to look at me with poker faces. They even look offended. There must be something wrong in what I've said, but I can't see what.

"Ralph, by how much are our bottlenecks overloaded?" I ask.

"They're not overloaded," he says flatly.

"No problem there," I conclude. "So let . . ."

"He didn't say that," Stacey cuts me off.

"I don't understand," I say. "If the bottlenecks are not overloaded then . . ."

Maintaining an expressionless face she says, "From time to time the bottlenecks are starved. Then the work comes to them in a big wave."

"And then," Bob continues, "we don't have a choice but to go into overtime. That's the case all over the plant. It looks like the bottlenecks are moving all the time."

I sit quietly. What can we do now?

"If it were as easy as determining some overloads," Stacey says, "don't you think we would easily solve it?"

She is right. I should have more confidence in them.

"My apologies," I mutter.

We sit quietly for a minute. Then Bob speaks up, "We can't handle it by shuffling priorities and going into overtime. We've already tried that for several days. It might help save some specific orders but it throws the entire plant into chaos and then many more orders are in trouble."

"Yes," Stacey agrees. "Brute force seems to push us more and more into the spiral. That's why we asked for this meeting."

I accept their criticism.

"Okay, it's obvious that we have to approach it systematically Anyone got an idea where to begin?"

"Maybe we should start by examining a situation where we have one bottleneck." Ralph suggests hesitantly.

"What's the point?" Bob objects. "We now have the opposite.

We are facing many, traveling bottlenecks." It's apparent that they've had that discussion before.

I don't have any other suggestion, nor does anybody else. I decide to gamble on Ralph's hunch. It worked in the past.

"Please proceed," I say to Ralph.

He goes to the board and takes the eraser.

"At least don't erase the five steps," Bob protests.

"They don't seem to help us much," Ralph laughs nervously. "Identify the system's constraints," he reads. "That is not the problem now. The problem is that the bottlenecks are moving all over the place."

Nevertheless, he puts the eraser down and turns to the flip chart. He draws a row of circles.

"Suppose that each circle represents a work center," he starts to explain. "The tasks are flowing from the left to the right. Now, let's suppose that this one is a bottleneck," and he marks one of the middle circles with a big X.

"Very nice," says Bob sarcastically. "Now what?"

"Now let's introduce Murphy into the picture," Ralph responds calmly. "Suppose that Murphy hits directly on the bottleneck."

"Then the only thing left to do is to curse wholeheartedly," Bob spits. "Throughput is lost."

"Correct," Ralph says. "But what happens when Murphy hits anywhere before the bottleneck? In such a case, the stream of tasks to the bottleneck is temporarily stopped and the bottleneck is starved. Isn't this our case?"

"Not at all," Bob brushes it away. "We never operated that way. We always make sure that some inventory accumulates in front of the bottleneck, so when an upstream resource goes down for some time, the bottleneck can continue to work. As a matter of fact, Ralph, we had so much inventory there that we had to choke the material release to the floor. Come on," he says impatiently, "that is exactly what you're doing on your computers. Why do we have to regurgitate what we all know by heart?"

Ralph goes back to his seat. "I just wondered if we really know how much inventory we should allow to accumulate in front of the bottlenecks?"

"Bob, he has a point," Stacey remarks.

"Of course I have," Ralph is really annoyed. "We wanted three days' inventory in front of each bottleneck. I started with releasing material two weeks before it was due at the bottleneck. Then it turned out that that's too much, so I cut it to one week and everything was okay. Now it's not okay."

"So increase it back," Bob says.

"I can't," Ralph sounds desperate. "It will increase our lead time beyond what we currently promise."

"What's the difference?" Bob roars. "In any event we're sliding on our promises."

"Wait, wait," I cut into their quarrel. "Before we do anything drastic, I want to understand better. Ralph, let's go back to your picture. As Bob pointed out, we do hold some stock in front of the bottleneck. Now let's suppose that Murphy hits somewhere before the bottleneck, then what?"

"Then," Ralph says patiently, "the flow of parts to the bottleneck stops, but the bottleneck, using the stock that accumulated right in front of it, continues to work. Of course that eats into the stock and so, if we don't build enough stock to start with, the bottleneck might go down."

"Something doesn't match." Stacey says. "According to what you just said, we have to guarantee the uninterrupted work of the bottleneck by building stock that will last more than the time to overcome Murphy on the upstream resource."

"Correct," says Ralph.

"Don't you see that it can't be the explanation?" Stacey says.

"Why?" Ralph doesn't get it, and neither do I.

"Because the time to overcome a problem upstream did not change, we haven't faced any major catastrophies lately. So if the stock was sufficient to protect the bottlenecks before, it must be sufficient now as well. No Ralph, it's not a matter of insufficient stocks, it's simply new wandering bottlenecks."

"I guess you're right."

Maybe Ralph is convinced by Stacey's argument, but I'm not.

"I think that Ralph might be right after all," I say. "We just have to carry his line of thought a little further. We said that when one of the upstream resources goes down, the bottleneck starts to eat into its stock. Once the problem is corrected, what do all the upstream resources have to do? Remember, if there is one thing that we can be sure of, it's that Murphy will strike again."

"All upstream resources," Stacey answers, "now have to re-build the inventory in front of the bottleneck, before Murphy hits again. But what's the problem? We released enough material for them."

"It's not the material that concerns me," I say. "It's the capacity. You see, when the problem that caused the stoppage is overcome, the upstream resources not only have to supply the current consumption of the bottleneck, at the same time they have to rebuild the inventory."

"That's right," Bob beams. "That means that there are times when the non-bottlenecks must have more capacity than the bottlenecks. *Now* I understand. The fact that we have bottlenecks and non-bottlenecks is not because we designed the plant very poorly. It's a must. If the upstream resources don't have spare capacity, we won't be able to utilize even one single resource to the maximum; starvation will preclude it."

"Yes," Ralph says. "But now the question is, how much spare capacity do we need?"

"No, that is not the question," I gently correct him. "Just as your previous question, 'how much inventory do we need?' is not the real question either."

"I see," Stacey says thoughtfully. "It's a trade-off. The more inventory we allow before the bottleneck, the more time is available for upstream resources to catch up, and so, on average, they need less spare capacity. The more inventory the less spare capacity and vice versa."

"Now it's clear what's happening," Bob continues. "The new orders have changed the balance. We took more orders, which by themselves didn't turn any resource into a new bottleneck, but they did drastically reduce the amount of spare capacity on the non-bottlenecks, and we didn't compensate with increased inventory in front of the bottleneck."

Everybody agrees. As usual, when the answer finally emerges it's plain common sense.

"Okay Bob," I say. "What do you think you should do now?"

He takes his time. We wait.

Finally he turns to Ralph and says, "We have outstanding promises for very short delivery times on only a small percent of our order intake. Can you identify those orders on an on-going basis?"

"No problem," answers Ralph.

"Okay," Bob continues. "For those orders, continue to release material one week in advance. For all others, increase it to two weeks. Let's hope that that will be enough. Now, we have to rebuild the inventory in front of the bottlenecks and in front of assembly. Stacey, take all the necessary steps to put the plant, and I mean all the non-bottlenecks, to work throughout the weekend. Don't accept any excuses, it's an emergency. I'll notify sales that until further notice they should not promise any delivery in less than four weeks from receipt of the order. It will jeopardize their new campaign, but that's life."

Right in front of our eyes the baton has been passed. It's obvious who is the boss now. I feel proud and jealous at the same time.

"Bob has taken over very nicely," Lou says as we enter my office. At least this front is covered."

"Yes," I agree. "But I hate to put him in a position where his first independent actions are so negative."

"Negative?" Lou asks. "What do you mean by negative?"

"All the actions he is forced to take are leading in the wrong direction." I answer. "Of course, he doesn't have any choice, the alternative is much worse, but still. . . ."

"Alex, I'm probably thicker than usual today, but I really don't understand. What do you mean by 'leading in the wrong direction?' "

"Don't you see?" I'm irritated by the whole situation. "What is the unavoidable result of telling sales that they should quote four weeks' delivery? Remember, just two weeks ago we went out of our way to persuade them to quote two weeks. They didn't have much confidence then. Now, it will cause them to drop the entire sales campaign."

"What else can we do?"

"Probably nothing. But this doesn't change the end result; future throughput is down."

"I see," says Lou. "On top of it, overtime is up significantly; putting the plant to work on the weekend will consume the entire overtime budget for the quarter."

"Forget the budget," I say. "When Bob has to report it, I'll be the divisional president. The increased overtime is increasing operating expense. The point is that throughput will be down, operating expense will be up and increasing the buffers means that inventory will be up. Everything is moving in the opposite direction of what it should."

"Yup," he agrees.

"Somewhere, I've made a mistake," I say. "A mistake that now is causing us to pull back. You know Lou, we still don't know what we're doing. Our ability to see what's in front of us resembles that of moles. We're reacting rather than planning."

"But you've got to agree that we are reacting much better than before."

"That's not a real comfort Lou, we're also moving much faster than before. I feel as if I'm driving looking only in the rear view mirror, and then, when it's almost too late, we make last minute course corrections. It's not good enough. It is definitely not good enough."

40

I'm driving back from headquarters with Lou. We've been doing this every day for the last two weeks. We are not in what one might call a cheerful mood. Now we know every little detail of what's going on in the division, and the picture doesn't look good at all. The only bright spot is my plant. No, I should get used to the fact that it's Donovan's plant. And it's not a bright spot, that's a gross understatement. It's the real savior.

Donovan succeeded getting everything under control before the clients had any reason to complain. It will take him some time to regain the confidence of our sales people, but with me pressing from the other side it will not take long before it will be okay.

This plant is so good that Lou and I were led astray for some time. The reports on the division gave us the impression that the situation is quite good. Only when we went through the elaborate work of separating out Donovan's plant was the real picture exposed. And it's not pretty. It's actually quite disastrous.

"Lou, I think we did the exact thing that we knew we shouldn't do."

"What are you talking about?" he says. "We haven't done anything yet."

"We have gathered data, tons of data."

"Yes, and there's a problem with the data," he says. "Frankly, I've never seen such a sloppy place. Every report is missing at least back-up details. You know what I found today? They don't even have a report on late receivables. The information is there but—can you believe—it's scattered in at least three different places. How can they operate this way?"

"Lou, you're missing the point."

"Am I? Do you know that with proper attention we can reduce the open receivables by at least four days?"

"And that will save the division," I say sarcastically.

"No," he grins. "But it will help."

"Will it?"

When Lou doesn't answer I continue, "Do you really believe it will help? Look Lou, what have we learned? What did you yourself say when you asked for the job? Do you still remember?"

Irritated he says, "I don't know what you're talking about. Don't you want me to correct things which are obviously wrong?"

How am I going to explain it to him? I try again.

"Lou, suppose that you do succeed in collecting four days out of the open receivables. By how much will throughput, inventory, and operating expense be improved?"

"They'll all be slightly improved," he says. "But the major impact will be on cash. You shouldn't sneeze at four days' cash. Besides, improving the division requires many small steps. If everyone does his share, together we can lift it."

I drive silently. What Lou said makes sense, but somehow I know that he is wrong. Deadly wrong.

"Lou, help me here. I know that improving the division will require many small improvements, but . . ."

"But what?" he says. "Alex, you are too impatient. You know what they say, Rome was not built in a day."

"We don't have hundreds of years."

Lou is right, I am impatient. But shouldn't I be? Did we save our plant by being patient? And then I see it. Yes, many small actions are needed, but that doesn't mean that we can afford to be satisfied with actions that improve the situation. We must carefully choose which ones to concentrate on, otherwise. . . .

"Lou, let me ask you. How much time will it take you to change, for internal purposes only, the way that we evaluate inventory?"

"The mechanical work is not a real problem, that won't take more than a few days. But if you're referring to the work it'll take to explain the ramifications, to explain to managers how this affects their day-to-day decisions, that's a different story. With concentrated effort, I'd say it'll take weeks."

Now I'm on solid ground.

"What, do you think, is the impact of the way we currently evaluate inventory on the levels of finished stocks that the division currently holds."

"Significant," he says.

"How significant," I press. "Can you give me a number?"

"I'm afraid not. Not even a meaningful evaluation."

"Let's try to do it together," I say. "Have you noticed the increase in finished goods that the division is holding?"

"Yes, I have," he answers. "But why are you surprised? It's exactly what should be expected. Sales are down and the pressure to show profits is up, so they build finished goods inventory to generate fictitious inventory profits. I see what you mean. We can take the increase in finished goods as an indicator of the impact of the way we value inventory. Wow, it's about seventy days!"

"Lovely," I say. "Compare it to your four days of receivables. On what should you work? Moreover," I keep on hammering, "what is the impact on throughput?"

"I don't see any," he answers. "I see very clearly the impact on cash, on inventory, and on operating expense, but not on throughput."

"Don't you?" I say mercilessly. "What was the reason that they gave us for not introducing the new models? Can you recall?"

"Yes," he says slowly. "They are convinced that introducing the new models will force them to declare all the old ones they're holding in stock as obsolete. That would cause a major blow to the bottom line."

"So, we continue to offer the old stuff rather than the new. We continue to lose market share, but it's better than to bite the bullet of write-offs. Do you understand now the impact it has on throughput?"

"Yes, I do. You are right. But Alex, you know what? With some extra effort I think that I can handle them both. I can work on the problem of the way we value inventory and at the same time arrange for more attention to the receivables."

He still doesn't get it but now I think I know how to handle it.

"What about the plant indicators?" I ask him.

"That's a real Pandora's box," he sighs.

"What is the damage there? Slightly bigger than four days? And what about the fact that sales continue to judge opportunities according to the formal 'product cost' and desirable margins. Or even worse, that they will look for anything they can sell above variable cost. What's the damage there? And what about the transfer prices between us and the other divisions; that's a real killer. Do you want more?"

"Stop, stop," he raised his hands. "You made your point. I guess I was inclined to deal with the open receivables issue just because there I know what to do, while in all the others . . ."

"Afraid?" I ask.

"Frankly, yes."

"So am I, so am I." I mutter. "Where do we start? Where do we continue? On what should we concentrate first, on what second? It's overwhelming."

"We need a process," he says. "That's obvious. It's too bad that the five-step process that we developed turned out to be false. No . . . Wait a minute Alex, that's not the case. At the end, the problem was not wandering bottlenecks. It was insufficient protection for the existing bottlenecks. Maybe we can use that five-step process?"

"I don't see how, but it's worthwhile to check it. Should we head to the plant and give it a try?"

"Certainly. I'll have to make some phone calls, but it's no problem."

"No," I say. "I have some commitments for tonight."

"You're right," he says. "It's very important but not urgent. It can wait for tomorrow."

"Identify the system's constraint(s)," Lou reads from the board. "Do we accept it as the first step?"

"I don't know," I say. "Let's examine the logic that brought us to write it. Do you remember what it was?"

"Roughly," he says. "It was something about the fact that we adopted throughput as the number-one measurement."

"I'm afraid that roughly is not good enough," I say. "At least not at such an early stage in our analysis. Let's try again, from first principles."

"I'm all for it," he groans, "But what do you call first principles?"

"I don't know. Something basic that we accept without hesitation."

"Fine. I have one for you. Every organization was built for a purpose. We haven't built any organization just for the sake of its mere existence."

"Correct," I laugh. "Even though I know some people in some organizations who seem to forget it."

"Washington, you mean?"

"That too. I thought about our corporation, but who cares. Let's keep going. Another basic fact is that any organization is comprised of more than one person, otherwise it's not an organization."

"Correct," says Lou. "But I don't see the point in all this. I can give you many more correct statements about organizations in general."

"Yes, you probably can, but look at the conclusion that we can derive already. If any organization was built for a purpose and any organization is composed of more than one person, then we must conclude that the purpose of the organization requires the synchronized efforts of more than one person."

"That makes sense," he says. "Otherwise we wouldn't need to create an organization; the efforts of individuals would suffice. So?"

"If we need synchronized efforts," I continue, "Then the contribution of any single person to the organization's purpose is strongly dependent upon the performance of others."

"Yes, that's obvious." With a bitter smile he adds, "Obvious to everybody except for our measurement system."

Even though I wholeheartedly agree, I ignore his last comment. "If synchronized efforts are required and the contribution of one link is strongly dependent on the performance of the other links, we cannot ignore the fact that organizations are not just a pile of different links, they should be regarded as chains."

"Or at least a grid," he corrects me.

"Yes, but you see, every grid can be viewed as composed of several independent chains. The more complex the organization —the more interdependencies between the various links—the smaller number of independent chains it's composed of."

Lou doesn't want to spend too much time on that point. "If you say so. But that's not so important. The important thing is you've just proven that any organization should be viewed as a chain. I can take it from here. Since the strength of the chain is determined by the weakest link, then the first step to improve an organization must be to identify the weakest link."

"Or links," I correct. "Remember, an organization may be comprised of several independent chains."

"Yes," he agrees impatiently. "But as you said, the complexity of our organizations almost guarantees that there are not many of them. In any event, it is taken care of by the S in parenthesis that we put at the end of the word 'constraint'. Fine, Alex, what do we do about the measurements?"

"Measurements?," I say in surprise. "Where did they come from?"

"Didn't we agree yesterday that the distorted measurements are the biggest constraint of the division?"

Bob Donovan is right. Lou certainly has a fixation on measurements. "They are definitely a big problem," I say carefully. "But I'm not convinced that they are the constraint."

"You're not?" Lou is astonished.

"No I'm not," I say firmly. "Do you think that the fact that most of our products are already outdated in comparison to what the competition is offering is not a major problem? Don't you realize that the attitude in engineering, claiming that the basic rule of nature is that a project never finishes on time, is an even bigger problem. And what about marketing, have you seen any marketing plan that has any chance of turning the situation around?"

"No," he grins. "As a matter of fact everything that I've seen of long term planning should be more appropriately categorized under 'long term bullshitting.' "

I'm on a roll. Today asking me about problems is like opening a dam. "Wait Lou, I haven't finished. What about the mentality that is so prevalent in headquarters, the mentality of covering your ass. Haven't you noticed that whenever we asked about something that doesn't go so well, everyone almost automatically started to blame everybody else?"

"How could I not notice. Okay, Alex, I get your point. There are major problems all over. It seems that in our division there is a whole herd of constraints, not just a few."

"I still claim that there are only few constraints. Our division is too complex to have more than a very few independent chains. Lou, don't you realize that everything we mentioned so far is closely connected? The lack of sensible long-term strategy, the measurement issues, the lag in product design, the long lead times in production, the general attitude of passing the ball, of apathy, are all connected. We must put our finger on the core problem, on the root that causes them all. That is what actually is meant by identify the constraint. It's not prioritizing the bad effects, it's identifying what causes them all."

"How are we going to do that? How are we going to identify the divisional constraints?"

"I don't know," I say. "But if we succeeded in doing it here, in our plant, it must be possible to do in the division."

He thinks about it for a minute and then says, "I don't think so. Here we were lucky. We were dealing with physical constraints, with bottlenecks, that's easy. But at the divisional level we'll have to deal with measurements, with policies, with procedures. Many of them are cast already into behavioral patterns."

"I don't see the difference," I disagree. "Here we had to deal with all of the above. Come to think about it, even here the constraints were never the machines. Yes, we called and still call the oven and the NCX10 bottlenecks, but if they were true bottlenecks how come we succeeded to squeeze almost twice as much out of them as before? How come we increased throughput so much without buying more capacity?"

"But we changed almost every aspect of how we operate them, and how we operate everything around them."

"That is exactly my point," I say. "What aspect of operation did we change?" Mimicking his voice I answer, "The measurements, the policies, the procedures. Many of them were cast into behavioral patterns. Lou, don't you see? The real constraints, even in our plant, were not the machines, they were the policies."

"Yes, I do see. But still there are differences," he says stubbornly.

"What differences? Name one."

"Alex, what's the use of pushing me to the corner? Don't you see that there must be major differences? If there weren't, how come we don't even have a clue of what the nature of the divisional constraint is?"

That stops me dead.

"Sorry. You're right. You know, Lou, maybe we were lucky here. We had physical constraints that helped us to focus our attention, to zoom in on the real policy constraint. That isn't the case in the division. Over there we have excess capacity going through our ears. We have excess engineering resources that we succeed so brilliantly in wasting. I'm sure that there is no lack of markets. We simply don't know how to put our act together to capitalize on what we have."

Pacified he says, "That brings us to the real question, how does one go about identifying the system's constraint? How can we zoom in on the most devastating erroneous policies. Or, to use your term, how does one go about identifying the core problem, the one that is responsible for the existence of so many undesirable effects?"

"Yes," I agree, "That's the question, no doubt."

Looking at the board I add, "What's written here is still valid. Identifying the system's constraint is the first step. What we now understand is that it also translates into a mandatory demand for a technique by which to do it. Lou, that's it. We found it."

The excitement causes me to stand up. "Here it is," I announce, "here is the answer to Jonah's question. I'm going to call him right now. You can imagine my first sentence: Jonah, I want you to teach me how to identify the core problem."

As I turn to leave I hear Lou, "Alex, I think that it might be a little premature."

"Why?" I ask, my hand on the doorknob. "Do you have any doubt that that is what I must learn first?"

"No," he says. "On that I'm quite convinced. I just think that maybe you should ask for more. Knowing the core problem exactly might be far from sufficient."

"You are right again," I calm down. "It's just that I was looking for the answer for so long."

"I understand, believe me, I understand," he smiles.

"Okay Lou." I sit down. "What else do you think I should ask Jonah to teach me?"

"I don't know," he answers. "But if the five steps are valid, maybe what you should ask for are the techniques required to enable us to carry those steps out. We already found the need for one technique, why don't we continue to examine the other four steps?"

"Good idea," I say enthusiastically. "Let's proceed. The second step is," I read from the board, "decide how to exploit the system's constraints. That doesn't make any sense to me. What is the point in trying to exploit an erroneous policy?"

"It makes sense only if the constraint is physical, but since we do deal with policy constraints, I guess we'd better move to the next one," Lou agrees with me.

"Subordinate everything else to the above decision," I read. "Same reservation. If the constraint is not physical this step is meaningless. The fourth step is, 'Elevate the system's constraint(s).' Hmm, what are we going to do with this one?"

"What's the problem?" Lou asks. "If we identify an erroneous policy we should elevate it, we should change the policy."

"How lovely. You make it sound so simple," I say sarcastically. "Change the policy! To what? Is it so simple to find a suitable replacement? Maybe for you, Lou, not for me."

"For me neither," he grins. "I know that cost accounting is erroneous, but that doesn't mean I've completely figured out what to replace it with. Alex, how does one go about correcting an erroneous measurement or any other policy?"

"First, I think that you need the light-bulb idea, the breakthrough. The management techniques that Jonah talks about must include the ability to trigger such ideas, otherwise those techniques can't be used by mere mortals. You know, Lou, Julie predicted that as I come to it I'll recognize that we are not dealing just with techniques but actually with thinking processes."

"It started to look like it," Lou agrees. "But triggering breakthrough ideas by itself is not enough. An even bigger obstacle is to verify that this idea really solves all the resulting bad effects."

"Without creating new ones," I add.

"Is it possible at all?" Lou sounds very skeptical.

"It must be, if we want to plan rather than just react." As I talk I find a much better answer. "Yes, Lou, it must be possible. Look what happened to us with our solution of getting more sales. As a direct result of the French order we threw the plant into a very unpleasant two weeks and we killed or at least delayed a good marketing campaign. If we just thought systematically before we implemented it, rather than after the fact, we could have prevented many problems. Don't tell me that it was impossible. All the facts were known to us, we simply didn't have a thinking process that would force and guide us to examine it early in the game."

"What do we change to?" Lou says.

That throws me off balance. "Pardon me?"

"If the first thinking process should lead us to answer the question 'what to change?' the second thinking process should lead us to answer the question 'what to change to?' I can already see the need for a third thinking process."

"Yes, so can I. 'How to cause the change.'" Pointing to the fifth step I add, "with the amount of inertia that we can expect in the division, the last one is probably the most important."

"So it seems," Lou says.

I stand up and start to pace. "Do you understand what we are asking for?" I cannot contain my feelings. "We are asking for the most fundamental things and at the same time we are asking for the world."

"I've lost you," Lou says quietly.

I stop and look at him. "What are we asking for? For the ability to answer three simple questions: 'what to change?', 'what to change to?', and 'how to cause the change?' Basically what we are asking for is the most fundamental abilities one would expect from a manager. Think about it. If a manager doesn't know how to answer those three questions, is he or she entitled to be called manager?"

Throughout Lou signals that he is following me.

"At the same time," I continue, "can you imagine what the meaning is to being able to hone in on the core problem even in a very complex environment? To be able to construct and check solutions that really solve all negative effects without creating new ones? And above all to cause such a major change smoothly, without creating resistance but the opposite, enthusiasm? Can you imagine having such abilities?"

"Alex, that is what you have done. That's exactly what you have done in our plant."

"Yes and no," I answer. "Yes, that's what we have done. No Lou, without Jonah's guidance all of us would be looking for new jobs today. Now I understand why he refused to continue advising us. Jonah said it to me in the clearest way. We should learn to be able to do it without any external help. I must learn these thinking processes, only then will I know that I'm doing my job."

"We should and can be our own Jonahs," Lou says and stands up. Then this reserved person surprises me. He puts his arm around my shoulder and says, "I'm proud to work for you."

AN INTERVIEW WITH
ELI GOLDRATT AND OTHERS
by David Whitford,
Editor at Large, Fortune Small Business.

DW: *The Goal* was published 20 years ago. Since then a lot has changed in operations. New, powerful methodologies to improve operations, such as LEAN and Six Sigma, are widespread. The emphasis on reducing lead time and improving due-date performance has become the norm. Even *The Goal's* subtitle - *a process of ongoing improvement* - is a statement that is now taken for granted by every organization. So, my first question: Is *The Goal* still relevant?

EG: How does a scientist go about judging the relevancy of a particular body of knowledge? I believe that the decisive way is to choose an organization where all the competing knowledge is implemented. We should choose a large company that is already using all the new methodologies you mentioned; an organization that is using these methodologies so extensively that there is an institutionalized organizational structure – like a formal "black-belt" central office. The next step is to choose a significant section of that organization, and properly implement in it the body of knowledge in question. In our case it will mean implementing TOC in one of the plants of that large company. Then, compare the performance of the chosen plant with the performance of the rest of the organization. Now we are able to reach a conclusion: if no real difference is detected then the conclusion will be that the examined body of knowledge in question is not relevant. But, if there is a decisive difference, then the conclusion must be that the examined body of knowledge has relevancy; the bigger and more significant the difference, the more relevant it is.

DW: Did you conduct such an experiment? And if so can you tell us about the results?

EG: Fortunately, I don't have to initiate such experiments, since many readers of *The Goal* are kind enough to write to me and share their experiences. From the letters that I received over the years let's pick one that fits our conditions. Since we are discussing relevancy, it must be a recent letter. It should be from a person who implemented TOC in a plant that is part of a large enough organization, an organization that is using black-belts. And it should contain comparisons between that plant and all other plants of that company.

Judge for yourself if this letter fits our bill perfectly.

> **Dow Corning Corporation**
> Healthcare Industries Materials Site
> 635 N. Gleaner Road
> Hemlock, MI 48626
>
> May 20, 2004
>
> Dear Dr. Goldratt:
>
> I wanted to share with you what we have accomplished within our organization by using the tools presented in your books, "The Goal" and "It's Not Luck."
>
> When a colleague gave me a copy of "The Goal," the plant at which I work was in a similar situation as Alex's plant in the book. At that time, in 1998, our plant's on-time delivery was approximately 50%. We were carrying over 100 days of inventory and we had customers on allocation because we could not meet the demand for orders. In addition, our management had given us six months to turn things around, or else. I was the new production team leader for approximately thirty percent of the plant sales and forty percent of the plant production employees. My units performance was similar to the plant's overall performance.
>
> As I read "The Goal" I quickly realized one person alone could

not solve the problems within my unit, or within our plant. I ordered several copies of "The Goal," and my colleague and I distributed them to our production manager, plant manager and manufacturing and quality engineers. Everyone was eager for a solution to our problems.

Within my unit we identified the bottleneck and began to focus our resources there. Our plant is a non-union facility and many of the workers were also interested in what we were doing. I ordered copies of "The Goal" for everyone who worked for me. By the time the six-month ultimatum came, my unit and another had started to make significant changes, and the plant was spared any ill recourse. However, the expectation was that we would continue to improve. For the five years that followed, we continued to work on breaking our bottlenecks. When one moved, we attacked it again. We got pretty good, and could determine where the bottleneck would occur next. Eventually, the bottleneck moved outside our plant as depicted in "The Goal." However, we knew this would happen ahead of time and had already begun the indoctrination of our sales and marketing group.

I recently moved out of production, but before I left, the results within my unit were: cycle time reduction of ~85%. Operator headcount reductions of 35% through attrition; no layoffs were needed. Work in process and finished goods inventory down ~70%. On-time delivery went from ~50% to ~90% and the number of material handling steps were cut by over half. Our plant, and business unit have done very well too. And me, I received a promotion while in that position, and a compensation award. Dow Corning, like many other corporations, has downsized multiple times in the past five years. During each one, our plant, and business unit were affected very little or completely passed over. I am convinced that if we hadn't read and followed the methods in "The Goal" and "It's Not Luck" the situation would be much different today. There is still much to do, as our business unit is the only one to really have embraced "The Goal." I am hoping in my new role in Six Sigma that I can further share your tools and methods.

Thank you for signing the book Dr. Sirias has forwarded to you on my behalf. I am honored.

Sincerely,
Robert (Rob) Kain P.E.
Six Sigma Black Belt
Dow Corning Corporation
Life Sciences/Specialty Chemical Business

DW: Impressive, but why is only one business unit of Dow Corning using TOC? What bothers me is that this person is talking about a span of over five years. If it worked so well, why didn't it spread to the other business units? Is it the Not-Invented-Here (NIH) syndrome?

EG: Before we dive into speculation about psychology of organizations, let's examine the facts. We are talking about a middle manager who works in one corner of a large company. Why should we be surprised that, in five years, this person was not yet able to take his whole company through a major paradigm shift? And, by the way, as you read in his letter, he is making nice progress; he has already moved into a much more influential position.

DW: Still, even with enough time, is it possible for a middle manager to influence his whole company?

EG: Yes. But of course, such a person will need a lot of stamina and patience.

DW: What makes you so sure that it is possible at all?

EG: What evidence will convince you that it is possible?

DW: Give me an example of a middle level manager working for a large company who has succeeded in institutionalizing the usage of the know-how written in *The Goal*. I mean institutionalizing it across the board.

EG: Given that General Motors is the largest manufacturing company in the world, you should get an outstanding proof by interviewing

Kevin Kohls. *(Eli Goldratt interview to be continued.)*

Interview with Kevin Kohls General Motors
Director of Throughput Analysis and Simulation for North American Assembly Plants.

DW: What drove you to seek help from *The Goal*?

KK: It goes back almost 15 years, when I was starting off as a controls engineer at the Cadillac Detroit-Hamtramck assembly plant, just returning from Purdue University after completing a masters degree in electrical engineering. When I left a year and half earlier, the plant was just starting production. When I returned, they had yet to hit their production targets; in fact they were far short. As you might imagine, everyone was frustrated about not hitting these targets, and there was a lot of effort being expended to improve the system, with minimal results.

I was frustrated as well. The solutions I was putting in place rarely had a significant impact on the production of the plant, and it wasn't clear why. About that same time, Dave VanderVeen from GM Research made a presentation to Larry Tibbetts, who was then plant manager. Dave was promoting a research tool that he said would help improve throughput in the plant. Larry was very impressed, and asked me to go see Dave to find out if we could use this tool at Hamtramck. When I went down to the Research Building at the GM Tech Center in Warren, Dave explained what a bottleneck was and how his tool identified it. He handed me a copy of *The Goal* and said if you want to understand bottlenecks and how to improve throughput, this is the book to read.

I took the book home and started to read it right away. The first thing that surprised me was that it was written in novel format. The second was how much I could identify with what was happening in Alex's plant. I finally had to put it down at 2 A.M. so I could get some sleep, but I finished it the next day. I wanted to apply the concepts immediately, so I began collecting data from the systems we had, and putting it into the bottleneck program. After about a week of effort, I was fairly certain I had found the bottleneck. The scary part is that it was not 20 feet away, on the production line right outside my office!

DW: What was the problem?

KK: It was an operation where they were installing the fuzzy, felt-like material that goes in the ceiling of the car—very big and very clunky. Our data said that the mean cycles between failures was about five minutes, and the mean time to repair was about a minute. I was amazed that the line was stopping that often, and thought maybe the data was wrong, so we went and looked for ourselves. Sure enough, we watched the operator run for five cycles, stop the line, walk away, pick up five more of these big, bulky items—they weren't heavy but they were big—drag them back, restart the line, and continue to install them. Every five cycles she would stop the line. Was it considered a major problem before we looked at it? No. It's not like we were losing an hour straight of production because something had broken down. We were only losing one minute. But it was happening every five cycles.

We could see immediately why the material wasn't closer to the line. There was a supervisor's office in the way. We found out there had been a request made some time ago to move the office, but it was considered very low priority and it wasn't getting done. So I got the office moved, and lo and behold, throughput of the entire plant went up, which was a surprise, because my experience told me that I couldn't expect that. Then we used the software to find the next bottleneck and continued on with that process until we were making our throughput goals very steadily, every day. That was a real change in the way that plant operated.

DW: Did you take your insights to other GM plants?

KK: Yes. We demonstrated the process when central office management visited the plant, and it became apparent a lot of plants in GM weren't hitting their throughput targets. Eventually, I left Detroit-Hamtramck and went to a central office position to help start a divisional group to implement this solution. Seventeen years later, I'm an executive at GM who owns the process for all of the North American plants, and it has been expanded to include the simulation of future manufacturing designs.

DW: And this is all TOC related?

KK: Yes, but there are other disciplines involved. You have to understand simulation, and how it predicts throughput, and why it's important to understand where the bottleneck will be for a future design. But TOC is the basis for what we do. I still teach a two-day course. We might go to a plant and train the whole staff in how to use TOC concepts. I always give out copies of *The Goal* ahead of time and ask them to read it before the training. It's gotten to the point in manufacturing, however, where there are not that many people left to go through the training. My internal customers are usually very savvy now about TOC, bottlenecks, data collection and analysis. So I rarely have to sell the concept anymore. Demand for data collection implementation to drive the bottleneck software, for example, exceeds our ability to install. And while I'm responsible for GM North America, this week alone I have people in China and in Europe working on these kinds of issues.

DW: How has your use of TOC concepts changed over the years?

KK: What we found when we first started out is that we were dealing with the low-hanging fruit. You look at that first example I told you about, and it was very obvious that the office was in the way, and the solution was just to move it. Over time, the solutions to the problems have become a lot more difficult to find. This doesn't mean you can't solve them, it just means you might have to use more scientific techniques. Now I might have to apply statistical methods as opposed to simple observation to understand what's driving the problem at a work station.

Another thing we're doing lately is applying what we've learned from *The Goal* to the design of new plants and production lines. In effect, we're solving problems before they arise. Eli Goldratt hasn't spent a lot of time talking about using TOC in that way, but we've taken his concepts and adopted them to our needs. That's been the beauty of it for me. If you understand the logic and the reason behind the methodology, then you can apply that stuff continuously.

DW: It's interesting that a way of thinking about production problems that you found useful 15 years ago you still find useful today. Does that surprise you?

KK: Yes and no. The Theory of Constraints is a very scientific, logical process. And because of that, when the game changes you can always go back to the logic. Originally we just had to find the bottleneck, walk out there, ask three or four questions, and we knew what to go and do. Now we can change the way we design whole manufacturing processes to make sure they're better from the start. But the logic behind TOC–the conflict clouds, the current reality trees, the way we ask questions to uncover the constraint–all that still applies.

I think the problem with too many other approaches is that once the first layer of problems goes away, and the crisis no longer exists, then it's, "Phew! We're done!" In the TOC world, you find yourself asking, "Where has the constraint gone, and what can I do to help break it?" So you're never done.

I'd like to be able to tell you that as soon as I started telling people about these concepts, the whole organization immediately changed to the new paradigm. The fact is that it has taken years to get the process going, and the leverage to make improvements is still significant, especially in a company as large as General Motors. It's much like the flywheel concept discussed in *Good to Great*, by Jim Collins. It's taken a while to get the flywheel turning, but it's starting to go at a pretty good clip right now!

Interview with Eli Goldratt continued . . .

DW: At Dow Corning it took about 5 years for TOC to spread from one section to a whole business unit. In General Motors it took over ten years to be institutionalized throughout North America. Does it always take years to spread from the origin to the whole company?

EG: Not necessarily. It depends on who took the initiative. If the initiative was taken by a middle level manager, it naturally takes much longer compared to the many cases where the initiative was taken by a top manager. What is amazing is that the complexity of the organization is playing almost no role. In very large and complex organizations it takes TOC about the same time to become the dominant culture as it takes in small, relatively simple organizations.

DW: Can you give an example?

EG: In order to prove my point let's take an extreme example. An example of an operation that is not only large and complex but also dominated by large uncertainties - a repair depot of the United States Marine Corps. This depot is overhauling helicopters. It's very large – several thousand people. It is very complex – the helicopters are disassembled to the smallest pieces. Even the paint is sandblasted off. Whatever has to be repaired is repaired. Whatever has to be replaced is replaced. And then you reassemble the whole airplane. One has to make sure that certain parts which were taken from the original airplane go back on the same airplane. What makes it even more complex is the fact that two intrinsically different modes of operation have to be synchronized. The disassembly/assembly lines are a multi-project environment. The repair shops that feed the lines are a production environment, and the two must work in tandem. The real challenge is the fact that the whole operation is dominated by high uncertainty – one doesn't know the content of the work until the helicopter is disassembled and inspected. Surprises all over the place. A real nightmare. Still, it took the commander less than a year to implement TOC. An implementation that was so solid that the process of on-going improvement continues with his successors.

Interview with Robert Leavitt, Colonel,
United States Marine Corps retired.
Manager, Sierra Management Technologies

DW: You were responsible for implementing a TOC-based program in the Marine Corps?

RL: Yes, when I was commanding officer at the Naval Air Depot in Cherry Point, North Carolina. I started the implementation there, which they have continued. As a colonel I had in essence a $625 million company and 4,000 people working for me. Everybody says the government is always the last to get the message. I don't know if that's true. My personal belief is that the government gives guys like me the opportunity to try things a little differently.

DW: Tell us about your implementation.

RL: We had problems delivering H-46s on time. The H-46 is a 25-to 30-year-old Boeing helicopter used extensively in the Marine Corps as part of their assault support role. Because the airplane is so old and in frequent need of maintenance, anything over a single-digit number of airplanes on our hangar deck meant that you took a shadow off the flightline. If you took a shadow off the flightline, that meant they didn't have an airplane to do their mission. Our negotiated norm for turnaround time was 130 days, and on average we were somewhere between 190 and 205 days.

DW: Sounds like you had a problem.

RL: A problem, yes. So we implemented critical chain, and ultimately cut the number of airplanes in flow from 28 to 14. We were able to sell that to our customers. And the turnaround time went from 200 days to about 135. Now that in and of itself is probably a significant improvement. But at the same time we were starting the process, they added 30 days more worth of corrosion work to be done to the cabin. We accommodated the 30 days within that 135-day delivery. So we went from what would have been about 230 or 240 days to 135.

DW: Why did this approach work where others had failed?

RL: We had looked at a lot of the project management solutions, including material resource planning (MRP). TOC was the one that worked from all dimensions; building teamwork, understanding variability, and with a grounding in scientific thought. It was a holistic approach to solving the problems. It looked at the entire system and said, hey, once you find the key leverage point you'll get some significant returns. And then you can go back and find the next leverage point, or constraint.

DW: Did it take you a long time to find the constraint?

RL: No, it didn't. And within about 120 days we were already beginning to see the results.

DW: What was the constraint that you found?

RL: It was the schedule—the way the schedule was developed. The biggest thing was the way we applied available resources; it didn't make any sense. The estimators and evaluators really had about two days worth of work and they were taking about 14. We figured out what was going on—why that was a problem, why the scheduler set that up—and then reorganized.

DW: Bottom line?

RL: Well, the way it worked with the government, we were funded for a certain number of airplanes each year. We started burning through the backlog and we actually produced a few extra airplanes. I know from talking to the new commanding officer down there that they've increased the amount of product every year as they've gone forward.

DW: And you had another example?

RL: I also implemented TOC in the tail rotor blade cell at Sikorsky Aircraft, the overhaul and repair division. We were averaging somewhere between 15 and 19 tail rotor blades a month. It took us about 73 days to finish a tail rotor blade and we had as many as 75 or 80 tail rotor blades in flow. Well, we changed the flow to more than 30 tail rotor blades in process, which means our turnaround time actually was about 28 days.

DW: How quickly did this improvement occur?

RL: Three months. Now you can understand why I'm trying to build a consulting practice around TOC.

Interview with Eli Goldratt continued ...

DW: I'd say almost everybody I've talked to who has read *The Goal* agrees with its messages. It also seems clear that many readers believe TOC to be founded on solid common sense. So why doesn't everybody implement TOC right away? Is it because TOC demands that cost accounting be discarded? Do the financial managers block the implementations?

EG: Not at all. The notion that financial managers try to protect cost accounting is completely false. As a matter of fact, financial managers are the only type of managers that knew, much before TOC, the fallacies of cost accounting. Moreover, in almost any company, the VP of finance is one of the few managers who sees the overall picture and is extremely frustrated to witness so many devastating local optima decisions which do not view the organization as a whole. What we see in reality is the exact opposite; the financial managers rarely oppose TOC. On the contrary, in many (if not most) implementations, they are the driving force.

DW: That's hard to believe. Can I interview such an enlightened financial manager?

EG: As many as you want. As I said, such financial managers are the norm rather than the exception.

Interview with Craig Mead, Book Manufacturing
Vice President Finance, Thomson-Shore, Dexter, Michigan.

DW: Tell me about Thomson-Shore.

CM: We're in Dexter, Michigan, just outside Ann Arbor. Approximately 40% of our customers are university presses. We would be considered a short-run printer, meaning we print runs of between 200 and 10,000 copies. We're also an ESOP company–98% of the stock is owned by the employees. We've had as many as 300 employees. Right now we're at 280.

DW: I understand that everybody in your company has read *The Goal*.

CM: We made it mandatory reading for all our employees.

DW: Top to bottom?

CM: Yes.

DW: So what was the problem you were trying to correct with the help of *The Goal*

CM: Our main problem was with on-time delivery. We also had problems with a department-type mentality at the company. People had a hard time looking beyond their departmental responsibilities. Everybody was functional in thought.

DW: Were you able to turn things around?

CM: Yes. Before we started, we were at around a 70% on-time delivery. After implementing the TOC policies and practices, we got up to around 95%.

DW: Your first step was to have everyone read *The Goal*?

CM: Yes, that was the first step. The next step was to bring in a TOC consultant. We put 30 people through a three-day training course on Theory of Constraints. From there the leadership group identified what we thought was the constraint and began to follow the Five Steps.

DW: What was the constraint you identified?

CM: In our business we have two areas of major investment. One is in the press room and one is in the bindery. We basically settled on the press room as the constraint and began to manage the business with that in mind. As we focused on the constraint and began to subordinate everything else to that, we began to break down departmental barriers. It took a lot of education and training. We developed our own internal course for employees. Basically we took the three-day course, pared it down to about an hour, and had every employee go through that. The course dealt with the major concepts of constraint management, subordination, flowing work, and removing localized thought processes.

DW: What changes did you make in the press room?

CM: We chartered some teams to look at the various products that we made and began to challenge assumptions on how we use the presses. We make two types of books, a perfect-bound paperback book and a casebound hardcover book. We have sheet-fed and web presses. We began to devise rules on what type of books went on what pieces of equipment, to maximize the capacities of the equipment and to meet customers' needs. By creating new standards we eliminated an incredible amount of waste. Before, we were constantly reworking jobs to meet what we thought were customer needs. In reality it was forever putting us farther and farther behind. Rethinking all our assumptions forced us to discipline ourselves and to maximize each component in the press room. That allowed us to flow the work more consistently.

DW: How did you involve the employees?

CM: Employees at Thomson-Shore have the ability to influence the standards and the way work moves within their area of expertise. When you're strictly localized in your thinking, every person wants the job designed to benefit themselves. And that creates chaos. Before we did our TOC implementation, we could never agree on anything without a long, involved discussion. If we wanted to make a change we had to get 12 people in a room and then try to reach a compromise on everything. We could never please everybody. Having everyone read *The Goal* helped everyone understand that the basis for everything we do wasn't localized thinking anymore. So, for example, if a job had to spend a little more time in the bindery, that's okay, as long as that's what's most effective for the press, which we had identified as the major constraint. In the end we got the throughput that we needed.

DW: As a finance guy, what was your specific contribution?

CM: The Theory of Constraints is built on the premise of breaking the barriers of the cost model of accounting, and we were a heavily cost-driven organization, as a lot of manufacturing companies are. Everything in the company was designed as the cost-system would dictate. That's where I began to add value—by helping to develop different measurement tools that we could use instead of the traditional cost tools. And that's what I believe began to drive real change in the organization. We are still struggling on the sales side but we've made progress in breaking away from the cost method of sales and estimating.

DW: How does that work?

CM: The cost method of accounting creates departments and it allocates indirect overhead expenses. TOC, however, says you're one big happy family, you have fixed expenses and you have variable expenses. Your variables are your materials and your fixed is everything else. And sitting around spending all your time trying to figure out how much electricity and square footage of air conditioning and cooling goes to the press room, how much to the bindery and the prepress and how much to the office doesn't help you manage your business.

DW: Because it distracts you from the goal.

CM: Yes! Of meeting the needs of the customer. And flowing the work in a timely fashion. When we began to concentrate on making the work flow, that is, maximizing the capacity of the press room, and subordinating everything else to that, we began to improve our on-time delivery. The critical issue is how you measure the performance of the organization. We use two methods.

DW: And they are?

CM: Eli Goldratt talks about developing a constraint management tool. Ours is called TCP, for throughput contribution per press hour. When the market isn't a constraint, you choose which products and which customers to bring in based on that number. That's how you build profitability. Assuming, of course, that the constraint is not in the market.

DW: And when the constraint *is* in the market?

CM: For that we came up with another internal measure. We call it CRH, for contribution margin per resource hour. We try only to capture hours that represent value that customers pay for. We take the contribution—which is sales less materials—and we divide by the hours consumed and come up with a relative measure that has validity across the whole organization. It has taught us an immense amount about what we do here.

DW: By confirming what you already suspected or by revealing what you hadn't known before?

CM: Both. It confirms that certain types of customers, certain types of work, are difficult and cost us more to manufacture—it clearly pointed that out. And then it also began to show us how technology affects our margins. I mean, we get most of our books on PDF files now, and the cost difference between working with a PDF file and working with what I'll call the old conventional way is incredible. What was happening was that we were being forced by the market to reduce our prices across the board, but then any job done the old way was not very profitable. Hah! Not profitable at all! People were expecting PDF pricing for conventional work, and that just doesn't work. Bottom line: In a harsh business climate, in which the market is the new constraint, and sales are declining, we've actually built profitability. Significantly.

DW: Does it help that you're an ESOP company? Does that make it easier for employees to align their interests with the goal?

CM: It depends on the individual. Someone who is ten years from retirement is more interested in the value of the stock. Someone who's been here three or four years, they're looking at the individual-based bonus. So we actually began to implement team bonuses instead of individual-based bonuses. Today we're working on disconnecting the link between compensation and performance feedback. Feedback is going to be all team-based.

DW: You said you had 300 employees before and now you're at 280. Is that the fault of a bad business climate or a benefit of being more efficient?

CM: It's both. The business climate has not been healthy. But at the same time, some of the changes we made freed up capacity, and as people quit we didn't replace them, which built profitability. No layoffs. We just didn't replace everyone who left. And we moved individuals around.

DW: Is the constraint still in the presses?

CM: Well, it shifted to the bindery.

DW: What about market constraints?

CM: Yeah, we have more capacity than the market's willing to give. That's an issue. I think we're prepared to meet the market when and if it comes back. And in order to do that we have to do three things. We have to fulfill the requirements of speed and delivery. We have to stay profitable to maintain our equipment and provide the quality that customers expect from us. And then, three, we have to have employees who are participating fully, who want to come to work every day, and who understand why they're here and why they're doing what they're doing. TOC has allowed us to do all three.

Interview with Eli Goldratt continued . . .

DW: I'm back to my previous question. How come most readers of *The Goal* do not rush to implement TOC?

EG: TOC is built on the realization that every complex environment/ system is based on inherent simplicity and the best way to manage, control and improve the system is by capitalizing on this inherent simplicity. That's why the constraints are the leverage points. That's why the five focusing steps are so powerful. But, what we have to bear in mind is that such an approach is a major paradigm shift. And people will do almost anything before they will shift their paradigm.

From observation, I can tell you that readers of *The Goal* proceed to implement it mainly when three conditions are met. First, there is a real pressure to improve. But that by itself is far from being enough. The second condition is that it is obvious to them that there is no remedy within their existing paradigm. In other words, they had already tried everything else. And the third condition is that something helped them to do the first step. This something might be a "how to" book, like *Production The TOC Way*, a course, a simulator, or a consultant.

DW: Can you guide me to a case where all the three conditions exist?

EG: Frankly, once the three conditions had crystallized in my mind it became easy to detect them in every case. It is just a matter of asking the right questions and the pattern is apparent. Actually, there is no need even to ask guiding questions, you just have to listen.

Interview with Stewart Witt, Ongoing Improvement
A consultant

DW: I understand that your introduction to *The Goal* came before you became a consultant.

SW: Right. I was VP of operations at the time for a small manufacturing company, Ohmart/Vega Company, in Cincinnati, Ohio. Someone gave me the book with the recommendation to read it. And I read it, and it was very entertaining and made a lot of sense, and I promptly put it right back on the shelf.

DW: I've heard stories like that before.

SW: Right. I just wasn't ready yet. This company had hired me specifically to improve their operations and prepare them for growth and make them more efficient, all that stuff. I had talked the president into hiring a consulting firm, saying, "I can do these things but we can get it done that much quicker with some help," and he was fine with that. So we hired Grant Thornton, and they came in. We rearranged everything, streamlined everything. They took a look at the software we were using and made some other recommendations. We paid them about $120,000 and in about 6-8 months we started to see some results. Everyone was very happy because we took lead times down from, like, two weeks to one week. It was, wow, that's pretty good! The problem was that the same improvements were happening in sales and marketing. So here comes 40% more orders in the same time frame, and as it trickled out into the shop, so trickled away my improvements. The capacity I had freed up was now being doubled up by all these extra orders and I was back in the same boat that I was in before.

DW: What were you manufacturing?

SW: Nuclear measuring devices for the oil industry. Essentially, it's a non-contact measuring system, kind of like a Geiger counter.

DW: So, you were back in the same boat.

SW: Yeah, I spent all this money, all this time. All the things I knew how to do I had done. I couldn't rearrange everything again. I couldn't look at the software and come up with any new ideas. I had already employed the best consultants that I knew.

DW: Right. So what did you do?

SW: I signed up for Porsche mechanic school in California. It must have been a weak moment in my life. I do amateur racing and there's a saying that goes: you didn't make any mistake when you spun the car and flew off the track; what you did was you went into the corner and ran out of talent. That's how I looked at it—I must not be cut out for this job, there must be something I'm missing. I couldn't figure it out

DW: How old were you?

SW: That was ten years ago; so, early 30s. Mechanic school wasn't a waste of time. I still use what I learned. I save 600 bucks doing my own tune-ups. But right before I left to go out there, someone said: "You know, in San Jose there's a software company that has been created to support the rules that are stated in *The Goal*, and by the way, the Goldratt Institute has just issued a self-learning kit that you might be interested in." So I went to my mechanic class, that was very fun. Then afterwards I stopped in San Jose, took a look at the software, and completed the workbook on the way home. I was so excited that on Monday morning I got my staff together and I said: "This is what we're going to do. We've got nothing to lose. It looks like it's possible. It almost looks too simple. Let's give it a try." They weren't very convinced. In fact they were pretty skeptical. I'd put them through a lot already. One more thing, huh?

DW: This was their first exposure to TOC?

SW: Yes. Short story is, it took us about a month to go through the training materials, which came with a tutor guide and a workbook for all the participants. I went through the tutor guide step by step, they went through the workbook, and eventually they said: "I think you're right, we can do this." So we started, and about two weeks later we began to see some things improve. Lead times were starting to come

down, our on-time deliveries were starting to go up. At first I thought
it was just a fluke.

DW: What changed your mind?

SW: Well, a month later here comes one of my welders and he says:
"Boss, I think my numbers are wrong. The lead time I've been measuring is now about a day and a half." I said: "How can that be?" We
were still running more orders. I had even had to fire a guy in the
meantime, so we were down resources. And we hadn't bought any
new equipment. So I said, "Okay, fine, let me check and I'll let you
know what I find out."

DW: What did you find when you examined the numbers?

SW: I told my welder: "You know what? You're right, the numbers are
wrong. The lead time is *less* than a day." Same resources, 40% more
orders, a fraction of the lead time. Took us two months to do that.
Cost us $500. The company was a hundred years old and they had the
best two quarters that they've ever had. One division that was losing a
million dollars a month was now making a million dollars a month. If
I hadn't seen it with my own eyes, I would never have believed it.

**DW: What was the constraint you exploited to make such a
huge difference?**

SW: We actually worked through about three of them. One of them
had to do with the fact that we were sending everything out to put a
protective coating on the pipes that held the measuring equipment.
It was a step that had been added at some point by the marketing
department, and it had developed into a constraint. So we had to go
and find one or two more suppliers to handle the load.

DW: And there were others?

SW: One was the saws that cut the pipes. We offloaded some of the
work to another machine that was just sitting there doing nothing. That
saw ran at half the speed of the other saw, no one ever wanted to use
it. But we identified just the right materials to run on it, which built
just enough capacity to eliminate the saw as a constraint. And then the

paint department was next, we did a couple of things there. At which point the constraint shifted to engineering. We were waiting for some new products to come out, and that's kind of where it ended up.

DW: Do you believe that TOC is an infinite process? In other words, is there always going to be another constraint you can find and exploit?

SW: Theoretically, it can go on forever. But from what I've seen, it goes through one or two cycles within a facility, and then you've kind of broken the constraint in the production operation. Then it may move to, say, engineering. Then you can apply Critical Chain to the engineering group and eliminate that as a constraint, and then the next constraint usually is the market, and typically it's the existing market. Unless you're Coke or GE or whoever, you probably don't have a dominant position in your market. So you can still find room to grow. Finally, there are plenty of cases where, using the same capabilities that you generated using TOC, you can attack new markets that you never thought you could compete in. At that point, you're probably doing all you can handle anyway.

Or maybe it goes back to manufacturing again. Could be, yeah, and you definitely know how to deal with that by then.

DW: Alright. So then you moved on?

SW: I actually went to Grant Thornton for two years and worked on developing other TOC skills and applying what I knew to an ERP [enterprise resource planning] implementation at a plant in Mexico, working with Navistar International. I did that for about two years. Traveled to Mexico a lot, gained about 40 pounds, got no exercise. But it was kind of fun. Then I went to work for a consulting firm. Within about a month I was put on my first project, involving TOC, at a manufacturing facility in Clarksville, Tennessee, where they made graphite electrodes for the steel industry. It was a big plant, had been there quite a while, and it was already their best plant of that kind in the world. They made it a challenge for us, saying, "If you can improve things here, then we'll consider applying your methods elsewhere."

DW: This was a large-scale implementation?

SW: Huge. The plant covered half of Tennessee, it seemed like, way out in the middle of nowhere. So we put a small team together. It was me and another guy and about half a dozen folks at the site, and we went through the exact same training I had done the first time at Ohmart/Vega. Was exactly the same concept, exactly the same ideas. The only thing different was the context. We had software systems we had to integrate–five different software systems that had the data in it we needed. We identified the constraint, and did all the usual things, like making sure there was a buffer in front of it, making sure the maintenance guys were giving it top priority so if there's any trouble they could fix things right away. We put a quality check in front of it so that we weren't wasting time processing any bad electrodes at that point in the process.

DW: What was the upshot?

SW: No change whatsoever in on-time delivery. The company already had an excellent record in that regard and by the time we had finished, it still had an excellent record. But the only reason they could deliver on time before was because they had more inventory than they really needed. They just stuffed the shelves full of electrodes, had them sitting all over the place. So you see, we didn't disrupt their delivery performance at all, they continued to deliver 100% on-time. But in the end they did it with about 40% less inventory. And they were very satisfied with that because that essentially freed up almost $20 million that they could now use elsewhere to run their business. Based on those results, the CEO stood up at a big meeting one day and said that this is what we're going to do worldwide. We brought representatives from Spain, Brazil, Italy and South Africa to Clarksville as part of a worldwide implementation team. It's become a classic case of phenomenal improvement and a very satisfied client.

DW: So this is what you do now? TOC-based consulting gigs?

SW: Yes.

DW: Do you offer TOC as one option among many, or is this your primary approach to problem-solving?

SW: Maybe there's a third way. If I'm invited to participate in some of the initial meetings with the client, I may approach it differently than some of my colleagues. They'll come in and say: "We have this line of services, which one do you want?" What I do is ask questions, like Jonah does in the book. That helps me decide if there is a fit for what I do. Basically, I try to help clients understand that if you address the core problems rather than the symptoms so many people focus on, you can almost promise good results.

Interview with Eli Goldratt continued . . .

DW: What are the limits of TOC? Can it be applied also to service-based organizations?

EG: Yes, but... And in our case the "but" is quite big.

Let me start with the "Yes." Yes, any system is based on inherent simplicity, in this sense there is no difference between a manufacturing organization and any other organization, including service organizations. Yes, the way to capitalize on the inherent simplicity is by following the five focusing steps; identify the constraint, decide how to exploit it, etcetera.

The "but" revolves around the fact that it might not be a triviality to figure out how to actually perform each of the five steps; to figure out the detailed procedures. In *The Goal*, I introduced the overall concept and, through the detailed procedures for production, proved its validity. In *It's Not Luck*, I've explained the thinking processes needed to develop the detailed procedures to perform each of the five steps. As teaching examples, I showed how the thinking processes are used to develop the detailed procedures for sales of several different cases of manufacturing organizations. So, as a result, manufacturing organizations are not presented only with the approach and the concepts but also with the detailed procedures. Detailed procedures are not available for most types of service organizations. Therefore, in order to implement TOC in a service organization, one has to follow this generic knowledge and first develop the specific procedures. This is, of course, a much bigger task.

DW: So why didn't you write another book for service organizations?

EG: As you know, we use the term service organization for a very broad spectrum of totally different types of organizations. Organizations that are different from each other no less than they are different from manufacturing. You are not talking about another book, you are talking more of a library.

DW: Can you give me an example of a TOC implementation in a service industry? Any type of service industry?

EG: Let's start with a company that does not design or manufacture anything, and therefore is called a service organization. Still they deal with physical products; something that you can touch. An office supply company.

DW: A distributor of office supply products?

EG: Correct. But before you go and interview them, let me stress one point. All the TOC detailed procedures for the logistical aspects of distribution had long been developed and tested in many companies. But this particular company still had to use heavily the thinking processes to properly develop the detailed procedures needed to properly position itself in the market.

Interview with Patrick Hoefsmit, Office Supply
Former managing director, TIM Voor Kantoor, 100-year-old office supply company in the Netherlands.

DW: What was your first exposure to *The Goal*?

PH: I was one of the owners of a printing company. Pretty big company. Couple of hundred people, 40 presses. I was taking a course from someone who was explaining to me the difference between debit and credit–I'm a technical engineer, so I needed some explanation. And I was such a pain in the ass during the course that he gave me a book, *The Goal.* He said, "This is something for you because all the other books are nothing for you." I read it with great pleasure. I thought finally I have found someone who can explain to me the meaning of business.

DW: That seems to be a large part of the appeal of The Goal, it's accessibility.

PH: Yes, *The Goal* doesn't go really deep into the financial difficulties of running a company. As a matter of fact it completely makes it irrelevant. So for me it was also a great message that I could just ignore all these economist Ph.D. people–if they couldn't explain to me what was going on, then forget about it! So that was my first experience with the Theory of Constraints. Then somebody gave me an article that said Eli Goldratt was in Holland to give a seminar. So I went there. At the seminar Eli told us that he just increased the price for his Jonah courses from $10,000 to $20,000 because otherwise top management wouldn't come; something like that. So I said to him, "I promise I will come, even at the old price!" He said he had a better deal for me. If I was to do the course, I could do so and I only had to pay him after the results were of such magnitude that the price of the course was irrelevant.

DW: Good deal.

PH: Yeah, it was a perfect deal. So I went to New Haven, to America. He had an institute there. Did the course, couldn't do anything with it. So a year later I went to a Jonah upgrade workshop; it was in Spain. Eli has a very good memory, so when he ran into me he said, "Hey, did you pay for your course yet?" I said, "No, no, I didn't see any reason why I should." So he invited me for a private session. Some people warned me about that! On Monday morning I had a private session here in Rotterdam. That was a hefty morning. All my homework and all the things I did were to him completely irrelevant. The point was, I was looking at my own company and looking for a production bottleneck when there was so much excess capacity and the constraint was obviously in the market! But for me that was thinking outside the box. It had never occurred to me that Theory of Constraints would apply also outside the company's walls.

DW: That's understandable, since *The Goal* describes a production problem.

PH: Yes. So I was one of those stupid people who couldn't see the whole picture. So then Eli explained the bigger picture and the bigger application of it. He slowly forced me to think—sometimes by yelling at me, "Think!" It was a hefty morning. And this story is described by him in *It's Not Luck* —the candy wrappers case. We finally made some money over there. Actually, a lot of money. Later I discovered that my nephew, who was the other 50% owner of the company, wasn't doing much and was taking out more money than we had agreed upon, so we decided to split the company in two. I did the split and he chose which part he wanted. I never imagined that he would keep the printing business, which I had been running, and leave me with the office supply business, which had been his responsibility.

DW: Did you know anything about the office supply?

PH: No, nothing at all. The company was pretty big, it was number four or five in the Netherlands. It was making an awful loss. Competition was suddenly fierce and only concentrated on price. Other companies were very subtly sending brochures to every small business in the Netherlands with prices on the front cover that I couldn't get for myself as a wholesaler. This was really awful. All our good customers became suddenly more and more interested in price. They said, "How is it possible that we pay twice as much as what's on the front cover of this brochure?"

DW: It sounds like an impossible situation.

PH: Well, it was, it was really awful. We had something like four or five thousand customers, 20 sales people. The only thing we could think of was to also lower prices, and do it only on items where we had to. That was not a long-term solution but that was what everybody else was doing. So the conventional way of doing business in office supplies was pretty soon completely gone. We got tenders for office supplies—which was unheard of—where you had to fight with three or four competitors. In the past, orders for office supplies were just given to a local good-performing company. Now everybody was focusing on price.

DW: So what did you do?

PH: We started to build, as Eli calls it, the current reality tree. And of course this time I didn't make the mistake of making it about our company but I made it about the customers' situation: Why is this customer complaining so heavily about price? After long thought and a lot of discussions with my sales people, the only thing we could come up with is that he's thinking this is the only way that he can decrease the total cost of office supplies; that he can't do anything about the tremendous cost of having to stock supplies, and store them, and the cost of bringing the stuff to the right people in the building. Well, I know what kind of a mess customers can make out of it. In most offices where you open drawers, there's more stock in the office than anybody can imagine. While at the same time they are screaming for a specific item which has to be brought to them by taxi in crazy short delivery times. In Rotterdam we are down to four-hour delivery times! Not even 24, just four-hour delivery times, which is completely crazy for office supplies. I mean, we're not saving lives here.

So this is what we offered our customers: That we would take over all this hassle of supplying everybody in the office with the right equipment, the right articles, at the right time. We offered them cabinets with office supplies in them. We owned both the cabinets and the contents. The supplies were for a specific working group. Whatever they took out was considered sold, whatever was left was still ours. We replenished these cabinets every week. We made it very easy for them to check on us. And more importantly, we could give specific data about each department, explaining that certain items were consumed fast. For instance you might need a new pair of scissors once in three months, but not every week.

DW: So you could discover theft?

PH: Well, we didn't call it theft, we called it overconsumption. But of course it was theft, yes. So suddenly this guy who was responsible for office supplies had much better tools to go after his dishonest personnel. He's not interested in how many pencils someone uses. Everybody knows that people take pencils home; you do that by accident and it doesn't cost anything. Toner cartridges, that's a bigger problem. So when the theft of these ink-jet cartridges went up very much, we advised them to buy bigger printer machines, which we could also supply, to make them different than the machines people had at home. Things like that. But those cabinets were a big, big invention. While our customers might have paid 20%-25% more for the actual articles, the total cost of providing office supplies for their workers dropped by 50% because they didn't have the internal hassle of misplacements, overstocking, and things like that. So they didn't care that much anymore about the original price we charged. When I sold my company a couple of years ago, the due diligence took a long time because they couldn't believe our added value.

DW: What were the numbers?

PH: Normal gross margins in the industry were very much below 20%. Above 20% was suspicious. We were above 30%, which makes a lot of difference. And we were not ripping people off. They were extremely satisfied with our service.

DW: How did you go about selling the concept to your customers?

PH: We had a department which was making appointments with financial directors, not the guy normally responsible for purchasing office supplies. That other guy was scared for his job when you came with this solution. And we made a short movie to show the current situation in their office and how people were screaming for office supplies and things like that, and how great it would be if we could take over their stock and their responsibility and solve this problem. And this worked really great. Something like 30% of the sales visits were successful sales. Again, the prices we were charging for supplies was no longer an issue

DW: For anyone?

PH: Not exactly. We still had some customers who were focused on price. We didn't chase them away. We just gave them completely different conditions. We told them that if price is what matters most, you have to buy big quantities and you shouldn't care about delivery times: "You can get the lowest price possible but you have to stand in line." Now a good thing for us about the cabinet system was that we had one-week advance notice on our purchasing needs. I mean, what the customer used last week I didn't bring the day I was checking. I would bring it the week later. So I hardly needed any stock anymore. My suppliers could deliver in a day but I had a week. So now I could start buying on price. And I could combine my orders with those of the bigger customers who still wanted to do business just on price.

DW: Those must have been a very satisfying couple of years for you as you explored this new way of doing business.

PH: Well, yes, for a couple of years it's really fun. Because you're winning a race. Of course at the beginning I was relatively small; I was number four or five in the country. I was really afraid the bigger companies would copy my cabinet system.

DW: Did they?

PH: Yes, a little bit. But they didn't get the message. It was actually really funny. They were prepared to deliver cabinets but the customer had to buy the cabinet and the content as well. They were never willing to do it on consignment terms, which is what made it work. So that was a big difference to start with. Secondly, they didn't understand my replenishing system of stuffing the cabinets full enough that you could survive a couple of weeks. What they offered was so different that we could immediately show the customer that with our competitors, you'll still have to do it yourself, you'll have to take responsibility. Whereas in my case, when you change a printer, for example, and you don't tell me, I will find out you don't use this cartridge any more and I'll adjust. These cartridges are very expensive, do you want the responsibility? That's the main difference of consignment.

DW: Later were you able to discover new constraints that opened the way to new growth?

PH: Ultimately the constraint moved back inside the company. The new constraint became; how quickly can we measure or install a new cabinet? At first we could only do something like two or three cabinets a day. People were standing in line for cabinets. We had waiting lists for three months. So we put a second person on the job. Not a big deal. But we were fully in charge. We could grow at the pace we wanted to grow. That's kind of funny in a race where everybody was yelling about price! There are other businesses in that situation. For example, if you go to a really good restaurant, they don't care about prices. They are booked for the next three or four months; they become arrogant. And we had the same situation! It was great! And to think that we had started with all those competitors, all the problems, and 20 sales guys who were really discouraged, they didn't know what to do. And here we came with this really simple solution. I'm amazed that to this day nobody's really copying it.

DW: Would you have discovered this breakthrough had you not been exposed to Goldratt's theories?

PH: First of all, I wouldn't have known how to attack the problem. Since I was working at the printing company and my nephew was working at the office supplies company, I never expected that we would change roles. Nevertheless, I knew how much loss they made. And by then I was so convinced that just by applying Theory of Constraints, I would figure out a way to solve the problem. It took me something like three or four weeks to see the light and understand what was going on and how to solve it. I survived that month by sitting back and saying, "Okay, no panic, no panic, let's not be hasty. As long as we don't have a breakthrough idea I'm not going to make any changes." I was just sitting back and thinking and discussing with people how we could solve the problem, until we solved it. And that's one of the good things about theory of constraints. You know in these cases that eventually you will come up with a breakthrough idea.

DW: You have only to find it.

PH: Yes, and I became better and better at it. It takes Eli about five minutes to find the constraint and how to brake it. In most cases, I can find the same within a week. Compare it to just doing more of the same. I very often use this funny story about two guys on a safari. And after a couple of days they hear the first tiger and they think, well, great! So they go for their guns and discover they forgot their bullets. So one of them puts his pack down and grabs his running shoes, and the other guy starts laughing: "Do you think you can outrun the tiger?" He says, "I don't need to outrun the tiger, I only have to outrun you!"

Interview with Eli Goldratt continued . . .

DW: Can you give me another example? Of a service company that does not deal with physical products?

EG: To demonstrate how different one type of service company is from another, I suggest you interview both a bank and a financial advisors company. Then interview another, obviously different, type of service industry, a hospital

Interview with Richard Putz, A Midwest Bank
Former CEO of Security Federal Bank.

DW: How did you conceive of applying the principles outlined in *The Goal* to the banking industry?

RP: I was flying back from Los Angeles one night. And I was remembering my days as a consultant at Coopers & Lybrand, working with the folks who were handling the manufacturing engagements. That's where I was first exposed to *The Goal.* And I began to think that when you look at how a bank operates–for example, how it moves through the process of putting loans together–it's really no different than manufacturing. Why couldn't I use something that worked in manufacturing and apply it to a bank? The process is the same, we just give it different labels. So I started testing that out.

DW: How did that go over with the staff?

RP: In the beginning they were skeptical. I got all of the people who report directly to me into the board room, we sat down, I passed out copies of *The Goal,* and I said: "Guys, we're going to come together every week on Friday. We'll have fun, we'll have food, the whole bit, but we're going to discuss how to translate *The Goal* into banking terms." I'm looking over there at my CFO, he has this constipated look on his face. I said, "Jim, is there something wrong?" He says, "Yeah." I said "What?" He says, "There's no index in the back of the book. How do we find anything?" I said, "You read it, it's a novel." He eventually became our biggest advocate. But he was totally skeptical.

DW: So how did you approach the problem?

RP: Traditionally the tough issue within banking is how you manage all the regulatory constraints that you're faced with. Banks are just immersed in regulations. And if you actually tried to manage according to the regulatory measurements, your bank would fail. You bring that up to the regulators and they laugh. There's just this whole slew of things, some of which contradict themselves. Some of them were created when lawmakers added them onto banking legislation because they looked good, or else to fit a particular situation at the time.

DW: You're talking about regulations that keep banks out of certain businesses?

RP: Right, as well as those that mandate certain loan mixes, how you approach a market, that type of thing.

DW: Preservation of asset ratios and so forth?

RP: You got it. We took a slightly different approach. We decided we had to figure out what our real market constraint was. Using TOC, we found it had to do with service levels and how we were solving problems for our customers, not with the specific products we were offering. So we ended up gearing the whole bank toward solving problems for our customers. Part of the solution—the injection that broke the conflict—was the creation of personal banking for everybody, not just for wealthy people. Banks normally assume it's not worth spending time with you if you have only $100,000 when they can spend that time with a guy who's got $10 million. We discovered that a guy who only has $100,000 isn't really going to spend a lot of time with you anyway; he's just not there very often. So we stopped worrying about that and began focusing on how to better manage our customer relationships across the board. People ended up coming to our bankers anytime they had a financial problem. If we couldn't solve it for them, then at least we could refer them to someone else, and we could give them good advice because we didn't have an ax to grind. All we asked is that they let us manage their cash flow. Most people gave us everything in that regard, plus all their loans.

DW: You had a large mortgage business, too?

RP: Right. We had more than 300 correspondent banks, all over the country. National City and Bank of America would sell us mortgages. What we discovered—also using TOC, and this is how we expanded this business—is that most people with a loan viewed the bank that serviced the loan as their bank. So, whether Freddie Mac or Fannie Mae or PNC or any other investor actually owned the loan, we wanted to own the servicing asset. It was more valuable in terms of building customer relationships than the loan itself.

Also, these days it's a lot easier, but it used to take forever to get a mortgage approved. That's because there are all these things you have to have in place—again, to satisfy the regulators. We looked at that and said, "Okay, what's the conflict here?" We built our conflict clouds, and we built a current reality tree, and we discovered there are only three things that end up deciding whether a loan is a go or a no-go. If we just focus on doing those three items, and worry about plugging everything else into the file later, we can speed things up. In fact we were able to cut the approval time almost in half. That made us really popular with realtors and mortgage brokers, which brought us more business.

DW: What effect did TOC have on customers' ordinary day-to-day interactions with tellers?

RP: Most of the tellers said they wanted to do this TOC thing, too. Well, what do they really need to do? They really don't need to know how to do future reality trees because their everyday life is not involved in future reality trees. But a teller is often dealing with conflict resolution. Tellers represent the frontline defense, especially at savings and loans. People come up to them and say: "This doesn't work, this is out of balance, they screwed this up," and it's the tellers who have to solve the problem. So we taught them how to do conflict clouds. We created conflict-cloud worksheets for them, pads of 50 sheets, eight and a half by eleven. On the back side were the instructions, just in case they forgot how to do it. And the teller could actually fill in the cloud as he or she was talking to the customer, work out the problem, then rip off the sheet and do the next one. We had that going throughout the bank.

DW: It sounds like one of the main conclusions you reached

was that the perceived constraint–the regulatory climate–was not the actual constraint.

RP: Correct. I would walk into the office of my compliance officer and I'd say, "Jeff, I got this idea." And he would just automatically point to this poster on his wall that basically said: If you can dream it, there's a regulation for it.

DW: And yet even in that environment, you found ways to grow.

RP: We did things in the banking industry that were totally unheard of. We actually had regulators visit us more often than other banks because those other banks kept calling them and saying: "They've got to be doing something illegal, you need to check them out."

Interview with David Harrison, Administrative Services, Founder, Positive Solutions, Newcastle, U.K.

DW: Tell me about Positive Solutions.

DH: We provide management and administrative services to independent financial advisors. At present we have 755 of those people who rely upon us to help them with such things as compliance with financial services regulations, collection of commissions, and so forth. That's the company we built, 60% of which we sold recently to the Aegon group, one of the world's largest insurers.

DW: How have you made use of *The Goal*?

DH: In a couple of ways. First and foremost we use the five focusing steps almost instinctively now, in that we seek to identify the constraint in any problem before we do anything else. That's sort of been my mantra, if you like–before we go any farther, let's identify the constraint.

Beyond that, a big part of what we do is acquire new independent financial advisors–we want people to join our organization, and the people we use to recruit them we call our business consultants. Oded

Cohen, of Goldratt UK, helped us build a process for that. He broke it down into very discrete steps and helped us program software which helps us track how each of our business consultants is succeeding, or not. At any point in time they may have 150-200 people they're having conversations with about joining Positive Solutions. We've got them to think of each of those people as a project. That streamlined the process and also got our business consultants to think in a more logical fashion.

DW: What distinguishes Theory of Constraints from other management techniques you've looked at?

DH: I think it can be very easily applied in a simple process. As I have said, the one I use more than anything else is the five focusing steps. A lot of the problems which arise in business are about lacking focus. I guess if people were to describe Positive Solutions, it would be as a very focused organization. We don't seek to be all things to all people. We stick to what we know will be the most profitable areas to us at any point in time. We've been working on the same constraint for five years.

DW: And that is?

DH: Our ability to recruit the right people at a pace which fits our business plan. The more people we have, the more profitable we become. A lot of companies by now would have given up at about 300 advisors, something of that nature. And they'd say the constraint is no longer recruiting people, what we should be doing is trying to improve the productivity of those people, or trying to get a better deal out of the manufacturers of financial products. But we've kept the focus on the fact that as long as the people that you are recruiting are profitable, then why stop recruiting them? Just because it's not getting any easier? Well, it's not actually getting any harder, either. It's just another day at the office. But we can work all of our financials back to simply the number of advisors that we have. Therefore, we don't go any farther.

DW: That's your focus?

DH: That's our focus. We've identified the constraint, now let's exploit it, make the most of it. Therefore we have easily one of the best recruiting machines in the UK in this sector. We approach recruitment very differently from all our competitors. Our competitors will advertise, they'll try to acquire businesses, for example, rather than the approach that we have, which is to recruit people one by one. Our rate of growth might at first appear to be slow. But because our advisors have been recruited in the right way, we don't lose many of them. That's the beauty of TOC: as you really dig in to identify the constraints, you begin to understand these things.

DW: Have you thought about what the next constraint will be?

DH: Of course, at present there is still a market for further independent financial advisors to join us. There are about 25,000 of these people in the UK and we have less than 1000 of them. Now the quality of some of those 25,000, and the fact that not everybody will join us in any case, means at some point the effort needed to increase the capacity just won't be worth it versus the energy we could put into something else. At that point, you say, "We've now changed our plan. What is the constraint in our new plan?" Frankly, it's about retaining the clients' money. At present what we do is introduce clients to a variety of manufacturers of financial services. The money goes to the manufacturers and they give some of it back to us in the form of commissions or fees. The next step really is for the clients to give us the money, and for us then to give some of it to the fund managers and the life insurers. So once we're a certain size, the constraint will begin to move. We'll have a brand, and the revenue needed to communicate that brand, so there won't be quite as much effort to get people to join us. At that point the constraint shifts.

Interview with Dr. Antoine Van Gelder
A South African Hospital, University of Pretoria

DW: You're not a typical Eli Goldratt disciple, are you?

AV: I'm a university professor with a dual appointment, head of the department of internal medicine at the University of Pretoria and head of the department of internal medicine at Pretoria Academic

Hospital. In 1992 I got an invitation to attend one of Eli Goldratt's courses in Pretoria. Not one run by him, himself, but by a subsidiary of the Goldratt Institute. At that time I knew nothing about Theory of Constraints and I had not read *The Goal.* I got myself into this out of curiosity more than anything else.

DW: Why? What kind of help were you looking for?

AV: Let me put it this way. I was literally sitting in my office, with my head in my hands, highly frustrated, with piles of paper all around me, going through correspondence. I opened a letter, saw that it was another invitation to a course, threw it away, and as I threw it in my wastepaper basket my eye caught the price of this particular course. It was the South African equivalent of about $18,000. That caught my attention. I thought if any course was worth that amount it was worth looking at. This was a two-week course in production management; the invitation was addressed to the engineering faculty. It had gotten to the medical faculty by mistake. The course was actually offered free to university professors. So because of my deep frustration with some of the management issues I had in my department, and because I had some time off the next week, I phoned. I planned to only go for the first week, because this was the time I had available. I was told that I had to attend the full two-week course. I said, "Yeah, we'll see about that."

DW: But you went?

AV: I went the first week. The course was taught with reference to a production environment and the logic around it. Now you don't find much of this logic–the reality trees and that sort of thing–in *The Goal.* Quite a lot of that is in *It's Not Luck,* which was published later. But the logic grabbed me because I was this frustrated man who was running a department of medicine and I had not been trained to do that. I had no insight into management issues. Suddenly I saw that here was a potential way of analyzing my department.

DW: What were the parallels?

AV: My department was in chaos, total chaos. Everything coming and going, not knowing what was what–much as things were in the factory that is the setting of *The Goal.* During the course, *The Goal* was mentioned. I bought it, read it through in one night, and I thought to myself, that's *my* environment. A chaotic system is not necessarily a factory. It could be a hospital with people coming and going. It could be a department with a whole lot of prima donnas—the doctors—who need to be managed. That parallel struck me.

Now if I can answer your question a bit more precisely. When one is introduced to Theory of Constraints, the first thing you see is a system where the causality is hidden. In other words, it's chaotic. Things happen, you have no control. Suddenly, though, it becomes a system that can be analyzed in terms of certain key points—leverage points. And one learns that addressing these key points—rather than launching a symptomatic firefight—is the way to exert control over these systems. Remember, this was in the early 1990s, before frameworks like systems theory had moved to the forefront and become part of the main buzz. Though the Theory of Constraints doesn't talk about systems theory, already it was offering an approach by which a complex system could be managed in terms of a few key leverage points.

DW: Did you wind up attending both weeks of the course?

AV: Correct. Then I came back to the hospital. There are two points I want to make. The first was that I underwent a mental change. Instead of thinking that things were too complicated, too complex and not manageable, I now saw that if I could analyze the system correctly, it *was* manageable. That was the first important breakthrough that I had, and many people I've taught this to subsequently have had the same breakthrough. There is a way—find it!

Second, our outpatient clinic, like most hospital outpatient clinics at that time, and even now in many parts of the world, was plagued by inefficiencies and long waiting lists. The more we fought the inefficiencies, the more money we poured into the system, the longer the waiting lists seemed to become. This is the problem with the national health system in Britain as we speak. Now in my department, it seemed to me as though the processing of patients by doctors could really be viewed as a production line, just as in *The Goal.* The times are different, and obviously people aren't machines. All of those issues I acknowledged. But I saw that parallel.

DW: How did you attack the problem?

AV: The manager in charge of that clinic and I sat down and I told her about the principles used in *The Goal.* Between the two of us—with her doing most of the work—we identified our constraint. We realized that we lost a tremendous amount of capacity whenever patients or doctors wouldn't show up for scheduled appointments. That time lost was not recoverable. So we developed a call-in list, which we called the patient buffer. A day or two before a scheduled appointment we would phone patients and make sure that they would be coming into the clinic. If not, we would find substitute patients. The result was less loss of capacity. Our waiting list at that time was about eight or nine months long, which is common for this type of waiting list. As a matter of fact in the UK now some of these waiting lists are over one year. In about a six month period we got our waiting list below four months, which was roughly half of what most other hospitals were doing in South Africa at that time.

DW: Yours is a public hospital?

AV: Yes, we're part of the state health system. In other words, not for profit. Patients pay only a small amount for services. Later on, after I started consulting with the Goldratt Institute in South Africa, we looked at a large private hospital, 600 beds, a flagship hospital with neurosurgery and all the high-tech stuff. The issue there was loss of capacity in the operating rooms. The spin-off effect of that was that surgeons were leaving the hospital and going to other private hospitals. It was a serious situation. We found that instead of focusing on local optima—making sure that my little department comes first—the real question people should be asking is, what can I do to achieve the larger goal of the hospital, which is to throughput new patients? It's a simple concept, but implementing it took about two months of meeting with staff. Each person then developed an action plan aimed at making sure more patients moved through the system more efficiently. In a period of a year, this hospital moved from a 20% shortfall on its budget to where it began showing a profit.

DW: So you've become a Goldratt consultant yourself?

AV: Yes. I presented the results from our hospital's outpatient clinic at one of the Goldratt symposia in the early 1990s. This was the first report of a medical implementation of the Theory of Constraints. Eli Goldratt was there to hear my presentation, and afterwards he invited me to join the Goldratt Institute as an academic associate. I was based at the university but involved in the implementations of his consulting company. I did quite a bit of work in the mining industry—nothing to do with medicine! It was pure theory of constraints, straight out of the book. It allowed me to develop my own skills.

DW: What's a doctor doing advising mining companies?

AV: It's interesting that you say that. I'm a physician, not a surgeon, In other words, I'm a thinker, not a doer. I say that facetiously, but as a physician, it's all about diagnosis. And the whole process of diagnosis, whether it's a patient or an organization, is the application of the scientific method. Eli Goldratt says that his Theory of Constraints is simply the application of the scientific method. So it's almost natural that an advisor to a mining company—in terms of diagnosing what's wrong and what to do about it—could be a physician. In fact, some of the teaching materials that the Goldratt Institute uses refer to the medical model. It asks trainee consultants: How does a doctor approach the problem? It gives them a parallel for how you diagnose problems in organizations.

DW: That's interesting. Eli has said that his overriding ambition in life is to teach the world how to think.

AV: Right. And nothing he has done in the almost 14 years that I have known him suggests to me that that is a facetious statement. The Theory of Constraints is about thinking processes, it's a subset of logic. In other words, the scientific method.

DW: Has any of this made you a better teacher of physicians?

AV: Absolutely. Absolutely. I've told you that diagnosing a patient and diagnosing a business is the same thing. But a doctor learns to diagnose by watching other doctors. It's not taught as a science. The processes of diagnosis are taught, but what might be called the philosophy of diagnosis is not taught as it is in the Theory of Constraints. The traditional approach is, watch what I do. The approach that I've since followed is, let's look at how the scientific method works, then let's see if we can apply this to a patient. Most students take to this very well.

Interview with Eli Goldratt continued . . .

DW: That will do it.

EG: Please, one more. The jewel in the crown, at least in my eyes, is the usage of TOC in education. Yes, in kindergartens and elementary schools. Don't you agree that there is no need to wait until we are adults to learn how to effectively insert some common sense into our surrounding?

Interview with Kathy Suerken, CEO
TOC For Education,
An international nonprofit dedicated to teaching TOC thinking processes to schoolchildren.

DW: You're a middle school teacher, not a plant manager. How does *The Goal* fit with the work you do with children?

KS: Well, it all started almost 15 years ago. I was kind of a new teacher at a middle school but I had been a parent volunteer for a while. I was running a voluntary math program for kids and my husband was giving me advice on how to manage it. The program was already a success; we had 100% participation. I asked him, "Well, what do I do now? Go to a different school?" And he said, "Kathy, you'll have to find another goal." Six months later he said, "There's a book you have to read, we're passing it around at our office and everyone's signing the back if they recommend it." That was my introduction to *The Goal.* Within six months, I wrote a letter to Eli Goldratt that began, "Dear Dr. Goldratt, if you were to walk into the office of Frank Fuller, Ruckle Middle School's principal, on his desk you would find a copy of *The Goal . . .* and thereby hangs a tale." I went on to say how I was using the ideas and concepts to run this project.

DW: Did you hear back from Eli?

KS: Within four days, with a copy of his newly revised book. And then within about a week or so I heard from Bob Fox, who was president of the Goldratt Institute at that time, and they offered to send me to Jonah school on scholarship. So I went through the course. Later I went through a facilitator program on how to become a trainer of Jonah processes. And then I went back and taught a pilot course to kids. By the end of the year my kids were using the thinking processes, which they learned brilliantly. They were the most Socratic learners and teachers of other kids that you ever saw. It was pretty convincing evidence to me that this stuff works with kids, and it launched me into the role I have now.

DW: Was it a course about TOC or a course that used TOC methods to teach other content?

KS: It was a class on world cultures–basically a class on perspectives, which of course this is so aligned with. We used methods derived from TOC to advance the curriculum. Later I taught a critical thinking skills course that was pure TOC. In that course I was teaching cause and effect as a skill. We used concepts like the conflict cloud to analyze conflicts in real-life situations.

DW: What evidence do you have that the kids were absorbing the concepts?

KS: Here's an example. One day I read to the students the section about the hike from *The Goal,* and then I gave them an evaluation sheet. I asked them, "How is this relevant to real life? What's the weakest link?" Stuff like that. It wasn't a test. I just wanted to know if they were getting it. That night I looked at their answers and I realized maybe half of them got it and half of them didn't. So I went back the next day and I asked them again, "What determines the strength of the chain?" I called on one boy–let's say his name was Mike–who I knew was struggling. He was rambling on and on. He did not get it. And I did not know what to ask Mike to get the answer out of him. So then I looked at my other students. And I knew if I called on John, for example, who did get it, he would just tell Mike the answer, and that's not what I wanted. So I said, "No one can give Mike the answer. You can ask Mike a question to help him think of the answer." And that is when one of my other students raised her hand. She said,

"Remember when we were doing the cloud on teach fast, teach slow? The problem of making sure everyone understands but the fast ones don't get bored?" That's when I saw what was happening. As the other students began asking Mike questions designed to draw the answer out of him, I could see that everyone was engaged. It was a wonderful example of cooperative learning. Because everyone had to think. Even if they already knew the answer, they were thinking hard about how to guide others to the answer.

DW: How do you introduce TOC to schools where it has never been taught before?

KS: We usually start with teaching TOC as a generic process, then figure out how to apply it to a specific curriculum. Initially it was easier to get it in through the counseling element of the school the behavior application. That seemed to be the most obvious way in.

DW: How do counselors use TOC?

KS: Let's say the child is sent in to the guidance office with a behavioral problem. The counselor who's been trained in TOC will use tools like the negative and positive branch: "What did you do? Why were you sent here?" And then they go into the cause and effect consequences of the behavior, and how that leads to negatives for the student. The student will say, "If I do this, I get in trouble, I get grounded, I get sent up here, my parents get called." It's almost predictable, this branch. Then the counselor asks, "Okay, what would happen if you didn't do these things?" Then the student writes the other branch, the positive one. Then the counselor asks, "Okay, which would you prefer? It's up to you."

One of the first teachers that was using this in a classroom in California was working with at-risk students. They were at risk of failing academically and behaviorally. She was teaching the process outright, as a skill. And she had her students do cause and effect branches. One boy did it on, "I'm going to steal a car, go on a joy ride." She went to help him, because he couldn't get the branch started. She said, "What's the problem?" He said, "This is the first time I've ever thought of something ahead of time." In the end he had to go to the driver education teacher and get some information to finish the branch, which is great. He found out what would happen to him if he got caught, because he didn't really know. How do you quantify the results of something like that?

DW: You've since developed other applications?

KS: Yes, and they're interconnected. Because behavior changes attitudes. Or maybe I should say that attitudes impact behavior. If a student can make a more responsible decision, and he gets a favorable impact, his attitude toward the teacher and what he's doing in school changes. That's bound to have some impact on his learning. But additionally, we have, in the past two years, really worked on how to deliver the TOC learning process through curriculum content. Or, again, maybe it's the other way around: How to teach content using the TOC processes. Because teachers do not want to interrupt class to teach a life skill. They have to teach the curriculum.

DW: I understand you've introduced TOC to young people in prison settings.

KS: I went into a juvenile jail in California about five years ago. I spoke to a new group of juvenile offenders; this was their first day. They were all gang members. Later the teacher who invited me told me he had been very worried because I was female and most of them had been abused by their moms. He was afraid they would back me into a corner and be quite rude. There I stood in a polka dot dress, from Niceville, Florida, looking like the person who had put them in jail. I'm sure I didn't look very empathetic. But I tried to get them to tell me what they wanted out of life. They said things like. "We just want to get out of here, lady." I said, "Do you think that's enough to keep you out of here?"

Finally, one boy said to me, "I just want a better life for my kids." These were 16-19-year-old old black and Hispanic males. I looked at this guy and I said, "I'm sorry, I don't understand. What do you mean? You have kids?" He said, "Yes, I have a two-year-old and a baby."

Anyway we had this goal on this rickety old chalkboard, "A better life." I said, "Okay, what is preventing you from having a better life?" They said, "Jealous people." I turned around and I said again, "I'm sorry,

I don't understand what you mean by jealous." Because I'm thinking to myself, and not facetiously, "who could be jealous of them, they're in jail?" And that's when they said, "Oh, but if you go back and try to get out of the gang they'll be jealous, they don't want you to leave the gang, you can't leave."

They also mentioned prejudice as an obstacle. And as I'm making this list I am thinking, "I am in over my head." There was nothing I could think of that would overcome the obstacles these kids were facing. But I didn't need to worry about it. Because they had the answer. They went down the list and they added more obstacles like, "my past," and "criticism," and about halfway through they gave me something brilliant: "Me. Myself. I have to change myself. Right away."

I later received letters from some of those kids. One of them said, "Before we had that talk, even making it to 21 was hard to see in my future. But you gave me hope." Now I ask you, did I give him the hope? No! It came from him! But he wrote, "You gave me hope that I can make it if I just follow those steps." That last part is so important. This is not just wishful thinking. It's giving somebody a process they can use, so that when the person who's giving them the attaboys isn't there, they have the know-why, not just the know-how to keep going.

DW: Does TOC have the same relevance to kids who don't have such severe obstacles to overcome?

KS: Absolutely. What it helps people do is to make sense of things. Many times, even in affluent communities, students are motivated only because their parents want them to achieve. But learning does not make sense to them. It doesn't seem relevant. They're doing it only because they have all the right environmental factors. What could be unleashed from those children if we could present information to them in such a way that they could derive their own answers instead of providing answers that were simply memorized? It's all about unleashing people's potential. I have felt many times as a teacher that disruptive behavior comes from the high achievers as well as the low achievers—because the high achievers are bored! In TOC we have a way to differentiate instruction with one learning process. To bring them all with you.

DW: What is your goal for TOC For Education?

KS: I see empowered learners, enabled learners, and the real joy of lifelong discovery. All those platitudes that we aspire to, I see them being practically achieved. As well as people being kinder to each other. I see this as the real language of civility. Once I had to give a presentation about TOC to a group of teachers. We put on a play with some of my students. And afterwards the students were saying, "Mrs. Suerken, what's going to happen? This is so effective, there won't be any problems left." I thought, that will probably never happen! But that's the way they saw it. I wish you could come to our conference in Serbia in May! We're going into Thailand this month through an organization called the Girl's Brigade, like the Girl Scouts. We have somebody in Singapore who is taking it into the sports council, into sports applications. We're in Malaysia. My new director in the United States, he's going to start a private school next fall and he's writing all of the curriculum based on TOC. Really, I think we've just touched the tip of the iceberg.

For information about other books on the
Theory of Constraints (TOC)
please visit our web site at:
www.northriverpress.com